ENVIRONMENTAL IMPACT ASSESSMENT (EIA)

Cutting edge for the twenty-first century

ALAN GILPIN

CAMBRIDGE
UNIVERSITY PRESS

Published by the Press Syndicate of the University of Cambridge
The Pitt Building, Trumpington Street, Cambridge CB2 1RP, UK
40 West 20th Street, New York, NY 10011–4211, USA
10 Stamford Road, Oakleigh, Melbourne 3166, Australia

First published 1995
Reprinted 1995

Printed in Hong Kong by Colorcraft

National Library of Australia cataloguing-in-publication data

Gilpin, Alan, 1924– .
Environmental impact assessment (EIA).
Bibliography.
Includes index.
1. Environmental impact analysis. 2. Environmental policy.
3. Environmental impact analysis – Case studies. I. Title.
333.714

Library of Congress cataloguing-in-publication data

Gilpin, Alan.
Environmental impact assessment (EIA): cutting edge for the
twenty-first century/Alan Gilpin.
Includes bibliographical references and index.
1. Environmental impact analysis. 2. Environmental impact
analysis – Case studies. I. Title.
TD194.6.G54 1994
333.7′14 – dc20   94-8970
                                                                CIP

A catalogue record for this book is available from the British Library.

ISBN 0 521 41931 X Hardback
ISBN 0 521 42967 6 Paperback

To
Alexandria, Jenny, Jordan,
Ruth, Ryan, and Stephanie

CONTENTS

ABBREVIATIONS

ADB	Asian Development Bank
Brundtland Commission	World Commission on Environment and Development
CBA	cost-benefit analysis
CEQ	Council on Environmental Quality (US)
DA	development application
EA	environmental assessment
EARP	environmental assessment and review process (Canada)
EC	European Community
ECE	Economic Commission for Europe (UN)
EHIA	environmental health impact assessment
EIA	environmental impact assessment
EIS	environmental impact statement
EPA	Environmental Protection Agency (US)
ER	environmental report
ESCAP	Economic and Social Commission for Asia and the Pacific (UN)
FEARO	Federal Environmental Assessment Review Office (Canada)
NEPA	National Environmental Policy Act (US)
NSW	New South Wales (Australia)
PPA	Post-project analysis
RAC	Resource Assessment Commission (Australia)
UN	United Nations
UN ECE	United Nations Economic Commission for Europe
UNEP	United Nations Environment Program
USA	United States of America
WHO	World Health Organisation

CHECKLISTS

Chapter 4

Chapter 5

Chapter 6

Chapter 7

FIGURES

TABLES

MAPS

PREFACE

Material in this book has been used in undergraduate and postgraduate courses at several Australian universities, and now in the degrees of Master of Business and Technology and Master of Environmental Engineering Science in the School of Civil Engineering, University of New South Wales; and the degree of Master of Natural Resources Law, Faculty of Law, University of Wollongong.

The work reflects my experience of conducting over 50 public inquiries in New South Wales and Victoria into controversial planning, environmental, and heritage policies, plans, programs, and projects. It captures experience before 1980 in the assessment of environmental impact statements (EISs); the development of environmental planning instruments; the identification of regional administrative centres; the evolution of natural resource accounting; and the management of major pollution control programs, both in Australia and Britain.

The text has been reinforced by consultations overseas into environmental policy procedures in Asia and the Pacific, North America, and Europe. Of particular note are meetings: in Taiwan at the National Cheng-Kung University and the Environmental Protection Administration; in Seoul and Daejon organised by the Korean Office of the Environment and the Korean Institute of Energy and Resources; in Tokyo and Tsubuka with the Environment Agency and the National Institute for Environmental Studies, Japan; Environment Canada, Ottawa; the US Environmental Protection Agency, Washington; and the US East-West Center in Hawaii; the World Resources Institute, Washington; in Britain with the Department of the Environment and the universities of Oxford, Manchester, and Aberdeen, and several environmental agencies in mainland Europe and the Nordic countries.

Assistance from many countries has been much appreciated; however, the focus of the book is by-and-large on countries which have been at the cutting edge of the environmental impact assessment (EIA) process, although some promising developments elsewhere have been noted.

In this work, much reliance has been placed on the world data provided by various *Britannica* Books of the Year; and on the reports of individual countries to the United Nations Conference on Environment and Development held in 1992 in Rio de Janeiro, Brazil. I have supplied as much information as is available to date. Every effort has been made to be up-to-date, taking account of events in 1993, but it has been difficult to gain information after 1992 for several countries.

Late in 1993 the European Community became the European Union which is to be enlarged from 12 members.

I am particularly grateful to Robin Derricourt and Phillipa McGuinness of Cambridge University Press, and Robin Appleton, for their encouragement, care, and skill.

Alan Gilpin

CHAPTER 1

EIA approaches

1.1 The meaning of the word 'environment'

Essentially, and in its broadest sense, the word 'environment' embraces the conditions or influences under which any individual or thing exists, lives, or develops. These surroundings can be placed into three categories:

(1) the combination of physical conditions that affect and influence the growth and development of an individual or community;
(2) the social and cultural conditions that affect the nature of an individual or community;
(3) the surroundings of an inanimate object of intrinsic social value.

The environment of the human being includes the abiotic (devoid of life) factors of land, water, atmosphere, climate, sound, odours, and tastes; the biotic factors of human beings, fauna, flora, ecology, bacteria, and viruses; and all those social factors which make up the 'quality of life'. The concept has emerged of the environment as an assembly of people and things which render a stream of services and disservices to the individual and which take their place alongside the stream of services rendered by real income, commodities, homes, infrastructure, and markets generally.

The European Commission, the governing body of the European Community (EC), has defined the environment as 'the combination of elements whose complex inter-relationships make up the settings, the surroundings and the conditions of life of the individual and of society, as they are or as they are felt'. All these approaches place humanity at the centre of things; there are no environmental values which cannot be traced to the welfare of human beings. There is no room, on the face of it, for compassion to other species, but perhaps the evolution of the word 'environment' still has some way to go.

However, we should not overlook how far the word has already come; for it is only since the 1970s that environment has become identified as an entity to be addressed by international conferences, to command segments of national legislation, and to have received an appropriate allocation of financial resources in the public and private sectors of the economy.

On the one hand, origins can be traced to the nineteenth century in the area of public health: insanitary dwellings and streets, contaminated public water supplies, drains and sanitation, public nuisances (these include noxious accumulations, vermin, animal faeces), unhygienic food processing, overcrowding, noxious effluvia, offensive trades, refuse dumps, and epidemics. The responses by government were largely in the area of public water and sewerage schemes, slum-clearance programs, food hygiene drives, regular sanitary inspections, and elementary pollution control.

On the other hand, increasing interest was being taken in nature; the conservation of natural areas and the creation of national parks, and reserves. These appeared at the time to be two completely separate developments.

Tracing the evolution of environmental management, embodied in many display boxes throughout this book, reveals a common path shared by many diverse countries. However, it was not until the 1960s that the two paths began to coalesce; new strands were added; new agencies were created for pollution control initially, and later for environment protection as a whole; and it became possible to conduct the first United Nations (UN) conference in Stockholm in 1972, the second in Nairobi, Kenya, in 1982, and the third in Rio de Janeiro in 1992. See checklist 1.1.

Pollution control and nature conservation have merged into the general subject of environment

---

CHECKLIST 1.1

Ingredients of the word 'environment' as reflected in most national legislation

1   all aspects of the surroundings of human beings, whether affecting human beings as individuals or in social groupings;

2   natural resources including air, land, and water;

3   ecosystems and biological diversity;

4   fauna and flora;

5   social, economic, and cultural circumstances;

6   infrastructure and associated equipment;

7   any solid, liquid, gas, odour, heat, noise, vibration, or radiation resulting directly or indirectly from the activities of human beings;

8   identified natural assets such as natural beauty, outlooks, and scenic routes;

9   identified historical and heritage assets;

10 identified cultural and religious assets;

11 aesthetic assets;

12 public health characteristics;

13 identifiable environmental planning, environmental protection, environmental management, pollution control, nature conservation, and other mitigation measures.

---

protection, culminating in the all-embracing process of environmental impact assessment (EIA), some embryonic subjects have matured and become incorporated such as environmental economics, risk assessment, and relevant cultural, social, and heritage considerations. International environmental concerns and concepts such as ecologically sustainable development have also entered the arena.

The workplace environment and the domestic environment tend to be excluded, save those practices that pollute the general environment, although pollution control measures have penetrated the garden gate to restrict open-burning and chimney emissions. Occasionally studies are published comparing internal atmospheres with external atmospheres.

However, many of these matters have been considered in environmental planning, statutory planning, and zoning, to effectively separate incompatible uses and to manage cumulative effects. Planning is the strategic arm for tackling environmental problems and supporting individual project assessment.

The word 'environment' arises in many other common situations: the 'business environment', 'economic environment', 'political environment', or even the 'musical environment'. It is clear that environment protection and EIA are primarily about the physical environment outside the workplace and the home, and its relevant social and economic considerations.

1.2   The historical development of EIA

Since the passage of the US National Environmental Policy Act (NEPA) 1969 which incorporated a requirement for assessing the environmental impact of 'major federal actions significantly affecting the quality of the human environment', the concept of environmental impact has spread throughout many countries. Some countries have introduced specific legislation, setting out formal requirements for environmental assessment (EA), while other countries with well-established land-use planning procedures responded initially by adapting existing environmental and planning legislation to place greater emphasis on the assessment of environmental impacts or effects.

The formal approach is one in which:

• EIA procedures are defined by statute with guidance as to when these are to be applied, and how;

• EIS (or environmental reports [ER]) are prepared for specified development projects;

• all levels of government and all public agencies must take environmental assessment (EA) into account during decision-making;

• the public is consulted and encouraged through meetings, hearings, and public inquiries, to participate actively in the decision-making process;

• avenues for appeal against official decisions and against apparent irregularities in administration and the process of decision-making exist, allowing administrative and judicial review, and dispute resolution.

See checklist 1.2.

Initially, Britain, the Federal Republic of Germany, and most of the Nordic countries responded by adapting their well-developed land-use planning systems, though all have now created specific legislation by way of Acts and regulations. Britain, the Federal Republic of Germany, and Denmark, were obliged to meet the European Community (EC) 1985 directive on EIA.

Many other countries have followed the US lead from the outset, creating separate EIA legislation in the first instance. Table 1 indicates those countries

CHECKLIST 1.2

The role of EIA in society

1 provides a procedure for the full consideration of the possible adverse environmental impacts of policies, programs, activities, and projects before any decision to proceed; it precludes 'behind-closed doors' decision-making in the public and private sectors;

2 there is opportunity to present recommendations to the decision-maker on the suitability of the policy, program (groups of projects, either sequential or concurrent), activity, or project, to proceed or not, on environmental grounds;

3 for proposals which proceed, there is the opportunity to present the incorporation of conditions of consent that should mitigate some of the adverse environmental effects;

4 it is an avenue for the public to contribute to the decision-making process, through written and oral contributions to the decision-maker(s), appearances at public inquiries and hearings, and possible participation in mediation processes;

5 the whole process of development is open to scrutiny for the benefit of all the key players: proponent (applicant), government, and public, resulting in better projects more carefully thought out;

6 basically unsatisfactory projects (including otherwise satisfactory projects on the wrong site) tend to weed themselves out before advancing far into the EIA process, and certainly before reaching a public inquiry stage;

7 conditions of approval may ensure monitoring, annual reporting by the proponent, post-project analyses (PPA), and independent auditing;

8 alternative approaches, mixes of technology, and sites, can be thoroughly examined;

9 EIA is seen, however, as the servant of development: promoting better developments, at best, but basically supporting economic growth;

10 the process endorses waste discharges, the emission of greenhouse gases in many cases, and the profligate use, mining, extraction, and processing of natural resources;

11 the whole process as a creature of government, is subject to political pressures; key players within government have no security of employment whatever;

12 officers of integrity have little chance when confronted by a combination of hostile interests at a political level;

13 on the other hand, a vigilant public, skilled objectors, and organisations with a range of legal rights to object, access to the courts, and a supportive media with some political sympathy, can exercise countervailing power and influence.

Table 1 Introduction of formal EIA requirements

Country	Year
Australia	1974
Austria	pending*
Bangladesh	pending*
Belgium	1985
Britain	1988
Canada	1973
China	1979
Czechoslovakia	1991
(the Czech and Slovak republics, 1992)	
Denmark	1989
Finland	pending*
France	1976
Germany	1975
Greece	1986
Hong Kong	1972
Iceland	pending*
India	pending*
Indonesia	1982
Ireland	1988
Italy	1988
Japan	1972
Korea, South	1981
Luxembourg	1990
Malaysia	1985
Netherlands, The	1986
New Zealand	1991
Norway	1989
Pakistan	pending*
Philippines, The	1977
Poland	1989
Portugal	1987
Singapore	1972
Spain	1986
Sri Lanka	pending*
Sweden	1987
Switzerland	1983
Taiwan	1979
Thailand	1984
United States of America	1969
* at July 1993	

(Source: The survey of countries later in this book).

which appear to have been most effective in this area; and whose activities are the subject of cameos in this book and a source of case studies.

The UN Economic Commission for Europe (UNECE) (1987) has stated that:

the purpose of environmental impact assessment (EIA) is to give the environment its due place in the decision-making process by clearly evaluating the environmental consequences of a proposed activity before action is taken. The concept has ramifications in the long run for almost all development activity because sustainable development depends on protecting the natural resources which is the foundation for further development.

The introduction of EIA is to be seen as an end product of a very long evolutionary process, starting with rudimentary but evolving pollution control measures for air, water, noise, land, and chemicals, each governed by separate, and separately administered pieces of legislation. These have only been coordinated since the 1970s. Parallel activities were taking place about the natural environment, in the establishment of national parks and nature reserves, and the protection of fauna and flora. EIA is an important step in the integration within the planning system of all these efforts. See checklist 1.3.

CHECKLIST 1.3

Characteristics of EIA processes

1 *Status, scoping, and data assembly* Identifying the status of the project within the context of planning and environmental law; national, state, provincial, and local planning requirements and policies; clarifying, in principle, the potential economic, social, and environmental benefits and disbenefits of the proposed policy, plan, program, or project. Meetings with the decision-making body, affected and interested individuals, groups, agencies, and departments at all levels of government, to help identify the scope of the issues to be addressed. Preparing the terms of reference (TOR) for the EIS/EIA on the proposal.

2 *Consideration of alternatives* Identifying alternative means of meeting similar or identical objectives, including alternative sites; and the consequences of 'no action' (no proceeding). Further consideration of the benefits and disbenefits (disadvantages) of the policy, program, or project, looking at considered alternatives. Uncertainties should be clearly identified; possible cumulative adverse effects should be noted. For projects and alternative sites, data on the existing environments should be assembled and compared.

3 *Review of proposed mitigation measures* Mitigation measures about possible adverse effects that might be adopted for all feasible alternatives should be carefully reviewed, embracing pollution control, nature conservation, and environmental management, generally.

Buffer and transitional zones might have an important role to play.

4 *Screening* The beneficial and detrimental short- and long-term effects of each alternative are compared and summarised, to facilitate discussion and evaluation by interested parties and the interested and affected general public. This draft EA document also identifies the preferred alternative and the reasons for it. The limits of acceptability of change, risk, and uncertainty, should be identified, explained, and discussed.

5 *Communication* The full involvement of the public should be sought at all stages of the development of the draft and final EA. Public inquiries and hearings should be held, and small mediation-type meetings, as appropriate. The proposed mitigation measures should be fully discussed. New issues and aspects might be raised by the public which require elucidation. A final document should be issued to the public focusing on the reasons for the preferred decision.

6 *The decision* The decision of the decision-making body should be publicly released, noting the avenues of appeal that are available to the proponent and members of the public.

7 *PPA* Monitoring is generally undertaken before, during, and following, the construction of a project. A condition of approval might be the preparation of an annual report for public release, consolidating the environmental data obtained, and reviewing progress with the implementation of all consent conditions. The project might be subject to an annual independent environmental audit. Individual government agencies become responsible for the surveillance of different aspects of the project and the legal enforcement of conditions. Many consider this phase to be part of the EIA process, which previously had terminated at the decision stage.

1.3   Terminology

The EA terminology used in the countries of Asia, Australasia, North America, and Europe, tends to vary both in the meaning of terms and the scope of their application. Some of those concepts and terms are defined here:

Environmental impact assessment (EIA) The official appraisal of the likely effects of a proposed policy, program, or project on the environment; alternatives to the proposal; and measures to be adopted to protect the environment. The concept might apply from inception to operation, but might embrace PPA.

The European Council EIA Directive 85/337/EEC of 27 June 1985 applies the term 'environmental impact assessment' to the identification, description, and assessment, of the direct and indirect effects of a project on: human beings, fauna and flora; soil, water, air, climate, and the landscape; the interaction of these factors; and on material assets, and the cultural heritage.

Environmental impact statement (EIS) A document prepared by a proponent or developer applicant describing a proposed policy, program, or project; alternatives to the proposal; and measures to be adopted to protect the environment. An EIS in draft or final form will then be subject to an EIA. The EIS might thus be one step only within the framework of an EIA. In some countries the EIS might simply be known as an EIA report, the term 'EIS' not being used. In other countries, the EIS in its final form is recognised as the EIA, after official approval.

Environmental assessment (EA) process Essentially, this involves the complete EIA process leading to a decision. In the USA the term used is 'environmental review (ER) process' and is applied not only to physical projects but can also apply to plans, programs, policies, legislation and regulations, which could cause potentially significant environmental impacts.

Environmental assessment (EA) A document containing information in sufficient detail to determine whether a proposal will impose significant adverse impacts on the environment. In the USA, an EA provides sufficient evidence for determining whether to prepare an EIS or whether to issue a 'finding of no significant impact' (FONSI) on the human environment.

The National Environmental Policy Act (NEPA) process In the USA is the evaluation of the environmental effects of a federal undertaking, including its alternatives. There are three levels of analysis: at the first level, an undertaking might be categorically excluded from detailed analysis as having no significant impact; at the second level, an EA might find significant impact, or no significant impact; and at the third level an EIS might be necessary, followed by the decision of the relevant federal agency being placed on public record.

The British system In Britain, 'environmental assessment' is often used instead of 'environmental impact assessment' and 'environmental statement' is often used instead of 'environmental impact statement'. In both cases the word 'impact' is removed.

1.4 What is 'impact'?

In the context of environmental impact, what is meant by 'impact'? Essentially, in this context, 'it is the effect of one thing upon another'; as such an impact can range from the effects of mine-blasting or the striking of a hammer to the insidious effects of radiation or ozone destruction. It is difficult to think of an impact, however, as being anything but a sharp blow and perhaps the description 'environmental impact statement' or 'assessment' is a misnomer, or perhaps not the description to be preferred. Perhaps initially the available possible alternatives were not fully examined. There is certainly evidence of different national usage.

In 1978, the Victorian government, Australia, introduced the Environmental Effects Act, the word 'effects', was derived from the 1973 report to the Victorian government on the 'environmental effects of the proposed Newport D power station, Melbourne' (Gilpin, 1973). That report had carefully rejected the use of the word 'impact' as inappropriate to the consideration of a gas-fired power station.

However, the horse has bolted and the word 'impact' is so widely used that I use it throughout this book not with a sense of correctness but simply as a surrender to its common misuse.

Before considering the key word 'significant' it is desirable to identify some of the many impacts or effects that might occur, significant, or otherwise. See checklist 1.4.

CHECKLIST 1.4

Examples of environmental impacts or effects

Pollution and ecological

1 effects on air, water, noise, and vibration levels, radiation levels, flora, and fauna, ecology, biological diversity, contamination levels, health, areas of outstanding natural beauty, natural and artificial landscape, historical and cultural heritage; visual environment and aesthetics, traffic generation and management, soil erosion and land degradation, drainage and sewerage, open space, waste generation and management, and climate;

Natural resource

2 effects on agricultural land, forest resources, water supplies (including ground water), minerals and marine resources, energy resources, building materials, wetlands, mangroves, coral, rainforest, wilderness, and bush;

Social

3 effects on settlement patterns, employment, land use, housing, social life, welfare, recreational facilities, community facilities and services, accessibility, safety, residential amenity, Aboriginal communities, minority groups, youth, unemployed, aged, disabled, women, and the socio-economic profile of the affected community;

Economic

4 effects on employment opportunities; accessibility to facilities, services, and employment opportunities; urban infrastructure; choice and affordability of goods and services; the local rate base; infrastructure costs and contributions; real income; land prices and the likely multiplier effect.

It is also possible and instructive to divide these impacts or effects into two categories: microenvironmental impacts, effects, or problems which immediately affect the lives of citizens; and macroenvironmental impacts, effects, or problems which are problems of a regional, national, and international character. See checklists 1.5 and 1.6.

1.5   The meaning of the word 'significant'

In the USA under NEPA (1969) and the executive orders and regulations of the Council on Environmental Quality (CEQ), EIA is mandatory for every recommendation or report on proposals for legislation and other major federal actions significantly affecting the quality of the human environment. NEPA is deemed to be complied with, without the filing of an EIS, for actions which will have no significant impact on the human environment. See checklist 1.7.

The word 'significant' appears in the EC EIA directive of 1985, and in the UN ECE convention of EIA in a transboundary context. It appears several times in the United Nations Environment Program (UNEP) principles of EIA; and in the World Bank 1992 operational directive on EA. It appears again in such national documents as the Canadian cooperative principles for EA, and the national principles for EIA in Australia. The word 'significant' occurs in most of the national EIA legislation examined.

Yet, at no point, is 'significant' defined. General dictionary definitions merely suggest 'meaningful', 'important', or 'notable'; these are highly subjective terms. Specialised dictionaries suggest 'something

---

CHECKLIST 1.5

Microenvironmental problems immediately affecting the lives of citizens

1   dereliction, slums, and blight in certain localities;

2   unsafe water supplies;

3   inadequate or non-existent sewerage systems;

4   vector breeding;

5   air, water, and noise pollution;

6   fumes and vibration from industrial processes;

7   hazards from traffic in the street;

8   poorly located industrial plant;

9   loss of light and over-shadowing from other buildings and overhead roads;

10 severance of communities and neighbourhoods by highways, railways, traffic management schemes, or large-scale developments;

11 lack of space for play or recreation;

12 visual squalor because of litter, garbage, abandoned vehicles and equipment, and overhead wirescape;

13 dereliction arising from abandoned and closed dwellings, business premises, and factories;

14 inadequate street maintenance, and drainage;

15 loss of heritage buildings and the special character of areas;

16 inequitable, obtrusive, and antisocial developments;

17 loss of privacy;

18 loss of views;

19 loss or deterioration of natural assets in the immediate neighbourhood;

20 loss of existence value, that is the loss of things elsewhere whose existence has been appreciated such as rainforest, or brown bears.

---

outside of acceptable limits'; the usual level adopted in the social sciences is 5 per cent.

As a measure of 'significance', a variation of 5 per cent of a component in the physical environment might well have some validity; for example, a deterioration of this size in the salinity of irrigation water or in the presence of heavy metals. However, 'significance' is much more difficult to apply to the loss of a view, or the habitat of a rare or endangered species. The concept of 'significance' remains, therefore, highly subjective, depending

CHECKLIST 1.6

Macroenvironmental problems: regional, national, and international

1 dereliction, slums, and blight in most of the cities and rural districts of the world;

2 unsafe water supplies;

3 inadequate or non-existent sewerage systems, and the pollution of waterways;

4 vector breeding;

5 regional, transboundary, and global air pollution;

6 floods and associated threat to life and property;

7 incidence of drought and famine;

8 desertification;

9 soil degradation;

10 Population growth in relation to resources;

11 mortality and morbidity arising from environmental sources;

12 threats to natural resources including ecosystems, forests, woodland, and mangroves;

13 threats to endangered fauna and flora;

14 increasing noise levels;

15 the disposal of toxic and nuclear wastes;

16 threats to regional seas and marine resources;

17 the location of hazardous industries;

18 visual pollution;

19 atmospheric warming, and climatic change;

20 threats to the ozone layer.

CHECKLIST 1.7

USA Council on Environmental Quality (CEQ)
Guidance on the word 'significance' provided in CEQ regulations

1 Context: the significance of an action must be analysed within the context of society as a whole; the affected region; the affected interest; and the locality, as appropriate. Both short-term and long-term effects are relevant;

2 Intensity:

(a) the degree to which the proposed action affects public health and safety;

(b) proximity to historical or cultural resources, parklands, prime farmlands, wetlands, wild and scenic rivers, or ecologically critical areas;

(c) the degree to which the effects are likely to be highly controversial;

(d) the degree to which the possible effects are highly uncertain or involve unique or unknown risks;

(e) the degree to which the action might establish a precedent or affect future considerations;

(f) the implications for cumulatively significant impacts;

(g) the degree to which the action might adversely affect districts, structures, or objects listed in, or eligible for, listing in the National Register of Historic Places;

(h) the degree to which the action might cause loss or destruction of significant, cultural, or historical resources;

(i) the degree to which the action might adversely affect an endangered or threatened species or its habitat that has been determined as critical under the Endangered Species Act;

(j) whether the action threatens a violation of federal, state, or local law, or requirements imposed for the protection of the environment.

perhaps, initially, upon the opinion of an assessment officer. But such an opinion is likely to be a professional judgement, based on accumulated knowledge and experience, mixed with due regard to the likely reaction of the decision-maker, who (or which) will receive the initial assessment on which to decide the question of 'significance'; and that reaction will always be strongly influenced by the degree of public and media furore which has arisen, or is likely to arise.

Some governments have sought to resolve the problem in advance by scheduling categories of activities which must have an EIS followed by an EIA; these statutory schedules remove the responsibility of decision-makers to decide on 'significance'. The uniformity of these schedules reveals the degree of unanimity, internationally, on what kind of activity will have a significant (no doubt negative) effect on the environment.

Significance is, in the end, a collective judgement of officers, elected persons, and the public. A '5 per cent' criterion will be found in practice to have a certain relevance only for certain elements in the situation; and will have little relevance at all to the outcome.

1.6 Political determinants

The institutional structure and the evolution and strength of environmental law are of vital importance, as little or nothing can be achieved without means and resources, but the political background remains a dominating influence. Political will is like a powerful spring operating the machinery of administration, surveillance, and enforcement; a loss of will becomes a lead weight for all involved.

For example, with the election of Ronald Reagan in 1980 as US president, the administration that came into power was not noted for its commitment to environmentally sound decision-making (Kennedy, 1987). Although the Reaganites did not attempt to repeal or amend the National Environmental Policy Act or the pollution control Acts, the progressive appointment of political appointees opposed to such legislation to federal agencies (even to positions that had previously been the domain of career civil servants) reversed many of the gains made. Poorer EISs was one of the outcomes, and an extensive collapse of morale.

In another example, the advent of a new administration in the state of Victoria, Australia, in 1972, witnessed a surge of new conservation and environmental legislation, and the creation of an independent environment protection authority. However, while such legislation was significant in winning an election, it did not have the full support of much of the parliamentary party, including its conservation committee. Measures were adopted to effectively remove the independence of the environment protection authority, without amending the legislation. The ultimate step was the dismissal of the chairman of the environment protection authority in 1974. The grounds given were that the chairman was behaving independently (Gilpin, 1980).

However, the underlying tide might go in a reverse direction with a progressive program of new and amended legislation, introducing innovative measures in the form of a say in an improved and more responsive and effective planning system, with enhanced opportunities for public participation in the decision-making process.

This occurred in New South Wales, Australia, in the late 1970s, with new planning and heritage legislation and the creation of a land and environment court. However, conflicts soon arose, and before long the same government had introduced 10 pieces of separate legislation taking specific development projects out of the planning system, thus precluding normal EIA procedures and public inquiries.

Such measures are not, of course, unique to New South Wales, or Australia; they are 'worldwide'. The preferred project, perhaps involving foreign investment, will be, as often as not, driven through regardless, there being no consultative process.

Officials, aware of political decisions made behind cabinet and ministerial doors, might hurry to the government's bidding or might brace themselves to achieve the best for the environment out of a foregone conclusion.

Fortunately, there are departmental and agency chiefs, and commissioners of inquiry, who will, from time to time, stand by their prescribed duties and face ministerial wrath. Many officers in environmental agencies have done so; some have suffered for it.

Politicians vary enormously in ability and quality, and carry a great deal of responsibility. But their first response is always to think of survival, before seeking martyrdom.

1.7 EIA and the World Commission on Environment and Development (the Brundtland Commission)

The preeminent report of the World Commission on Environment and Development (known as the Brundtland Commission) recognises EIA as an essential component in the promotion of sustainable development. The report envisages greater public participation in decisions that affect the environment, giving communities an effective say over the use of local resources (Brundtland Commission, 1987). Further, some large-scale projects require participation through public inquiries and hearings.

The report also comments that 'when the environmental impact of a proposed project is particularly high, public scrutiny of the case should be mandatory and, wherever feasible, the decision should be subject to earlier public approval, perhaps by referendum'.

Beyond this, the report urges that a broader EA should be applied to products, policies, programs, and projects, especially major macroeconomic, financial, and sectoral policies that induce significant impacts on the environment. This principle should be applied also to bilateral aid programs, as recommended in 1986 by the Organisation for Economic Cooperation and Development (OECD).

The Brundtland Commission was clearly building on the 1972 Stockholm Declaration and the 1982 Nairobi Declaration, products of those two UN conferences. However, it noted the problems arising from lack of institutional capacity, skilled personnel, quality checks, and second opinions on environmental documentation.

1.8 EIA and the UN Conference on Environment and Development

The UN Conference on the Human Environment, held in Stockholm in June 1972, endorsed a declaration of 26 principles, essentially about sustainable development and EIA, although these terms did not appear in the text of the declaration. The precise concept of sustainable development was to become central, however, to the World Conservation Strategy launched in 1980 by the International Union for the Conservation of Nature and Natural Resources, the UN Environment Program, and the World Wide Fund for Nature. Further, the concept of EIA, which had been embodied in the US and NEPA, and operational two years before the UN conference, had begun to be progressively incorporated in environmental and planning legislation throughout the world.

By the time of the Brundtland Commission, created by the General Assembly of the UN in 1983 and reporting in 1987, both expressions were popular currency. The commission's report, *Our Common Future*, accentuated the crucial importance of sustainable development and EIA to the future well-being of humanity.

The UN Conference on Environment and Development met in Rio de Janeiro in June 1992, 20 years after the Stockholm conference. It reaffirmed and sought to build on the original declaration. In the new declaration of 27 principles, sustainable development is referred to frequently while principle 17 is devoted to the national instrument of EIA.

A final product of the 1992 Rio de Janeiro conference was Agenda 21 (UN Conference on Environment and Development, 1992), establishing a program for the immediate future and for the twenty-first century. There can be little doubt that to find solutions to the problems of poverty, lack of access to clean and safe water, inadequate housing and sanitation, lack of access to primary education, to name only a few of the identified problems, will provide an agenda for the next 100 years.

One of the administrative problems addressed at that conference, of immediate relevance here (from chapter 8 of Agenda 21), is that of integrating environment and development in decision-making. It was stressed that in many countries prevailing systems for decision-making tend to separate economic, social, and environmental factors at the policy, planning, and management levels. It was argued that environment and development should be put at the centre of economic and political decision-making, in effect achieving a full integration of these factors. In many countries these are, no

doubt, grave deficiencies that need to be rectified, particularly at the policy, and national, and regional program levels. The most advanced countries are beginning to tackle the problem.

However, Agenda 21 does not acknowledge the contribution of EIA procedures at the very least at project level to the problem of integrating environmental and development considerations, before any decision is made by the decision-making body. Here an important instrument needs solely to be extended from the project to policy, regional, and national program level for integration to be complete.

1.9 EIA and sustainable development

The concepts of sustainability, sustainable yield, and sustainable development, enjoy an enormous popularity in current statements of policy, pronouncements by agencies, and in professional literature. While the possibility of natural resource constraints to human development and multiplication dates from at least the Malthusian theory these ideas have now moved to centre stage. The theory stated that population tended to increase in a geometrical progression, whereas the means of subsistence increased in only arithmetical progression. Hence population tends to outstrip the means of feeding itself, if not kept down by vice, misery, or self-restraint.

Initially, these concepts found a place in the area of renewable biological resources such as fisheries and forests, 'sustainability' meaning 'using the incremental increase without reducing the total physical stock'. In other words, living resources should be used at levels of harvesting that allow those resources to survive indefinitely; sustainable yield has meant living off the interest, rather than the capital, of a resource. Sustainable yield aims to maintain essential ecological processes and life-supporting systems, to preserve genetic diversity, and to maintain and to enhance environmental qualities relevant to productivity. It seeks to avoid disadvantage to future generations.

'Sustainable development' has, however, been extended to embrace living and non-living resources. It has been defined as 'development which provides economic, social, and environmental benefits in the long term'. Thus sustainable development must have regard to the living and non-living resource base; conservation of resources; the long-term character of the market; and the advantages and disadvantages of alternative courses of action for future generations.

The concept of sustainable development is wider than sustainable yield, and differs in one important respect: it allows the use of resources, which are decreasing, such as fossil fuels, in an efficient manner with an eye to the substitution of other resources in due course. The objective is no longer the sustainability of a physical stock, or the physical production from an ecosystem over time, but a sustained increase in the level of human welfare. The Brundtland Commission defined sustainable development as development that 'meets the needs of the present without compromising the ability of future generations to meet their own needs'. The objective is seen by most as desirable; the debate is how to pursue it. Does it not just mean 'business as usual'; and how could it possibly affect the EIA of a policy, plan, program, or project?

This is one of the more serious questions to be answered. This book outlines what factors need to be considered when balancing development with environment protection, viewed as an exercise in using human resources. Are there further considerations then to be considered, when viewing the interests and needs of generations yet unborn?

Certainly much greater emphasis on natural resource conservation is needed to prevent or to compensate for the loss of a natural resource base upon which future development itself depends. There is, therefore, much scope for the better management of the use, renewal, and conservation of all natural resources through the EIA process. For example, there must be a bias towards the development of alternative, sustainable, and renewable forms of energy; a development of a world strategy for the global commons; and much better care for all living resources including forests, fisheries, and wildlife. We cannot predict the needs of future generations with any degree, even of approximation, but we can ensure the maximum possible range of options and opportunities. In the absence of firm government guidelines, yet to emerge, this may prove a tough one for EIA writers and reviewers with the indispensable assistance of the public.

1.10   EIA and the quality of life

As a matter of perspective, it is important to recognise that consideration of the economic, social, environmental, and political aspects of a policy, plan, program, or project, does not actually exhaust the full potential effect on human society; the 'quality of life' is to be considered. This phrase, particularly popular following the UN conference in Stockholm in 1972, embraces a host of desirable things not necessarily recognised, or adequately recognised, in the marketplace; and not necessarily reflected in the gross domestic product (GDP).

Some qualities of life escape the EIA net, however broadly interpreted and applied, but these are clearly valuable to most people: civil liberties, justice, integrity, fair play, compassion, health, education, law, order, recreation, and national self-respect. The quality of an individual's life is strongly influenced by personal, family, and community relationships, housing, and working conditions, discrimination, ethnic differences, domestic violence, gender, and spiritual influences.

Material success in a community with fair distribution of that success, is a vital key in combating poverty and affording an adequate level of social welfare and environmental protection, but it remains only half the story. Thus the conduct of EIA, it must be recognised, is to tackle simply one important aspect of human welfare.

1.11   National principles for EIA

Countries that have produced a statement of principles for the conduct of EIA include Canada and Australia; both with somewhat similar federal systems.

The Canadian Council of Ministers of the Environment approved a set of principles in May 1991. See checklist 1.8. The principles emphasise the need for cost-effectiveness in the process, assessment before a development decision, public participation and encouragement, scoping, that is 'early identification of issues', innovative procedures, consistent application of EIA throughout the country, with emphasis on cooperative arrangements between governments at various levels.

In 1992, the Australian and New Zealand Environment and Conservation Council approved a set of national principles, enunciated for assessment authorities, with provision for public participation, and PPA; for government, with emphasis on policy and planning frameworks, consistent approaches and integrity; for proponents, with an emphasis on consultation with the public and the decision-maker, taking the opportunity to improve projects; and for the public, with advice on how to become effectively involved. Details are outlined in checklist 1.9. Figure 1, from the same source, places EIA within a framework of policies promoting ecologically sustainable development. It emphasises, also, the importance of strategic environmental planning.

In both statements, there is an emphasis on collaboration and cooperation, particularly between governments at, say, national, state or provincial, and local level. Checklist 1.10 suggests a form of agreement between two governments to achieve more harmonious collaboration when major projects arise in a transboundary or transjurisdictional situation.

CHECKLIST 1.8

Canada: cooperative principles for EA

General

It is critical that the environmental assessment process be cost effective, provide for a minimum of uncertainty and duplication and encourage cooperative action.

Assessment timing

Environmental impacts should be assessed prior to any irrevocable decisions being made.

Common elements

In order to ensure consistent and effective environmental assessment across the country, several common elements should be integral to each process:

Public participation. Accessible information, consistent terminology, the opportunity for public involvement (such as public hearings, public meetings, open houses, mediation or other mechanisms) and participant assistance, whether financial or technical, are important to encourage public participation in the environmental assessment process;

Scope of the review. Recognising that the scope of assessment will vary with the size and complexity of the project, environmental assessment should address as appropriate: public comments and concerns, the biophysical environment, socio-economic considerations, project need and justification, alternative means of carrying out a project, cumulative effects, follow-up requirements, sustainable development, and mitigation measures.

Proponent pays. Preparation of the environmental assessment statement, mitigation measures and follow-up programs will be undertaken at the expense of the proponent in conformity with the terms of reference or guidelines set down by the regulator. The proponent may also be responsible for costs related to public consultation;

Project approval/rejection. Each environmental assessment process should result in the provision of information to allow the decision-maker to approve, modify or reject the project;

Issue identification. Issues should be defined as early as possible in the process, in consultation with the public and other affected jurisdictions, to ensure that they are addressed in a timely and effective manner;

Innovative procedures. Each process should have provision for innovative procedures to allow the process to remain both effective and efficient under a variety of circumstances involving, for example, mediation, class assessments, compensation, performance bonds, development of standards and guidelines, cooperative assessments, or mandatory study lists.

Decision-making

Decisions arising from environmental assessments will be made by each jurisdiction within the limits of its legislative competence. Decisions cannot be delegated to another jurisdiction.

Consistent application

To avoid jurisdictional or 'forum' shopping, it is important that there be consistent application of the environmental assessment process. Projects which are likely to have significant environmental impacts should be subject to consistent environmental assessments wherever they are located.

Cooperative mechanisms

The necessity for federal/provincial and inter-provincial cooperation in the environmental assessment process must be recognised and all jurisdictions should adopt a range of cooperative mechanisms to facilitate harmonised environmental assessment, such as:

Consultation. Consulting with other jurisdictions early in the process to determine the extent and scope of the environmental assessment;

Process flexibility. Using another jurisdiction's environmental assessment process or a joint process, where appropriate, as the information gathering mechanism (recognising that the decisions must still be taken by the respective jurisdiction);

Administrative agreements. Developing administrative agreements between jurisdictions, to set out the principles and protocols for cooperation on both a general and project specific basis; and to include such topics as project screening, formation and membership of panels, cost sharing arrangements, hearing procedures, and participant assistance;

Communication. Establishing clearly defined points of contact between environmental assessment officers to ensure that any administrative or procedural difficulties can be dealt with quickly and effectively;

Scope and timing. Establishing the scope of an assessment and to set reasonable time frames for the environmental assessment process; and

Public participation. Designing mechanisms for public participation to allow for cooperative environmental assessment processes.

(Source: Canadian Council of Ministers of the Environment, approved at a meeting of the council, 6–7 May 1991)

CHECKLIST 1.9

National principles for EIA in Australia (Australian and New Zealand Environment and Conservation Council, 1992)

Principles for Assessing Authorities

1 Provide clear guidance on types of proposals likely to attract environmental impact assessment and on levels of assessment.

2 Provide proposal-specific guidelines (or a procedure for their generation) focussed on key issues and incorporating public concerns; and a clear outline of the EIA process. Amendments to guidelines should only be based on significant issues that arise after guidelines have been adopted.

3 Provide guidance to all participants in the EIA process on criteria for environmental acceptability of potential impacts including such things as the principles of ecologically sustainable development, maintenance of environmental health, relevant local and national standards and guidelines, codes of practice and regulations.

4 Negotiate with key participants to set an assessment timetable on a proposal-specific basis and commit to using best endeavours to meet it.

5 Seek and promote public participation throughout the process, with techniques and mechanisms tailored appropriately to specific proposals and specific publics.

6 Ensure that the total and cumulative effects of using or altering community environmental assets (for example air, water, amenity) receive explicit consideration.

7 Report publicly on the assessment of proposals.

8 Ensure predicted environmental impacts are monitored, the results assessed by a nominated responsible authority and feedback provided to improve continuing environmental management of proposals.

9 Monitor properly the efficiency and effectiveness of the environmental impact assessment process to learn from the past, streamline requirements and help maintain consistency.

10 Review, adapt and implement techniques and mechanisms which can improve the process and minimise uncertainty and delays.

11 Ensure that educational opportunities inherent in the EIA process are actively pursued.

Principles for Government

1 Provide policy and planning frameworks which set contexts for the environmental assessment of proposals.

2 Base decisions on proposals having potentially significant environmental impact on advice resulting from the EIA process and include provisions for effective protection and management of the environment.

3 Apply the EIA process equally to proposals from both the public and private sectors.

4 Within each jurisdiction (Commonwealth, State/Territory) provide for a coordinated government decision-making process to which the outcomes of EIA can be directed; and develop mechanisms to synchronise processes for decision-making such that, where possible, the opportunity exists for decisions to be made in parallel rather than sequentially for proposals requiring multiple approvals.

5 Ensure assessment reports are available to the public before or at the time of decision-making.

6 Establish one national agreement to ensure a single orderly process is in place where the EIA responsibilities of several governments are involved.

7 Provide support, if and when appropriate, to participants in the process to enable better and informed involvement.

8 Provide opportunities for reasonable public and proponent objections, on decisions made other than at Ministerial level, regarding the requirement for and level of assessment, adherence to due process, and environmental advice given to decision-makers.

9 Implement this national approach including, where appropriate, progressive amendment of statutory provisions, to increase consistency in the process.

10 Maintain the integrity of the EIA process.

Principles for Proponents

1 Take responsibility for preparing the case required for assessment of a proposal.

2 Consult the assessing authority and the community as early as possible.

3 Incorporate environmental factors fully into proposal planning, including a proper examination of reasonable alternatives.

4 Agree on a proposal-specific evaluation timetable and commit to using best endeavours to meet it.

5 Take the opportunity offered by the EIA process to improve the proposal environmentally.

6 Make commitments to avoid where possible and otherwise minimise, ameliorate, monitor and manage environmental impacts; and implement these commitments.

7 Amend environmental management practices responsibly, following provision and dissemination of environmental monitoring results.

8 Identify and implement responsible corporate environmental policies, strategies and management practices, with periodic review.

Principles for the Public

1 Participate in the evaluation of proposals through offering advice, expressing opinions, providing local knowledge, proposing alternatives and commenting on how a proposal might be changed to better protect the environment.

2 Become involved in the early stage of the process as that is the most effective and efficient time to raise concerns. Participate in associated and earlier policy, planning and program activities as appropriate, since these influence the development and evaluation of proposals.

3 Become informed and involved in the administration and outcomes of the environmental impact assessment process, including:
   - assessment reports of the assessing authority
   - policies determined, approvals given and conditions set
   - monitoring and compliance audit activities
   - environmental advice and reasons for acceptance or rejection by decision-makers.

4 Take a responsible approach to opportunities for public participation in the EIA process, including the seeking out of objective information about issues of concern.

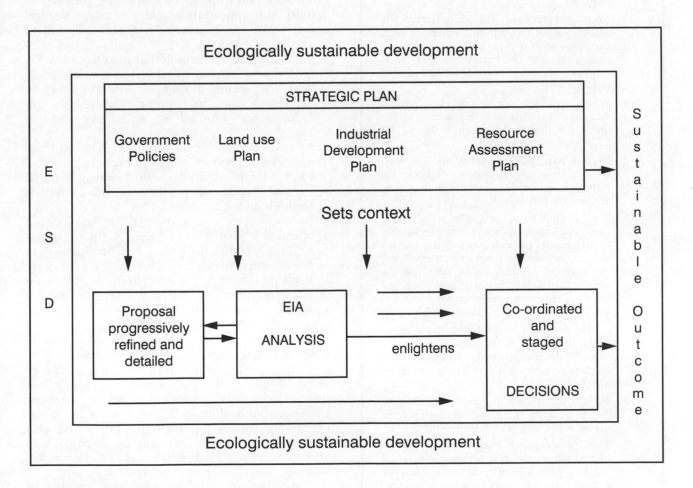

Figure 1 Setting the context for EIA
(Source: Australian and New Zealand Environment and Conservation Council, 1992)

Form of agreement between two governments to deal with transboundary or transjurisdictional situations arising from proposed activities

Object of the Agreement:

Arrangements for the reciprocal sharing of information about developments appearing to come within the respective environment protection legislation of the two governments; and to establish working arrangements for EIA of proposals involving both governments.

Procedural arrangements:

1   Both governments agree that only one EIS shall be produced to meet the requirements of both governments;

2   The respective governments and relevant departments or authorities shall inform immediately the other party of any proposal of which it becomes aware which is environmentally significant and likely to require EIA;

3   Each government (or department or agency) shall consult the other on each proposal with a view to reaching agreement on the information that each requires, having regard to legislative requirements;

4   Where an EIS is required, the two parties will consult with a view to reaching agreement on the matters that should be addressed in that EIS;

5   Each department or agency shall seek to ensure that the environmental impact statement is made available to both parties at the same time;

6   The EIS shall be made available for public comment in accordance with the legislative requirements of both parties; the parties will consult on the form of public notice, the method of advertising, the specific requirements of each party, and the party who will receive the comments;

7   The party receiving the comments shall convey copies of all comments to the other party; independent assessment of the outcome of the public display of the EIS will be conducted by both parties in consultation;

8   Should the need for a public hearing or inquiry emerge, the parties shall consult on the arrangements for such an inquiry;

9   The independent assessments shall be placed before the respective ministers of the two governments; in the event of a public inquiry that report shall be addressed to both ministers;

10   The responsible ministers shall confer to seek a common agreement on the outcome, the granting or refusal of development consent, the conditions to be attached to any approval granted, and the form and manner of any public announcement;

11   In the event of approval, the distribution of responsibility for the surveillance of the project shall be decided by the respective governments; also the reporting responsibilities of the proponent;

12   The rights of appellants shall be safeguarded by both parties.

1.12   Life cycle EIA (LEIA)

Life cycle EIA is a procedure for evaluating the environmental impacts of a product, process, or activity, throughout its whole life cycle; a vertical exercise running from cradle to grave. The main purposes of LEIA are:

- to assess the environmental effects of the retrieval and consumption of the raw materials and other inputs during the different life cycle phases of a product, process, or activity, including the fate of all pollutants and residuals;
- to assess the disposal problem, if any, of the superseded product, process, or activity;
- to provide information useful for an aggregated EIA of products, processes, and activities, throughout the life cycle;
- to evaluate the environmental consequences of alternative processes and design concepts, permitting a comparison between products, processes, and activities.

Each phase might be accorded a score on an environmental index, for example, for: natural resources, raw materials, land use; emissions to air, water, and soil; noise; manufacturing procedures about economy, energy, work and public safety; waste handling; recycling, and ultimate disposal.

A LEIA extends beyond the boundaries of responsibility of the individual company or producer, backwards and forwards, into matters entering the public domain. It goes beyond the realm of private ownership into the full social and resource implications of, say, car manufacture and ownership, including the disposal of car tyres, batteries, and abandoned vehicles.

The principle could be applied as readily to household appliances, beverage containers, packaging materials, paints, plastics, steels, fuels, lubricants, detergents, cables, fast food, fertilisers, energy production and use, and major infrastructure developments.

It is distinct from project EIA, which is much concerned with location, focusing on the life cycle of individual projects rather than the life cycle of infrastructure; its scope may be readily enlarged to embrace communication and transport systems.

The concept appears to have limited application so far, although some work by the Federation of Swedish Industries, the Swedish Environmental Research Institute, and the Volvo Car Corporation, has direct relevance (Ryding, 1991).

CHAPTER 2

EIA procedures

2.1 The environmental impact statement (EIS)

The EIS, sometimes known as the environmental effects statement (EES), the environmental statement (ES), or as the environmental impact assessment (EIA), depending upon country, is a document, prepared by a proponent, describing a proposed development, or activity (or a plan, or program) and disclosing the possible, probable, or certain effects of that proposal on the environment. An EIS should be comprehensive in its treatment of the subject matter, objective in its approach, and should be sufficiently specific for a reasonably intelligent mind to examine the potential environmental consequences, good and bad, of carrying out, or not carrying out, that proposal.

An EIS should meet the requirement that it alerts the decision-maker, the proponent, members of the public, and the government, to the consequences for the community; it should also explore possible alternatives to the project that might maximise the benefits while minimising the disbenefits (disadvantages). The primary purpose of an EIS, however, is to assist the decision-maker (usually government at some level, or a government agency) to arrive at a better informed decision than would otherwise have been the case. A decision might involve the outright rejection of the proposal or its deferment for further studies or revision, though more usually the project is approved, subject to a range of legal conditions and requirements that are attached to the development consent, approval, or permit.

In addition to an EIS and its assessment or review by a responsible agency or branch of government, a controversial and highly sensitive issue might involve an independent public inquiry by commissioners specially appointed for that pur-

pose. The principle of the EIS was introduced to the USA through the National Environmental Policy Act 1969, and has since been widely adopted in many countries including Australia, Canada, the members of the EC, the Nordic countries, and many Asian countries, as described in this book.

An EIS usually includes the following: a full description of the proposed project, or activity; a statement of the objectives of the proposal; an adequate description of the existing environment likely to be affected by the proposal; the identification and analysis of the likely environmental interactions between the proposal and the environment; the justification of the proposal; economic, social, and environmental considerations; the measures to be taken with the proposal for the protection of the environment, and an assessment of the likely effects of those measures; any feasible alternatives to the proposal; and the consequences of not carrying out the proposal for the proponent, community, region, and state. Checklist 2.1 sets out in much greater detail the characteristics of a good EIS. Checklist 2.2 provides a summary of the contents of an EIS for a proposed major third runway at the Sydney (Kingsford Smith) Airport, Australia, a proposal ultimately approved by the Australian federal government.

Although an EIS should take full account of all matters affecting, or likely to affect, the environment, there are reasonable limits to this. Sometimes an EIS does not and cannot address every aspect of a problem that experts, analysts, and members of the public, consider it should explore. The responsible government agency or commission of inquiry must then decide if further work and research is justified, given available time and costs. An adjournment in the EIA process might prove necessary, although sometimes it is possible to cover a 'loose end' through the legal conditions imposed. For example, emergency procedures and fire-fighting arrangements might not have been finalised; these become part of the development consent requirements imposed, stipulating also the authority or agency that must be satisfied about these measures.

We turn next to some of the more important considerations in the EIS.

CHECKLIST 2.1

Characteristics of a good EIS, environmental effects statement (EES), or environmental statement (ES)

1 A summary of the EIS, intelligible to non-specialists and the public, should precede the main text.

2 Acronyms and initials should be defined; a glossary of technical terms can be relegated to an appendix.

3 The list of contents should permit quick identification of the main issues.

4 The authors of the EIS should be clearly identified.

5 A brief outline of the history of the proposed development should be given, including details of early consultations.

6 A full description of the proposed project or activity, its objectives and geographical boundaries; its inputs and outputs and the movement of these; also the inputs and outputs specifically during the construction phase. Diagrams, plans, and maps will be necessary to illustrate these features, with a clear presentation of the likely appearance of the finished project.

7 A full description of the existing environment likely to be affected by the proposal; the baseline conditions; deficiencies in information; data sources; the proximity of people, other enterprises, and characteristics of the area of ecological or cultural importance.

8 The alternative locations considered, or alternative processes, resulting in the preferred choice of site; evidence of credible studies will be needed here.

9 The justification of the proposal in terms of economic, social, and environmental considerations; the consequences of not carrying out the proposal for the proponent, the locality, the region, and the nation.

10 The planning framework, relevant statutory planning instruments, zoning, planning, and environmental objectives.

11 The identification and analysis of the likely environmental interactions between the proposed activity and the environment.

12 The measures to be taken with the proposal for the protection of the environment and an assessment of their likely effectiveness, particularly about pollution control, land management, erosion, aesthetics, rehabilitation, ecological protection measures, and decommissioning. Measures to achieve clean production and recycling; the management of residuals.

13 The effect on the transport system of carrying people, goods, services, and raw materials, to and from the project.

14 The duration of the construction phase, operational phase, and decommissioning phase; housing the workforce, both construction and permanent.

15 The implications for public infrastructure such as housing, schools, hospitals, water supply, garbage removal, sewerage, electricity, roads, recreational facilities, fire, police, emergency services, parks, gardens, and nature reserves; the implications for endangered species and threatened ecological features and ecosystems; the prospective financial contributions of the proponent.

16 Any transboundary or transborder implications of the proposal.

17 Any cumulative effects from similar enterprises should be considered, being either short-term or long-term, permanent or temporary, direct or indirect.

18 Proposals for annual reporting to the decision-making body on the implementation of the conditions of consent; PPA and environmental auditing.

19 Arrangements for consultation with the relevant government agencies, planners, the public and interested bodies during the concept, preliminary, screening, scoping phases, the preparation of the EIS, the EIA stage, the construction, operational, and decommissioning stages; the communication of results.

20 Any unique features of the proposal of national or community importance such as technology, employment characteristics, training, contributions to exports or import replacement, defence, landscaping, recreational facilities; foreign investment, or marked multiplier effects.

21 The contribution to sustainable development, and the containment of global environmental problems.

2.2   The existing environment

An accurate and adequate description of the existing environment of the site and environs of a proposed development is a vital component in an EIS, for it is the possible effects on this environment that are next considered. Such a study might serve also as a protection for the proponent against later unjustified claims of damage to the environment by the project, during the construction or operational phases of the project.

CHECKLIST 2.2

EIS Proposed third runway, Sydney (Kingsford Smith) Airport, Australia

Summary of contents

1   Objective and context of the proposal
2   Relationship to the Sydney Airport planning strategy
3   The proponent
4   Public consultation procedures
5   The role and significance of Sydney Airport
6   Forecast demand and its implications
7   Airport system alternatives
8   Third runway alternatives
9   Evaluation of alternatives
10   Layout of Sydney Airport with the proposed third runway
11   Construction of the proposed runway
12   Operation of the proposed runway
13   Aboriginal and European heritage
14   Groundwater and surface hydrology
15   Terrestrial ecology
16   Aesthetics
17   Sources of bulk fill
18   Coastal hydrodynamics of Botany Bay
19   Marine ecology of Botany Bay
20   Aircraft noise
21   Economics and land use
22   Social and demographic environment
23   Hazards of airport operation
24   Air quality and emissions
25   Surface transport and the road network
26   Wake turbulence and jet blast
27   Monitoring programs
28   Construction management
29   Noise management and minimisation of impacts
30   Emergency planning
31   Bird strike potential
32   Relationship with Badgerys Creek
33   Implications of all issues for management
34   Guidelines for the EIS prepared by the Commonwealth (federal) Government

(Source: Technical documents and working papers derived from Kinhill Engineers Pty. Ltd., Sydney, Australia)

However, a survey of the environment conducted during a necessarily limited period (at, say, a particular time of year) gives only a snapshot impression, though this might be invaluable. It is important to identify some of the changes that might be taking place in the character of that environment in its ecological, archaeological, cultural, and urban aspects, in order to assess the future of the site should the development not take place.

Furthermore, some aspects of the environment might require monitoring and thorough analysis over an extended period to establish all the existing background levels of possible concern. This could apply to air and water pollutants such as fluorides, or heavy metals, which might be attributed to the new plant.

A proposed major power plant, for example, might well require a study conducted for 2 or even 5 years before development approval, to establish backgrounds for meteorological characteristics, existing air pollutants, or radiation. This stresses that a background survey cannot start soon enough.

The total area surveyed must be large enough to embrace all possible adverse environmental effects from the proposed project; this is a matter of judgement. Much depends, for example, on the nature and characteristics of pollutants discharged and the level of discharge. Potential effects, if any, might be quite close or at great range. Further, some potential adverse effects might be confined to the construction phase, while other adverse effects might only occur in very unlikely circumstances. The question then of area and the potential nature of adverse effects remains, therefore, a difficult one, not likely to satisfy everyone. Whatever boundary is defined, the rationale must be included in the EIS.

A company carrying out a well-researched, thorough study is better placed to advance its case, assuming adequate mitigating measures; and is in a very strong position to meet any later challenges.

Checklist 2.3 indicates the kind of matters which a survey of the existing environment should try to encompass.

CHECKLIST 2.3

EIA

The existing environment: components to be surveyed

1 topography, geology, and geomorphology;

2 surface and underground waters; coastal waters, if any;

3 meteorology and microclimate, by season;

4 principal ecological systems;

5 flora characteristics;

6 fauna characteristics;

7 endangered species;

8 history of ecological and natural events; for example, outbreaks of blue-green algae, dust clouds, fire, storm, flood and drought, soil erosion;

9 land uses and trends, for example, agriculture and horticulture, logging and forestry activities, and recreational activities;

10 aesthetic characteristics;

11 infrastructure, for example, communication and transmission facilities;

12 industrial, commercial, and residential developments;

13 evidence of air, water, land, and noise pollution, and the characteristics of each;

14 social characteristics;

15 archaeological, historical, cultural, Aboriginal, heritage, or religious, features of the area;

16 any public health characteristics of the area;

17 any risks and hazards associated with the area;

18 applicable environmental planning, and conservation instruments.

2.3 Scoping

Experience of NEPA in the USA led many to a conclusion that with EIAs there should be a process that starts early, involves all affected parties, and enables agencies and the writers of EISs to pinpoint significant issues warranting study and analysis. Such a process, it was felt, could lead to fewer delays and greater satisfaction with completed EISs.

Consequently, in 1978, the US CEQ introduced,

as a NEPA regulation, that 'there shall be an early and open process for determining the scope of issues to be addressed and for identifying the significant issues relating to a proposed action. This process was to be called "scoping"'.

Thus the scope of an EIS might vary greatly depending on the input from scoping meetings which usually last one day. Sometimes the meetings can involve large numbers of people and resemble fully fledged public hearings and inquiries. However, more often than not, scoping meetings are small informal gatherings of representatives of the key players: the proponent, the government agency involved, the environmental agency, state and local agencies, and citizens' environmental groups. They meet and, with the help of presentations, decide together on the scope of the EIS, the alternatives to consider, and the types of effects to closely examine and assess.

Kennedy (1987) has noted two problems with scoping:

• Although the main purpose of scoping is to identify the significant issues and eliminate the insignificant ones, experience has shown that environmentalists rarely agree to eliminate any issue. As a result, more issues often come from scoping meetings than were originally included by the proponent, lead, or environmental agency.

• The criteria used to determine the 'significance' of an impact or alternative are highly subjective, 'public concern' is often cited as a factor in determining 'significance'.

Nevertheless, Kennedy concludes that 'international experience has shown that where scoping does not take place, delays often occur along with extra costs because of time spent in assessing impacts that were not identified early-on and eventually proved significant'.

It is important that the community understands the issues well enough to participate in the process, and this involves adequate steps to inform the public and its voluntary organisations as soon as possible. The role of the media here is clearly pertinent.

Not all countries accept scoping. The concept was considered and rejected in New South Wales, Australia, in the late 1970s on the grounds that such meetings might well resemble, and be treated by some, as full-scale public inquiries, requiring very skilful chairing to conclude a meeting in one or two days. There was, and still is, a patent shortage of such people available to undertake this, in addition to their normal public inquiry activities towards the end of the process. However, many proponents have conducted their own scoping meetings with members of the local communities.

2.4 Terms of reference (TOR)

EIA processes require proponents to consult the review body or decision-making body for initial guidance on the prospective content of an EIS. In Thailand the purpose of setting TOR is to stipulate the requirements for the EIS to be prepared by the agency or proponent proposing to undertake the project. The TOR may be set by the Office of the National Environment Board; an example of such TOR is illustrated in checklist 2.4. Such consultation is another aspect of the scoping process. The EIS might be undertaken by the agency or proponent directly or through the employment of a consultant. The object of TOR is to improve the prospects of a competent report. The proponent should not rely, however, on official guidance alone and is never restricted to official TOR. Other sample TORs have been published by the Economic and Social Commission for Asia and the Pacific (ESCAP) in the Environment and Development series (see Bibliography).

For a proposed third runway at Sydney (Kingsford Smith) Airport, the proponent, the Federal Airports Corporation, sought the guidance of both the federal and the New South Wales governments. From this consultation process, draft guidelines or TOR were developed and made widely available for public comment. Advertisements advising availability of the draft guidelines were placed in local and state newspapers. A period of 1 month was allowed for written submissions by the public; more than 250 submissions were received and considered before finalising the TOR for issue to the consultants preparing the EIS. In this way scoping extended to two governments, local councils, other agencies, and the general public.

2.5 Alternatives

In all prescriptions for EISs, there is a quite proper emphasis on the question of alternatives: alternative techniques and alternative sites. Furthermore, it has been stressed by the US CEQ, this search must be genuine and well-documented, done before, not after, a choice has been made. Examples in this book illustrate the benefits of searching for alternatives (see Britain, 6.1, and case study 6A).

In a range of industries, reasonable alternative sites within a region are often appropriate. Power stations, aluminium smelters, oil refineries, dams, airports, highways, chemical processing works, light industry, incinerators, transmission lines, urban developments, landfills, nuclear facilities, defence facilities, forestry operations and so on, lend themselves often to much debate on the choice of site.

CHECKLIST 2.4

TOR for the preparation of an EIS: outline

1   Introduction
   1.1 Purpose of terms of reference
   1.2 Responsibility for preparing EIA report
2   General EIA guidelines
3   Background information
   3.1 Specific background studies and reports
   3.2 General background studies and reports
4   Specific EIA guidelines
   4.1 Specific environmental effects
   4.2 Corrective measures
   4.3 Monitoring
   4.4 EIA study proposal
      4.4.1 Work tasks
      4.4.2 Study schedule
      4.4.3 Review sessions
      4.4.4 Printing or reproduction of EIA report
      4.4.5 Study team
5   Time constraints
   5.1 EIA report
   5.2 Proposals for conducting the EIA study
6   Budget
7   Outside assistance
8   Additional information
Appendices (not included)
I   General guidelines for preparing EIA reports
II   Guidelines for preparing an EIA report for specific types of projects
III   Recommended format for preparing EIA proposals

(Source: Office of the National Environment Board, Bangkok, Thailand)

Many proposals are site-specific:
- the mining or extraction or use of natural resources;
- port facilities often depend on deep-water access;
- coalmining operations require immediate access to coal deposits;
- oil and gas operations to those resources;
- bauxite mining;
- mineral sand extraction usually only on the coast;

- communications towers only at advantageous points;
- sewage effluent outfalls serving existing systems;
- some harbour crossings;
- major buildings viable only in the central business district on acquired sites;
- major restoration and rehabilitation projects;
- tourist facilities to serve specific tourist attractions;
- additions and extensions to existing installations such as oil refineries;
- steelworks;
- chemical processing plants;
- shopping complexes;
- road systems;
- housing developments;
- public infrastructure.

In these instances where there cannot be an alternative site, an EIS is pointless to discuss the issue, save to stress that the project is site-specific. The issue here is simply 'yes' or 'no', without alternative locations being discussed, although there may be a range of choices about scale, appearance, technology, waste discharges, mitigation measures, and traffic management.

2.6 The quality of EISs

Lee and Colley (1990) have reviewed the results of several surveys and studies carried out on the subject of the quality of EISs and have concluded that there is mounting evidence from a number of countries 'that the quality of a significant proportion of these statements is unsatisfactory'.

Certainly, in Britain and no doubt in other countries, part of the problem, it is argued, is because of a lack of grasp (possibly the result of inexperience) on the part of some proponents and consultancies, of what is involved in the EA of projects, and what is expected in EISs. Another part of the problem lies in the understandable temptation for developers to present EISs which are designed to support the case for project approval.

However, Lee and Colley concede that, given the limited research evidence available to date, any conclusions about the quality of EISs have to be tentative.

Experience in New South Wales, Australia

The Department of Environment and Planning, New South Wales, summed up several years' experience of EISs in its manual of EIA (DEP, 1985), listing a variety of shortcomings. These include:
- overly technical or complex presentation which precludes general comprehension;
- insufficient information relating to the proposal and environmental impacts;

- concentration on extolling the virtues of a proposal rather than objective presentation of information;
- poor base information which leads to deficiencies in analysis;
- omission of information which is relevant to decision-making;
- inclusion of considerable scientific data which may be largely irrelevant to decision-making, or which is not employed in the analysis of environmental impacts;
- poor presentation of information, unclear text, lack of readily understood illustrative data;
- incomplete identification of proposal/environmental interactions and consequent impacts;
- lack of appreciation of indirect impacts or of potential impacts outside the proposed development site;
- use of complicated systems of value judgements rather than factual statements concerning environmental impacts.

Other problems in the preparation of EISs and the conduct of EIAs have also been pinpointed by the New South Wales Science and Technology Council (1983), summarised as follows:
- Often information on the physical and biological environments, necessary for scientifically adequate environmental studies, is both limited and fragmentary particularly in rapidly developing parts of the state.
- The absence of an effective information retrieval system results in information which does exist not being fully utilised.
- The time constraints for the review of project proposals often means that the scientific background for individual projects is not in place before the EIA process starts.
- The process is handicapped by the small number of trained personnel available and the lack of guidelines and methodology manuals.
- Cumulative impacts are not always addressed in EISs in an effective manner.
- Individual projects often need consideration in a wider regional context and such wider regional environmental plans might not exist.
- Sometimes the scoping of key issues has proved inadequate.
- Some information provided in an EIS could be extraneous or non-essential.
- There can be too much reliance on 'professional opinions', rather than substantive scientific evidence.

However, the report notes that there had been a considerable improvement in the substantive content of New South Wales EISs so that a satisfactory review of many project proposals is now possible. Further improvements are, however, both desirable and possible.

The evidence of Smyth (1987), a former New South Wales Director of Planning, is much more emphatic, drawing on experience over 10 years. He identifies the main deficiencies in EISs, in summary, as:

- a failure to address real environmental issues relevant to the local community;
- the descriptive nature of much information given and its superficiality;
- a narrow focus on the engineering aspects of the proposal, rather than a broader environmental planning approach;
- misleading, absent, contradictory, and biased information, and a lack of objective findings;
- the use of complex technical jargon, incomprehensible to the community;
- failure to adequately justify the proposals and address alternatives;
- offering only a justification for a previous decision.

This is a severe judgement. Smyth argues that over 50 per cent of all EISs fail to address the issues relevant to decision-making; and that over 75 per cent of all EISs fail to adequately communicate with the public, facilitating participation.

However, Smyth offers much useful advice on how the quality of EISs could be improved. He also stresses that choosing the right site is just as important as producing a good EIS.

My opinion over a similar period, is perhaps not so severe. I argue that about 75 per cent of EISs examined, were adequate for public exhibition and public challenge through the public inquiry system. However, there have been some conspicuous failures.

2.7 NSW Land and Environment Court

The NSW Land and Environment Court has made observations about the adequacy of the EISs during its judgements on appeal. These points are summarised below:

- The purpose of an EIS is to bring matters to the attention of members of the public, the decision-maker, and the Department of Planning so the environmental consequences of a development proposal can be properly understood.
- The purpose of an EIS is to assist the decision-maker.
- An EIS is not a decision-making end in itself, but a means to a decision-making end.
- The EIS must be sufficiently specific to direct a reasonably intelligent and informed mind to possible or potential environmental consequences.

- The EIS should be written in understandable language.
- The EIS should contain material which would alert both lay persons and specialists to potential problems.
- An EIS would be unacceptable if it is superficial, subjective, or non-informative.
- An EIS would be acceptable if it is comprehensive in its treatment of subject matter, objective in its approach, and alerts relevant parties to the environmental effects and community consequences of the carrying out, or not, of the proposed development.

2.8 An ethical dilemma

EISs are prepared by the proponent (developer). To accomplish this, it is common practice for either in-house staff to be employed, or more commonly, outside consultants. As a consequence, some people feel that the process is essentially flawed from the outset. In-house and outside consultants are employed, it is argued, to please those who employ them, and not to meet the needs of the wider community, and the decision-making body. An EIS, it is felt, must necessarily be no more than a shop-window with the better goods prominently displayed and inferior stock carefully hidden. Certainly, it is true that everyone seeks to survive, while individuals and consultancies look also to future business.

In all organisations, whether public or private, people with strong social consciences or religious zeal, or sound integrity, often find that they are excluded from crucial discussions, and excluded from major projects calling for 'flexibility'. When an individual of high competence challenges the emerging pattern, there is invariably some reference to a 'lack of confidence' somewhere in the higher management in that individual.

Some feel that EISs are essentially 'sleazy' documents, a product of a single interest, lacking objectivity, full of carefully selected words to disguise a multitude of shortcomings. Professional individuals working within organisations recognise the occasional 'ethical dilemma', of either stating the truth reasonably and objectively, or serving the narrow interest of the employer, even though such service might prove to be a disservice to that same employer in the end.

Clearly, some of the shortcomings of EISs indicated elsewhere in this text must be a result, surely, of this compromising factor. Consequently, EISs should be carried out by independent bodies, though at the expense of the proponent. This approach does not seem to have attracted much support.

Probably this is because of an emerging quality in EISs, where the better, franker, documents have a much better track record in gaining the golden fleece – the development approval (DA). Further, many governments require consultation with the proponent on the contents of the forthcoming EIS, and there is an increasing trend to scoping meetings at which the whole range of possible issues might emerge. As deficient EISs tend to 'foul-up' in the EIA process, matters are referred to the proponent for further exposition and research. Deficient work can be costly in time and effort. Better to get it right in the first place! Particularly if the outcome is a public hearing or public inquiry and the third parties have rights of appeal to the courts on non-complying documents.

The key factor is that an EIS as a basic document is only one input to the EIA process; and there is really no escape from the necessity of good work. Poor quality, dishonesty, unskilled presentation, and unconvincing conclusions often lead to increased costs to the proponent, and the in-house staff, or consultants who provide the EIS. Sound integrity can be achieved by employing, for particular sections of an EIS, experts and authorities whose interests are not closely tied to the interests of the proponent, financially, or otherwise.

At all times the analyst should try to reduce the subjective element and increase the objective content of all assessments. Some suggestions are incorporated in checklist 2.5.

All-in-all, EISs of good quality are an advantage to all parties: the public, the relevant government agencies, and the proponent. Apart from gaining development consent with a minimum of delay and indirect costs, proponents frequently find that appropriate mitigation measures and correct siting, result in reduced direct costs of production, or implementation. The additional effort in the preparation of EISs giving attention to many procedures and processes often yield, in practice, a more competent enterprise.

2.9 Decision-making

Before the more formal or statutory part of an EIA process, both proponents and decision-makers might make decisions of major importance for potential development; this is called 'ad hoc' decision-making. This category of decision-making is an assessment of potential costs and benefits, but in a context of business policy and political considerations. For proponents, it is usually a decision not to proceed with a project on the grounds of actual or anticipated public concern; for governments it is often a decision to proceed regardless of public opinion.

CHECKLIST 2.5

EIA or review
How to reduce subjectivity and increase objectivity

1. Take up a 'Rio' approach, balancing development with environment protection.
2. Review carefully the policy, legal, political, and media-interest framework within which the assessment or review takes place.
3. Take note of public expectations and reservations expressed at scoping meetings.
4. Take note of the performance of similar programs, projects, or activities previously approved within the nation and elsewhere, with particular reference to the results of environmental audits, PPAs, and court actions.
5. Refer to the proponent's track record.
6. Take note of the thoughts and reflections of those colleagues with the best proven professional judgements.
7. Take note of the principles of natural justice when considering the distributional effects of the proposal.
8. Take note of relevant cultural, religious, sacred, archaeological, historical, economic, and social factors.
9. Attempt to define the public interest.
10. Resist intimidation, threats, inducements, bribes, and 'advice' from whatever quarter it might come.
11. Establish liaison groups early in the procedure, such between the local community and voluntary conservation bodies and the proponent; these will serve as a continuous sounding board for the proponent and involved levels of government.

In the early 1960s an application did not proceed to construct and to operate a major power station in London on an otherwise excellent site, solely on the grounds that the stack top, it was discovered, would be in direct view of the terraces of the House of Commons.

In the 1980s, in New South Wales, Australia, major projects did not proceed because of public unrest; the location of an open-cut mine too close to a major residential district; and the abandonment of proposed sand-mining in an ecologically sensitive bay. In both cases, the proponents found that they could not confront a public inquiry and hope to succeed. These are both examples of EIAs conducted by proponents behind closed doors.

For governments, decisions are also made behind closed ministerial and cabinet doors, and lead to a major project proceeding on a particular site to a particular schedule, the decision and any financial arrangement with the proponent embodied in a separate piece of legislation. Environmental planning and pollution control officers learn of the decision in the evening newspapers. When the legislation comes before parliament, these officers discover that the project has been exempted, in whole or substantial part, from all normal planning and assessment processes, and from all pollution licensing.

These vital matters are usually referred to in general terms for consideration only by the development minister. There is thus an ad hoc agreement between a government and a proponent of a private nature, the exemptions applying to planning permits and to subsequent policing. The explanation is to be readily found. Ministers of development and their senior people travel overseas and interstate to attract industrial development in their regions. Once gained, nothing and nobody must stand in the way of bringing home the golden fleece. Existing safeguards and all public participation have been bypassed. Rights of appeal and the right or need for a public inquiry are also set aside. Government-initiated and financed projects might also receive similar protection, announced with enthusiasm with half the issues unexamined.

Public opinion, environmental groups, and the media, can create a stir; and this does happen. Without such vigilance, the ad hoc decision, typical of the past could once again become the norm. The 'behind closed doors' scenario sometimes lends itself to ministerial corruption whether it be simply the acceptance of the proponent's cut-price shares, or the offer of free holiday accommodation; or the acceptance of secret commissions of a large and illegal nature. EIA emerges as a healthy tonic for the body politic.

The results of an EIA must be placed, finally, before the decision-making body. This might be a local elected council, a minister, an agency board, a cabinet, or other nominated body. In a dictatorship it might be the president or a military junta.

At this stage, experience at the political level suggests, nothing complex should be presented. Any discussion of options, alternatives, variants, values, weightings, let alone any reference to a three-dimensional matrix, should be assiduously avoided. On a single sheet of paper with substantial margins, a single recommendation should be advanced. If the recommendation is the rejection of a DA or proposal, the reasons should be confined to not more than 50 words. If the recommendation is positive, there will be a need to refer to a range of conditions set out in the text, but again confined at this stage, to no more than 50 words.

Attached to this simple statement should be a summary of no more than two or three pages, in simple language, summing up the entire case, for and against.

The presentation of a recommendation to the decision-making body will always be a tense experience for the presenter. Among an elected body there will be a range of interests, some of which will be known. With other decision-makers, there may be a number of interests which cannot be ascertained in advance. The presenter will run a risk, always, of experiencing impact at the point of presentation: delight, dismay, mixed reactions, grumblings, wrath, outbursts, or apoplectic anger.

The presenter must remain self-composed and persuasive however unassuring the environment; there must be no expressions of doubt or reservation, no betrayal of the multi-disciplinary team who worked with the presenter. Questions must be answered without hesitation and confidently.

Beyond this, and indeed, beyond the documentation itself, it is often necessary to offer some political guidance by drawing attention to the attitudes of the proponent and the opponents of the project. The decision-maker must know something of the climate surrounding the EIA process; if politicians or parties participated, if the proponent willingly accepted suggestions for change and improvement, and what conservation bodies participated. All of this should be summarised in the body of the EIA report, but an oral presentation is invariably required.

In the end, the decision-maker reaches a determination; the EIA is simply an input to that process. There might be other important considerations known only to the government. A minister might not like a project within her or his own constituency, however satisfactory, where objectors have included members of her or his own preselection committee. A project not recommended might prove to be the premier's personal ambition for state development. There might be, from time to time, a corrupt influence such as a minister having her or his holidays at the expense of the proponent. Such is the rich fabric of political life!

At this stage, for the presenter, the matrix and checklist can often seem very far away. Personal survival, career-wise, can often become the prime sensation. Yet in reality, many recommendations are accepted as of professional quality and appropriately respected.

Checklist 2.6 sets out the essential structure of an environmental impact review report; while checklist 2.7 suggests how to handle such a report in conditions of uncertainty and lack of knowledge.

CHECKLIST 2.6

Structure of an EIA report

1. letter of transmittal to the decision-making body or person, signed by the responsible official;

2. recommendation(s) and proposed conditions, if relevant;

3. principal findings;

4. background to the proposal;

5. the proposal and the EIS;

6. the issues:
   (a) environmental;
   (b) economic;
   (c) social;

7. mitigation measures;

8. the planning context: local and regional;

9. appendixes:
   (a) list of submissions from the public, departments, and agencies;
   (b) location and site boundaries;
   (c) layout of buildings;
   (d) transport network;
   (e) visual assessment;
   (f) air and water quality;
   (g) noise, equipment, and traffic;
   (h) industrial wastes;
   (i) alternatives;
   (j) energy considerations;
   (k) risks and hazards;
   (l) emergency arrangements;
   (m) rehabilitation.

CHECKLIST 2.7

How to handle EIA in conditions of uncertainty and lack of knowledge

1. If the uncertainties are great (with possible grave consequences to the community) and there is no way of reducing these uncertainties to acceptable proportions, within a framework of conditions, reject the development application.

2. If the uncertainties are great, but might be reduced by further studies over a short period (say, 6 months) and there are prospects of controlling the remaining uncertainties by reasonable and enforceable conditions (say, temporary shut down of production), defer the development application until completion of further studies.

3. If uncertainties might be reduced by further studies, and there is every likelihood (based on experience elsewhere) that the outcomes would not be serious and could be contained by conditions, then development consent might be granted, subject to further studies over a limited period and restrictive conditions.

4. If the uncertainties are tolerable, grant development consent, subject to conditions including audit at specified intervals.

5. Adopt the precautionary principle (see glossary).

6. In all cases of development consent, specify criteria for the suspension of hazardous operations and arrangements for review.

2.10 The cost of EIA

Direct costs

The direct compliance costs of the assessment process do not appear to have proved a significant problem for large companies, especially if EA is integrated with feasibility studies. Usually these costs represent only a small proportion of total project costs.

The Bureau of Industry Economics (1990) in Australia has estimated these direct costs as generally less than 1 per cent of total project costs. The Environmental Protection Administration (1985) in Taiwan has estimated the costs in that country as ranging from about 0.1 per cent to 1.5 per cent of a project's total cost. It does not appear that these costs are of particular concern.

Indirect costs

A corporation's planning horizon needs to be extended to allow for the whole of the planning, environmental, public inquiry, and licensing procedures. In some instances this involves planning 5 to 10 years ahead, or even longer in the case of electricity generation, or requirements. Much of what might be described as 'delays' can be avoided by forward planning. However, unexpected problems and delays might arise which could not reasonably have been anticipated.

These delays could arise from:
- a lack of coordination between the responsible authorities or levels of government involved;
- conflicting demands between agencies and levels of government;
- the failure of agencies and governments to observe time limits;

- an increase in the number of authorities and agencies involved;
- an unexpectedly large volume of public opposition;
- a public inquiry not reasonably expected;
- parliamentary opposition not reasonably anticipated;
- significant deficiencies identified in the EIS by a discerning public and by agencies.

These often require further studies to be undertaken and perhaps involve adjournments during a public inquiry.

These indirect costs can be considerable, amounting to about 10 per cent of total project costs. They are particularly onerous in the case of a large electricity generating system and transmission network. Here delay incurs the operation of more expensive plant beyond the planned time through the exclusion of more efficient plant with lower generating costs from the system.

Some of these unexpected delays and interruptions are beyond the control of the company and its officers; others might have been avoided or minimised perhaps with better public and agency consultation. The ultimate rejection of a DA inflicts the maximum burden of costs, both direct and indirect.

Pollution control costs

The direct and indirect costs of EIA should be set, however, in the context of other environmental costs such as the costs of pollution control measures which must be subsequently incurred during construction. Typically, pollution control costs as a percentage of total plant and equipment costs, for the following industries in Europe and North America, have been: iron and steel industry, 20 per cent; non-ferrous metals, 12 per cent; electricity generating plant, 11 per cent. Other costs are also incurred in the acquisition of buffer zones, landscaping, time, and operating restrictions (Gilpin, 1990).

2.11   Tax relief for EIA studies

From March 1991, the Australian government allowed taxpayers a tax deduction for capital expenditure incurred primarily and principally in undertaking an environmental impact study.

Expenditure, other than on plant and equipment, became deductible on a straight-line basis over the lesser of the life of the project or 10 years. For this purpose, the life of the project would include any period involved in completing the environmental impact study and between completing the study and the beginning of operations. Where the project does not proceed, expenditure on the environmental impact study is deductible

over 10 years. Expenditure on plant and equipment used in such studies is also deductible under the general depreciation provisions, as if used to produce assessable income.

Environmental costs

The costs of EIA procedures, direct and indirect, and the costs of appropriate mitigation measures, must be set within the framework of environmental costs as a whole. Projects rarely become entirely innocuous as a result of EIA processes. There are quite commonly losers in the process.

Mitigation procedures do not necessarily protect all sections of the community such as a new airport or extension which introduces a noise element not previously experienced. This larger view of costs and benefits must not be overlooked, and is discussed elsewhere in this work. (See chapter 3.)

2.12   Post-project analysis PPA (auditing)

A most effective tool for improving the entire EIA process is the PPA or audit. Its primary purpose is to ensure that the development has taken place under the terms and conditions imposed by the initial EIA process and its associated development consent or planning approval. PPA also has other uses.

A UN ECE task force (UN ECE 1990) concluded that PPAs are very effective and necessary for continuing the EIA process into the implementation phase, and serve the following purposes:

- to monitor compliance with the agreed conditions set out in construction permits and operating licences;
- to review predicted environmental impacts for proper management of risks and uncertainties;
- to modify the activity or develop mitigation measures in case of unpredicted harmful effects on the environment;
- to determine the accuracy of past impact predictions and the effectiveness of mitigation measures in order to transfer this experience to future activities of the same type;
- to review the effectiveness of environmental management for the activity.

In summary PPA should be used to complete the EIA process by providing necessary feedback in the project implementation phase for proper and cost-effective management and for EIA process development. See checklist 2.8.

A preliminary plan for PPA should be prepared during the EIA process, and fully developed when a favourable decision is made. See figure 2.

CHECKLIST 2.8

Classifications for PPA

Project management PPA
Undertaken for the purpose of managing the environmental impacts of the activity.

Process development PPA
Undertaken to identify the lessons to be learned from the activity for future benefit.

Classification by type of PPA study

Scientific and technical PPA
Deals with the scientific accuracy of impact predictions, or the technical suitability of mitigation measures.

Procedural and administrative PPA
Deals with EIA process effectiveness (either with the EIA process or with the project as implemented).

(Derived from UN ECE, *Post-project analysis in environmental impact assessment*, environmental series 3, UN, New York, USA, 1990, p. 10).

The UN ECE task force also recommended that:

- As a tool for managing PPAS [PPAs], advisory boards consisting of industry, government, contractors, independent experts and public representatives should be used.
- Public participation in the PPA should be encouraged.
- PPA reports should be made public.
- The conditions of approval for a project should be such that the management of that project should take account of the findings of the PPA.

These recommendations are clearly a doctrine of the ideal. Many societies are still wrestling with the basic idea of public participation in the EIA process, let alone in the initial scoping process, and now PPA.

So far, few countries appear to have adopted the principle of PPA at least as an aspect of EIA. PPA is required as a formal component of the EIA process in The Netherlands; EIA legislation explicitly requires subsequent investigation of the environmental consequences of any activity reviewed under the IEA Act. Britain also endorses the

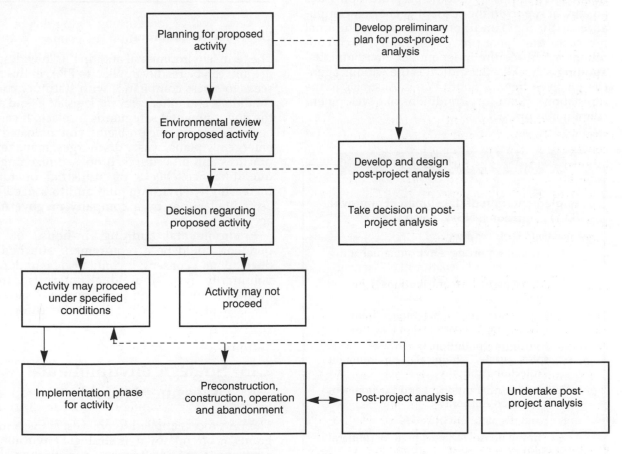

Figure 2 The PPA framework linked to the EIA process
(Source: UN ECE, *Post-project analysis in environmental impact assessment*, environmental series 3, UN, New York, USA, 1990, p. 29)

principle that the actual effects of a development project on the environment should be evaluated, after development consent has been given, both during the construction phase and subsequently during the project's operation. Britain has long-standing provisions of this kind, applying to all relevant installations, not only those which have been subject to EIA. The recommendations of the UN ECE task force would not apparently improve on the existing arrangements in that country.

Similarly, in Australia, it seems likely that a statutory requirement for PPA would not add much (or anything) to present arrangements. The reason is that the completion of the EIA for a major project (with or without a public inquiry), leading to the granting of development consent (subject to a range of conditions), is not the end of the process. On the contrary, it marks the beginning of a process whereby a whole range of departments and statutory bodies is involved in translating the conditions of approval into satisfactory measures consistent with those conditions and their own respective statutory duties and functions. Further, the process is often assisted by a statutory condition, often imposed, that the proponent provides an annual report to the consent agency on compliance with the conditions and any additional measures that have proved necessary; such conditions might require independent environmental auditing. Checklist 2.9 indicates the various agencies involved in New South Wales, Australia, in the translation of statutory conditions of development consent into practice.

CHECKLIST 2.9

Implementation of development approval (DA) conditions, NSW, Australia

Condition/Agency or proponent

1. Annual reporting; environmental auditing/Proponent Department of Planning
2. Infrastructure contributions; bonds; levies/Treasury; local council
3. Implications for zoning and environmental planning/Department of Planning
4. Control of pollution (air, water, noise, solid waste, chemicals)/Environment Protection Authority
5. Monitoring/Proponent and Environment Protection Authority
6. Land/Department of Lands
7. Mining leases/Department of Mineral Resources
8. Implications for agriculture/Department of Agriculture
9. Soil conservation/Department of Conservation and Land Management Service
10. Fauna and flora/National Parks and Wildlife Service
11. Roads, highways, traffic/Roads and Traffic Authority
12. Rail connections/State Rail Authority
13. Emergency plans and services/Proponent; State Emergency Service; Fire Brigade
14. Water, drainage and sewerage/Water Board
15. Electricity supplies/Sydney Electricity or regional body
16. Catchment protection/Catchment Areas Protection Board
17. Forestry/Forestry Commission
18. Landscaping/Local council
19. Heritage, culture/Heritage Council
20. Public health/Health Department
21. Harbours and marine waters/Maritime Services Board/Port Authority/Waterways Authority

---

Environmental auditing

The term 'environmental auditing' is in widespread use and can be readily applied to PPA; in this role it seeks to assess compliance with statutory consent conditions and other relevant legislation and assess the environmental safeguards in place. It can also be applied to specific problems: contaminated sites, emergency plans, waste discharges, management practices and procedures, proposed rezoning; and due diligence checks of industrial operations. Increasingly, environmental auditors need to be accredited either by a company or government agency.

Environmental auditing, in-house or independent, could be a requirement attached to a development consent; it could also be undertaken voluntarily by an individual enterprise. In any event, the cost falls on the proponent. However, the cost of checks will fall on the enforcement agency.

2.13 Strategic environmental assessment (SEA)

The EA process applied to policies, plans, and programs, is often known as strategic environmental assessment or SEA. It achieves more than simply complementing the normal EIA procedures applied to individual projects, providing a framework within which individual EIAs can take place. Some important matters such as cumulative effects, greenhouse policies, conservation of resources, and the issue of sustainability are at least partially taken into account in this framework.

In effect SEA introduces a two-stage EIA, going further than some earlier initiatives in Britain, and initiating two-stage public inquiries into particularly complex schemes. The first inquiry is essentially a policy-and-need inquiry, while the second is a site-specific inquiry. SEA might embrace, say, national energy policy, dealing with many crucial issues, examining a national energy development program, setting the standards and targets for individual projects. Later each individual project would undergo a separate EIA, a second stage in the process. The inquiry into hard rock resources in New South Wales, Australia, represented an initial step into a two-stage approach to EIA.

According to Lee and Walsh (1992), relatively small numbers of countries and organisations have created mandatory SEA provisions with features broadly corresponding to those found in EIA. Greater numbers of countries have incorporated some elements of a limited form of environmental evaluation (EE) into their planning procedures. Many more countries and organisations are addressing the issue.

The European Commission has indicated in its environment program that it intends to propose a directive for the application of SEA to certain policies, plans, and programs in member states (Commission of the European Communities, 1992). The UNECE (1992) has also reviewed the issue. Since 1975, a German guideline has made provision for the EA of federal policies, plans, and programs, but this appears to have had limited application. France and The Netherlands have also made provision for the EA of certain policies, plans, and programs only.

Canada has established a procedure for the EA of policy decisions at the federal level (Couch, 1991). Under the US NEPA, 1969, there is provision for 'programmatic' EIAs, but this provision has only been used to a limited extent; California is the only state in the USA that has a fully operational, tiered EIA system (Bass, 1990).

Australia has engaged in strategic forms of EA largely through Royal Commissions into specific issues such as the Great Barrier Reef and nuclear testing; through the Ranger Uranium Environmental Inquiry conducted under the Environment Protection (Impact of Proposals) Act, 1974; and through the activities of the Resource Assessment Commission (RAC). The commission has held public inquiries and presented reports to the federal government on forestry, coastal lands, and on aspects of Kakadu national park.

Checklists 2.10, 2.11, and 2.12 offer some guidance on what might be considered in the SEA of the energy, forestry, and transportation sectors of the economy.

CHECKLIST 2.10

Energy policy and program impact assessment
Checklist: matters for consideration

1   the probable validity of forecast energy demands in all their forms;

2   the components of the program according to fuel and other sources of energy, and the economics of choice;

3   the economic factors influencing the location of electricity generating units;

4   the environmental and social factors to be considered in the final choice of input energies;

5   the environmental implications of transmission networks;

6   energy efficiency in generation, transmission, and use;

7   conservation measures which might be adopted;

8   the size of fossil fuel, natural gas, petroleum, uranium, and hydro reserves;

9   trends in motor vehicle fuel consumption;

10   the physical location of major primary sources, together with environmental and social considerations;

11   the influence on energy consumption of taxes and subsidies;

12   incentives for energy efficiency and conservation;

13   energy efficiency targets;

14   availability and cost of capital for energy installations and the promotion of efficiency;

15   research and development;

16   the energy needs for rural and outlying districts;

17   integration of energy, development, and environmental policies;

18   the levels of air pollution attributable to energy use; the nature and significance of each pollutant and the implications for health and the environment;

19   the synergistic effects of air pollutants; the levels and significance of photochemical smog;

20   the cumulative effects of air pollutants in valley situations for health and the environment;

21   the levels of water pollution attributable to energy exploration, mining and use; the nature and significance of each pollutant for health and the environment;

22   the levels of noise pollution created by activities associated with the use of energy; the implications for health and the environment;

23   the aesthetics of energy use;

24   the disposal of energy wastes from fossil fuels and nuclear installations;

25   energy in relation to sustainable development;

26   energy in relation to the greenhouse effect;

27   the environmental effects of energy exports;

28   transportation of energy by sea, road, and pipeline;

29   mitigation measures that have been and can be adopted about the adverse effects of energy exploration, processing, and use;

30   the implications of the recommendations for individual projects yet to be proposed.

8   economic and other incentives or compensation packages introduced in areas experiencing deforestation;

9   alternative opportunities for those displaced by deforestation;

10   the involvement of people and employment opportunities provided for the local community;

11   resource security: the principles, and the issues;

12   the woodchip industry and its environmental and economic significance;

13   national parks, nature reserves, wilderness, and the conservation of nature;

14   fauna, flora, and endangered species;

15   the implications for biological diversity;

16   the implications for climate change;

17   the implications for sustainable development;

18   the status of rainforest;

19   public reaction to various forestry activities;

20   the traditional rights of Aborigines and forest users;

21   mitigation measures proposed by the forestry industry, and by community and conservation groups;

22   identification of the ingredients of a successful future plan and program;

23   provisions for the continuous involvement of the public.

CHECKLIST 2.11

Forestry policy and program impact assessment
Checklist: matters for consideration

1   the relationship of the program to the community's needs for food, fodder, fuel, timber, and other products;

2   the effects on income distribution;

3   the effects on the economic performance of forestry, particularly the long-term productivity of natural resources;

4   the social and economic costs of deforestation, including clear felling;

5   the objectives of reforestation program objectives to assess whether they are clearly formulated to promote: social forestry, agroforestry, commercial/plantation forestry, natural forests, and protected areas;

6   the long-term ecological and socio-economic impacts on local residents as a result of large-scale mono-species plantation forests;

7   the criteria used for reporting rates of deforestation and reforestation, with reference to types/species of trees;

CHECKLIST 2.12

Transport policy and program impact assessment
Checklist: matters for consideration

1   the results of transportation studies which assess the present demand for movement, how the demand is met, and the characteristics of the study area; estimate future travel demands, and outlines of the possible ways of meeting those demands; and evaluate transportation proposals which would provide maximum benefit to the community at minimum cost;

2   the trends in modal split between forms of transport with implications for highways and roads, rail transport, ports and harbours, and airports;

3 current policies and objectives of transport planning and its implications for urban development;

4 the prospective roles of private and public transport in providing access to opportunities within the region under consideration, particularly employment, shopping, recreational centres, harbour, and industrial centres;

5 the prospective improvements in safety, reductions in existing congestion, reductions in through traffic on residential streets and traffic passing through shopping centres, and the provisions for parking;

6 the provision of routes for vehicles and tankers carrying inflammable, explosive, or hazardous loads, to avoid residential streets and densely populated districts;

7 the progressive reduction of all heavy vehicle traffic through city, town, and village centres;

8 the implications of the volume and characteristics of future traffic for air quality and noise by category;

9 the future trends in vehicle design, emission, and noise controls; and the future trends in noise from aircraft;

10 the future trends in the use of lead-free petrol and catalytic converters;

11 the future prospects of the electric car;

12 the promotion of public transport as part of an integrated transport system, particularly to reduce congestion in the business centres; the provision of a rapid transit system;

13 the encouragement of the use of bicycles with safe bicycle paths;

14 the provision of noise bunds (screens) and barriers along major roads;

15 the landscaping of highways to help absorb noise and improve the aesthetics of the routes;

16 the provision and availability of emergency services to deal with spills and fires and the utility of dangerous goods legislation;

17 minimising conflict between vehicular and pedestrian traffic;

18 the improvement in design and appearance of transportation facilities;

19 minimising social impact in the construction of new highways and freeways;

20 the encouragement, through pricing and taxing policies, of the purchase of energy conserving vehicles.

2.14 Regional environmental plans (REPs)

SEA has been largely about policies, plans, and programs, various sectors or segments of the economy. Individual projects might be better served if adequate considerations were given to many important environmental matters.

It is unlikely, however, that all relevant matters are covered sufficiently in a region where a major project might be established. For example, it is necessary to consider the possible cumulative physical and biological effects (both additive and synergistic) of multiple projects of both similar and widely different types.

Cumulative impacts can be defined as 'effects which combine from different projects and which persist to the long-term detriment of the environment'.

• Developments could imply a progressive loss of quality agricultural land.
• Mine drainage could lead to salt-rich or sulphur-rich water reaching streams.
• Successive sewage or industrial waste outfalls could cause progressive deterioration of rivers, lakes, harbours, and coastal waters.
• Different sources of enrichment could cause eutrophication of bodies of water.
• An increase in irrigation activities could raise watertables with increased risks of soil salinity.
• Dust, noise and traffic problems could multiply with an increasing number of open-cut mines.
• The progressive development of holiday and recreational facilities could damage fragile ecosystems such as coastal dunes, swamps, and estuaries.

These cumulative or incremental matters are difficult to consider within the context of an individual project. They are often considered outside the individual proponent's area of responsibility and more in the area of responsibility of government and bureaucracy.

It becomes clear that REPs can substantially contribute to the assessment of cumulative effects and establish planning objectives of an economic, social, and environmental nature. The region can also be a meeting point for the EIA results of policies, plans, and programs, as they are undertaken. The assessment of individual projects can be much more adequately undertaken within such a framework. Indeed it can be argued that regional planning should precede the planning of individual projects, although the effect might be to delay urgently needed development.

Many countries have national, regional, and local planning systems in varying degrees. Planning legislation in the Australian states embraces regional planning, with New South Wales endorsing the 'regional environmental plan'. An REP must be preceded by an environmental study and a published draft of the plan. Both must be exhibited publicly and the public given every opportunity to comment and make written submissions. A public inquiry might be held. Any REP must be consistent with relevant state environmental planning policies. After becoming law, local environmental plans introduced by individual elected councils must be consistent with the regional plan.

The main purpose of an REP is to provide a framework for coordinated action so that the public and private sectors might help to ensure the best use of land resources, meeting regional needs, and improving the quality of life.

In Britain, REPs are known simply as 'regional plans'; an REP is a plan which illustrates the basic land-use distribution and communications network, providing also a framework for planning at the district level. It must conform with any strategy plan which applies to a much larger area, say, the whole of south-east England. Structure plans need to be approved by the central government; local plans are made and adopted by local government but must conform with the relevant structure plan. Structure plans must broadly link the economic, social, and environmental concerns of the region with land and urban development.

In Canada, the strategic planning program of British Columbia and the federal regional assessments carried out in connection with the Beaufort Sea review should be noted (see case study 8A). Other noteworthy regional studies include the James Bay region of Quebec; and the foothills land-use allocative program, Alberta.

The US Department of Housing and Urban Development (1981) applies the concept of area-wide EIA. This has been applied to developments near several metropolitan areas, such as Denver, Colorado, USA.

The essential ingredients of an REP are outlined in checklist 2.13 and the nature of area-wide EIA in checklist 2.14.

2.15 Regional economic, social, and environmental database

The role of EIA would be facilitated by strengthening regional environmental planning, particularly in its capacity to handle cumulative and secondary environmental effects, and through the establishment of a regional database.

Established within the regional office for planning or environment, such a regional database

---

CHECKLIST 2.13

The regional environmental plan (REP) Checklist: matters for consideration

1 the boundaries of the area under consideration; the topography, geology, soils, meteorology, hydrology, catchments and other physical, biological, and ecological characteristics;

2 the results of resource surveys (geology, soil, water resources, erosion, vegetation, and fauna);

3 the pattern of settlement, growth, and decline, agricultural, forestry, and industrial activities;

4 the economics of the region;

5 the social structure of the region;

6 the environmental features of the region (sensitive and high-value areas, recreational opportunities, marsh and wetland areas, national parks, nature reserves, wildlife habitats, rare and endangered species, mangroves, coral, forests and bushland, amenity areas);

7 relevant national, state, and regional, environmental and planning policies;

8 local planning policies for zoning, urban settlement, rural development, roads, and communications, traffic control, utility corridors, alternative land uses, erosion control, protection of sensitive areas, local subdivision, local, and regional infrastructure, future development options, population distribution, housing standards, land-use patterns, land-use constraints, environmental quality targets, floods, sewerage and drainage, provision of other services, agriculture, recreational and tourist activities, landscape;

9 zones for industrial development; prospective sites for major developments linked with regional resources; protection of catchments; provision of drainage and sewerage systems with sewage treatment;

10 evidence of pollution of air and water, salinity, eutrophication, noise and blasting, blue-green algae, sedimentation, erosion, abandoned quarries and industrial sites, destruction of landscape and natural assets;

11 mitigation measures against pollution and damage to the environment in the public and private sectors; minimising waste discharges;

12 evidence of cumulative environmental effects and countermeasures;

13 restraints on future development of various categories;

14 opportunities for future development in various categories;

15 avoid sterilisation of resources;

16 promote an efficient transport system;

17 monitor trends in all key areas;

18 environmental quality targets and objectives;

19 quality of life objectives and attainability;

20 arrangements for the involvement of the public, government at all levels, the private sector, and local and national organisations, in future development plans and project decision-making;

21 responsibility for the regional environment plan and its implementation involving possibly a regional authority;

22 relating to planning in contiguous areas.

CHECKLIST 2.14

Area-wide EIA: advantages and procedures

1 to determine the need for and feasibility of the project or program;

2 to define the boundaries of the project or program;

3 to define the units for the analysis and database;

4 to identify and allocate area-wide development alternatives;

5 to identify the main issues through scoping;

6 to carry out environmental analysis;

7 to conduct impact synthesis and evaluation;

8 to identify all impacts and synergistic effects, favourable and unfavourable;

9 to ensure that environmental considerations are introduced early in the decision-making process.

(Derived from Department of Housing and Urban Development, *Areawide environmental impact assessment: a guidebook*, DHUD, Washington, DC, USA, 1981)

---

could reflect a wide consideration of social and environmental costs and social and environmental benefits arising from economic development.

The data stored in a variety of forms from a rich variety of sources, would be accessible to the public, consultants, advisers, analysts, and participants generally, in the EIA process. At these offices also, EISs would be placed on public exhibition for study and scrutiny, with photocopying facilities and additional copies for sale.

A database would include such items relevant to the region as:
• demographic and census material;
• economic and social data;
• land-use information;
• natural resource accounting;
• meteorology;
• hydrology;
• geomorphology;
• industrial activity;
• local plans;
• energy use;
• air and water quality;
• noise levels;
• use of fertilisers and pesticides;
• sustainable development issues;
• company reports;
• copies of all permits and approvals with conditions attached, issued by government about all significant development in the region;
• copies of all environmental audits;
• records of public inquiries and reports;
• monitoring results;
• emission inventories;
• prosecutions for environmental offences;
• waste management and recycling;
• special environmental studies;
• risks and hazards;
• environmental management generally.

Existing databases such as those relating to soil, land suitability, biological, and census data, would need to be locked into the more comprehensive system. Established probably at public expense, the enlarged database could be maintained on a user-pays basis.

2.16   Introduction of EIA into foreign aid programs and projects

With EIA processes taking root in many lands it perhaps was inevitable that the process would be applied sooner or later to aid extended by more fortunate countries to less fortunate countries through loans or grants. In 1975, the US Agency for International Development was sued by a public interest group to enforce the preparation of EISs on its loans and grants to other countries (see USA, 8.2). Subsequently, an EIA process was introduced with which federal agencies were expected to conform. This was probably the start of the EIA process in foreign aid (Mathews and Carpenter, 1981).

It was not until 1985 that the OECD (see OECD, 5.4) adopted a recommendation on EA of development assistance projects, and programs. The 24 member governments were asked to ensure that significant development assistance projects are assessed at as early a stage as possible. In 1986 detailed procedures were issued.

There appears to have been a general implementation of these proposals since 1985. Two members of OECD, Britain and Australia at least, have issued publications and guides on the matter (Overseas Development Administration, 1992; Australian International Development Assistance Bureau, 1991).

About the time of the UN Conference on the Human Environment, the World Bank took some uncertain steps into the domain of EIA. It later faced severe criticism (see World Bank, 5.9). In 1989, the World Bank introduced its operational directive on EIA with a more vigorous policy. The Asian Development Bank (ADB) and the African Development Bank have also taken a strong interest in this question, as have all international funding agencies. Indeed, the international agencies have shown considerable interest in sponsoring training courses, particularly in developing countries.

It was an unfortunate omission from the 1992 Rio Declaration on Environment and Development that while EIA procedures were strongly endorsed, there was no specific endorsement for foreign aid. However, principle 2 did stress the responsibility of nations to avoid causing damage to the environments of other nations or of areas beyond the limits of national jurisdiction.

CHAPTER 3

EIA methodologies

3.1 Optimisation or making the most of resources

EIA is essentially about optimising resources through an allocation of all resources, to achieve a balance between sustainable development and environment protection. Of the factors of production, natural resources (referred to in traditional economics simply as 'land'), embrace land, water, air, forests, fishing grounds, fauna, flora, and minerals.

The idea of the economic optimum has pervaded economic literature for a considerable time. Named after Vifredo Pareto (1848–1923), the concept of Pareto optimality is an economic situation from which it is impossible to deviate so as to make one person or group better off without placing some other person or group at a disadvantage. This criterion is not about the distribution of income, hence a situation might be Pareto optimal even if the distribution it represents is totally unacceptable on other grounds. It does not identify the best or optimal social state.

Later, Nicholas Kaldor, the economist, developed a compensation principle to deal with situations in which there are winners and losers; this principle states that if those who gain from a policy could fully compensate those who lose, and still remain better off, then the policy should be implemented. However, the compensation is only hypothetical. In a situation where the overall gains exceed the losses, in narrow financial terms, there could be social and political repercussions.

The problems of achieving economic optimality alone, underscore the problems of achieving optimality in human welfare as a whole. EIA cannot achieve this, but it can achieve a modest contribution to balancing development and environmental protection at the workface of the policy, plan, program, or project. This requires an evaluation of the worth of many things which are not otherwise likely to be considered in narrower financial calculations, common to projects in the public and private sectors; and it means attempting to value aspects of the environment through a series of objective and subjective routes when no market measurements are necessarily available. It calls for great judgement to arrive at a right recommendation, and often it takes great courage. The key lies in the identification, first, of all costs and of all benefits which might arise, followed by efforts to assess what it is all worth and in whose opinion.

Approaches to an EIA methodology in the 1970s followed in the tracks of economic science, in the direction of models, matrices, numbers, networks, inputs and outputs, with subjective weightings provided by expert analysts, who often worked independently. Much of the earlier EIA methodology still renders valuable exercises in specific cases; but much has yielded to the influence of the political interaction, public involvement, prescriptive legislation, standards and regulations, the effects of recession, and environmental conflict. It is not possible for the analyst or commissioner to stray too far, too often, from the current framework within which they all must work. But there are ways and means in the real world to score brilliant victories and achieve dramatic political turnarounds. The analyst, assessor, reviewer, commissioner, investigator, activist, judge, and report writer, become part of the game.

3.2 Cost-benefit analysis (CBA)

Cost-benefit analysis (often referred to as 'benefit-cost analysis', particularly in the USA), is a procedure for comparing the social costs with the social benefits of a program or project, all expressed, as far as practicable, in monetary terms. Costs and benefits which cannot be valued are identified as 'intangibles'. The difference between the social benefits and social costs is called the 'net social benefits'. Clearly, in general terms, programs and projects showing the greatest net social benefit are preferred.

CBA has been used by government and agencies to:

- accept or reject a single project;
- choose one of a number of discrete alternative projects;
- choose a smaller number from a larger number of discrete alternative projects;
- accept or reject a number of projects;
- choose one of a number of mutually exclusive projects;
- help decide whether a proposed program should be undertaken or an existing program continued;
- help choose the appropriate scale and timing for a project.

The method is usually and preferably applied before it is undertaken (ex ante) but can be applied after it has been completed (ex post).

The perspective of CBA is 'global'; it does not reflect the interests of any individual, organisation, or group. CBA is often used in situations where the signals that market prices normally provide are either absent or fail to reflect adequately the opportunity cost of the resources involved. Valuations are made about such matters as:

- savings in travel time resulting from transport projects;
- external or spillover effects arising from pollution;
- multiplier effects in the community flowing from investment;
- costs and benefits imposed on third parties;
- the effects on employment in the wider community;
- the implications for infrastructure.

CBA can be applied to policies, plans, programs, and projects. It can be applied widely to such matters as the labour market, education, scientific research, and the environment, with particular reference to EIA.

The 'toolkit' of the CBA includes the following basic concepts:

- opportunity cost (the cost of the sacrifice of alternative activities or earnings);
- contingent valuation (establishing a monetary valuation of a good or amenity by asking people how much they are prepared to pay for it);
- shadow prices (reflecting the true scarcity of environmental resources to society as a whole);
- discounting (in which all future costs and benefits are reduced to present values);
- the Pareto optimum (when it is impossible to make one person better off without placing some other person at a disadvantage);
- the cost-benefit rule (that a project is acceptable

where the net social benefits are positive, that is the benefit-cost ratio is positive, rather than negative).

Within this context a public transport system, bound to operate at a loss in commercial terms might have a high benefit-cost ratio, but a chemical factory designed to make corporate profits might have a negative rating because of risks, hazards, and pollution arising from a poor choice of site.

The cost-benefit approach might explain costs and benefits not normally revealed within a corporation's financial evaluation of a program or project, and assist in identifying when the marginal social costs of a project might exceed the marginal social benefits; for example, when additional incremental costs for pollution control measures exceed any possible benefit to the public.

Figure 3 outlines the steps in the cost-benefit analysis process (Department of Finance, 1991).

Evolution of CBA

The concept of CBA has its origins with the French engineer A-J-E-J Dupuit. Through his professional activities, Dupuit became interested in the economic problems of constructing public works and charging for their use. He developed a number of economic concepts and introduced CBA for public works. But his work in this area became dormant for almost 100 years following his death in 1866.

In 1936, the theory and practice of CBA developed when the US Flood Control Act, required that projects be undertaken only '. . . if the benefits to whomsoever they may accrue are in excess of the estimated costs . . .' The implementation of this requirement led to the publication of the 'green book', codifying the general principles of economic analysis as they were to be applied for federal water resource projects. The authors drew on the emerging field of welfare economics (Little, 1957).

In 1958, three influential books on CBA (Eckstein, Krutilla and Eckstein, and McKean) were published. These were followed in 1962 by a seminal work on water resources by Maass and Hufschmidt et al (1962). Subsequently, Dorfman (1965) extended the application to areas other than water resources. The use of the technique spread rapidly to other countries, notably Britain.

Prest and Turvey (1965) published an economic review article on CBA. There has been continuous input and there is now substantial literature. This was continued by Mishan with his famous introductory text on CBA (1976). Hammond (1958) was one of the first to apply the principles of CBA to pollution control; and later advances were made at Resources for the Future in the USA (Kneese and Bower 1968; Kneese, Ayres, and D'Arge 1970; Kneese, Rolfe, and Harned 1971).

Concurrently, environmental economics and the

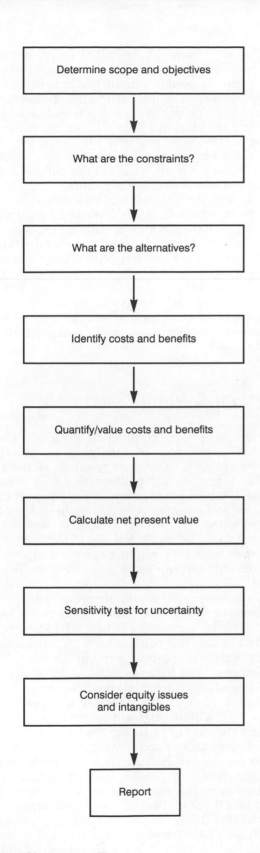

Figure 3 Key steps in CBA
(Source: Department of Finance, *Handbook of cost-benefit analysis*, Australian Government Publishing Service, Canberra, Australia, 1991, p. 6)

related field of natural resource economics acquired recognition (Fisher and Peterson, 1976; Ciriacy-Wantrup, 1952; Scott, 1955; Barnett and Morse, 1963; and Herfindahl and Kneese, 1974). Attention was being given to developing countries (Little and Mirlees, 1974; Squire and van der Tak, 1975; United Nations Environment Program (UNEP), 1980; Ahmad and Sammy, 1985; Economic and Social Commission for Asia and the Pacific (ESCAP), 1985, 1990; Interim Mekong Committee, 1979, 1982; Lohani and Kan, 1983; National Environment Board, Thailand, 1979, 1986).

Useful additional references on CBA include: Baumol (1968); Baumol and Oates (1979); Department of Home Affairs and Environment (1980); Department of Science and the Environment (1979); Environment and Policy Institute (1980); Fisher (1981); Gilpin and Hartmann (1981); Herfindahl and Kneese (1974); Hufschmidt (1980, 1981); Industry Commission (1991); James and Boer (1987); Pigou (1946); among other references included in the bibliography and elsewhere in this book.

Today, many EISs or EIAs take on the appearance of CBAs in all or many respects; for proponents wish to demonstrate that their projects possess attributes of a social character beyond the narrow calculations of return on capital.

Not all, or perhaps any, of these attributes are measured in monetary terms, or discounted over a lengthy period at a social rate of interest. Nevertheless, the similarity remains. CBA certainly started the process, so evident in environmental debate and EA, of listing all likely gains and losses in a systematic manner, attempting to measure the size of those gains and losses, weighing their significance and, as appropriate, revealing the distribution of those gains and losses between different groups of people.

Checklist 3.1 gives some examples of social and environmental costs and benefits. It is often assumed in EIA that the private benefits will exceed the private costs where the proponent is in the private sector, although this is sometimes challenged. In the public sector much depends on whether the project is a commercial one or a non-profit service such as much public transport.

3.3 Cost-effectiveness analysis (CEA)

In some situations, CBA might be impracticable or inappropriate, if not in theory, then certainly in practice. Particular objectives might have corporate or political approval while the benefits, though obvious and real, cannot be readily measured in

CHECKLIST 3.1

**CBA
Examples of social and
environmental costs and social and
environmental benefits**

Natural resource depletion	Sustainable development
Social dislocation	Economic growth
Restricted employment	More efficient use of resources; multiplier effects
Risks and hazards	Buffer zones
Traffic congestion	Reduced average travel times
Despoliation of landscape	Landscape and re-habilitation program
Threats to wildlife	Protection of wildlife areas
Pollution of air, water, and land	Reduction of pollution through scrapping of old plant; best available technology
Infrastructure demands	Proponent contributions to infrastructure
Intrusion into high-value conservation area	Avoidance of high-value conservation areas
Threat to cultural heritage	Preservation of cultural assets

monetary or material terms. The benefits might be ecological (such as preserving the Great Barrier Reef, or establishing a system of national parks); social (such as setting standards for consumer protection or child care); defence (such as building warships or establishing bases); or educational or research (such as the establishment of university centres of excellence).

However, formal CBA might falter, but cost-effectiveness analysis (CEA) can remain relevant. For given the benefits, or alleged benefits, CEA is about the least-cost approach to the objective; with an examination of the costs of alternative ways of meeting the objective(s) to achieve the maximum value for the dollar invested. Of course, CEA cannot be used to compare projects that have different objectives. CEA is often used in the difficult area of social and educational infrastructure.

For example, a decision to establish a new university to serve essentially a certain geographical area might have obvious benefits, in the medium-term and long-term. However, the evaluation of those benefits in monetary terms over the next 50 years or so, would no doubt stretch CBA. CEA remains, however, relevant: whether to combine some existing facilities, to have one or several campuses, the staging of construction, all essential considerations in making the project more affordable.

3.4 Opportunity cost

The concept of opportunity cost is relevant also to EIA. It is the cost of satisfying an objective, measured by the value those resources would have had in other attractive alternative uses. For example, if capital funds committed to a project could have earned a higher return elsewhere, then that return is the opportunity cost of those funds in present use. There is a real cost if funds perform less well than they might have done elsewhere, even though this cost is not revealed in any balance sheet.

Governments are constantly presented with this dilemma of how to use public works funds to the best advantage, choosing between building better highways, say, and better schools. A consideration of opportunity costs assists in ensuring that resources are put to the best use and that all costs, explicit and implicit, are taken into account.

On the basis of this principle it is possible to argue that a particular government program or project should not be undertaken (not because of an inherent lack of social merit or environmental performance), but because the funds could be better used elsewhere, possibly with less impact on the environment. It is an argument perhaps not often used and it enters the political arena. It might be argued that this is not a matter of methodology so much as one of optimisation but optimisation comes back to method in the allocation of funds. It is a fundamental question that is often not raised in considering alternatives, supporting possibly a 'no action' outcome resting upon an allocative issue.

3.5   The multiplier

The concept of the multiplier is frequently introduced into EISs and EIAs. It implies social benefits far beyond the initial capital investment of a program or project. The multiplier is a ratio indicating the estimated effect on total employment or on total real income of a specific amount of capital investment or stream of expenditure.

Investment or expenditure represents income for the factors of production (land, or natural resources, labour, and capital); after tax some of that income is saved, the balance is spent. This expenditure becomes, in turn, the income of others, along an almost endless chain. If the factors (people) were previously unemployed the benefits are considerable; employing one additional person might well create, through the multiplier effect, the equivalent of work for another. Whatever the factor of production, there is a chain reaction.

The growth of income continues throughout the economy until the original investment or expenditure has been siphoned into savings or taxes; the multiplier is a crucial concept in Keynesian economics. At the time, it was thought the multiplier was about two; employing one person previously unemployed would have led to the equivalent of employment and wages for one other person. Claims by proponents need to be closely examined, for assessors are asked to weigh these claims against environmental and other disadvantages.

3.6   Contingent valuation

Contingent valuation, a surrogate market approach, is a method of establishing a monetary value for a good or service by asking people what they are prepared to pay for it. The good or service in this context would be an environmental amenity, clearly of value but falling beyond the range of the market economy and therefore unpriced. The method seeks to determine a level of payment acceptable to most people; it can determine a willingness to pay for a better environment, or accept compensation for a degraded environment.

The method takes several forms as described by Freeman (1979); Hufschmidt et al (1983); Hyman (1981); Imber (1991); James and Boer (1987); Nichols and Hyman (1982); Sinden (1991); Sinden and Worrell (1979).

(1)   *Bidding games.* The simplest approach here is direct questioning; individuals are asked how much they are prepared to pay (or how much extra) to enjoy a particular environmental amenity, or bring about some environmental improvement. Bidding games can be applied also to the willingness to accept compensation for a loss of environmental amenity. Examples are to be found in Hufschmidt et al (1983). Bidding games can embrace such concepts as:

- option value, which refers to the price that people are willing to pay to maintain the possibility of using or visiting an amenity or site;
- existence value, being the price that people are willing to pay just to know that certain things are being preserved but which the individual might never see, such as whales, polar bears, tropical rainforest, coral reefs, or Antarctica.

(2)   *Convergent direct questioning.* This is a development of point (1) above. Each individual is given a high value likely to exceed any reasonable willingness to pay, and a low value which almost certainly would be paid. The higher value is reduced and the lower value increased until the two values converge at an equilibrium value. The answers can be analysed in various ways.

(3)   *Trade-off games.* Here each person is asked to rank various combinations of two objects, such as a sum of money and some environmental attribute (such as water of a certain quality, or the preservation of a natural area). For any pair of combinations, the person is asked to indicate either a preference of one over the other, or indifference. The marginal rate of trade-off of money for an environmental amenity is identified at the point of indifference.

(4)   *Moneyless choice method.* Instead of using money as one of the objects, only specified commodities are used in combination with environmental attributes. The trade-off is again identified at the point of indifference. The monetary valuation of an environmental attribute is then obtained by substituting the current market value for the commodities chosen.

(5)   *Priority evaluation method.* In this method each person is given a hypothetical sum of money to spend on conventional goods and environmental attributes at assumed prices. The game might have five objects (four goods and an environmental attribute) in three different quantities (giving 15 possible choices). As the budget is limited, clear choices must be made. True preferences and marginal valuations can be derived.

However, all these methods must be viewed with caution. A willingness to pay might be overstated to encourage preservation of an area (turning more into a public opinion poll); or might be understated to minimise the possibility of a significant user-charge or levy. The questions might condition the responses; or bias might be introduced by the interviewer or into published briefings. The conduct of the survey could exaggerate the importance of the issue. Certainly, all questions and briefings should aim at being true, fair, and reasonable.

Contingent valuation has been used in Australia since the mid-1970s by many kinds of agencies and organisations, to value a great variety of things (Sinden, 1991). A contingent valuation study was undertaken in 1991 to estimate the value attached to a portion of land contiguous with the Kakadu national park in the Northern Territory; this was part of a review by the Resource Assessment Commission to help the federal government to decide whether this territory of 2000 square kilometres called the 'conservation zone' should be used, at least in part, for mining, or incorporated in its entirety in the existing national park. About 2500 Australians were asked to value the zone. It was a landmark event, as it was the first attempt to assess environmental values for the express purpose of being part of a report to the federal government (Imber, 1991).

The Kakadu contingent valuation was severely criticised by the Australian Bureau of Agricultural and Resource Economics and the Tasman Institute, and the Resource Assessment Commission had some reservations. However, it remained a significant contribution, although the final decision to incorporate the conservation zone in the national park was made out of concern for the views of the Aboriginal community.

3.7   Travel cost approach

This is another surrogate market technique, particularly useful for assessing the economic value of natural areas or recreational areas where no price is directly charged. In this case, the willingness to pay for an environmental amenity is assumed to be measured in the costs incurred by people when travelling to chosen locations.

Travel costs from each concentric zone around the site are used as a surrogate for price, the quantity being determined by head counts of the number of visitors from each zone. The relationship between cost and visitor rates becomes a demand curve for the recreational experience which might involve a number of activities. The travel cost approach is well accepted, probably underestimating real benefits since it does not try to establish the maximum willingness to pay.

When the survey of how frequently each person or group makes a visit to the area is taken, travelling distance and cost can be gauged. The total

population in each zone must be known. From this the rate of visits is calculated. By fitting a regression equation to the data, a visitation rate as a function of travel costs is determined. Sometimes an entrance fee can be simulated by including it in the regression equation; the process can be repeated for successively higher simulated charges until no visits are made; an optimal charge can then be considered.

A travel cost study has been undertaken for Lumpinee public park in Bangkok, the details of which are reported in Dixon and Hufschmidt (1986). Other examples have been provided in Sinden and Worrell (1979). The method is reviewed in Hyman (1981).

3.8   Hedonic price technique

The hedonic price technique (or property value method) is yet another surrogate market approach, attempting to assess the value attributed by buyers to the environmental attributes of a dwelling. It is generally accepted that, all other things being equal, a house located in a poor environment (broadly considered) will sell for a lower price than a similar house in a better environment. Thus the difference in house prices can be used as an estimate of buyers' willingness to pay for a better environment. The differential paid for the superior environment is known as the 'hedonic price'.

The proposition is simple, but complex in application. Houses are rarely of the same age, size, suitability, character, structure, number of rooms, quality, materials, and presentation. These factors vary. What is true is that houses with similar costs of construction command different selling prices, depending on location.

If the basic quality and character of a house with a similar cost of construction can be held constant, then the difference in market price, if significant, must be because of the quality of the environment. This is not, however, a simple entity confined to outlook, cleaner air, lower levels of noise, or remoteness to unsightly industrial plants. It has much to do with access to better schools, shopping centres, recreational facilities, entertainment, nicer neighbours, and a district with a better reputation for law and order, with better standing and access to better things generally. Such elements ensure that any given house will command a better price (and that the land chosen for it will also command a better price).

Determining the size of the differential in the prices for similar houses is challenging; yet it reveals what financial value buyers are willing to place on environmental quality (and perhaps particular elements in environmental quality). Such a finding helps, as members of the community indicate environmental matters impinging on immediate personal and family well-being; and perhaps it explains, in part, some of the unknown values placed by the community on environmental elements.

Research in this difficult area might be simplified by talking with real estate agents; direct contact with the market enables them to form sound opinions about the effects of different environments on property prices. Thus a hypothetical house can be placed in a variety of hypothetical locations with an experienced real estate agent (or valuer) offering a very good guide on the market value.

Hedonic pricing has been used for a variety of purposes; in the USA for vehicles, and, in Australia,

on the effects of aircraft noise on property prices, and on the effects of a water-supply pipeline on the value of properties in the wheatbelt.

Relevant references include Freeman (1979); Hufschmidt et al (1983); James and Boer (1987); Hyman (1981); Sinden (1991); Sinden and Worrell (1979). See checklist 3.2.

3.9 Ecological evaluation

To place a value on a commodity or service as described, is to try to assess what might be gained or lost in environmental terms. However, these methods are limited and do not take other environmental attributes into account for which it is

---

CHECKLIST 3.2

Methods to value unpriced benefits and costs

Method	What is valued?	What data are required?
Observed data from actual market exchanges		
1 Travel-cost	Net social benefit	Quantities consumed, and costs for persons in each of several travel zones
2 Cost-saving	Total benefit (values benefit as a saving in cost)	Actual money costs before and after a change
3 Replacement-cost	Total benefit (gives a range for the total benefit)	Actual and likely costs or replacement
4 Opportunity-cost	Total cost (values cost as a loss in income)	Money incomes before and after a change
Observed data from related markets		
5 Hedonic pricing	Value of a change in a characteristic of a good (as the change in purchase price of the good)	Prices and characteristics of a good from many exchanges of the good
6 Input valuation	Value of an input (as increase in value of output from using more input)	Value of the changes in output due to change in input
7 Interpret past decisions	Benefit or cost implicit in decisions	Considerable data on each of many comparable decisions
8 Value proxy goods	The benefit or cost of interest	Willingness to pay for a proxy good
Questionnaire data		
9 Contingent valuation	Consumer surplus or total benefit	Responses to questionnaire surveys

(Derived from Sinden, J. A., *An assessment of our environmental valuations*, 20th Annual Conference of Economists, University of Tasmania, Hobart, Australia, 1991)

impossible, save in a most arbitrary way, to attribute monetary value. Beyond the limits of reasonable valuation, in monetary terms, the task of valuing (or evaluating) in ecological terms many environmental attributes, has continued to develop, and is of inestimable value in overall appraisals.

Ecological evaluations seek to identify the importance of conservation and the intrinsic value of nature. Thus they fill an essential role within the context of CBA, yet cannot be priced readily or at all. Such evaluations can be applied to any natural asset such as wetlands, mangroves, wilderness, natural coastlands, fauna, and flora.

A habitat evaluation procedure (HEP) was devised in 1976 by the US Fish and Wildlife Service for use in the evaluation of habitats near major federal water projects. Using functional curves HEP determines the quality of a habitat-type relating habitat quality to the quantitative biotic and abiotic characteristics of a habitat. Habitat sizes and quality are combined to assess possible project impact. As shown in figure 4 the HEP involves six steps for the evaluation of the impacts of a proposed development.

3.10 Matrices and checklists

Once a project is before a multi-disciplinary group for drafting an ES or EA, the question of the precise procedure or methodology to be adopted comes to the fore. Costs and benefits need to be defined and orders of magnitude identified.

An approach has been the use of the matrix. White (1968) was one of the first to adopt this approach. He defined eight interacting systems affected by the construction of a dam, but stressed the need for wider considerations than the immediate physical results of the construction. Leopold et al (1971) with the US Geological Survey (1971), developing circular 645, produced one of the first systematic methodologies for the entire field of EIA. The procedure centred around a large matrix containing 8800 cells; the horizontal axis has 100 columns for activities that might cause positive or negative environmental impacts. The vertical axis consisted of 88 rows of environmental quality variables grouped in four categories: physical and chemical; biological; cultural; and ecological.

To use the matrix, the analyst identifies those activities that are likely to (or will certainly) be as-

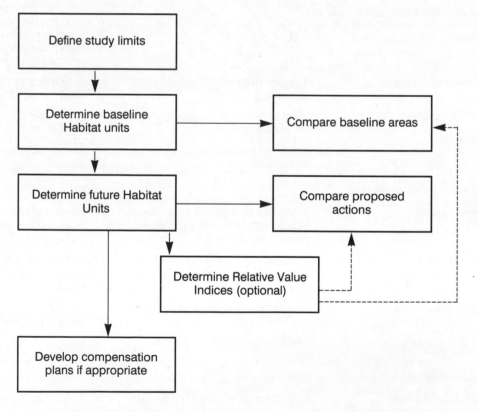

Figure 4 Generalised evaluation process using the US Fish and Wildlife Service habitat evaluation procedure (HEP) (Source: US Fish and Wildlife Service, 1976)

sociated with the project; then the analyst examines the entire row of environmental factors and inserts a slash in each of the cells where impacts are possible for each activity already marked. The identified effects are then evaluated according to their magnitude and importance on scales 1-10. The results are entered in the relevant cells. The matrix serves as a checklist and a summary of the impact assessment. However, an accompanying text should explain and justify high scores for magnitude and importance (Nichols and Hyman, 1982).

The Leopold matrix has a number of drawbacks. There might be uncertainties hidden within the ratings as it becomes impossible to distinguish between a highly probable low impact event and a catastrophic event with low probability. It cannot reflect indirect or feedback events; the time horizon of events is not revealed; the matrix is cumbersome; it is not conducive to a comparison of alternative plans; there are no criteria for measuring magnitude and importance; the matrix fails to handle important secondary impacts; and tends to neglect social, and economic values. The most serious defect is that the Leopold matrix depends on the subjective evaluation of experts; and the judgement is then converted into numbers. Granted such judgement might be influenced by scoping exercises; but much is lost in the conversion to numbers. The system is not suitable for public presentation; yet among analysts it can serve as a focal point for discussion following the gathering of information during the initial stage of an environmental analysis. Even here there is a danger that the analyst will try to count the numbers to achieve the overall effect.

The final EIS can be prepared using a matrix only as a guide; the matrix itself should not be included, or if it is, include it only as an appendix. The report should stand alone; it should never be an explanation and discussion of a matrix. Matrices are strong, however, in identifying effects and are still used in some evaluations.

The methodology used by the National Environment Board (1979) of Thailand for EIA provides an example of the current use of the matrix concept. An item-by-item review of possible effects on the environment is undertaken in an attempt to identify and to quantify those effects so far as is practicable. The matrix is then used as a summary display of EIA.

Figure 5 provides an example of an effective matrix or grid which has been used in Australia as an aid to identifying likely environmental interactions. Such a matrix is not a substitute for analysis. It and other matrices are only an adjunct to the orderly and systematic identification of possible interactions.

Both economic science and EIA are casualties of much theorising. Nichols and Hyman (1982) reviewed no fewer than 12 representative methods for EA, describing, evaluating, and comparing these using 7 evaluation criteria; treatment of the probabilistic nature of environmental quality, incorporation of indirect and feedback effects, dynamic characteristics, multiple-objectives approach to social welfare, clear separation of facts and values, facilitation of participation by the public and decision-makers, and efficiency in resource and time requirements. None of the methods satisfied the criteria as a whole, and many not even substantially.

Nichols and Hyman concluded that most of the methodologies reviewed relied on experts or a small group of experts and key decision-makers to carry out EIA. Few methods addressed the problem of eliciting and incorporating environmental values from the broad array of groups in affected communities. Improved methods are needed to accommodate more direct public consultation and to recognise that EIA is part of a larger political decision-making process.

Since 1985 EIA procedures and methodologies have been reviewed by ESCAP (1985, 1990); but reference should also be made to other valuable contributions: Ahmad and Sammy (1985); Andrews and Waits (1978); Battelle Pacific Northwest Laboratories (1974); Bisset (1980); Burchell and Listokin (1975); Canter (1977); Dixon and Hufschmidt (1986); Fabos, Green and Joyner (1978); Holling (1978); Hyman (1981); Hyman and Stiftel (1981); Interim Meking Committee (1979, 1982); Lapping (1975); Lohani and Kan (1983); Maass and Hufschmidt (1962); McHarg (1969); Nichols and Hyman (1980); Solomon et al (1977); Stiftel and Hyman (1980); The Netherlands (1990); United Nations Environment Program (UNEP) (1980); Water Resources Council (US) (1973, 1978); and also other works listed in the references and bibliography.

Of all the methodologies, checklists have tended to survive as a guide to the potential impacts of a project. Such checklists may initiate preliminary analysis to provide first approximation answers, or to identify areas of ignorance; they are not, however, final analyses in the sense that an assessment is. Checklists are another approach to sorting out often complex situations, strong in impact identification. All types of checklists, simple, descriptive, scaling, and weighting, are valuable. They can be drawn from specialist literature or created on the basis of previous experience of similar projects. PPA can yield valuable inputs for future checklists.

This work offers a series of examples of simple checklists. Checklist 3.3 offers the 'mother of all'

A: CHARACTERISTIC OF THE PROPOSED DEVELOPMENT

OPERATION

Land clearing	
Earthworks	
Drainage construction	
Location of buildings or works	
Building construction	
Raw material inputs	
Equipment operation	
Labour requirements	
Proponent's expenditure patterns	
Traffic movements	
Potential emergencies (including hazards)	
Landscaping	

CONSTRUCTION

Location of buildings or works	
Raw material inputs	
Equipment operation	
Storage/stockpiling	
Water demand	
Waste disposal	
Demand for services	
Labour requirements	
Proponent's expenditure patterns	
Production outputs	
Traffic movements	
Transport requirements	
Potential emergencies (including hazards)	
Landscaping	

B: CHARACTERISTIC OF THE EXISTING ENVIRONMENT

Land use · Land form · Visual quality · Drainage pattern · Surface water · Groundwater · Soils/land stability · Vegetation · Fauna · Air quality · Noise and vibration · Resident population · Employment · Housing · Local/regional economy · Historic/archaeological sites · Road/transport system · Utilities provision (eg water, sewer, wastes) · Services provision (eg education/recreation/health)

NOTE:
- A: actions which are part of the proposed development are identified (these will alter from project to project).
- B: characteristics of the environment which is likely to be effected are identified (these will alter from area to area).
- Where a characteristic of the existing environment is potentially affected by a characteristic of the proposed development the appropriate matrix cell should be noted. This indicates likely environmental interactions.
- The text of the EIS should describe the likely interactions and then analyse the scale and significance of the interactions ie: environmental impact.

Figure 5 Example of an environmental interaction matrix
(Derived from Department of Planning, *Manual for environmental impact assessment*, Sydney, Australia, 1985)

checklists, as it is of general application in EIA. Checklists 3.4 to 3.12 are for the assessment of:

- air quality impact;
- ecological impact;
- economic impact;
- environmental health impact;
- hazard and risk impact;
- noise impact;
- social impact;
- urban impact;
- water quality impact.

The relevance of the lists of matters for consideration depends upon the nature of the project under consideration; in some cases only one or two lists are relevant; in some, all.

CHECKLIST 3.3

EIA
Checklist: matters for consideration

In determining a DA, a consent authority should consider such of the following matters that are relevant to the proposed development:

1 the provisions of:

   (a) any environmental planning instrument; national, regional, or local, plan relevant to any proposed and alternative sites, and any draft instruments or policies; any development, conservation, or management plan; and any national parks or reserves, existing or proposed; and any national, state, or provincial conservation strategies;

   (b) the provisions of any government strategies for the development of the land for energy generation and distribution; for the mining or extraction of natural resources; for logging; and for the specific protection of ecological resources such as fauna and flora, wetlands, mangroves, coral, forest and bushland, agricultural land, pasture, and waterways;

   (c) the results of any specific ecological, social, hazard, health, urban impact assessments, or EIAs;

2 the nature and character of the existing environment and something of its natural or industrial history; the nature and character of alternative sites which might be available;

3 the impact of the proposed development on the environment and, where harm to the environment is likely to be caused, any means that might be used to protect the environment or to mitigate that harm. Such harm that might arise from air, water, land, or noise pollution, environmentally hazardous chemicals, hazards and risks, land clearing, ecological disturbance, changes in land use, or patterns of activity. The nature of mitigation measures in technology and management; and the economic implications;

4 the effect of that development on the landscape or scenic quality of the locality;

5 the effect of that development on any wilderness area within the locality;

6 whether there is likely to be a significant effect on the environment of protected fauna;

7 the social effect and the economic effect of that development in the locality;

8 the character, location, siting, bulk, scale, shape, size, height, density, design, or external appearance of that development;

9 the size and shape of the land to which that DA relates, the siting of any building or works thereon, and the area to be occupied by that development;

10 whether the land to which that DA relates is unsuitable for that development by reason of its being, or being likely to be, subject to flooding, tidal inundation, subsidence, slip or bushfire, or to any other risk;

11 the relationship of that development to development on adjoining land, or on other land in the locality;

12 whether the proposed means of entrance to and exit from that development and the land to which that DA relates are adequate and whether adequate provision has been made for the loading, unloading, manoeuvring and parking of vehicles within that development, or on that land;

13 the amount of traffic likely to be generated by the development, particularly for the capacity of the road system in the locality and the probable effect of that traffic on the movement of traffic on that road system;

14 whether public transport services are necessary and, if so, whether they are available and adequate for that development;

15 whether services are available and adequate for that development;

16 whether adequate provision has been made for the landscaping of the land to which that development application relates, and whether any trees or other vegetation on the land should be preserved;

17 whether that development is likely to cause soil erosion;

18 any representations made by a public authority for that DA, or to the development of the area, and the rights and powers of that public authority;

19 any submissions and objections by the public;

20 the existing and likely future amenity of the neighbourhood;

21 any special circumstances of the case;

22 the public interest as it may be argued by government departments and agencies, at all levels, by voluntary conservation bodies, by individuals, or groups of individuals.

(Based, in part, on the NSW Environmental Planning and Assessment Act, and augmented by more advanced studies)

CHECKLIST 3.4

Air quality impact assessment
Checklist: matters for consideration

In determining a DA for the emission of wastes to atmosphere, a consent authority should consider such of the following matters that are relevant to the proposed development:

1 Identification of air pollutants by source; weight and volume of discharge; temperature and level of discharge; and by other characteristics. Air pollutants should include carbon dioxide, dioxins, furons, and radiation; as well as the more familiar categories such as the oxides of sulphur and nitrogen, grit and dust, smoke, haze, odours and mercaptans, vapours, hydrocarbons, carbon monoxide, metals, organic compounds, fluorides, carcinogens, CFCs, halons (halogens), PCBs, and other residual intractables.

2 Description of existing air quality levels and variations for the above and products of synergistic effects such as ozone and other complex compounds such as peroxyacetylnitrate (PAN).

3 Meteorological characteristics diurnal, seasonal, and annual, with particular attention to wind directions and speeds; temperature inversions, incidence, type and depth; and variations in turbulence, both vertical and horizontal. Data relating to abnormal meteorological events in recent years. Macro-, meso-, and micro-meteorological characteristics should be noted.

4 Determination from the data obtained from (1), (2), and (3) of the capacity of the atmosphere for the dispersal of pollutants to a harmless degree.

5 The assembly of acceptable air quality standards which should be achieved by the community either in the short term or medium term. Such standards may be those adopted by the WHO or the US EPA; or may be a set of standards appropriate to the circumstances of the country concerned and its stage of development.

6 Details of the mitigation measures to be adopted by the project; and details of any substantial mitigation measures to be adopted in the rest of the community in the industrial, commercial, or residential sectors. Any trade-offs to be offered by the proponent by way, say, of closing down or relegating to stand-by status of other plant on-site; these steps in the context of the above will determine the air quality impacts of the proposed project and alternatives at both the macro-scale, meso-scale, and micro-scale levels; the micro-scale assessment takes account of the calculated concentrations of air pollutants at specific locations in the vicinity of the site. The other assessments take account of regional, national, and international effects, if any.

7 The above assessments might involve complex mathematical disperion modelling, wind tunnel analysis, or simpler prediction calculations; mitigation or abatement measures might involve review of the various control technologies that can be used for various kinds of emission.

8 Consideration should be had to persistent air quality problems characteristic of the region such as acid rain, photochemical smog, brown haze, or trapping of pollutants for extended periods by temperature inversions.

CHECKLIST 3.5

Ecological impact assessment
Checklist: matters for consideration

In determining a DA development application, a consent authority should consider such of the following matters that are relevant to the proposed development:

1 The general character of the existing site in terms of fauna and flora; landscape and geological features, lakes, creeks, marsh, mangroves, coral, forest and bush, and aesthetics.

2 The natural history of the site; the importance of the area in national, regional, and local terms.

3 The consistency of the proposed development with any relevant statutory instruments, planning policies, heritage orders, measures under Aboriginal legislation, or international conventions (protecting, say, wetlands and migratory birds, or threatened or endangered species).

4 Alternative sites for the proposed development, or alternative designs or techniques, which might pose reduced ecological risks. Reasons why this site is clearly preferable to all others.

5 In that event, an ecological inventory of at least the most prominent and common species with major plant and animal habitats, particularly habitats critical to the preservation of threatened or endangered species. The geographical relationship of species on the site.

6 Artificial features of the site as existing, such as roads, railways, buildings and other facilities relating current uses to the local ecology: agricultural activities.

7 A history of Aboriginal activity on the site, with reference to archaeological, cultural, and heritage items.

8 The present use of the area by natural history societies, youth groups, bushwalkers, birdwatchers, and so on.

9 Outstanding individuals such as the oldest or largest of the trees; rare or uncommon species, races, variants, and populations; unique or scarce habitats. Communities threatened or endangered.

10 Plants or animals that could affect public health or safety: allergenic plants, poisonous and venomous species, pest or nuisance populations; populations that might expand dramatically if the immediate environment were changed.

11 The possible effects of the proposed development on land species (plants and animals); on aquatic species (fauna, fish, coral); on habitats; on the aesthetics of the site; on natural resources such as soil, geological formations, dunes, beaches, lakes, forest (including rainforest), coral reefs, mangroves, swamps, outcrops, and the atmosphere; including the possible effects of noise.

12 Primary and secondary impacts, temporary and long-term, unavoidable impacts and risks; synergism; transboundary effects; possible irreversible changes.

13 The possible mitigation of effects by technical, or financial measures, by redesigning.

14 Proposed monitoring and PPA.

15 The existing and likely future amenity of the neighbourhood.

16 The implications of clear felling or selective logging for timber and other forest products; the effects of road-building, drainage of wet areas, and the skidding, hauling and yarding of logs; the possibility of replacement by monoculture plantations; the danger of forest fragmentation causing genetic isolation of animal populations.

17 The possibility of upsetting the species composition by excessive harvesting of fish, molluscs, crustaceans, seaweed, and other creatures and organisms.

18 The possibility of the mining of coral for cement, lime, road-building and construction purposes; and other damage to coral.

19 The threat to mangroves from clearing and development, and from pollutants.

20 Other related developments in the area which might have a cumulative ecological impact.

21 In sum, the ecological significance of the site for the community and the potential for genuine loss should development proceed.

(Derived from Prieur, Michel and Lambrechts, Mrs Claude, *Model outline environmental impact statement from the standpoint of integrated management or planning of the natural environment*, Council of Europe, Strasbourg, 1980, and other publications)

CHECKLIST 3.6

Economic impact assessment
Checklist: matters for consideration

In determining a DA, a consent authority should consider such of the following matters that are relevant to the proposed development and can be circulated without commercial compromise:

1 The general economic viability of the proposal and hence the ability of the proponent to meet all obligations and responsibilities imposed by development consent conditions, including rehabilitation.

2 The ability of the proponent to begin the project promptly and not be seeking consent merely as a basis for starting the search for possible contracts.

3 The previous performance of the proponent in respect of social and environmental responsibilities.

4 The generation or reduction of employment opportunities; the effect on full-time and part-time employment; the

effect on female employment, and on Aboriginal groups.

5 The multiplier effects on the local, regional, or national economy through investment and other expenditure, salaries, and wages.

6 For the community, improved or reduced accessibility to facilities, services, and employment opportunities in the locality.

7 The effect of supply and demand in the local area for whatever is being proposed.

8 The effect on the choice and affordability of goods and services.

9 Better use or redundancy of existing urban infrastructure.

10 The effects on the local rate base and costs likely to be imposed on local rate revenue.

11 The possible effects of the development on commercial competition.

12 The relationship between the proposal and national or state economic, social, and environmental policies.

13 The likely cost to the proponent of proposed pollution control and environmental protection measures.

14 The requirements imposed on government and hence the public by provision of infrastructure.

15 The requirements imposed on government and hence the public for the provision of finance, grants, loans, and other forms of assistance by guarantees or protection, or reduction or abolition of risk.

16 When it is the public purse, full public disclosure of expected cash flow; debt and taxation commitments; public cost implications on-site and off-site; equity impacts; hidden costs, private and public; sources of finance, both overseas and local, and a complete cost-benefit analysis (CBA).

(Source: Gilpin, Alan, *The case for the economic impact statement* 20th Conference of Economists, University of Tasmania, Hobart, Australia, 1991)

CHECKLIST 3.7

Environmental health impact assessment (EHIA)
Checklist: matters for consideration

In determining a DA, a consent authority should consider such of the following matters that are relevant to the proposed development:

1 Within the framework of EIA, those aspects of the proposed development which might present adverse risks to the health and well-being of the community, either near or far, in the short term or long term, either directly or indirectly; or any particularly vulnerable section of the community (the young, the old, the disadvantaged, the sick, females, ethnic minorities, Aborigines).

2 Emissions from the proposed development that might have a detrimental effect on the quality of air or water to the detriment of human beings either directly, or indirectly through the food chain; an inventory of pollutants with details of the handling or dispersal of these.

3 The risks of contamination of land from leachates or the dumping or storage of toxic materials; risk of contamination of aquifers.

4 Solid wastes from the development and their management; possible dust and grit from wastepiles, disposal areas, vehicles, roads, and tipping operations.

5 The levels of noise, blast and vibration that may occur, during the day, night, or weekend.

6 Odours likely to emanate at various times from various processes and disposal practices.

7 The volume of traffic likely to be generated by the development, particularly heavy vehicles; the implications for community noise, and for the safety of drivers and pedestrians, particularly children, the elderly, the physically disadvantaged.

8 The risks and hazards of the activity: fire, explosion, sudden harmful fumes, major spills of toxic materials within the plant or on the roads, radiation, failures of safety systems, effects of sustained temperature inversions in the atmosphere, failure of flares, unexpected discharges of toxic materials such as dioxins, chain reactions, failure of treatment plant, asbestos risks, sewage discharge, floods, failure of emergency procedures.

9 Possible synergistic effects of several pollutants reacting together.

10 Possible promotion of vector breeding such as flies or mosquitoes; the effects of water resource development.

11 Cumulative effects of other developments in the region or locality, for example, effects on safety of drinking water.

12 Other effects likely to have a negative effect on physical or mental well-being such as split communities, ecological damage, loss of access to recreational facilities, bright night-lighting, loss of amenities, overhead transmission lines, surface pipelines, increased closure of

railway-crossing gates; night-time noise from, say, aircraft or power plant, generators and transformers; increased stress; deterioration of the visual environment or amenities, anxiety about the future; isolation; adverse effects on local businesses in some cases, absence of facilities for the mediation of disputes or ventilation of opinion.

13 The effect on workers at home who are exposed to detrimental conditions at both work and home, such as air pollution and odours.

14 The existing environment, land uses, and current levels of pollution and risk; characteristics of the population and its current health status; other environmental degradation; existing standard of living of the population; Aboriginal issues.

15 Mitigation measures proposed for the adverse effects of the development; proposals for monitoring and PPA for effects on health.

16 Contributions by the proponent to improving the health, social, and recreational facilities of the immediate locality.

17 Public perception of the risks and hazards; interaction with the media.

18 The incorporation of environmental health standards in development consent conditions; and annual reporting requirements to the environmental, planning, and public health agencies.

(Derived from World Health Organisation, *Environmental impact assessment: an assessment of methodological and substantive issues affecting human health considerations*, WHO report no. 41, University of London, 1989, and other related literature)

CHECKLIST 3.8

Hazard and risk impact assessment Checklist: matters for consideration

In determining a DA, a consent authority should consider such of the following matters that are relevant to the proposed development:

1 The choice of the location for the project, in particular the proximity of dwellings, other centres of employment, other vulnerable facilities such as schools and hospitals, and storage areas for inflammable and explosive materials.

2 Any proposed buffer zones, and any other planning restrictions.

3 The routeing of vehicles and trucks into and out of the proposed installation; the risk to life and limb of moving heavy trucks and road tankers through towns.

4 The nature of each process, identifying inputs, outputs, instrumentation, and controls.

5 The location of chemical and hazardous waste storage areas, process areas where hazardous materials are used, equipment fuelling areas, routes of pipelines carrying dangerous materials, electrical equipment, and transmission lines.

6 The location and nature of wastewater treatment plant and air pollution control equipment; the disposal of their sludges and solids.

7 The risks of component, vessel, or system failure through material failure, leakage, corrosion, stress, explosion, breakdown, excessive pressure, fire, uncontrolled reactions, vibration, shock, collision, incorrect operation, inadequate design, lack of back-up and duplication of controls, inadequate monitoring; the risks of a boiling liquid expanding vapour explosion (BLEVE), or unconfined vapour cloud explosion (UVCE).

8 The proposed use of techniques to minimise hazards and risks, for example, the use of bunds (screens), sand-covered storage tanks, drip trays, or barriers; indicators and alarms; leak detection systems; ground-water monitoring; soil testing; automatic diversion systems; stormwater controls; secondary containment arrangements; clear identification of chemicals.

9 Compliance with all standards for the storage, movement, and use of dangerous goods; poisons and environmentally hazardous chemicals legislation; occupational health criteria; and probable licence conditions.

10 The history of similar plant at other locations about safety and the lessons learnt.

11 The disposal of all wastes, with clear identification; recycling.

12 Emergency measures, plans, and procedures.

13 Periodic review of safety measures and monitoring results; arrangements for independent audits.

14 Laboratory facilities; sampling and testing.

15 Management and operational controls; hazards procedures manual; fines and penalties.

16 Training of staff and allocation of duties.

(Sources: various)

CHECKLIST 3.9

Noise impact assessment
Checklist: matters for consideration

In determining a DA involving the emission of noise, a consent authority should consider such of the following matters that are relevant to the proposed development:

1   Identification of sources of noise from the proposed development and the prospective noise levels in dB(A).* This step takes account of every piece of equipment, vehicle, operation, and activity on the site. The prospective noise levels should be correlated to distance, with emphasis upon noise levels beyond the site boundaries varying with meteorological conditions.

2   Description and measurement of existing noise levels, their incidence and characteristics, particularly during the day and hours of darkness; the background level. The history of the surrounding area about noise.

3   Noise standards and criteria; acceptability of noise according to the nature of the surrounding area such as agricultural, open space, commercial, industrial, or residential. Existing published noise standards, being the recommendations of a national or international body.

4   The predicted noise levels in relation to (2) and (3) and their acceptability in this locality, or alternative localities; the characteristics of the noise(s) emitted and their incidence over time.

5   Mitigation measures to be adopted for the proposed development, with particular attention to the noisiest activities. The use of less noisy equipment and practices, the positioning of equipment and buildings, the noise-proofing of buildings, the erection of bunds (screens) and sound barriers, the management of traffic noise, restrictions on working hours or the operational hours of certain equipment.

6   For airfields, the use of curfews.

*See glossary

CHECKLIST 3.10

Social impact assessment (SIA)
Checklist: matters for consideration

In determining a DA, a consent authority should consider such of the following matters that are relevant to the proposed development:

1   Generally, those changes in social relations among members of a community, society, or institution, resulting from external change attributable to the proposed development; for example, where, in the case of hydroelectric dams, it will be necessary to relocate large populations into alien environments.

2   Changes in circumstance which are likely to result in social discontent, unhappiness, increased illness, and a loss of productivity, leading to loss of income.

3   The consequences of the severance of communities by major developments, both physical and psychological.

4   The effects of a development on general lifestyle.

5   The effects of a development on group relationships.

6   The effects of a development on cultural life.

7   The effects of a development on social tranquillity and attitudes and values.

8   Assessment of the services and infrastructure required by the new development and those required to ensure social sustainability; likely financial and other contributions by the developer.

9   The likely effect of the proposed development on neighbourhood property values by, for example, interfering with views and amenities, or introducing streams of noisy traffic.

10 The potential loss of ecological assets such as bushland, wetlands, rainforest, distinctive geological features, fauna and flora, mangrove, swamp, lakes and creeks, forest and walking trails, lookouts, and recreational areas and facilities, and natural areas, all of value to people.

11 The effects of extra cars and extra noisy people; the impact of numerous heavy vehicles and the implications for driver and pedestrian safety; parking, and congestion.

12 The health impacts of the proposed development.

13 The effect of the development in displacing low-income people and other disadvantaged people.

14 The effects on public transport, open space, community facilities such as child care and youth centres, pedestrian access, and roads.

15 The changing character of the area affected.

16 The implications of the development for social policy.

17 The integration of social, economic, and environmental factors with the aim of sustainable development.

(Derived from Gilpin, Alan, *Environmental planning: a condensed encyclopedia*, Noyes Publications, Park Ridge, New Jersey, 1986, and other literature)

CHECKLIST 3.11

Urban impact assessment
Checklist: matters for consideration

In determining a DA, a consent authority should consider such of the following matters as are relevant to the proposed development:

1 The general character of the proposed site and any possible alternative; the natural, urban, commercial, or industrial history of the site.

2 The consistency of the proposed development with any relevant statutory instruments, planning policies, heritage orders, or measures under Aboriginal legislation; and with any planning studies and recommendations under consideration.

3 The provisions of any government strategies or policies for the development or redevelopment of the business centres or urban area in question.

4 The results of any specific social, health, economic, or ecological impact assessments.

5 The nature and character of the existing environment in the vicinity of the proposed development.

6 The commercial and economic basis of the proposal.

7 The character, location, siting, bulk, scale, shape, size, height, density, design, or external appearance of that development.

8 The size and shape of the land to which that DA relates, the siting of any building, or works thereon, and the area to be occupied by that development.

9 The relationship of that development to development on adjoining land or on other land in the locality.

10 Whether the proposed means of entrance to and exit from that development and the land to which that DA relates are adequate.

11 Whether adequate provision has been made for the loading, unloading, manoeuvring and parking of vehicles within that development or on that land.

12 The amount of traffic likely to be generated by the development, particularly for the capacity of the road system in the locality and further afield; repercussions throughout the entire metropolitan road system.

13 The effect of traffic to and from the development on the immediate road system.

14 Whether additional public transport services are necessary to help serve the development; and whether they will be adequate.

15 Whether utilities generally are adequate for the development.

16 Whether adequate provision has been made for the landscaping of the land and the aesthetic treatment of the building.

17 The effect of the building on the meteorology of the district by blocking sunlight or casting shadows; or causing wind turbulence or wind tunnelling.

18 The effect of the building on the general character of the area through being excessively dominating or high, significantly varying a generally accepted character; or creating ravines, or reducing areas of relaxation in the city area.

19 The effect of the types of employment offered, on the nature and character of employment in the central business district or suburban centre; the implications for the employment and advancement of women, and ethnic minorities.

20 Any multiplier effect such as support services that the development might induce.

21 The implications for the heritage values of the city or suburban centre.

22 The implications for public space generally in the area.

23 The implications for existing occupants in the vicinity in any aspect.

24 Whether the development adds status to the urban and city scene.

25 The implications of additional office space for the supply and demand situation generally.

26 The effect on suburban centres following a further concentration of services in the city centre.

27 The effects on air pollution.

28 The effects on noise levels.

29 The implications for garbage removal services.

30 The financial implications at local government level.

(Sources: various)

CHECKLIST 3.12

**Water quality impact assessment
Checklist: matters for consideration**

In determining a DA involving the emission of wastes, run-off, or soil erosion affecting the quality of water resources, a consent authority should consider such of the following matters that are relevant to the proposed development:

1   The characteristics of the water resources at risk: rivers, tributaries, lakes, streams, creeks, aquifers and aquifer recharge areas; the topography and ecological characteristics; seasonal and annual flows; rainfall and run-off; storage facilities; and other features.

2   Use of the present water resources: domestic, commercial, and industrial, agricultural or recreational.

3   Existing waste discharges and run-offs which may be detrimental to existing water quality; remedial measures already adopted or planned.

4   Pending developments for water resources likely to affect the present and future scenarios.

5   The history of pollution or misuse of water resources; the incidence, for example, of eutrophication, blue-green algae, or acidification; and any evidence of events detrimental to the health, safety, welfare, or property of persons, or harmful to animals, aquatic life, birds, or fish.

6   Identified sources of waste discharges from the proposed development after all measures of waste minimisation, recycling, treatment, dilution, ponding, filtering, or otherwise, have been adopted.

7   The likely effects of soil disturbance during the construction phase and, subsequently, mitigation measures to be adopted.

8   The likely effects of run-off from surfaces, sealed and unsealed; mitigation measures to be adopted.

9   The likely effects under conditions of drought and flood.

10   The significance of the likely emissions, discharges, and run-offs, particularly for state regulations, standards and classifications, and environmental objectives; the total ecological, chemical, and physical effects, and salinisation. Specific pollutants by toxic substances, minerals, metals, sludges, oil, pesticides, radioactive substances, acids, alkalis, intractable wastes, processing effluents, sewage effluents, phosphorus and nitrogen, suspended and dissolved solids; the likely biochemical oxygen demand (BOD) and chemical oxygen demand (COD).

11   The likely effects on fish, wildlife, communities, and vegetation.

12   The possible effects of the development on water flows, depths and widths of channels, erosion of banks, deposition rates (upstream and downstream), and turbulence.

13   The results of discussions at scoping meetings, with individual groups, and with authorities, on the general and specific effects of the proposed development about water quantity and quality.

14   The implications for other water users, existing, and prospective.

15   The economic and social effects of prospective changes in watercourses, water quantity, and water quality for the wider community.

Following these checklists, checklists 3.13 to 3.21 outline the economic, social, and environmental matters to be considered for a range of projects of a specific character such as:

- a community centre;
- an expressway;
- a hydroelectric power plant;
- a marina;
- a nuclear power plant;
- an open-cut mining operation;
- a sand and gravel extraction operation;
- a sewage treatment plant;
- a thermal electricity generating plant.

CHECKLIST 3.13

Community centre: economic, social, and environmental elements for consideration

1   The contribution the community centre might make to an identified need for recreational and entertainment facilities within its catchment.

2   Alternative locations for the centre; alternative uses for the site.

3   The consistency of the proposal with national, regional, or local planning instruments and objectives; the present zoning and use of the site.

4   The general character of the proposal: the precise boundaries of the site; the vicinity of residences and other facilities; ingress and egress from the site; internal parking areas; location and capacity of buildings; nature of recreation and entertainment

(sports ground, tracks, theatres, bars and restaurants, library, cinemas, child care centre); workforce; management structure; funding; landscaping.

5 Present ownership of land, and consent of the owner(s) to the present development application.

6 The potential for noise from traffic, crowds, loudspeakers, and activities; the potential for noise nuisance to residents.

7 The volume and timing of traffic entering and leaving the site; traffic management at peak times; the risks of traffic congestion; risks of parking in neighbouring streets.

8 Meteorological information.

9 Potential traffic movement for established traffic movement in the area; traffic counts.

10 Risks to children, elderly, and the public in general; invasion of privacy; risks of drunkenness and antisocial behaviour.

11 Aims and objectives of the centre, and corporate status.

12 Evidence of need and support for the centre.

13 The need for the individual components of the complex.

14 The loss if the centre is not proceeded with.

15 The relationship with other community centres.

16 Emergency services and responses.

17 The maintenance of records.

18 The political implications of the operation.

19 An environmental management plan for the whole operation.

20 Facilities for monitoring and PPA.

21 Arrangements for continuing public involvement after the initial EIA.

22 Annual report to the environmental and planning agencies.

23 Prospective future developments in the same district or region, which suggest cumulative impacts.

CHECKLIST 3.14

Expressway: economic, social, and environmental elements for consideration

1 The route of the proposed expressway, design, and number of lanes, volume and nature of traffic, construction, tolls, management, landscaping, bridges, overpasses and underpasses, flow of traffic to and from the expressway, coordination of upgrading of entry and exit roads.

2 The need for the expressway and the possibility of alternative arrangements and routes.

3 The consistency of the proposal with national, regional, and local planning instruments and highway development strategies.

4 The potential contribution to reducing traffic congestion and improving travel times and safety; effects on local road hierarchy.

5 The cost-benefit framework for the proposal and implications for remaining road network; implications for public transport, and bicycles.

6 The proximity of residential districts and likely social impacts; implications for population growth.

7 The environmental impact of the proposal in respect of separation of communities, noise, air pollution, water pollution, drainage, hydrology, aesthetics, rehabilitation of disturbed areas, soil erosion, landslips, rockfalls, effects of bushland and creeks, effects on property, and physical services, lighting.

8 The environmental implications of the construction phase with particular reference to heavy traffic, noise, construction vehicle movement, closures, safety, hazards, water pollution, soil erosion, landslip and rockfalls, blasting, earthworks.

9 Measures to be undertaken to minimise adverse environmental effects during the construction and operational phases.

10 The relationship between road surfaces and noise; sound screening and barriers.

11 The implications for existing commercial centres.

12 The safety of motorists and pedestrians.

13 The landscaping of the entire route.

14 The implications for railways, existing and prospective.

15 The implications for the freeway of future traffic growth.

16 Alternatives to the expressway.

17 Community concerns regarding psychological impact, impact on health and safety, social displacement and relocation, community divisions; noise, water and air pollution; aesthetic impacts, lighting disruption, property resumption, reduced and impaired lifestyle, property value reduction, accessibility changes, leisure and recreational impacts, land-use changes, access restrictions, impacts on schools, loss of bushland, the diversion of

scarce capital from other more socially useful sectors including rail-based public transport, exacerbation of the levels of fossil fuel consumption contributing further to greenhouse/ozone problems, aggravation of the balance-of-payments problem, loss of residential amenity, need for pedestrian road bridges, visual impacts.

18   Emergency services and responses; hazardous incidents.

19   Energy considerations.

20   Arrangements for the acquisition of land, properties and houses which are needed for the construction of the expressway.

21   Special measures for the protection of fauna and flora, scenic features, national parks, nature reserves and sanctuaries, wetlands, mangroves, rainforest, bushland, sensitive ecological areas, historic, and cultural sites, and heritage values.

22   The political implications of the project.

23   The arrangements for continuing public involvement following the initial EIA.

24   Annual report to the environmental, planning, and public roads agencies.

CHECKLIST 3.15

Hydroelectric power plant: economic, social, and environmental elements for consideration

1   The contribution to a balanced system for the generation and supply of electricity to meet present and anticipated demand.

2   The alternatives to the proposal by way of alternative sites, alternative ways of generating electricity, or modifying the demand for electricity.

3   Hydroelectric power as a form of sustainable development using a naturally renewable resource.

4   Hydroelectric power as a preferable alternative to conventional thermal power stations using coal or oil, which emit greenhouse gases and other effluents to air and water.

5   The consistency of the proposal with national, regional, or local planning instruments; the relationship with national parks, wilderness areas, or nature reserves.

6   The problem of resettlement if people are to be displaced; the economic and social consequences of displacement.

7   The environmental implications of construction by way of quarrying, road-building, seepage, and landslides.

8   The housing of the construction workforce.

9   The possible geological effects of the dam by way of increased landslip, seepage, or seismic activity.

10   Water management issues such as the quantity and timing of the release of water.

11   The disposal of stagnant water or colder water from the lower layers within the dam.

12   The utilisation of the impounded water for purposes other than electricity generation, for example, for recreational or irrigation purposes.

13   Changes in water characteristics.

14   The effects on habitats.

15   The effects on fish spawning.

16   The implications for flood mitigation.

17   The problem of siltation.

18   The implications of downstream alluvial loss.

19   The overall effects on the health of communities immediately affected or downstream; nearby residential districts.

20   The implications for vector breeding.

21   Potential damage to, or destruction of, archaeological or historic sites.

22   The implications for sacred and cultural sites.

23   The rotting of vegetative matter drowned under dam waters and the removal of obstacles.

24   The reduction in biodiversity and the destruction of wildlife.

25   The implications for local industry.

26   The implications for ethnic minorities.

27   Environmental management of the dam.

28   Facilities for monitoring and PPA.

29   The risks and hazards of a major structure.

30   The implications for training.

31   The implications for technology in a national context.

32   The implications for foreign investment.

33   The implications for trade and the balance of payments.

34   The political implications of the project.

35   The arrangements for continuing public involvement following the initial EIA.

36   The proponent's contribution to local infrastructure development and social facilities.

37   The implications for aesthetics, amenities, and ecology on: site, and elsewhere; landscaping.

38 Electricity transmission lines, easements, and access roads; prospective routes.

39 Housing for the permanent workforce.

40 Facilities to be provided for tourists; parking.

41 Emergency services and responses.

42 Clearing of debris after construction, and restoration of vegetation; site rehabilitation.

43 Annual report to the environmental, planning, and energy agencies.

44 Prospective future developments in the same district, or region, which might suggest cumulative impacts.

CHECKLIST 3.16

A marina: economic, social, and environmental elements for consideration

1 The contribution the marina might make to growing recreational demands.

2 Alternative sites for the proposal.

3 The consistency of the proposal with national, regional, or local planning instruments; the relationship with other amenities.

4 The general character of the proposal, including the structure of the breakwaters, depth of water, number and type of boats for which the marina is planned, water and power supply, roads, dry docks, boat maintenance and repair facilities, slipways, housing units, hotel accommodation, restaurants, commercial areas, and parking.

5 Drainage and sewerage systems, solid waste disposal, and fuel supply for boats.

6 Means for the disposal of sanitary waste both on land and sea.

7 The proposed stages of construction and timetable.

8 Measures for the maintenance of water quality; details of dredging that may be necessary.

9 The structures in relation to the natural landscape.

10 Expected movement of people during the construction and operating stages.

11 The existing environment and proximity of dwellings including physical site characteristics, hydrographic, and meteorological information, sedimentological information, biological conditions, and present land uses on the area.

12 Topographic and bathymetric changes likely to occur during and after construction.

13 Sand movements and sites where increased sand accumulation and coastal erosion is likely to occur.

14 Oceanographic changes likely to occur in the future, including the location and risk of wave reflection on adjacent shores, and the concentration of wave energy and currents which could endanger swimming, or disturb fisheries.

15 Risks of sea pollution inside and outside the marina by uncontrolled sewage, polluted surface run-off, oil and petrol, paints and anti-fouling materials.

16 Adverse effects on flora and fauna in the area such as the risk of loss of habitat, changes in existing habitats, and the impact of barriers to movement of migrating species.

17 Likely impacts on land use.

18 Visual impacts during the construction and operational phase.

19 The possible effects on the quality of bathing water and on the cleanliness of beach sand.

20 The measures proposed to prevent, reduce, or mitigate the negative effects of the proposal.

21 The environmental management of the marina.

22 Monitoring arrangements.

23 Enforcement procedures by the management; the managerial structure.

24 Emergency services and responses.

25 The proponent's contribution to the provision of public facilities necessary to the marina.

26 Prospective future developments in the same locality which might suggest cumulative impacts.

27 Annual report for environmental, planning, and recreational agencies.

CHECKLIST 3.17

Nuclear power plant: economic, social and environmental elements for consideration

1 The need for a nuclear power plant.

2 The contribution to a balanced system for the generation and supply of electricity to meet present and anticipated demand.

3 The alternatives to the proposal, of alternative sites, alternative ways of generating electricity, or modifying the demand for electricity.

4 The consistency of the proposal with national, regional, or local planning instruments; the relationship with settlements, national parks, wilderness areas, or nature reserves.

5 The generating capacity of the proposed power station, the number and capacity of the individual generating sets.

6 The type of nuclear reactor and its safety characteristics.

7 The source and type of uranium fuel, the mode of transport to the site, mode of loading and unloading, and the storage or dispatch of spent fuel elements.

8 The risks and hazards of the discharge of high-level and low-level radioactive elements; precautions against leakages, and measures for coping with major mishaps.

9 Emergency procedures in relation to the population.

10 Predictions for the dispersal of radioactive elements in the atmosphere; local, regional, national, and transboundary implications.

11 The cooling water system, either direct to a body of water or indirect via cooling towers.

12 The visual and humidity effects of cooling towers.

13 The potential effects of thermal discharges into water on fauna and flora, including coral, and mangroves.

14 The environmental implications of construction by site preparation, road and railway construction, and other supporting infrastructure.

15 The housing of the construction workforce.

16 The implications for employment and local industry.

17 The implications for aesthetics, amenities, and ecology at the site and elsewhere; landscaping.

18 Electricity transmission lines, easements, and access roads; prospective routes.

19 Housing for the permanent workforce.

20 The proponent's contribution to local infrastructure development, and social facilities.

21 Facilities for monitoring and PPA.

22 Potential damage to, or destruction of, archaeological or historic sites.

23 The implications for sacred, and cultural sites.

24 The implications for training, and the provision of a highly skilled workforce.

25 The implications for technology in a

national context, and the development of new industrial manufacturing skills.

26 The implications for foreign investment.

27 The implications for the balance of payments.

28 Environmental management of the power station.

29 Proposals for decommissioning, and site rehabilitation at the end of the power station's useful economic life.

30 Proposals for the disposal of nuclear wastes during the operational life of the station, and on decommissioning.

31 The known public and political reactions to the proposal.

32 The proponent's detailed comments on, and reactions to, the Three Mile Island and Chernobyl events.

33 The potential contribution of the proposed power station to a reduction of greenhouse gases.

34 The arrangements for continuing public involvement following the initial EIA.

35 Annual report to the environmental, planning, nuclear, and energy agencies.

36 The risks and hazards in a local, regional, national, and international context; the track records of similar power stations elsewhere; trends in the utilisation of nuclear energy elsewhere; the ultimate disposal of nuclear wastes.

37 The long-term public interest.

CHECKLIST 3.18

Open-cut mining operation: economic, social, and environmental elements for consideration

1 The contribution to fulfilling energy demands, including export opportunities, that the mine might meet.

2 The alternatives to the proposal of alternative sites, or alternative ways of meeting energy demands.

3 The consistency of the proposal with national, regional, or local planning instruments; the relationship with national parks, wilderness areas, or nature reserves.

4 The prospective life of the mine, and the staging of operations.

5 Coal-handling, processing, and stockpiling facilities.

6 Rail-loading facilities.

7   Road-loading facilities.

8   Rail-spur lines.

9   Access roads.

10 The industrial area of the site including bathhouse amenities, plant maintenance workshops, administrative buildings, and ancillary facilities.

11 The various water management structures, site haul roads, construction facilities, and dragline erection area.

12 The rehabilitation program.

13 Landscaping and site perimeter screen planting.

14 Vegetation and topsoil stripping; topsoil stockpiles.

15 Overburden removal and dumping areas.

16 Details of the coal-preparation plant and stockpiles.

17 Handling of tailings from the coal-preparation plant.

18 Water for the washery and for road dust suppression.

19 Details of the sewerage treatment system.

20 Heavy vehicle access and movement during the construction phase, and the operational phases.

21 The routes chosen for heavy vehicles.

22 Project employment during the construction, and operational phases; the housing of employees.

23 The existing environment and its modification as a result of the intended mining operation.

24 The arrangements for mine drainage and prevention of water pollution.

25 Unwanted rock waste and backfilling.

26 The effect of the mine on habitats, fishing, biodiversity, and wildlife.

27 Pollution consequences in terms of air, water, and noise.

28 The implications for aesthetics, amenities, ecology, and health; nearby residential districts.

29 The implications for local industry.

30 Environmental management of the mine.

31 Potential damage to, or destruction of, archaeological or historic sites.

32 The implications for sacred, and cultural sites.

33 Facilities for monitoring and PPA.

34 The risks and hazards of a major industrial project.

35 The implications for training.

36 The implications for technology in a national context.

37 The implications for foreign investment.

38 The implications for trade and the balance of payments.

39 The political implications of the project.

40 The arrangements for continuing public involvement following the initial EIA.

41 The proponent's contribution to local infrastructure development, and social facilities; improved roads, underpasses and overpasses for people and farm animals.

42 Electricity transmission lines, easements, and access roads; prospective routes.

43 Emergency services, and responses.

44 Annual report to the environmental, planning, and energy agencies.

45 Prospective future developments in the same district or region, which might suggest cumulative impacts.

46 Arrangements for the acquisition of houses and properties which are likely to impede the progress of the mine or otherwise be adversely affected.

47 Proposals by the government for mine bonding.*

*See glossary

CHECKLIST 3.19

Sand and gravel extraction: economic, social, and environmental elements for consideration

1   The contribution the project might make to the growing demand for building and road materials.

2   Alternative sources for the material which might be used instead.

3   The consistency of the proposal with national, regional, or local planning instruments.

4   The general character of the proposal: the total volume to be extracted in each year over the life of the project; the planned life; the precise location of the site; the proposed stages of operation; basic operating cell sizes; hours of operation; proximity of dwellings; workforce; the market for sand and gravel and its proximity; transportation; dry extraction or wet dredging.

5   The precise methods of dry extraction or wet dredging; the use of suction dredges or other equipment; washing plant; disposal of wastes; stockpiles; tailings ponds; backfilling.

6   The rehabilitation plan to achieve stability and minimise pollution; to return it possibly to productive agricultural or recreational use; to restore the aesthetics of the site; to remove all items of mining equipment and rubbish; to return the topsoil and reshape the land to the required contours; to revegetate.

7   The trees and shrubs that are intended to be protected throughout the whole operation; the identification of land that will not be disturbed.

8   Other features of the existing environment that would be disturbed by the operation.

9   The volume of heavy traffic by road or rail that would be generated.

10 The effects of the entire operation including transport on the community by noise, disturbance, dust and grit, or road damage; the effects on flora and fauna, and heritage items.

11 If extraction is from a river, the likely effects downstream and upstream; the effects on water quality with urban pressures; the risks of blue-green algae blooms.

12 The disposal of all trees, shrubs, and undergrowth that are inevitably removed during the staged operations.

13 The provision of fencing around all areas to be extracted.

14 The avoidance of interference with the free use of the river, if any, for navigation.

15 The provision and maintenance of access roads.

16 The covering of all vehicles leaving the site, with loads trimmed.

17 The payment of bonds, guarantees, and levies to cover the risks of default in respect of development conditions, in particular, progressive rehabilitation.

18 An environmental management plan for the whole operation.

19 The maintenance of records.

20 Facilities for monitoring and PPA.

21 The political implications of the operation.

22 The arrangements for continuing public involvement following the initial EIA.

23 Emergency services and responses.

24 Annual report to the environmental and planning agencies.

25 Prospective future developments in the same district or region, which suggest cumulative impacts.

CHECKLIST 3.20

Sewage treatment plant: economic, social, and environmental elements for consideration

1   The contribution the sewage treatment plant would make to improving the environment of the community served, through the elimination of septic tank and other systems, and the protection of the effluent-receiving waters.

2   Alternative sites for the proposal and alternative treatment systems.

3   The consistency of the proposal with national, regional, or local planning instruments; the relationship to neighbouring residential or tourist areas.

4   The types of sewage and waste to be treated (domestic, industrial, hospital, agricultural).

5   The number of inhabitants to be served by the plant both now and in the future; arrangements for extension.

6   Quantity of sewage and wastes involved, cubic metres per day, per year, per season.

7   Characteristics of sewage and wastes to be treated.

8   Layout of the plant.

9   Final disposal of treated effluent (for agriculture, to sea or river); chemical, physical and bacteriological characteristics of the treated effluent.

10 Sludge quantity and characteristics.

11 Method of sludge treatment and disposal (incineration, discharge into the ocean after stabilisation, improving fertility of soils, providing compost for the horticultural industry, land rehabilitation, landfill).

12 The measures to maintain the reliability of the sewage treatment plant, so that plant bypasses, which lead to raw sewage discharges, are reduced to a minimum.

13 The measures to reduce overflows from the sewerage system resulting from illegal stormwater connections.

14 The arrangements for the separation of stormwater from the sewerage system, and the mode of disposal of stormwater.

15 The measures to reduce the emission of odours from the treatment and disposal activities; use of odour scrubbers.

16 The provision of additional sewerage services to reduce the pollution of waterways caused by run-off from on-site sewage disposal systems.

17 Measures which could be adopted for reducing the deleterious effects of urban run-off.

18 The possible impacts of measures on drinking water quality, and recreational beaches.

19 The effects of the project on flora and fauna.

20 Proposals for landscaping and screening of plant.

21 The construction impacts should extensive construction of sewers be required.

22 In certain climates, the risks of mosquito breeding.

23 Measures to improve the quality of influents into the system, domestic, industrial, and commercial.

24 Proposals for the monitoring of the entire system.

25 Proposals for the education of the public in environmentally sound practices.

26 Measures for the progressive improvement of plant performance, and environmental management of the entire system over coming years.

27 The existing environment: physical site characteristics; climatological, and meteorological conditions; geological, and hydrological condition; present land use of site and surroundings; any other particular characteristics.

28 Enforcement procedures by management; the management structure.

29 Emergency services, and responses.

30 Prospective future developments in the same locality which might suggest incompatibilities.

31 The political implications of the project.

32 The implications for aesthetics, amenities, ecology and health; nearby residential districts, schools, hospitals, and so on.

33 The arrangements for continuing public involvement following the initial EIA.

34 Annual report to the environmental, planning, and public works agencies.

CHECKLIST 3.21

Thermal electricity generation plant: economic, social, and environmental elements for consideration

1 The contribution to a balanced system for the generation and supply of electricity to meet present and anticipated demand.

2 The alternatives to the proposal, of alternative sites, alternative ways of generating electricity, or modifying the demand for electricity.

3 The consistency of the proposal with national, regional, or local planning instruments; the relationship with national parks, wilderness areas, or nature reserves.

4 The generating capacity of the proposed power station, the number and capacity of the individual generating sets.

5 The proposed fuel (oil, coal, or gas) and its sources.

6 The mode of transportation of fuel to the site; the storage of same.

7 The composition of the fuel to be used with particular reference to ash and sulphur content.

8 The types of steam generators and mode of combustion of the fuel.

9 The arrangements for dust arresters and flue gas scrubbing.

10 The characteristics and composition of the final emissions to atmosphere, with particular reference to greenhouse gases.

11 The number and heights of stacks; internal flue arrangement; efflux velocity, and temperature.

12 Measures against downwash and down draught, and adverse meteorological conditions.

13 Predictions for the dispersal of the final effluent in the atmosphere; local, regional, national, and transboundary implications.

14 The ash disposal system, and dust suppression arrangements.

15 The disposal of exhausted scrubber reagents.

16 The cooling water system, either direct to a body of water or indirect via cooling towers.

17 The visual and humidity effects of cooling towers.

18 The potential effects of thermal discharges into water on fauna and flora, including coral, and mangroves.

19 The environmental implications of construction, of site preparation, road and railway construction, and other supporting infrastructure.

20 The housing of the construction workforce.

21 The overall effects on the health of communities.

22 The risks and hazards of a major structure.

23 The implications for employment and local industry.

24 The implications for aesthetics, amenities, and ecology at site and elsewhere; landscaping.

25 Electricity transmission lines, easements, and access roads; prospective routes.

26 Housing for the permanent workforce.

27 The proponent's contribution to local infrastructure development and social facilities.

28 Facilities for monitoring and PPA.

29 Potential damage to, or destruction of, archaeological, or historic sites.

30 The implications for sacred, and cultural sites.

31 The implications for training.

32 The implications for technology in a national context.

33 The implications for foreign investment.

34 The implications for trade and the balance of payments.

35 Emergency services and responses.

36 Environmental management of the power station.

37 Proposals for site rehabilitation at the end of the power station's useful economic life.

38 The political implications of the project.

39 The arrangements for continuing public involvement following the initial EIA.

40 Annual report to the environmental, planning, and energy agencies.

41 Prospective future developments in the same district, or region, which might suggest cumulative impacts.

3.11 The multi-disciplinary team

Within an organisation specialising in EIS or EA, or undertaking reviews of such studies, it is important to have assembled a multi-disciplinary team able to comprehend and analyse a whole range of issues and provide answers. Thus a team might include people with specific skills in the following: forestry, ecological, scientific, engineering, biological, social, and economic areas. It is impracticable, however, to include skilled people in areas that might be drawn on infrequently or which might present great complexity in development situations.

Areas of knowledge that come readily to mind include:

- noise predictions, assessments and mitigation measures;
- rehabilitation issues requiring great experience;
- issues entailing unfamiliar, rare and endangered species;
- matters including environmentally hazardous chemicals;
- social issues where communities are split or displaced;
- situations requiring considerable insight into meteorological contexts;
- cumulative impacts involving, say, soil erosion and salinity;
- situations involving risks, hazards and health implications;
- emergency procedures;
- high-temperature incineration and air pollution dispersal studies.

To bring together a competent multi-disciplinary team, it is always necessary to seek and to harness knowledge and experience in special areas. Checklists might well take teams a considerable way along the track, but rare skills or bodies of knowledge (perhaps local), are often necessary. The subject of air pollution and its control, for example, breaks down into a whole range of special areas of knowledge and expertise.

The air pollution and control technologies of, say, the petrochemical industry, the iron and steel industry, the non-ferrous metals industry, the ceramic and brickmaking industries, the glass industry, the sugar industry, the metal-working industries, the scrap recovery industry, the fertiliser industry, the chemical industries, the transport industry – most notably the motor vehicle, the gas industry, the cement industry, the modest iron foundry, incineration in all industries, can all present formidable problems involving considerable specialist expertise. In these areas alone, the relevant literature is immense. Entire careers can be absorbed in a single aspect of one of these topics.

The control of air pollution from the main stack of a major power station burning a traditional fuel such as pulverised coal has been referred to in two checklists, checklist 3.4 on air quality impact assessment in general, and checklist 3.21, specifically on thermal electricity generation: the economic, social, and environmental elements for consideration. All, or certainly most, of the key issues are embraced, but important questions still need to be answered.

There is a problem in achieving a completely satisfactory understanding of the nature and dispersal of pollutants from high stacks, in a local, regional, and transboundary context; and how such pollution can be restricted or controlled to achieve the protection of both people and the natural and urban environment, at a cost which the industry (and hence the public) can afford to carry. Power stations using fossil fuels are a major source of pollution including the greenhouse gas, carbon dioxide. How this can be managed, until something better and cheaper comes along, is addressed in checklist 3.22.

CHECKLIST 3.22

EIA
A pulverised coal-fired power station:
requirements for stack emissions

1 The expected maximum plant load factor and overall thermal efficiency of the generating plant in determining heat input; the energy value of the fuel to be consumed; the composition of the fuel for ash and sulphur; the estimated maximum rates of emission to the atmosphere of key pollutants such as smoke, grit and dust, the oxides of sulphur and nitrogen, and carbon dioxide, after any mitigation measures adopted.

2 The preparation of the fuel and the mode of firing; measures for controlling combustion, minimising smoke and the formation of oxides of nitrogen; the distribution of fly ash between the furnace bottom and that carried forward in the flues; the stack temperature of flue gases after all heat recovery and pre-heating of primary combustion air; the final efflux velocity at stack top.

3 The provision of dust-arresting equipment by way of electrostatic precipitators or bag filters; the removal of dust from the flue gas stream at efficiencies ranging from 99.3 to 99.9 per cent; the rate of discharge of the residual amount to the atmosphere; the size distribution of the residual discharge with characteristic free-falling speeds; the proportion falling into the respirable range of less than 5 micrometres.

4 Proposals to limit sulphur dioxide emissions through sulphur limitations in the coal; sampling procedures to guarantee this.

5 The proposed height of the principal stack, multiple-flue arrangements, efflux velocity, measures against aerodynamic effects at stack top; the estimated effective height of emission under average meteorological conditions and normal load factor.

6 The modelling of the dispersal of pollutants under a whole range of meteorological conditions to determine the worst pollution readings at ground level; those conditions including variations in wind speed and direction, variations in turbulence both vertical and horizontal, and variations in lapse rates.

7 The effects of temperature inversions at various heights and of various intensities on the dispersal of pollutants; the effects of the break-up of inversions and the risk of fumigation.

8 The modelling of the dispersal of pollutants in the context of the actual meteorological characteristics of the site, diurnal, seasonal, and annual; and taking account of abnormal meteorological conditions and any adverse topographical features.

9 The effects of variations in the proposed stack height, gas temperatures or efflux velocities on the dispersal of pollutants.

10 The relationship between predicted concentrations and deposition rates and measured levels of existing pollution, by season, within the context of recognised or accepted air quality standards such as those of the WHO, or US EPA, or standards more appropriate to the situation under consideration.

11 Any particularly sensitive features of the existing environment such as agricultural or horticultural research establishments, or sensitive crops.

12 The need for flue gas scrubbing to minimise regional or transboundary effects, the scrubber arrangements, and reagents.

13 The economics and practical aspects of marginal changes in stack height, arrester, and scrubber efficiencies.

14 The implications for air quality of supplementary equipment such as gas turbines.

15 Monitoring and sampling arrangements, in-stack and around the site, both fixed and mobile, periodic, and continuous.

16 For carbon dioxide emissions, compensatory arrangements for decommissioning older and less efficient plant, extension of solar energy schemes, conservation and efficiency measures, insulation programs, and demand-management policies.

(Source: Gilpin, A., *Control of air pollution*, Butterworths, London, Britain, 1963, pp. 326-343, 449-465; Gilpin, A., *Air pollution* (2nd edn), University of Queensland Press, St Lucia, Brisbane, Australia, 1978; Gilpin, A., *Dictionary of Energy Technology*, Butterworth Scientific/Ann Arbor Science, London, Britain, 1982)

3.12   Best professional judgement

Finalising an EIS or EIA (such as the completion of a report by a commission of inquiry), requires a degree of judgement which often lies beyond methodology.

Even with the matrix, the checklist, and the advice of outside consultants and the results of exhaustive analyses, there might still be some doubt about the outcome: that is whether the document is now ready and able to withstand challenge by the public and the decision-makers.

One of the basic problems is that in all assessments there are winners and losers. A new or extended airport will lead to increased noise levels for some, or a hydroelectric dam could involve the relocation of residents. In other words, many issues have to be balanced; not simply development for environment protection as an optimisation exercise, but a balance for interests and people's welfare. A political framework must be considered; the nature of the government and its attitude to economic growth, employment, and controversial planning, and environmental matters. It is here that maturity of judgement is called for, considering the many matters in the relevant checklists and the many matters outside those factors.

Best professional judgement tries to embrace all relevant facts and values, incomplete data and uncertainties, the whole political context, and the history of similar ventures at home or elsewhere; it tries also to assess the future. Such judgement, as a contribution to decision-making, often irks academic researchers for it cannot be probed and objectively assessed. But often it is indispensable to the outcome.

CHAPTER 4

Public participation, inquiries, and mediation

4.1 Public participation

Public participation in deliberations which lead to important environmental planning and development decisions is a characteristic of the planning and EIA systems in many countries. That governments were elected to govern and should be free to govern without public 'interference' has tended to wither in democratic countries. Democracy is increasingly seen as a continuous and dynamic process in which governments carry ultimate responsibility but only with the most careful public scrutiny. Constant vigilance is necessary for, as Lord John Acton stated, 'All power tends to corrupt, and absolute power corrupts absolutely.'

This is true of most democracies in which a freedom to change governments exists, but many governments are autocracies or dictatorships in which opposition or even criticism of a project might readily be seen as disloyal or even treasonable. In such political systems, there is little hope for EIA in the enlightened forums that this book describes and recommends. *Agenda 21*, which resulted from the UN conference in Rio de Janeiro in 1992, and its associated declaration of principles, is not simply a statement of immediate and urgent tasks; it represents the agenda for the whole of the twenty-first century.

However, in many democratic countries progress should be recognised; some have long histories of public participation, a cornerstone of the US National Environmental Policy Act (NEPA). Since 1969, under NEPA regulations, agencies are required to make 'diligent' efforts to involve the public in the various statutory procedures and provide notice of hearings, public meetings, and the availability of environmental documents.

In the USA when an agency is considering a project whose anticipated effects are of national concern, public notices must include an advertisement in the US *Federal Register* and direct written notice to national organisations reasonably expected to be interested in the matter.

An agency must arrange for public hearings or public meetings whenever there is: environmental controversy about the proposed actions; substantial interest in holding a hearing expressed by members of the public; or a request for a hearing by another agency with jurisdiction over the action, or project.

When a draft EIS is to be considered at a public hearing, the agency must make the EIS and any relevant supporting documents available to the public at least 15 days in advance. Scoping provides another opportunity for public participation at an early stage in the decision-making process. The NEPA process, many aspects of which have been adopted by individual US states, has shown that the public will be heard and listened to.

In 1977, in an environmental message, the US president, Jimmy Carter, emphasised the importance of NEPA to the development of sound federal decisions and to public involvement in government in the USA.

Public hearings are widespread throughout the US planning systems. In Los Angeles, for example, members of the Los Angeles Planning Commission, known as 'examiners', conduct hearings about zoning changes, conditional uses, building lines and building height, completing reports for the commission; the commission's decision then rests on the contents of these reports.

In Britain, public inquiries have been a characteristic of approval processes for most of the twentieth century. Public inquiries conducted by Whitehall inspectors were common during the great slum-clearance drive of the 1930s; and again during the postwar years. The first public inquiry under the Clean Air Act was held in the Black Country town of West Bromwich in 1956, to hear objections to the first proposed smoke control area in Britain (Gilpin, 1963).

On a large infrastructure application in Britain the inspector's report to the minister was unfavourable. The report emphasised a number of environmental aspects of the proposal such as dust and other air pollutants, noise, visual exposure and aesthetics, and the disruptive effects of an additional 40 trains a day passing through level crossings in the metropolitan area. On these grounds consent was refused (Gilpin, 1936b). See case study 6A.

Today public inquiries with full public participation about town planning applications, proposed motorways, airports, and energy installations are quite common in Britain. When a proposal is of national significance, the British government may call in a DA and hold a public inquiry, and make the final consent conditions. Many of the inquiries have been held over a few days or at most a few weeks, and certain key issues have commanded a great deal of time and resources leading up to the inquiry.

The Roskill Commission was charged with the task of identifying the best site for a third London airport; reporting in 1971, the inquiry occupied 258 sitting days extending over 22 months. Another major inquiry was the Parker Windscale Inquiry, about a proposed major expansion of the Windscale nuclear waste reprocessing plant to convert uranium oxide waste into reuseable uranium and plutonium. The inquiry was broad as it was not dealing with a specific proposal; it was a policy-and-need inquiry and not a site-specific inquiry. Reporting in 1978, after many months, the House of Commons endorsed the inquiry's recommendations.

However, public inquiries in Britain, whether short or long, have their critics. An inspector, even sitting with technical assessors, lacks an investigative arm to help with major and technically demanding public inquiries. In some cases, the evidence of major bodies cannot always be as searchingly examined as warranted. Sometimes the proponent has a virtual monopoly of expertise in the area of controversy.

Further, it is difficult for members of the public to be sufficiently well-equipped to stand up to professional cross-examination, and to find the time and resources to participate. The problem of limited public knowledge has been accentuated by the more recent emphasis on risks and hazards as matters of major concern.

Nevertheless, Her Majesty's inspectors enjoy a high reputation as a body of independence, integrity, and objectivity.

Much Australian planning and environmental legislation provides for public participation in planning schemes and in holding public environmental inquiries in various circumstances which directly affect the quality of life or area. However, only the states of New South Wales and Victoria undertake inquiries and hearings as a normal part of the environmental planning and EIA process. New South Wales employs a small number of full-time commissioners of inquiry; Victoria has created a panel system of more than 100 qualified and experienced people, drawn on as required, to conduct hearings. The commonwealth (federal) government has conducted few public inquiries, and in some states any public inquiry is rare.

In New South Wales from the 1980s to 1992 there have been 250 public inquiries into environmental planning and heritage matters. The time taken for each inquiry has been generally less than 3 months, though exceptions occur. A handbook describes commissions of inquiry and how they work (Office of Commissioners of Inquiry, 1988). Checklist 4.1 gives readers an insight into public inquiry procedures, and checklist 4.2 lists typical matters dealt with in proposed conditions to be attached to development consents. Not all projects survive the public inquiry process, DAs having been refused, for example, for a coalmine, an agricultural and veterinary products plant, and an expressway.

Environmental inquiries in New South Wales, Australia, have proved efficient and effective as they are:
- relatively short;
- conducted at arm's length from any department, agency, or other participating party;
- conducted independently of the minister whose sole function is to initiate the inquiry and receive the report;
- a review of all available material including any EIA already conducted by the Department of Planning;
- an avenue and forum for more information sought by objectors and the commissioner(s);
- a forum exposing often important differences of opinion among government departments;
- a means through which a proponent might offer substantial changes to a proposal which would better meet or ameliorate environmental concerns;
- a process within which a measure of conciliation or mediation might occur;
- a source of succinct reports with a single recommendation (and, as appropriate, draft conditions of consent) which enable the minister (as decision-maker) to make better- informed decisions;
- an independent source when it comes to recommending a rejection of a DA.

However, the environmental planning and public inquiry system has its critics; improvements in the planning system are being pursued, again with public participation. Yet no one doubts that, compared with the pre-1979 situation, the quality of decision-making has much improved. Before that date the public was not necessarily invited to participate in hearings.

For further illustration of New South Wales procedures, checklist 4.3 provides the text of the commissioner's opening address to the Port Kembla grain-handling terminal inquiry.

CHECKLIST 4.1

NSW (Australia): public inquiry procedures

Environmental Planning and Assessment Act, 1979

Minister for Planning directs that a Commission of Inquiry be held into a proposed development and appoints a Commissioner of Inquiry for this purpose.

Notice of the Commission of Inquiry appears in newspapers indicating where and when the inquiry will commence; known interested parties are advised directly. Procedures to be followed are included in the notice.

Persons seeking to make submissions to the inquiry are required to register by lodging a primary submission with the Registrar of the Office of Commissioners of Inquiry.

Before the inquiry and the expiry date for primary submissions any person may examine the development application, the EIS, the initial EIA, and other related documents at specified venues.

Questions in written form should be available at the commencement of the inquiry. Further questions during the inquiry are dealt with at the Commission's direction.

Primary and subsequent submissions are to be made available to all parties.

Proceedings are generally as follows:

- Opening statement by Commissioner
- Preliminary matters such as procedures and personal difficulties
- Primary submissions (in stated order)
- Questions and replies to questions, in writing
- Submissions in reply (in reverse order)

Inquiries are conducted in accordance with the rules of natural justice; each person is treated on an equal footing whether legally represented or not; evidence is not generally on oath; cross-examination is rarely allowed.

Adjournments, usually of short duration, may be granted following an application from a party and argument by other parties.

All communication with the Commission is public and queries are through the Registrar. No private communication with a Commissioner may occur.

Following the conclusion of the inquiry, the Commission prepares its report to the Minister, setting out and discussing the issues, summarising the views of the parties, concluding with findings and a specific recommendation. Options may be discussed but only one is recommended as a course of action for government. The report must take account of criteria laid down in the legislation, State environmental policies, the stipulations of planning instruments, and the public interest as perceived by the Commission.

The Commission presents its report to the Minister, usually personally and with a verbal briefing. However, the report is final and becomes a public document the moment it passes over the Minister's desk.

The Minister is not in any way bound by the recommendation of the report and may consult others; however, departure from such recommendations is rare including the often quite stringent conditions laid down in respect of projects thought fit to proceed.

CHECKLIST 4.2

Typical matters dealt with in proposed conditions of development consent by NSW Commissions of Inquiry

Approvals, licences and permits to be obtained from statutory authorities, boards, departments, and local councils;

Conformity with certain specifications contained in the EIS;

Compatibility with all applicable planning instruments;

Control of air, water, and noise pollution including discharges to catchments, protection of aquifers, control of leachates, blasting controls, incineration, waste disposal, oil contamination, sewage treatment, drainage, stormwater and run-off management, and dust suppression;

Life of project;

Location of buildings and individual items of equipment;

Sequence of mining, quarrying, and extractive operations;

Working hours;

Buffer zones;

Access roads, junctions, traffic, rail, pipeline, and transmission routes;

Risks and hazards;

Emergency procedures: fire-fighting, evacuation;

Water supplies and storage;

Heritage items;

Visual amenity, trees, vegetation, screening;

Rehabilitation;

Social and economic effects of proposal;

Housing of workforce;

Monitoring and recording of results;

Environmentally hazardous chemicals;

Heights of buildings and stacks;

Acquisition of properties;

Protection of wetlands, parks, and reserves, oyster leases, mangroves, rainforest, and other natural resources;

Subsidence;

Closure of existing plant and replacement of less efficient plant;

Effects on residents, schools, and hospitals, industries;

Lodging of guarantee funds about performance, payment of levies towards future management of the site, contributions towards infrastructure costs, and road improvements;

Appointment of environmental management officers by proponent;

Independent auditing of risks and hazards;

Annual reports to the Department of Planning;

Arrangements for continuous liaison with the public, local councils, conservation bodies, and resident action groups.

CHECKLIST 4.3

Commission of Inquiry

Port Kembla* Grain-Handling Terminal: Opening Statement by Commissioner

1 This is the opening session of a Commission of Inquiry, appointed by the Minister for Planning, concerning a development application to the Wollongong City Council for the construction and operation of a grain-handling terminal at Port Kembla.

2 I have been specially appointed by the Minister to conduct this inquiry and report accordingly. I have no connection with any government department or agency, with the Wollongong City Council, or with any other party seeking to make a submission to this inquiry.

3 After reporting my findings and recommendation to the Minister, the Minister will determine the application. My report will be published immediately after the Minister's decision. A copy will be forwarded to all parties who have made submissions to the inquiry.

4 During or at the end of this inquiry, as proves convenient, it is my intention to conduct an inspection of the site and surrounding area, together with all parties who wish to be present. No fresh evidence will be heard during the visit.

5 The inquiry will be conducted in the manner as outlined in the Commission's letter to interested persons making inquiries concerning the matter.

6 For those who may not have received such a letter, additional copies are available from the registrar to this inquiry.

7 The inquiry will be conducted in four sessions, as follows:

   (a) Preliminary matters.

   (b) Primary submissions: the order of appearance will be the applicant (proponent) followed by other parties [the list is then read]. Primary submissions and additional information shall be in writing (typed or handwritten).

   (c) Question and discussion time: questions should be in writing, with copies served on the parties asked to respond and a copy handed to the registrar. Answers should be in writing and handed to the relevant party with a copy given to the registrar.

   (d) Submissions in reply: this session will provide an opportunity for each party (if desired) to make a submission by way of reply. The submission in reply will be in writing and read to the inquiry. It may simply sum up the primary submission and/or address any other matter raised before the inquiry, including answers to questions. The order of appearance of parties in reply will be the reverse order of primary submissions, the applicant (proponent) concluding.

8 It is stressed that all statements shall be in writing, as there is no transcript of these proceedings.

9 Copies of all statements shall be made available to all other parties; any difficulties in this respect should be discussed with the registrar.

10 All documents tendered to the inquiry will be available for public viewing dur-

ing the course of the inquiry. Any document may be subject to claims, in whole or part, of confidentiality.

11 All documents tendered will be systematically numbered by the registrar.

12 All parties, whether they are legally represented or not, will be treated on an equal footing; all parties will be afforded the opportunity of presenting their submissions and putting their views and of replying, if they wish, to the submissions made by others.

13 Parties may sit or stand when presenting submissions.

14 No objection is raised to any party who wishes, for its own purposes, to take notes or record the proceedings, providing such activity does not interfere with the course of the inquiry. Any such records will not be regarded as official.

15 The inquiry will be conducted during the following times: daily from 10am to 4pm, with breaks of 15 minutes at 11.15am and one hour at 1.00pm.

16 Parties having difficulty meeting the inquiry's program should discuss the matter with the registrar. Some flexibility will be exercised about order of appearance, and timing.

17 Certain documents are already held by the Commission, most of which have been public documents for some time.

These are:

(a) The development application and the accompanying environmental impact statement.

(b) Written submissions from the public to the exhibited environmental impact statement.

(c) An environmental impact assessment prepared by the Department of Planning.

(d) The Minister's direction and instrument of appointment for the Commission of Inquiry.

(e) Copies of planning instruments relevant to the land.

(f) Copies of the advertisements for the environmental impact statement and for this public inquiry.

18 Applications for the temporary adjournment of this inquiry at any stage shall be presented formally, and subject to comment by other parties.

*New South Wales, Australia

4.2 Resource Assessment Commission (RAC)

The Resource Assessment Commission (RAC) was created by the Commonwealth Resource Assessment Commission Act, 1989 to provide independent, comprehensive, informed, and unbiased information and advice to the federal government on complex resource-use issues referred to it by the prime minister. The commission comprises a chairperson, and special commissioners who are appointed for the duration of each inquiry. The commission proceeds by way of public inquiries. The entire costs of the commission and support staff are met by the federal government.

The RAC, an independent body, reports to the Australian prime minister on environmental, cultural, social, industrial, economic, and other aspects of Australia's resources and their uses. The RAC assembles and analyses information on specific resource issues, and provides a process by which all interested parties can have their views impartially and independently considered.

The RAC is not bound to act formally in conducting its inquiries, but it has the power to require people to provide information or documents if necessary. The RAC may investigate the matter under inquiry in any way it wishes, including through written submissions, public hearings, consultations, and research. See figure 6.

The prime minister initiates an inquiry by referring a matter to the RAC in writing, setting out the scope and time frame of the inquiry. The RAC is expected to hold public hearings, circulate a draft report to the public, and submit a final report to the prime minister, who must then table the report in the federal parliament. Of the draft report, the public must be invited to comment on its findings, and further public hearings may be held to review those comments on the draft report. The RAC may initiate research into relevant topics and publish background papers.

At the conclusion of each inquiry, the RAC presents a report to the prime minister. The report might propose possible courses of action or provide an overview of an issue, depending on the terms of reference (TOR) for each inquiry. The decision whether to implement any option identified by the RAC rests with the Australian government.

In considering resource-use questions, the RAC must be guided by the principles that are set out in the Act. These principles are:

(1) There should be an integrated approach to conservation (including all environmental and ecological considerations) and development by taking both conservation and development aspects into account at an early stage.

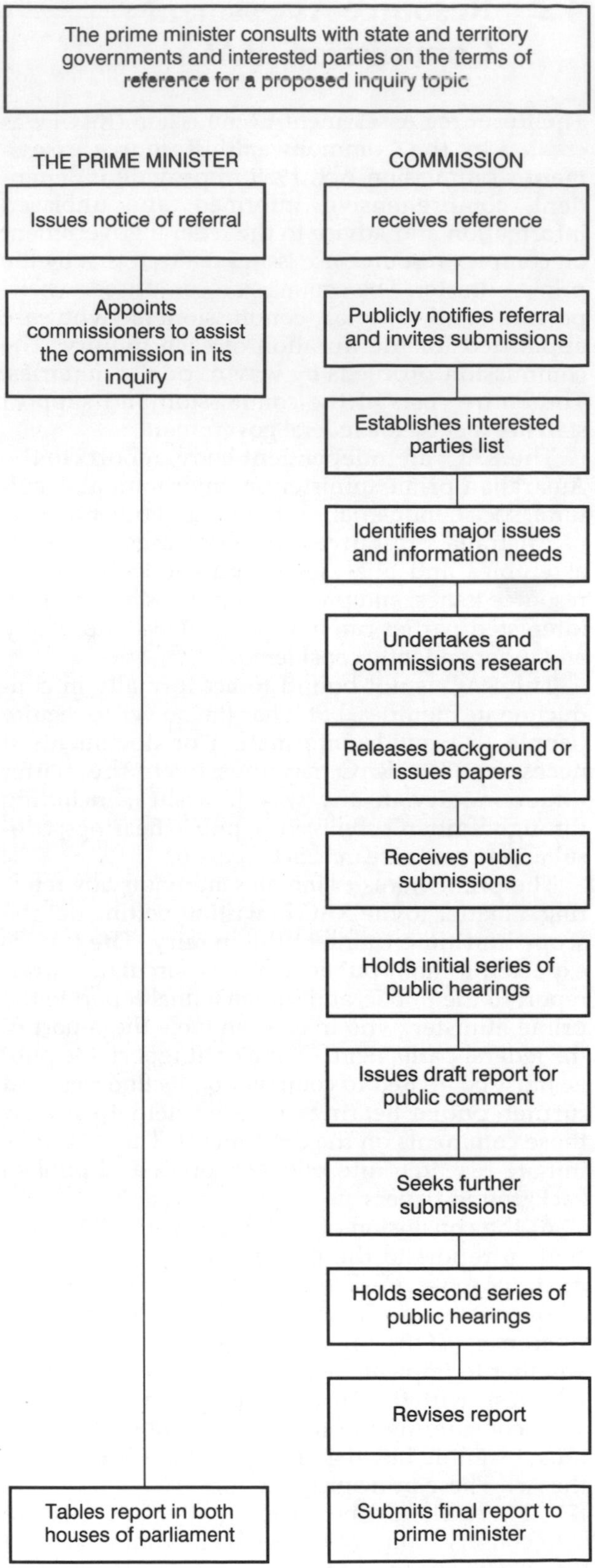

THE PRIME MINISTER	COMMISSION

The prime minister consults with state and territory governments and interested parties on the terms of reference for a proposed inquiry topic

THE PRIME MINISTER

Issues notice of referral

Appoints commissioners to assist the commission in its inquiry

Tables report in both houses of parliament

COMMISSION

receives reference

Publicly notifies referral and invites submissions

Establishes interested parties list

Identifies major issues and information needs

Undertakes and commissions research

Releases background or issues papers

Receives public submissions

Holds initial series of public hearings

Issues draft report for public comment

Seeks further submissions

Holds second series of public hearings

Revises report

Submits final report to prime minister

Figure 6 Australia
How the RAC conducts a public inquiry

(2) Resource use decisions should seek to optimise the net benefits to the community from the nation's resources, having regard to efficiency of resource use, environmental considerations, ecosystem integrity and sustainability, the sustainability of any development, and an equitable distribution of the return on resources.

(3) Commonwealth (federal) decisions, policies and management regimes may provide for additional uses that are compatible with the primary purpose values of the area, recognising that in some cases both conservation and development interests can be accommodated concurrently or sequentially; and, in other cases, choices must be made between alternative uses or combinations of uses.

By 1992, the RAC had reported upon its inquiries into the Kakadu conservation zone, and forest and timber resources, and had launched an extensive coastal zone inquiry. The Kakadu report led directly to the banning of mining at Coronation Hill in 1992, and the whole of the zone became part of the Kakadu national park (Northern Territory). The other two inquiries were about large and general, though highly controversial, issues. These inquiries undoubtedly help establish a framework within which EIA processes may take place for specific projects.

In 1984, Canada introduced an EIA public review phase at federal level to be conducted by an independent EA panel, for projects with potentially significant environmental impacts. A whole range of projects has now been embraced by these panel reviews.

The public exhibition of EIS associated with public meetings is well illustrated by the two case studies in this book on the Banff national park and the Beaufort sea hydrocarbon project. (See case studies 8A, 8B.)

The provinces have tended to emulate federal EIA requirements. In 1978, Quebec introduced EIA procedures similar to those at federal level. Checklist 4.4 illustrates the procedures adopted by the Quebec government for public hearings.

CHECKLIST 4.4

Quebec Government, Canada

Environmental Public Hearings Bureau

Bureau d'audiences publique sur l'environnement

Public hearing procedures

Minister of the Environment instructs the bureau to hold a public hearing; a special commission is established.

The commission's task is to ascertain public opinion in respect of a specific project: to recommend what should be accepted, changed or rejected.

The rules of procedure require that each public hearing should take place in two parts, with a minimum of twenty-one days between them. Each of those parts may extend over a period of days, which may or may not be consecutive.

The first part of each hearing is devoted essentially to receiving documentation; at this stage the principal speaker is the proponent who summarises details of the project and outlines the major elements in the environmental impact statement. The commissioners or members of the public may seek clarification from the proponent; in many cases, representatives of government departments and experts attend.

People with questions to put to the proponent are generally asked to enter their names in a register located in the hearing room; and are heard in that order. Each person is entitled to three questions, and may register again to ask a second series of questions. All questions must be addressed to the commissioner, who will direct the appropriate person to answer. This first part of a hearing gives members of the public an opportunity to learn in greater detail of the proponent's intentions and to further study documentation; they thus prepare for the second part of the hearing.

The second part of each hearing offers an opportunity for individuals, alone or in groups, government departments and municipalities to express opinions on the project; opinions may be written or oral. Written briefs must be submitted four days in advance, however, to the registrar of the hearing. Briefs are heard in the order that they are filed.

Following the hearing, the commission prepares a report for the Minister of the Environment. This report contains a synthesis of all the opinions voiced on the project, an analysis of the issues, and the commission's conclusions. The report must be submitted to the minister not later than four months after the bureau is instructed to hold a public inquiry.

After reading the report, the minister analyses the project in the light of all its implications, and submits a recommendation to Cabinet.

The Quebec Cabinet has the final decision and may authorise the project, with or without conditions, or may refuse it.

The Environmental Quality Act of Quebec provides that the report shall become public in sixty days after submission to the minister, unless the minister decides to release it sooner.

The bureau sends a copy of the report to the proponent, to each person making a submission, and to every individual, group or municipality asking for one.

(Source: Quebec Government, Environmental Public Hearings Bureau, 1992)

In Europe, reference has already been made to the widespread opportunities for public participation in decision-making in Britain. In France, public exhibitions of EISs and conduct of public inquiries have taken place since 1983. In Italy, since 1991, the public inquiry has been introduced. Generally, throughout the European Community (EC), opportunities for public involvement have progressively improved. This is also true for members of the Nordic Council.

Apart from Australia and New Zealand, where opportunities for public involvement are well established, the principle of public involvement has spread throughout the Asian community, with the exception of China. Public inquiries have been held in Japan since 1972. All other Asian countries invite public participation as outlined in this book.

4.3 UN Economic Commission for Europe (UN ECE)

The activities of the UN ECE are reviewed in Chapter 5, with particular attention to the European convention on EIA in a transboundary context, adopted in 1991.

In addition to an obligation imposed on the European partners to notify and consult each other on all major projects likely to cause significant adverse environmental effects across national boundaries and to carry out EIA in all appropriate cases, machinery was set up to provide for arbitration and public inquiries in the event of conflict of interests.

Checklist 4.5 sets out the arbitration procedures adopted for the settlement of disputes generally arising out of the interpretation of the convention. The procedures embrace notification, setting up an arbitral tribunal, adopting rules of procedure, taking evidence, expenses, and awards. The arbitrators are impartial and provision is made to preclude the more obvious conflicts of interest.

CHECKLIST 4.5

UN Economic Commission for Europe (UN ECE)

Convention on EIA in a transboundary context

Arbitration (Appendix 7)

Key points

1 The claimant party or parties shall notify the secretariat that the parties have agreed to submit the dispute to arbitration pursuant to article 15, paragraph 2, of this convention. The notification shall state the subject matter of arbitration

and include, in particular, the articles of this convention the interpretation or application of which are at issue. The secretariat shall forward the information received to all parties to this convention.

2   The arbitral tribunal shall consist of three members. Both the claimant party or parties and the other party or parties to the dispute shall appoint an arbitrator, and the two arbitrators so appointed shall designate by common agreement the third arbitrator, who shall be the president of the arbitral tribunal. The latter shall not be a national of one of the parties to the dispute, nor have his or her usual place of residence in the territory of one of these parties, nor be employed by any of them, nor have dealt with the case in any other capacity.

3   The arbitral tribunal shall render its decision in accordance with international law and in accordance with the provisions of this convention.

4   Any arbitral tribunal constituted under the provisions set out herein shall draw up its own rules of procedure.

5   The decisions of the arbitral tribunal, both on procedure and on substance, shall be taken by majority vote of its members.

6   The tribunal may take all appropriate measures in order to establish the facts.

7   The parties to the dispute shall facilitate the work of the arbitral tribunal and, in particular, using all means at their disposal, shall: provide it with all relevant documents, facilities and information; and enable it, where necessary, to call witnesses or experts and receive their evidence.

8   The parties and the arbitrators shall protect the confidentiality of any information they receive in confidence during the proceedings of the arbitral tribunal.

9   The arbitral tribunal may hear and determine counter claims arising directly out of the subject matter of the dispute.

10   Normally, the expenses of the tribunal shall be borne by the parties to the dispute in equal shares.

11   The arbitral tribunal shall render its award within five months of the date on which it is established, unless it finds it necessary to extend the time limit for a period which should not exceed five months.

12   The award of the arbitral tribunal shall be accompanied by a statement of reasons. It shall be final and binding upon all parties to the dispute.

Checklist 4.6 sets out inquiry procedures to be applied only to those differences about the interpretation of 'significance' in relation to possible transboundary adverse impacts. The procedures similarly embrace notification, appointing a commission of inquiry, adopting rules of procedure, taking evidence, expenses, and the announcement of the commission's opinion. Again an effort is made to preclude the more obvious conflicts of interest. There is no presumption in the procedures that an inquiry will be public; probably this would be decided by the commission.

CHECKLIST 4.6

UN Economic Commission for Europe (UN ECE)

Convention on EIA in a transboundary context

Inquiry procedure (Appendix 4)

Key points

1   The requesting party or parties shall notify the secretariat that it or they submit(s) the question of whether a proposed activity listed in the convention is likely to have a significant adverse transboundary impact to a commission of inquiry. The secretariat shall notify all parties to the convention of this submission.

2   The commission of inquiry shall consist of three members. Both parties to the inquiry shall appoint a scientific or technical expert, and the two experts so appointed shall designate by common agreement a third expert, who shall be president of the inquiry. The third expert shall not be a national of one of the parties to the inquiry, nor have his or her usual place of residence in the territory of one of these parties, nor be employed by any of them, nor have dealt with the matter in any other capacity.

3   The commission of inquiry shall adopt its own rules of procedure, and may take all appropriate measures to carry out its functions.

4   The parties to the inquiry shall facilitate the work of the commission and, in particular, using all means at their disposal, shall: provide it with all relevant documents, facilities and information; and enable it, where necessary, to call witnesses or experts and receive their evidence.

5   The parties and the experts shall protect the confidentiality of any information they receive in confidence during the work of the commission of inquiry.

6　The expenses of the inquiry shall be borne by the parties to the inquiry, in equal shares.

7　The decisions of the commission of inquiry on matters of procedure shall be taken by a majority vote of its members; the final opinion of the inquiry shall reflect the view of the majority of its members and shall include any dissenting view.

8　The commission of inquiry shall present its final opinion within two months of the date on which it was established, unless it finds it necessary to extend this time limit; such extension shall not exceed two months.

4.4　Mediation

Businesses and individuals have gradually discovered the benefits of using alternative methods of dispute resolution. Traditionally, it was standard practice to refer a dispute to a legal firm, to initiate legal action in an appropriate court that might lead to a hearing and resolution of the issue. This traditional procedure is cumbersome, tedious, time-consuming, and costly. More direct and less costly approaches are now used (Coulson, 1989).

These methods entail arbitration, negotiation, and mediation; alternatives that fall into the category of 'alternative dispute resolution'(ADR). Arbitration is the submission of a dispute to an impartial third person or panel; the function of arbitration is to obtain a decision, usually binding, upon the parties. Some courts in the USA have 'court-annexed' arbitration systems under which civil claims are arbitrated by a panel of lawyers. This is to be distinguished from adjudication when a case goes to court for a decision, before any trial. Two individuals or parties talking directly to each other, without a third party, negotiate; when there is a third party, negotiation becomes mediation.

Thus mediation is a process whereby an independent third party assists parties in dispute to reach a solution to that dispute. The role of the mediator is to act as a facilitator of consensus.

The mediator is essentially a catalyst who facilitates an agreement between the parties; the mediator has no authority to impose a decision. A mediator can only translate, suggest, advise, persuade, and at times, recommend a possible way of resolving the dispute. Successful mediation can certainly avoid animosity, cost, and delay.

Mediation is an important additional element in the settlement of environmental, planning, local government, and development disputes.

The mediation of disputes over land use and other environmental issues in the USA is traced back to 1973, when a 15-year-old dispute over a proposal to build a dam on a river near Seattle was handled by mediation. Two mediators held discussions with affected farmers, residents, fishing enthusiasts, environmentalists, and the federal agency. This resulted in the parties signing an agreement that the site for the dam be moved to a location providing reduced flood protection but causing less environmental disruption.

Since the mid-1970s, hundreds of major public disputes have been resolved in the USA by mediation. Examples have been disputes over the clean-up of hazardous waste sites; location of infrastructure such as hydroelectric sites, and prisons; asbestos removal; the size and nature of public housing developments; and apportioning the costs of water and sewerage systems.

Mediation has also been used to assist in the formulation of government regulations. Once government has determined principles or policies in a certain area of its jurisdiction, mediators have been asked to organise and convene committees or round tables of representatives of groups from the public with a possible interest in the final legislation or regulations which might result from that policy. This is 'legislation negotiation' (leg-neg), or 'regulation negotiation' (reg-neg).

The US Environmental Protection Agency (EPA), which issues a large number of regulations each year, most, detailed and technical, has seen close to 80 per cent of its rules challenged in court. Consequently, the EPA (US) now uses mediators to assist it in the formulation of regulations for a wide variety of situations.

Another striking example of mediation was in the development of the Hawaiian water code legislation. After a state constitutional referendum in 1978, the state of Hawaii was authorised to develop a legislative code for the protection, control, and regulation of the use of Hawaii's waters. Between 1978 and 1986, the first versions of a state water code were proposed without success, resulting in several major court cases.

In 1986, the Hawaiian Center for Alternative Dispute Resolution (part of the Hawaiian judiciary) was asked to organise, convene, and mediate an informal and voluntary policy dialogue about this impasse.

Representatives from key groups, government agencies, farmers' groups, county legislators, conservation groups, developers, and native Hawaiian groups, were invited to the initial meeting at which a draft concept paper was presented; this suggested round table discussions. This meeting resulted in an agreement to proceed with such mediated discussions. It was assumed by all that some kind of state water legislation was inevitable.

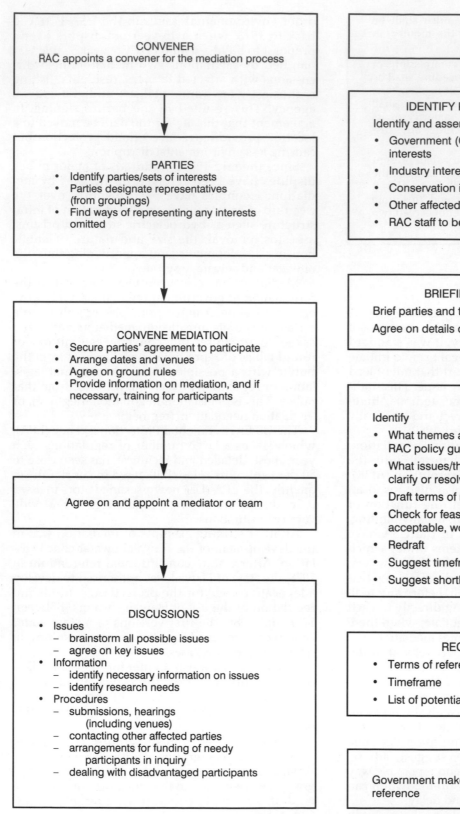

Figure 7 Mediation of inquiry scope and procedure
(Source: Boer, B., Craig, D., Handmer, J., and Ross, H.,
RAC discussion paper no. 1, 1991)

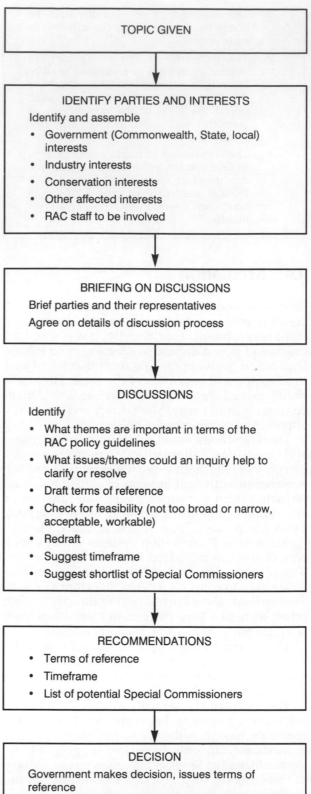

Figure 8 Mediation of terms of reference (TOR)
(Source: Boer, B., Craig, D., Handmer, J., and Ross, H.,
RAC discussion paper no. 1, 1991)

In 1987, an agreement in principle was drawn up and forwarded to interested people; at the same time it was released to the public. The proposals were discussed and debated in various public hearings. By May 1987, the new water code embracing many of the round table key proposals passed through the state legislature and became law.

Priscoli (1987) has explained that the essential element of the facilitation role (mediation) has been to listen to the values and interests of others, which are underlying their positions. Once those values and interests are identified and understood clearly by all parties, the role then is to look at options for dealing with the problem. However, Priscoli has warned that many issues cannot be negotiated. Many occupational and health regulations had been prepared after such facilitation; energy and wetlands policy had also been developed in this way.

In Australia, mediation has been described by Street (1990) as:

> a structured process which is chosen by the parties as the means through which to reach agreement for the resolution of their dispute ... it is throughout an entirely voluntary, without-prejudice process. Either party is free to walk away from the negotiations at any stage ... the mediator, as such, does not decide any aspect of the dispute or purport to impose any determination on the parties. Inherent within the personal dynamics of a structured mediation is a significantly enhanced prospect of satisfactory agreed resolution of the dispute.

The RAC (Boer, 1991) has outlined the possible role of mediation in its public inquiry procedures. It envisages the use of mediation by the Australian government in the formulation of the TOR for inquiries. See figure 7. It also envisages the use of mediation in the determination of inquiry scope and procedure. See figure 8.

The commission also sees the use of mediation in the PPA of an inquiry. After tabling a commission report, the federal government might need to consult or negotiate with the state and territory governments, as well as industry and conservation groups, about the acceptance and implementation of the commission report. Further, any party which opts to stay outside the commission's inquiry might well wish to lobby or protest at this stage; mediation with such parties could be essential for success. Mediation could also be vital in developing an implementation strategy for particular kinds of options and recommendations.

In 1991, the NSW Land and Environment Court, Australia, introduced an option of mediation of disputes in several classes of the court's jurisdiction. The aim of this decision is to give parties the opportunity of attempting to resolve their dispute without going to the expense of a full court hearing. A mediation session or sessions can be requested at any time between the filing of the documents in court and the date the matter is set down for hearing. At least 7 days before mediation the parties are required to serve on the other side a statement of their position and the issues as that party sees them.

The Environmental Assessment Board of Ontario, Canada, as a quasi-judicial administrative tribunal, investigates environmental disputes and attempts to resolve these by a hearing process. This process is generally adversarial in nature; however, there are opportunities for mediation to be used in those cases seen as appropriate by the chairperson.

Such mediation is not a substitute for the existing rights of parties and members of the public; but it has proved effective in addressing such issues as: public participation (the representation of the various interests involved); information gathering; inequality among the parties; and public interest considerations.

CHAPTER 5

International organisations

5.1 European Community (EC)

The EC is made up of 12 member states at present: Belgium, Germany, Denmark, Greece, Spain, France, Ireland, Italy, Luxembourg, The Netherlands, Portugal, and Britain. This is the order in which they take the chair of the European Council, the governing body of the EC. Under the Single European Act 1987 the aim of the EC is to work towards European unity.

The EC is home to 340 million people. About 80 per cent of the combined territory is agricultural, 15 per cent is urbanised. The average population density of 139 persons per square kilometre hides very wide variations, from less than 20 to over 700 per square kilometre. The proportion of urban to rural population shows similar differences; for example, 97 per cent of the Belgian population is urban, but only 32 per cent of the Portuguese is urban. The economic structure of the EC shows equally important variations, and marked differences in gross domestic product (GDP) per head with significant regional differences (Commission of the European Communities, 1992a).

The EC has recognised that environmental concerns are a priority inseparable from most other policy areas; the EC has thus come to adopt a broad approach to environmental policy formulation within the EC, complemented by reflection and action on global issues. The first EC environment program was adopted in 1973, shortly after the UN Conference on the Human Environment, held in Stockholm (1972).

This program involved three broad categories of action: to reduce and prevent pollution and nuisances; to improve the environment and the quality of life; and action through international organisations on environmental questions.

The second environmental action program, agreed by the EEC environment ministers in 1977, accepted that the measure initiated in the first program would continue. The 1977 agreement placed a new emphasis on preventive action, particularly about pollution, land misuse, and the production of waste. An important aspect of that program was a study of how appropriate environmental impact procedures might be introduced into the EC. The polluter-pays principle was also endorsed.

Directives, decisions, and regulations, are intended to be adopted by member countries and embodied in national legislation; hence EC rules affecting the environment follows this same process. Any member country failing to implement EC directives can be brought before the European Court of Justice. From 1970 to 1985 and the EIA directive in 1985, there were 23 directives about the environment (Gilpin, 1986). In 1980, a draft directive on EIA was issued, followed, in 1982, by a second draft directive.

Finally a European Council directive on EIA was finalised on 27 June 1985. It was noted by the European Council, that the disparities between the existing laws in the various member countries about the EA of public and private projects could create unfavourable competitive conditions, and affect the functioning of the European common market. A greater degree of uniformity than then existed and more effective and adequate laws were the primary aim of the EC.

The 1985 directive distinguishes between those projects that are likely to have significant effects on the environment and hence should be subject to rigorous EIA procedures (see checklist 5.1); and those which might have significant effects and should receive close preliminary study (see checklist 5.2). For all projects requiring EIA, the kind of information needed is presented in checklist 5.3.

CHECKLIST 5.1

European Community

Council Directive, 27 June 1985 on the assessment of the effects of certain public and private works on the environment

Projects generally subject to EIA (known as Annex 1)

1 Crude-oil refineries (save for those only manufacturing lubricants) and installations for the gasification and liquefaction of 500 tonnes or more of coal or bituminous shale per day.

2 Thermal power stations and other combustion installations with a heat output of 300 MW or more, and nuclear power stations and other nuclear reactors (except for very small research installations).

3 Installations solely designed for the permanent storage or final disposal of radioactive waste.

4 Integrated works for the initial melting of cast-iron and steel.

5 Installations for the extraction of asbestos and for the processing and transformation of asbestos, and products containing asbestos such as asbestos-cement.

6 Integrated chemical installations.

7 Construction of motorways and express roads, major railways and larger airports.

8 Trading ports and certain inland waterways.

9 Waste-disposal installations for the incineration, chemical treatment or land-fill of toxic and dangerous wastes.

(Note The original text contains more detail on capacities)

CHECKLIST 5.2

European Community

Council Directive, 27 June 1985 on the assessment of the effects of certain public and private works on the environment

Projects and activities that might require EIA (known as Annex 2)

1 Major agricultural activities

2 Extractive industry

3 Energy industry

4 Processing of metals

5 Manufacture of glass

6 Chemical industry

7 Food industry

8 Textile, leather, wood and paper industries

9 Rubber industry

10 Infrastructure projects

11 Installations for the disposal of industrial and domestic waste

12 Waste water treatment plants

13 Sludge-deposition sites

14 Knacker's yards

15 Racing and test tracks

16 Test benches for engines

17 Storage of scrap iron

18 Manufacture of artificial mineral fibres

19 Manufacture, packing, or loading of explosives

20 Holiday villages and hotel complexes

(Note The original text contains much more detail under several headings. In 1992, Annex 2 came under review; the outcome may be the elevation of certain works to Annex 1)

CHECKLIST 5.3

European Community

Council Directive, 27 June 1985 on the assessment of the effects of certain public and private works on the environment

Information required for projects subject to EIA

1 Description of the object, including in particular:

(a) A description of the physical characteristics of the whole project and the land-use requirements during the construction and operational phases;

(b) A description of the main characteristics of the production processes, for instance, the nature and quantity of the materials used;

(c) An estimate, by type and quantity, of expected residues and emissions (water, air and soil pollution, noise, vibration, light, heat and radiation) resulting from the operation of the proposed project.

2 Where appropriate, an outline of the main alternatives studied by the developer and an indication of the main reasons for the choice, taking into account the environmental effects.

3 A description of the aspects of the environment likely to be significantly affected by the proposed project, in particular, population, fauna, flora, soil,

water, air, climatic factors, material assets, including the architectural and archaeological heritage, landscape and the interrelationship between the above factors.

4   A description of the likely significant effects of the proposed project on the environment resulting from;

(a) The existence of the project;

(b) The use of natural resources;

(c) The emission of pollutants, the creation of nuisances and the elimination of waste; and a description by the developer of the forecasting methods used to assess the effects on the environment.

5   A description of the measures envisaged to prevent, reduce, and where possible offset any significant adverse effects on the environment.

6   A non-technical summary of the information provided under the above headings.

7   An indication of any difficulties (technical deficiencies or lack of know-how) encountered by the developer in compiling the required information.

(Note Under (4) above, the description should cover the direct effects and any indirect, secondary, cumulative, short, medium and long-term, permanent and temporary, positive and negative effects of the project)

However, the directive recognises three classes of exemption, which is disturbing. First, the directive 'shall not apply to projects the details of which are adopted by a specific Act of national legislation'. The fact is that too many projects attract their own separate piece of national, state or provincial legislation and quite often are taken right out all normal planning, assessment and licensing procedures. The preferred action is to have a requirement that EIA procedures are built into all legislation, whether of general application in the community, or specific to a major project. The directive conceded that 'it may be appropriate in exceptional cases to exempt a specific project from the assessment procedures, subject to appropriate information being supplied to the European Commission'. Projects serving national defence purposes are also exempt from the directive. No explanation is given in these three categories as to why these exemptions should be granted, but experience suggests that the projects exempted under these headings are quite often the most important and controversial. This aspect of the directive represents a flaw, but is no doubt the result of governments wishing to keep ultimate power.

Further, the directive is confined to projects and not extended to programs and policies. However, the term 'project' embraces not only construction works and also other installations and schemes, but includes the extraction of natural resources and other activities which might be detrimental to the natural surroundings and landscape. More importantly, the term 'developer' embraces the proponent in respect of both private and public works.

The member countries were given three years to comply with the directive, through national legislation. The review of the EC countries in this work indicates wide application of the principles. While deficiencies are apparent, the measure represents a great leap forward.

Nor is it the end of the road. At the UN Conference on Environment and Development in 1992, the European Commission (Commission of the European Communities 1992a, p. 61) stated that it was necessary to extend the EIA principle 'upstream' to the policy-making and planning stages of development. The main argument here was that it is often too late to take alternatives or cumulative effects into account at a project stage.

It also helps to ensure the integration of an environmental dimension into the economic, industrial, agricultural, and other policies of the EC and its member states. The EC supports the convention on EIA in a transboundary context.

An extension of the EIA principle also facilitated the implementation of directives, such as the habitats directive in preparation, which aims to cover the protection of fauna and flora and their habitats.

EIA principles have permeated the work of the European Bank for Reconstruction and Development, a bank created by western governments and financial institutions in 1991 to assist the private and public sectors in eastern European countries. The bank's role is to coordinate and channel western aid and investment into the region, helping to ensure an orderly transition from command to market economies. EIAs are now required for projects financed by the bank. The bank has also promoted reviews, guides, and EIA training.

5.2   Nordic Council, The

The Nordic Council of Ministers was established in 1971 to facilitate consultation and cooperation between the Nordic countries of Denmark, Finland, Iceland, Norway, and Sweden; its formal decisions are usually binding upon the members. The Nordic Council provides funds for a large number of joint Nordic institutions and projects in such fields as scientific research and development, culture, education, social welfare, health, and environment protection.

In 1974, the Nordic countries signed an environmental protection convention. Under this convention, the EIA of a project must place equal weight on potential damage to a neighbouring Nordic country as within its own country.

In 1990, a working party was established to review EIA procedures. The mandate of the group has been to 'work for the introduction of analysis and assessment of environmental impacts as a natural element in all sectoral planning and in decision-making at all levels'. Other studies have been initiated into the promotion of EIA responsibilities; methods of reporting and presenting EIAs; the relationship between EIA and land-use planning practices; and provision for training in EIA in the Nordic countries.

Checklist 5.4 summarises the status of EIA legislation in the Nordic countries.

CHECKLIST 5.4

The Nordic Countries

Status of EIA legislation

Country	Status of EIA legislation
Denmark	National and Regional Planning Act 1989; EIA Order 1989
Finland	EIA legislation pending, probably of a narrower kind
Iceland	Under consideration
Norway	Planning and Building Act 1989: EIA provisions in force 1990
Sweden	Natural Resources Act 1987; Planning and Building Act 1987; EIA provisions in force

---

5.3 UN Economic Commission for Europe (UN ECE)

The UN ECE was set up in 1947 by the Economic and Social Council of the UN initially to raise the level of postwar European economic activity, and to maintain and strengthen the economic relations of European countries, among themselves and with other countries. The membership is made up of European and North American countries.

Early, the UN ECE developed a test cycle for the measurement of gaseous emissions from the exhaust of motor vehicles. It was based on European patterns of driving. Still, in the absence of other information, it was adopted in Australia from 1974 as the most appropriate cycle for testing motor vehicle compliance with Australian design rule 27.

It was the first serious attempt to reduce hydrocarbon and carbon monoxide emissions to a significant extent in that country.

The environmental activities of the UN ECE have broadened considerably. The UN ECE is served in this area of environmental activities by a group of senior advisers representing each member country. Member countries now submit biennial monographs on their environmental policies and strategies. Working parties look at specific subjects such as air pollution, and long-range transboundary air pollution controls which the UN ECE pioneered to curb acid rain. The convention was signed in 1979 and came into effect in 1983.

The UN ECE is also active in environmental policy and strategy; integration of environmental and economic objectives and policies; environmental management because of changing socio-economic conditions; water, soil, and waste management; environmentally sound technology and products; environmentally sound management of chemicals and dangerous goods; energy efficiency and conservation; natural resources assessment and management; monitoring; public awareness; and EIA.

Particular attention has been paid to the need to prevent the harmful transboundary environmental effect of projects and activities. The Convention on EIA in a Transboundary Context was adopted by the senior advisers at Espoo, Finland, in February 1991. The convention led to the first multilateral treaty to specify the procedural rights and duties of nations about the transboundary impacts of their proposed activities.

The convention stipulates the obligations of parties to carry out EIA, and to arrange for assessment, at an early stage of planning, about activities likely to cause significant adverse transboundary effects. Checklist 5.5 lists the projects and activities thought likely to cause significant adverse transboundary effects; while checklist 5.6 indicates the kind of information that is needed in an assessment. Figure 9 indicates the EIA procedure as planned under the convention.

The convention defines the general obligation of countries to notify and consult each other on all major projects under consideration, ranging from nuclear power stations to major road construction and deforestation projects that are likely to cause significant adverse environmental effects across national boundaries.

The convention stipulates that public participation in the assessment procedure should be encouraged by each party, and that foreign participants be given the same opportunities as those given to the local public.

At Espoo, the ministers of the countries involved gave their full support to the implementation of the convention as soon as possible, urging cooperation during the interim period before the convention comes into force. By 1992, 28 countries and the European Community had signed the 1991 Espoo convention; many of these countries are devising legislation or adapting existing legislation to meet the requirements of the convention.

See chapter 4 for details relating to UN ECE arbitration and public inquiry procedures.

CHECKLIST 5.5

UN Economic Commission for Europe (UN ECE)

Convention on EIA in a transboundary context

Projects and activities likely to cause significant adverse transboundary impact (Appendix 1)

Summary

1   Crude-oil refineries and installations for the gasification and liquefaction of coal or bituminous shale.

2   Thermal and nuclear power stations, and other nuclear reactors.

3   Installations for the production or enrichment of nuclear fuels; for the reprocessing of irradiated nuclear fuels; or for the storage, disposal, and processing of radioactive waste.

4   Major installations for the initial smelting of cast-iron and steel and for the production of non-ferrous metals.

5   Major installations involving the extraction and processing of asbestos or products containing asbestos.

6   Integrated chemical installations.

7   Construction of major highways, railways and airports.

8   Large-diameter oil and gas pipelines.

9   Trading ports and major waterways.

10   Major waste-disposal installations for the incineration, chemical treatment or landfill of toxic and dangerous wastes.

11   Large dams and reservoirs.

12   Major ground-water abstraction activities.

13   Pulp and paper manufacturing.

14   Major mining activities and processing of ores or coal.

15   Offshore hydrocarbon production.

16   Major storage facilities for petroleum, petrochemical, and chemical products.

17   Deforestation of large areas.

CHECKLIST 5.6

UN Economic Commission for Europe (UN ECE)

Convention on EIA in a transboundary context

EIA documentation

Information required (Appendix 2)

Key points

1   A description of the proposed activity and its purpose.

2   A description, where appropriate, of reasonable alternatives locational or technological to the proposed activity, including the no-action alternative.

3   A description of the environment likely to be significantly affected by the proposed activity and its alternatives.

4   A description of the potential environmental impact of the proposed activity and its alternatives and an estimation of that significance.

5   A description of the proposed mitigation measures to minimise adverse environmental impacts.

6   An account of the predictive methods used and the underlying assumptions, as well as the relevant environmental data used; and an indication of the gaps in knowledge and uncertainties encountered.

7   An outline of monitoring and management programs and plans for PPA.

5.4   Organisation for Economic Cooperation and Development (OECD)

In 1961, an international organisation which succeeded the Organisation for European Economic Cooperation (OEEC) set up in 1948 to allocate aid received under the European Recovery Programme. The current membership of the OECD is Australia, Austria, Belgium, Britain, Canada, Denmark, Finland, France, Germany, Greece, Iceland, Ireland, Italy, Japan, Luxembourg, The Netherlands, New Zealand, Norway, Portugal, Spain, Sweden, Switzerland, Turkey, and the USA; 24 democratic countries with advanced market economies.

The objectives of the OECD are to:

• achieve the highest sustainable growth in member countries and thus to contribute to the development of the world economy;

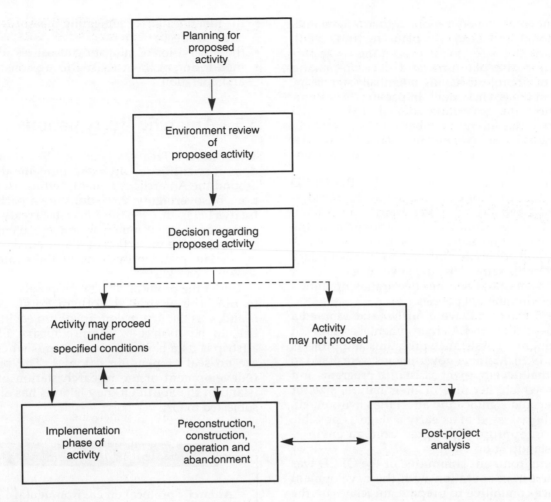

Figure 9 EIA process
(Source: UN ECE, 1992)

• contribute to sound economic expansion in member, as well as non-member, countries;
• contribute to the expansion of world trade on a multilateral, non-discriminating basis.

In 1970, the governing council of the OECD created an environment committee to advise on patterns of growth and development that would be in harmony with protection of the environment. From the work of the environment committee, the OECD took a lead promoting the polluter-pays principle, assigning the costs of pollution control; restricting the manufacture and use of polychlorinated biphenyls (PCBs); establishing a code for transboundary pollution; promoting the EA of new chemicals; encouraging energy conservation and the development of alternative energy sources; and the control of the disposal of radioactive wastes for OECD members.

In 1974, a Declaration on Environmental Policy was adopted. The text tends to mirror the principles embodied in the Declaration on the Human Environment, adopted at the UN Conference on the Human Environment, held in Stockholm, in 1972.

EIA

Paragraph nine of the Declaration on Environmental Policy stated that: 'In order to prevent future environmental deterioration, prior assessment of the environmental consequences of significant public and private activities should be an essential element of policies applied at the national, regional and local level.' Later in 1978, the governing council of the OECD added to this declaration with a recommendation on strengthening international cooperation on environmental protection in frontier regions.

In 1979, it was recommended (OECD, 1979) that member governments integrate substantive environmental considerations into arrangements for regional and land-use planning and, using environmental assessment procedures as appropriate, into the planning and decision-making process of all projects having potentially significant impact on the environment. In passing this recommendation, the governing council of the OECD was aware that many member countries already had various legislative, institutional, and administrative frameworks for the assessment of environmental impacts.

However, the governing council of the OECD stressed the need for coordination, early consideration, the avoidance of undue delays, consultation, and public participation, monitoring, and the enforcement of measures adopted during the EIA process, and adequate attention to transboundary effects. On the same date, the governing council of the OECD adopted another declaration on anticipatory environmental policies.

In 1985, the OECD went further and adopted a recommendation on EA environmental assessment of development assistance programs and projects (OECD, 1985). Member governments were asked to ensure that development assistance programs and projects which, because of their nature, size, or location could significantly affect the environment, should be assessed at as early a stage as possible and to an appropriate degree from an environmental standpoint.

The environment committee of the OECD was instructed in cooperation with the development assistance committee to prepare guidelines on the types of procedures, processes, organisation, and resources, needed to facilitate the assessment of environmental effects of development assistance programs and projects and to contribute to the early prevention and/or mitigation of potentially adverse environmental effects of certain aid programs or projects. The governing council of the OECD also adopted a schedule of those programs and projects most in need of EA.

The OECD had clearly recognised that the timely assessment of development assistance programs and projects could help reduce the risk of costly and potentially adverse effects on the environment. In 1986, the governing council of the OECD placed before the member countries details of the measures required to facilitate EA (OECD, 1986). The procedures incorporated:

- an initial screening process;
- assessment at a project proposal stage;
- examination of alternatives;
- identification of the most important issues necessary to making a decision;
- involvement of the host government, the public and other interested parties;

- the identification of mitigating measures for any adverse effects;
- the supervision of mitigating measures adopted;
- monitoring of the activity during construction and operation.

5.5 Antarctic Treaty nations

The Antarctic Treaty, signed in 1959, allows freedom of scientific research and movement on and around the Antarctic continent, setting aside questions of sovereignty; 25 nations are a party to the treaty (1993). In 1991, the Antarctic Treaty nations agreed on an environmental protocol to ensure the comprehensive protection of the Antarctic environment. The major provisions of the protocol are shown in checklist 5.7.

Under the protocol, all new proposals are subject to EIA. The airstrip at Rothera Point, Adelaide Island, was the first major capital project in Antarctica, to be subject to comprehensive EIA. The airstrip is on a barren gravel isthmus where there are no seal or penguin colonies. The proposed redevelopment of the research station on Signy Island in the South Orkney Islands has also been subjected to EIA.

CHECKLIST 5.7

Antarctic protocol on environmental protection

Major provisions

1 Antarctica is designated as a 'natural reserve devoted to peace and science'.

2 A ban on all mining for at least 50 years, except for scientific minerals research.

3 An EIA for all human activities before a program proceeds.

4 Increased international cooperation in the planning and conduct of activities.

5 The establishment of a committee for environmental protection to advise the parties to the protocol on its implementation.

6 Five agreed Annexes embrace:
   (a) EIA.
   (b) Waste disposal.
   (c) Prevention of marine pollution.
   (d) Conservation of flora and fauna.
   (e) Management of specially protected areas.

5.6 UN Economic and Social Commission for Asia and the Pacific (ESCAP)

A regional economic commission created by the Economic and Social Council of UN in 1987, ESCAP had the initial task of identifying major problems of industrial pollution in the region, especially among the agri-industries; determining various techniques and alternatives for pollution control in these industries; and estimating the costs of pollution control with an eye to minimising costs. Since then the activities of ESCAP on environmental matters have broadened considerably.

In 1990, ESCAP produced a report on the state of the environment in Asia and the Pacific and arranged for a meeting of ministers of the region in Bangkok in late 1990. This resulted in a ministerial declaration on environmentally sound and sustainable development in Asia and the Pacific, and presented a document representing the Asian and Pacific input to the 1992 UN Conference on Environment and Development held in Rio de Janeiro. These documents are listed in the references. ESCAP presents some stark facts to the UN conference:

(1) The current population of the Asian and Pacific region is 2.9 billion (a billion is one thousand million), more than 55 per cent of the world's total population. The population density is 93 people per square kilometre, compared with 24 people per square kilometre for the world as a whole. Population growth is 1.8 per cent per year.

(2) Rural–urban migration has fuelled the growth of cities; urban population in the ESCAP region increased from 360 million in 1960 to almost 860 million in 1990, resulting in the growth of urban slum and squatter settlements, overburdening urban infrastructure and degrading air and water quality.

(3) More than 800 million people in the ESCAP region are living below the poverty line.

(4) Of diseases 80 per cent are traceable directly to unsafe water and poor sanitation. Diarrhoeal diseases kill more than 1.5 million children every year, or three children every minute, in just seven countries of the region.

(5) A major cause of environmental degradation has been a lack of coherent sustainable development policies and an inefficient and reckless exploitation of natural resources. This exploitation has included deforestation, soil erosion, soil fertility loss, waterlogging, salinity and toxification of soils, loss of biological diversity,

damage to and destruction of coral reefs, mangroves, fisheries and other coastal and marine resources, and excessive extraction of underground water.

(6) The growth in food production and industry, though substantial, has taken place at the cost of the environment, evident from severe air and water pollution and the exhaustion of both renewable and non-renewable resources.

The conclusion is that environmentally sound and sustainable development adopted as a strategy by ESCAP countries will reap long-term benefits for the region. Within this strategy, reducing poverty is clearly a most urgent task.

ESCAP notes that at least 14 countries in the region now have ministries of the environment, others have central environmental agencies or environmental departments under other ministries. A range of environmental legislation had been introduced in the region from national environmental policies and pollution control measures to natural resource conservation and land management schemes. Most of the ESCAP countries have included environmental education at the primary level, many offer tertiary education in the environment and related fields. A regional strategy on environmentally sound and sustainable development has been evolved as a consequence of the ministerial conference held in Bangkok in October 1990, and support for international standards on the global environment.

The strategy provides a broad framework of priorities and actions by governments at various levels, and by private enterprise and citizens. It embraces the issues of population and human settlements: poverty, rural development and agriculture; natural resources and energy; trade, investment and tourism; and industry. It plans to have supporting policies in institutional and administrative procedures, such as economic instruments; environmental legislation, conventions and treaties; environmental education, communication, and public awareness; and development and transfer of environmentally sound technology.

Essentially, the concept of environmentally sound and sustainable development aims at improving the quality of life by securing the basic necessities such as food, shelter, safe drinking water, fuel, sanitation, primary and preventive health care, and education.

EIA

In its report to the UN, ESCAP notes that EIA is gaining wide acceptance in Asia and that many countries have introduced laws requiring EIA for major developments. It also notes that a major problem is an inadequate environmental database and inadequate monitoring.

In line with this, the regional strategy recommends that major investment projects, and foreign investments, should be assessed for their short- and medium-term environmental impact, and for their long-term impact on the sustainability of the natural resource base. Further, all relevant sectoral institutions should be made accountable for evaluating the environmental effects of their policies and programs.

ESCAP recognises the need to develop regional or subregional agreements on environment and development problems and EIA procedures for projects which might have significant transboundary environmental effects.

Of public involvement, ESCAP urges procedures to be developed for early assessment and reporting to the public of the environmental impacts and risks before approving policies, programs, or projects. Ways and means, it recommends, should be developed to promote public participation in decision-making and implementation procedures.

ESCAP urges that environmental parameters should be integrated into national economic policies, planning, budgetary, and development processes; in this the role of environmental agencies should be enhanced. Natural resource accounting should be introduced.

5.7   UN Environment Program (UNEP)

Created by the UN Conference on the Human Environment in Stockholm in 1972, UNEP has tried to implement the various recommendations of that conference. UNEP activities are financed from an environment fund to which all participating nations contribute. UNEP is subject to a governing council of 54 members, and is headed by an executive director.

An international referral system for sources of environmental information is in place. There has been much success gathering environmental information on regional seas. A global environmental monitoring system (GEMS) was initiated. In 1978, a division of EA was established within UNEP, to integrate assessment activity. In 1982, UNEP completed and published a comprehensive review of the state of the environment to identify trends in the 10 years following the Stockholm conference.

In 1982, a special session of the governing council of UNEP was held at its official headquarters in Nairobi, Kenya; it set the areas of priorities for the following 10 years. UNEP claimed 'fair-to-good progress' about some elements of its program. It

conceded 'very slow' progress in other areas. Progress in the implementation of plans to combat desertification, to improve water supply and management, and to improve human settlements, was described as 'distressingly slow'. An inhibitor has been that governments had been unwilling to provide the data needed to establish a register of radioactive releases to the atmosphere.

In sum, the arms race, pre-occupation with civil and transnational conflicts and survival, economic recession, and an energy crisis, had weakened the will of nations, and reduced the resources available for matters of environmental concern.

EIA

In 1987, the governing council of UNEP adopted goals and principles to be considered for use as a basis for EIA. The General Assembly of the UN, later that year, endorsed the goals and principles and the recommendations of the governing council for their application. The goals are as follows:

(1)   To establish that before decisions are taken by the competent authority or authorities to undertake or to authorize activities that are likely to significantly affect the environment, the environmental effects of those activities should be taken fully into account.

(2)   To promote the implementation of appropriate procedures in all countries consistent with national laws and decision-making processes, through which the foregoing goal may be realised.

(3)   To encourage the development of reciprocal procedures for information exchange, notification and consultation between States when proposed activities are likely to have significant transboundary effects on the environment of those States.

The principles are set out in checklist 5.8. Figure 10 indicates a suggested simplified flow chart of the EIA procedure (UNEP, 1990).

5.8   Asian Development Bank (ADB)

The ADB was established in 1966 by the UN ESCAP; ADB aims to foster economic growth within the Asian region through direct loans or technical assistance to any of the 30 or more regional countries largely in South and East Asia and the South Pacific. Members of the ADB also include some non-regional members in North America and Europe. ADB is the executive agency for the UN Development Program authorised to supervise national and regional projects. Its headquarters are in Manila, the Philippines.

CHECKLIST 5.8

UN Environment Program (UNEP)

Principles of EIA

1 States (countries, including their competent authorities) should not undertake or authorise activities without prior consideration, at an early stage, of their environmental effects. Where the extent, nature or location of a proposed activity is such that it is likely to significantly affect the environment, a comprehensive environmental impact assessment (EIA) should be undertaken in accordance with the following principles.

2 The criteria and procedures for determining whether an activity is likely to significantly affect the environment and is therefore subject to an EIA should be defined clearly by legislation, regulation, or other means, so that subject activities can be quickly and surely identified, and EIA can be applied to the activity as it is being planned.

3 In the EIA process, the relevant significant environmental issues should be identified and studied. Where appropriate, all efforts should be made to identify these issues at an early stage in the process.

4 An EIA should include, at a minimum:

(a) A description of the proposed activity;

(b) A description of the potentially affected environment, including specific information necessary for identifying and assessing the environmental effects of the proposed activity;

(c) A description of practical alternatives, as appropriate;

(d) An assessment of the likely or potential environmental impacts of the proposed activity and alternatives, including the direct, indirect, cumulative, short-term and long-term effects;

(e) An identification and description of measures available to mitigate adverse environmental impacts of the proposed activity and alternatives, and an assessment of those measures;

(f) An indication of the gaps in knowledge and uncertainties which may be encountered in compiling the required information;

(g) An indication of whether the environment of any other State or areas beyond national jurisdiction is likely to be affected by the proposed activity or alternatives;

(h) A brief, non-technical summary of the information provided under the above headings.

5 The environmental effects in an EIA should be assessed with a degree of detail commensurate with their likely environmental significance.

6 The information provided as part of an EIA should be examined impartially prior to the decision.

7 Before a decision is made on an activity, government agencies, members of the public, experts in relevant disciplines and interested groups should be allowed appropriate opportunity to comment on the EIA.

8 A decision as to whether a proposed activity should be authorized or undertaken should not be taken until an appropriate period has elapsed to consider comments pursuant to principles seven and twelve.

9 The decision on any proposed activity subject to an EIA should be in writing, state the reasons therefore, and include the provisions, if any, to prevent, reduce or mitigate damage to the environment. This decision should be made available to interested persons and groups.

10 Where it is justified, following a decision on an activity which has been subject to an EIA, the activity and its effects on the environment or the provisions (pursuant to principle nine) of the decision on this activity should be subject to appropriate supervision.

11 States should endeavour to conclude bilateral, regional or multilateral arrangements, as appropriate, so as to provide, on the basis of reciprocity, notification, exchange of information, and agreed-upon consultation on the potential environmental effects of activities under their control or jurisdiction which are likely to significantly affect other States or areas beyond national jurisdiction.

12 When information provided as part of an EIA indicates that the environment within another State is likely to be significantly affected by a proposed activity, the State in which the activity is being planned should, to the extent possible:

(a) Notify the potentially affected State of the proposed activity;

(b) Transmit to the potentially affected State any relevant information from the EIA, the transmission of which is not prohibited by national laws or regulations; and

> (c) When it is agreed between the States concerned, enter into timely consultations.
>
> 13   Appropriate measures should be established to ensure implementation of EIA procedures.
>
> (Source: From *Goals and Principles of Environmental Impact Assessment*, endorsed by decision 14/25 of the Governing Council of UNEP of 17 June 1987)

So far ADB's activities have included facilitating project preparation and implementation, policy formulation, institutional building, and sectoral studies. Interests and activities have naturally extended to environmental matters, the preparation of guidelines, environmental risk assessment, and arranging EIA training workshops (ADB, 1987, 1988a, 1988b, 1990a, 1990b, 1991a, 1991b). An environmental unit operates within the infrastructure department.

5.9   World Bank

An agency of the UN, the World Bank is made up of the International Bank for Reconstruction and Development (IBRD) and its affiliates, the International Development Association (IDA), the International Finance Corporation (IFC), and the Multilateral Investment Guarantee Agency (MIGA). Collectively, these bodies are sometimes referred to as the 'World Bank Group'. The common objective of these institutions has been to help raise the standards of living in developing countries by channelling financial resources from the more developed countries to the developing world. The bank was established in 1945.

In 1970, the bank created the position of environmental adviser, later converted into the Office of Environmental and Health Affairs. With this step, the bank became the first development assistance agency to screen development projects on a systematic basis for their environmental and health implications. However, screening at first tended to occur at the eleventh hour as decisions had to be made on projects that had already progressed far along the path of 'identification, preparation, appraisal and negotiation'. However, new borrowers were urged to take environmental and health issues into account when initiating projects. The matrix in figure 11 indicates the type of analysis suitable for each stage in the bank's project cycle.

The bank has provided much assistance for infrastructure projects including agricultural and rural developments; and water and sewerage facilities, as well as low-cost housing, nutrition, education, and family planning projects. In 1979, it supported a project to reduce air pollution in Ankara, Turkey. In that year, it was found that 700 projects in preparation had environmental implications, some requiring extensive studies. In most cases, major environmental and health measures were incorporated into the design or into the loan agreement.

Since 1979, investment and assistance began to extend to afforestation and reforestation, soil conservation, flood mitigation and control, range management, wildlife protection, measures against the encroachment of desert, as well as abatement of air and water pollution. However, in the late 1980s the bank had been accused of abandoning its original role of reducing poverty and of disregarding the environmental impact of development projects. It has, it is claimed, financed roads for settlers who devastated some of Brazil's jungles and dams forcing thousands of Brazilian Indians out of their homes.

EIA

Whatever the justice of these observations, in 1989, the bank introduced its *Operational directive on environmental assessment* and in 1992 the ADB published its *World development report* in advance of the UN Conference on Environment and Development in Rio de Janeiro.

The operational directive mandates an EA for all projects that might have a significant negative impact on the environment, so that problems can be tackled early in the project phase. From 1991, all projects were placed in one of four EA categories. Those falling into category A require detailed EA; for those falling into category B a more limited analysis might be appropriate. Those falling into category C do not require environmental analysis, while those in category D are about the abatement of environmental problems. In 1991, of 229 projects approved, 11 were rated as category A and 102 as category B (World Bank, 1991).

Several projects have been modified as a result of an EA. In the Botswana Tuli Block Roads project a road was rerouted to avoid an archaeological site; in the Lower Guayas Flood Control project, Ecuador, the floodways were redesigned to avoid disrupting a lagoon; in the Livestock Services project in Uganda, the carrying capacity of the rangeland was specifically analysed; and the Pak Mun hydro power project in Thailand underwent major design changes following assessment. The dam will be lower than originally planned to reduce resettlement of 20 000 people to about 1 000; the project was also relocated to preserve a series of rapids in a national park.

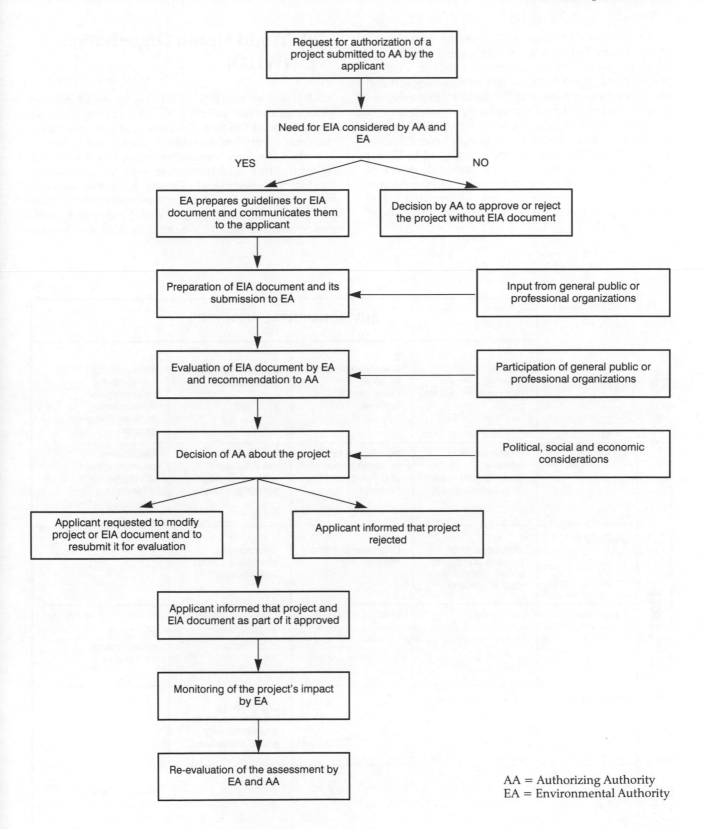

Figure 10 Simplified flow chart for the EIA procedure

(Source: UNEP, *An approach to environmental impact assessment for projects affecting the coastal and marine environment*, Nairobi, Kenya, 1990, p. 10)

In 1993, the Indian government cancelled a World Bank loan for a vast irrigation and hydro-electric project on the River Narmada in western India, unhappy about criticism from ecological and human rights groups and the bank's strict environmental and resettlement standards.

In 1992, the bank completed the publication of its three-volume *Environmental Assessment Sourcebook*, designed to assist all those involved in EIA. It supports a basic premise that sustainable development is achieved most efficiently when negative environmental impacts are identified and addressed at the earliest possible planning stage. See figure 11.

5.10 World Health Organisation (WHO)

An agency of the UN, WHO came into being in 1948, supported initially by 54 countries; it has proved one of the most effective and valuable international participants. Based in Geneva, WHO absorbed the health activities of the UN Relief and Rehabilitation Administration which had assisted the health departments of many market economies and underdeveloped countries with advice and practical aid, the Paris Office of Epidemic Intelligence and the Health Organisation of the former

		ENVIRONMENTAL ANALYSES			
		1. Elaboration of regional development pattern	2. Selection of location for given development scheme	3. Design of project for given location	4. Evaluation of compatibility between given development scheme and given location
PROJECT CYCLE	Identification	Promotion of efficient development pattern (e.g. infrastructure)	Selection of location for target sector (e.g. low-cost housing)	Selection of development scheme for target area (e.g. industry)	Identification of problem areas for environmental projects (e.g. drainage channels)
	Preparation	Detail design of projects promoting growth pattern (e.g. road alignment)	Detail site selection, site planning	Selection of alternatives, detail project design	
	Appraisal				Review of environmental soundness
	Supervision			Design and implementation of environmentally sound procedures	
	Evaluation				Review of actual environmental performance

Figure 11 Environmental analyses in the World Bank project cycle
(Source: World Bank, 1992)

League of Nations. WHO became the sole international health organisation, operating as the World Bank does, with a high degree of autonomy, though directed and guided by the World Health Assembly which meets annually.

The objective of WHO is the 'attainment of all peoples of the highest possible level of health'; 'health' is defined in the charter of WHO as 'a state of complete physical, mental and social well-being and not merely the absence of disease or infirmity'.

The work of WHO encompasses the control of communicable diseases; water supply and waste disposal; air and water pollution; standards for biological and chemical substances; nutrition, food hygiene and food standards; occupational health; the effects of radiation; psychosocial influences; carcinogenic risks; and environmental health impact assessment (EHIA) (Environmental Resources, 1985a, 1985b; WHO, 1987, 1989).

WHO has expressed the view that in the past, EISs had often failed to include adequate assessment of the effects of development decisions on the health and safety of affected communities (WHO, 1987). However, the increasing importance of EIA in many countries as a decision-making tool, provides an excellent opportunity for an improvement in assessing the health consequences of such decisions; this should apply to projects, and to policies, and plans. Thus an EIA should provide the best available factual information on the implications for health of projects, policies, and plans and the public should have access to this information.

WHO did not recommend a separate procedure for EHIA, but that it should remain within the overall framework of EIA. It has recommended the screening of secondary and higher-level impacts to assure that no possible health-related impacts are missed, particularly for groups at special risk; and for the development of mitigation measures to limit the exposure of people to health-related environmental factors.

Checklist 5.9 outlines the application of EHIA to chemical manufacturing facilities, as an indication of the steps involved.

5.11 International Association of Impact Assessment (IAIA)

Established in 1980, the IAIA is a voluntary body of EIA researchers and practitioners dealing with EIA, social impact assessment, risk assessment, technology assessment, and other forms of impact assessment. There are about 1 000 members from over 50 countries; people of many disciplines and professions. Regional chapters are active in Europe, and Brazil. The essential objective of IAIA is to promote the latest developments in impact assessment, and to foster its application locally to globally; from the individual project to the policy, plan, and program; from national to international considerations of trade and international assistance to improve the quality of life globally.

Through local, regional, and annual meetings, IAIA is a non-political forum for the exchange of ideas and experiences. It is an affiliated society of the American Association for the Advancement of Science and is a designated non-government organisation (NGO) of the UN. Members receive the Impact Assessment Bulletin, a quarterly publication of the IAIA.

The thirteenth annual meeting was held in Shanghai, China, in 1993. This was a forum for the discussion of large-scale developments in China including the Pudong New Area in Shanghai, and the Three Gorges hydroelectric scheme (see China, 9.2).

5A Case study: Sea-outfall for the Larnaca sewerage system, Cyprus

Larnaca is a port town on the south-east coast of the Republic of Cyprus, the population is about 52 000. Larnaca's prosperity depends largely upon tourism. The town has had no main sewerage system, and is dependent on septic tanks, absorption pits, and simple holding tanks. Discharges and seepage of sewage water have led to excess bacterial concentration in bathing waters. A sewerage system with treatment plant with outfall would improve this situation.

The municipality of Larnaca had planned to use treated water for irrigation. However, the high salinity of the water, as a result of the intrusion of sea water into the sewerage system, rendered this unsuitable. Then the municipality looked at the alternative of a sea outfall and requested a permit to build one.

Government policy required an EIA for any such development project, this being the first for Larnaca. It was also the first time the public was involved. The preparation of the EIA document was entrusted to the Fisheries Department of the Ministry of Agriculture and Natural Resources.

The draft EIA document was considered at a special review meeting in Nicosia in 1988. The meeting was hosted by the Agricultural Research Institute. It was attended by 27 participants from 7 ministries and departments, 1 non-government environmental organisation, and consultants. The conclusion of the EIA was accepted subject to some

---

CHECKLIST 5.9

World Health Organisation (WHO):
EHIA process applied to chemical manufacturing facilities

Step		*Activity*
1	Project description.	Toxic substances inventory.
2	Assessment of primary impacts on environmental parameters.	Normal EIA process.
3	Assessment of secondary and tertiary impacts on environmental parameters.	Normal EIA process.
4	Identification of impacted environmental parameters with health effects (environmental health factors). Preliminary assessment of environmental health impacts.	Epidemiological, toxicological information.
5	Prediction of exposure to environmental health factors.	Environmental behaviour, pathway analysis.
6	Identification of health risk groups.	Population analysis, lifestyle, diet information.
7	Estimation of predicted health impacts.	Chronic effects of routine releases, hazard analysis of accidental events.
8	Identification of mitigation measures to prevent or reduce significant adverse health impacts.	Process changes and/or protection measures for population.
9	Final decision on acceptability of adverse health impacts and whether or not the project should proceed.	Normal decision-making process, with due weight given to health effects.

(Source: World Health Organisation *Health and Safety Component of Environmental Impact Assessment: Report of a WHO meeting*, WHO Regional Office for Europe, Copenhagen, 1987, p. 4)

---

variations: the outfall was to be extended to 2.8 kilometres from 1.25 kilometres and to be located below the thermocline to achieve a better protection of the beaches. That the EIA procedure led to a modification of the project, though at a higher cost, contributed to a positive response among non-government organisations and the public, who had previously been sceptical.

The proposed outfall was to be located adjacent to Dates Point about 5 kilometres south of the town centre. The standards of the effluent from the treatment plant were defined. Clearly the impact of sewage effluent on the marine environment would depend on the proper functioning of the sewage treatment plant.

There was concern that the quality of effluent could deteriorate during the tourist season, with increased volume. Another concern was the dependence of the proposed activated sludge process on electricity supply. A power shortage for a few hours could make the activated sludge process anaerobic. To return the process back to normal operation could take about a week. Thus continuous monitoring would be necessary. This was another factor in the decision to lengthen the outfall from the original 1.25 kilometres to 2.8 kilometres. Other technical options for the treatment plant were also considered.

The overall aim was to achieve WHO/UNEP environmental quality standards for coastal recreation waters, shellfish, and shellfish growing areas. The project proceeded as modified. This EIA study has been a model for a corresponding study for a sewerage system for Limasol (south Cyprus), due for completion in 1995.

(Derived from UNEP, *Environmental impact assessment: sea-outfall for the Larnaca sewerage system*, Nairobi, Kenya, 1990)

5B Case study: Proposed sewage treatment plant for Port Said, Arab Republic of Egypt

Port Said is at the northern end of the Suez Canal; the other two cities on the canal are Ismailia and Suez. The population of Port Said is close to half-a-million people. During the 1980s, the government of the Arab Republic of Egypt initiated a program to reconstruct the basic infrastructure of the Suez Canal region, concentrating on the modernisation of the wastewater collection, treatment and disposal facilities in each of these three cities for public health and environmental reasons. These improvements would assist the economic development of the region and accommodate population growth.

The Egyptian Environmental Affairs Agency decided that an EIA document was required. Four treatment alternatives were considered for possible use at Port Said; aerated lagoons, activated sludge treatment, trickling filters, and deep shaft treatment. The use of aerobic lagoons emerged, after further studies, as the preferred treatment process. However, these would generate biological sludge and this would have to be removed from the aerobic lagoon cells every two or three years. This would be dried, stored, and finally removed to a sludge disposal site outside of the city of Port Said, or sold to agricultural enterprises as a soil conditioner.

Four alternatives were considered for the disposal of the treated wastewater. Land disposal was rejected because of lack of suitable land in the Port Said area. Discharge into the Mediterranean Sea was rejected as there is the potential for pollution on local bathing beaches and its adverse impact on tourism. Furthermore, Egypt had signed several international treaties to reduce pollution of the Mediterranean. Finally discharge to Lake Manzala, one of the largest of Egypt's delta lakes, being located near Port Said, was agreed upon, in preference to discharging wastewater into the Suez Canal. The assimilative capacity of Lake Manzala is much greater than that of the canal.

The EIA for this project was based on the objectives and principles for EIAs adopted by the governing council of UNEP and endorsed by the UN General Assembly. The preparation of the EIA document was entrusted to the National Organisation for Potable Water and Sanitary Drainage of the Ministry of Development, New Communities, Housing and Public Utilities. Consultations were held between staff and consultants.

In general, construction of the new Port Said treatment plant, with plant start-up in 1993, will have a positive environmental impact on the city and the immediate environment of Lake Manzala. Strict rules for monitoring have been laid down. The EIA process included public scoping meetings, at which interested parties raised environmental concerns and issues for inclusion in the assessment process.

(Derived from UNEP *Environmental impact assessment: sewage treatment plant for Port Said*, Nairobi, Kenya, 1991)

5C Case study: World Bank upland agricultural development project, Laos

Laos is a mountainous landlocked country bordered by China and Myanmar (formerly Burma), to the north-west, Vietnam to the north and east, Cambodia to the south, and Thailand to the west. Much of the country is in the catchment of the Mekong river. The population is 4.4 million, with a population density of 18.6 people per square kilometre. Most of the population engage in subsistence farming.

The country is relatively well-endowed with natural resources. Only a small proportion of the land is regularly cultivated, with much under shifting cultivation with upland rice as the major crop. There has been much deforestation through slash-and-burn methods. Laos is one of the poorest countries of the world.

For environmental reasons, government policies formulated in 1989 favour forest conservation with reduced logging. There have also been plans to encourage alternative crops to opium; in 1989, Laos was ranked the third-largest producer of opium in the world. Coffee is an important export.

The World Bank upland agricultural development project aims to reduce poverty, expand export earnings, improve food security, control soil erosion, and strengthen agricultural institutions; planning productivity gains. The principal beneficiaries are seen as farming families involved in highland coffee production, upland subsistence farming, and slash-and-burn cultivation. The program aims to introduce improved environmentally safe crop production technologies; to rehabilitate existing irrigation schemes and feeder roads and to provide technical assistance and training.

The project is expected to have beneficial environmental impacts in replacing existing land uses which have caused a progressive decline in soil fertility, increased soil erosion, siltation of waterways, and loss of biodiversity. New coffee plantings will replace slash-and-burn cultivation on relatively flat areas of secondary forest.

With improved irrigation and rehabilitation on the valley floors and on the less steep slopes, the need to cultivate steep hillsides will be reduced; this will lead to decreased siltation and flooding downstream in the wet season.

The World Bank recognises that the project will interact with ethnic groups, affecting their customary lifestyle; it is essential for those groups to recognise and to accept the new technologies and the need for conservation.

Overall, this project promises environmental improvements and the introduction of ecologically sustainable development. However, environmental monitoring is necessary with the promotion of community participation as a key to change.

Once again, the concept of EIA applies to projects of this kind as well as to major infrastructure developments.

(Derived from World Bank, 1992)

5D   Case study: Enterprise village reforestation project, Tanzania

The United Republic of Tanzania has a population of 25.8 million. Tanzania is bounded in the north and west by lakes Tanganyika, Malawi, and Victoria. Africa's highest peak, Mount Kilimanjaro, lies on the border with Kenya. With a mainly agricultural economy, Tanzania's exports are dominated by coffee, cotton, sisal, cashew nuts, tea and, from Zanzibar, cloves. The population distribution is 29 people per square kilometre, 67 per cent of whom are rural.

However, rural villages in north-west Tanzania are suffering acute shortages of wood for domestic cooking and building, as well as soil degradation

and falling timber yield. Severe deforestation has occurred here and, indeed, in all regions of Tanzania. Most of the population depends on wood for domestic cooking and heating. Population growth of 3.4 per cent per annum is exacerbating the problem and is contributing to the depletion of forest resources.

One of the areas worst affected by deforestation in Tanzania is the Kwimba district. The reforestation project was initiated to make the villages largely self-sufficient in firewood and building materials, to protect the soils, provide fodder for cattle, and fruit for consumption and sale. The potential environmental benefits from the reforestation program include reduction in soil erosion, improved water quality, and more natural regeneration in depleted forests.

Three components of the program, each conveying benefits are: the development of large village woodlots, the provision of fuel-efficient stoves to reduce the volume of wood consumed, and the establishment of an extension service to encourage the planting of fruit orchards on private land. The easing of pressures could allow people to spend more time on kitchen gardens.

Eucalypts planted in Tanzania are not African species but they are regarded as the best foreign species available for meeting the immediate needs of Tanzania. However, the long-term impacts of these plantings need to be monitored.

In sum, reforestation should have a positive effect on the environment, protecting bare soils from sheet and gully erosion, restoring the fertility and productivity of the land during fallow periods, increasing the organic material content of the soil and the water infiltration rate. The increased forest cover should improve the quality of watersheds with reduced excessive rainwater run-off; and siltation rates for dams and streams should be reduced. By 1992, the project appeared to be achieving its reforestation goals.

This project illustrates that the concept of EIA does not have to be restricted to major industrial and infrastructure projects. EIA is applicable to activities such as this which can yield substantial positive environmental benefits, efficiently carried through and monitored.

(Derived from Australian International Development Assistance Bureau, 1992)

CHAPTER 6

Europe

The 4 most populated countries in the European Community (EC) are treated first in this chapter. I then deal specifically with a number of other European countries.

6.1 Britain

Britain, an island nation, has a population of 57.6 million, 236 people per square kilometre; 91.5 per cent urban, and 8.5 per cent rural.

As the first of the industrialised nations, Britain has a long history of pollution and its control, and the resolution of environmental conflicts. Some of that history is recorded in checklist 6.1.

John Evelyn (1620–1706) was an eminent diarist and author of 30 books. He held senior positions under King Charles II and was life-time friend of Samuel Pepys. Evelyn's diary was published in 1818.

In 1661, Evelyn said of pollution in the city of London:

... her Inhabitants breathe nothing but an impure and thick Mist, accompanied with a fuliginous and filthy vapour, which renders them obnoxious to a thousand inconveniences, corrupting the Lungs, and disordering the entire habit of their Bodies; so that Catharrs, Phthisicks, Coughs and Consumptions, rage more in this one City, than in the whole Earth besides. (Evelyn, 1661)

However, apart from setting up an alkali inspectorate and giving local authorities a limited capacity to act against nuisances (see glossary) there was no clear objective until the passing of the Clean Air Act in 1956, following the London smog disaster of 4 years earlier. Measures to reduce water pollution and noise, and a general strengthening of the Town and Country Planning Acts, resulted.

In 1970, Britain formed a department of the environment. For the first time responsibility for planning and land use, pollution control, public building and construction, came under a single secretary of state. Since then, the aim has been to develop a strategic approach to environmental planning and protection, to replace the fragmented approach which previously handicapped effort. Local government, the basis of environmental planning, was extensively reorganised.

Regional structure plans pulled together all the diverse threads of strategic planning, location of industry, and housing, the improvement of transport, and conservation of nature. Water and sewerage services were reorganised. Public participation has been encouraged in the formulation of policy and proposals.

The Control of Pollution Act, 1974, significantly extended the powers of local councils to deal with noise problems, the deposit and disposal of waste on land, the prevention of water pollution, and the control of pollution of the atmosphere. Under the Clean Air Acts of 1956 and 1968, much progress was made with the control of industrial and domestic emissions. Smoke control areas were progressively introduced throughout the nation. Public inquiries have been a normal feature of these developments, sometimes leading to an application being rejected (see case study 6A).

Further, Britain has developed a comprehensive system for controlling changes in land use. The main features of this system are:
- Local councils (planning authorities) prepare development plans setting out policies and proposals for the development of land in their area.

Development Approval

Development Approval

CHECKLIST 6.1

Britain: Evolution of environmental management

1661 John Evelyn's thesis on London smog.

1848 Public Health Act.

1875 Public Health Act.

1906 Alkali etc Works Regulation Act.

1932 Town and Country Planning Act.

1936 Public Health Act; Housing Act.

1937 Food and Drugs Act.

1945 Water Act.

1947 Town and Country Planning Act.

1948 Rivers Boards Act.

1949 National Parks Act.

1951 Rivers (Prevention of Pollution) Act.

1952 Town Development Act.

1954 Report of the committee on air pollution (Beaver Report).

1956 Clean Air Act.

1960 Clean Rivers (Estuaries and Tidal Waters) Act; Noise Abatement Act; Radioactive Substances Act.

1961 Pippard Report on the pollution of the tidal Thames.

1964 Harbours Act.

1968 Town and Country Planning Act.

1970 Department of the Environment established; Royal Commission on environmental pollution created.

1971 Town and Country Planning Act; Merchant Shipping (Oil Pollution) Act.

1972 Poisonous Waste Act.

1974 Control of Pollution Act; Dumping at Sea Act; Health and Safety at Work Act.

1978 Commission on energy and the environment.

1980 Highways Act.

1988 Town and Country Planning (Assessment of Environmental Effects) Regulations.

1989 Electricity Act.

1990 Town and Country Planning Act.

1991 Environmental Protection Act; Planning and Compensation Act.

1992 Transport and Works Act; Town and Country Planning (Assessment of Environmental Effects) Regulations; Harbour Works (Assessment of Environmental Effects Regulations); EIA guides published by Kent and Essex Country Councils, the Passenger Transport Executive Group and the Department of the Environment.

- The development of land requires planning permission, and an application for planning permission must be made to the local council. If the council decides to grant permission for the proposed development, conditions might be imposed.

- If permission is refused, there is a right of appeal to the responsible minister. If an application raises major issues, the central government (Whitehall) might take the decision out of the hands of the local council, by 'calling in' the planning application for decision by the appropriate minister.

One of the major factors that must be considered about a DA is the potential effect on the environment. Her Majesty's inspectorate of pollution and the water authorities might be involved. Legislation such as the Control of Pollution Act 1974 is binding on any development whenever permission is granted. A public inquiry might be held by an independent inspector from Whitehall, before a ministerial decision.

At these inquiries, the proponent, the local council, the appropriate regulatory agencies, and members of the general public might put forward both oral and written arguments either in favour of or against the granting of permission, or the imposition of conditions, and might cross-examine the arguments put forward by other parties to the inquiry. About 2 000 such inquiries are held each year in Britain. See figure 12.

In Britain, therefore, the assessment of the environmental effects of proposed developments has been an integral part of the planning system (rather than a separate process) since 1947. Measures to mitigate adverse environmental effects have been commonly required by conditions attached to a planning permission or consent.

Britain has implemented the European Communities Directive on Environmental Assessment (85/337), though these procedures differ little from those previously in existence. The implementation of the EC directive is by a series of statutory regulations under the Town and Country Planning Acts. EISs are now prepared for major and environmentally significant projects; for so many proposals considered through the planning system, the preparation of elaborate environmental statements is inappropriate. Major projects directly under the central government are governed by similar requirements.

Reviews of the operation of the EIA system have appeared in various publications (Department of the Environment, 1989, 1990a, 1990b, 1991a, 1991b). See also checklist 6.2 applying EIA to government policies.

The Environmental Protection Act of 1991 places new responsibilities on industry to provide information on the environmental impacts of their

RESPONSE TO A PROPOSAL TO INTRODUCE LEGISLATION TO PERMIT THE CONSTRUCTION OF A RAILWAY BETWEEN LIVERPOOL AND MANCHESTER, ENGLAND 1824

On this becoming known, the canal companies prepared to resist the measure tooth and nail. The public were appealed to on the subject; pamphlets were written and newspapers were hired to revile the railway. It was declared that its formation would prevent cows grazing and hens laying. The poisoned air from the locomotives would kill birds as they flew over them, and render the preservation of pheasants and foxes no longer possible. Householders adjoining the projected line were told that their houses would be burnt up by the fire thrown from the engine-chimneys; while the air around would be polluted by clouds of smoke. There would no longer be any use for horses; and if railways extended, the species would become extinguished, and oats and hay be rendered unsaleable commodities. Travelling by rail would be highly dangerous, and country inns would be ruined. Boilers would burst and blow passengers to atoms.

Figure 12 An early case for a public inquiry

(Source: Samuel Smiles, *The Lives of George and Robert Stephenson* (1st edn, 1874), Folio Society, 1975, London, pp. 137-138)

CHECKLIST 6.2

Britain
Guide to the environmental implications of government policies
Checklist for policy appraisal

1. Be clear about priorities, objectives and constraints.
2. Consider the environment from the outset.
3. The key issues to take into account are:

   Irreversibility

   Distribution of costs and benefits between different groups in the population

   Uncertainty

   Monetary valuation.
4. Identify a wide range of options, and continue to look for new options.
5. Seek expert advice, and consider the need for research to reduce uncertainty.
6. Identify impacts to be analysed or ameliorated at the policy stage, and those to be dealt with at project level.
7. Use a broad cost-benefit approach, but try out different ways of analysing and presenting choices.
8. Keep the appraisal under review; new impacts may be found during the process of appraisal.
9. Monitor the effects of the policy and evaluate its effectiveness.

(Source: Department of the Environment UK, *Policy Appraisal and the Environment*, HMSO, London, 1991)

---

emissions. Many new proposed facilities require an EA to be undertaken before making a planning application.

Much research and training is undertaken in environmental studies and impacts in Britain, notably at the universities of Aberdeen, Manchester, Sheffield, and Oxford. Oxford Polytechnic has an impacts assessment unit. The Institute of Environmental Assessment, Horncastle, Lincolnshire, created in 1990, has promoted a national environmental auditors' registration scheme; drawn up guidelines with the aim of improving the biological and ecological aspects of EIAs; assisted with the EC eco-audit scheme; established the largest database for EISs in Britain; and helped with the introduction of BS 7750 (British standard) on environmental management with various corporations and organisations.

6.2 France

France, with a population of more than 57 million, has a population density of some 105 persons per square kilometre; of this population 10 million are concentrated in Greater Paris. About 60 per cent of France is cultivated agrarian land, with another 27 per cent forested.

With a long industrial history, the history of pollution to air and water is in France equally long; a variety of measures have been taken to combat these problems and to protect and enhance the natural environment (see checklist 6.3). The first national parks were dedicated in 1963, mainly in the south of France, and extensive regional parks were established throughout the country. Waste management is covered by a wide-ranging body of

---

CHECKLIST 6.3

France: evolution of environmental management

1913	Historic Monuments Act.
1921	Cultural Heritage Act.
1930	Act for the protection of national monuments and sites of artistic, historical, scientific, traditional or picturesque interest.
1942	Toxic and Hazardous Substances Act.
1948–49	Noise and Air Pollution Control Acts.
1957	Parks and Nature Reserves Act.
1958	Fauna and Flora Act.
1960	National Parks Act.
1961	Air Pollution and Wastes Act.
1962	Town and Country Planning Act; Urban Renewal Act
1963	First national parks established.
1964	Water Supply and River Management Act.
1971	Ministry for the Environment established.
1972	Protection of mountain regions directive.
1973	Amendments to pollution control and water Acts.
1974	Further amendments to environment protection Acts.
1975	Wastes Act.
1976	National Conservation Act; Marine Pollution Act; Environmental Impact Assessment Act.
1977	Chemical Products Act.
1980	Air Quality Agency set up.
1983	Environment Protection Zone Act; Oil Pollution Act; Environmental Impact Assessment Act.
1986	Coastal Protection Act.
1991	Comprehensive review of pollution control and environment protection legislation.

---

laws and regulations, with a principal Wastes Act in 1975. Town and country planning legislation has played a part in minimising problems of pollution and environmental protection, but some problems, such as noise, remain, with a high social cost.

In 1976, France introduced the initial measures for EIA, making assessments mandatory in many cases. This law was completed by a Council of State decree in 1972, and came into force in 1978. The contents of EISs are defined, and in the event of an inadequate study, appeals can be lodged with an administrative tribunal. After completion of works, the decision-making body carries a burden of responsibility, and might possibly be held responsible for any damage caused, with a commitment to provide compensation. About 5 000 to 6 000 impact studies are undertaken each year (Turlin and Lilin, 1992).

The measures adopted in France preceded those of EC countries that responded only to the EC directive of 1985. French legislation sought to meet three objectives: to help public or private developers to design projects with a minimal adverse effect on the environment; to help the decision-making authorities to make decisions based on better information; and to keep the public better informed and encourage participation in the decision-making process. The procedures are applied to all projects likely to have an adverse effect on the environment, such as major construction and development projects; activities with no immediate physical implications are exempted. The field of application of EIA procedures is now clearly defined in lists of activities, with low technical or financial thresholds.

The management of the process is a matter for the decision-making authority, responsible for granting or refusing planning permission. In some cases the Ministry for the Environment has responsibility; in other cases the appropriate regional bodies have. The administrative courts play an important role in the system, pronouncing on the correctness of administrative procedures and giving greater precision to EIA regulations.

Impact assessment studies must be placed on public exhibition; and a project might be subject to a public inquiry. The public must be informed before a decision is taken. The Act of 1983 on the 'democratisation of public inquiries and the protection of the environment' was intended to improve the effectiveness of public inquiries, increasing the range of projects subject to inquiries, and improving the procedures adopted for inquiries with greater powers for the commissioner.

6.3   Germany

The Federal Republic of Germany has a population of 80 million; the population density is 225 people per square kilometre. It is one of the most densely populated countries in Europe, and, yet, of the total land area almost 30 per cent is covered by forests, and 55 per cent is devoted to agriculture.

Within the German federal system, there is a sharing of environmental responsibilities between the federal government and the states; the image is more of a partnership. The UN Conference on the Human Environment in 1972 provided the impetus for the creation of the Federal Environmental Agency; yet, as in other cases, this was simply an evolutionary step from previous activities.

The federal Ministry for the Environment, Nature Conservation and Nuclear Safety co-ordinates the environmental policies of the federal government. The Federal Environmental Agency coordinates the development of environmental controls, prepares legislative and administrative regulations, and formulates procedures for EISs. The Conference of Ministers for the Environment is a major forum for the coordination of the state and federal environmental policies.

In Germany, the first statutory regulations on the preservation of the environment from air pol-lution and noise were promulgated as far back as the trade regulations of 1869 (see checklist 6.4). However, pollution did not become a public issue until the 1960s. In 1962, when the state parliament was being re-elected in North Rhine–Westphalia, the slogan of one of the contesting parties was: 'Make the sky above the Rhine blue once more.' In 1969, in a federal government policy statement Chancellor Brandt announced that his government would pay 'more attention to the conservation of nature, recreational areas and wildlife'; that 'com-prehensive and coordinated measures to protect the public from the risks to health caused by tech-nological development and automation' would be instituted; and that 'appropriate laws would be introduced to provide adequate protection against air and water pollution and to promote noise abate-ment (Ministry of the Interior, 1972).

EIA

On 22 August 1975, the federal government adopted a set of principles for EIA. These principles were intended to be applied to federal public works undertaken by departments, agencies, corporate bodies, institutions and foundations; also to plans, programs, administrative, and legal acts (Federal Republic of Germany, 1975).

It was stated that the purpose of assessing en-vironmental compatibility is to protect people as well as fauna and flora, and sensitive areas against harmful environmental effects arising from federal public works, by taking precautions to prevent or minimise these adverse effects. These possible adverse effects should be examined 'at the earliest possible stage'.

Arrangements were made for consultations between federal ministers, and the Federal En-vironmental Agency by other bodies. As a rule, the assessment of environmental compatibility was to proceed along lines set out in a flow pattern and to

---

CHECKLIST 6.4

Germany: evolution of environmental management

1869	Trade regulations restraining air pol-lution and noise.
1935	Nature Conservation Act.
1957	Federal Water Law.
1969	Federal Government policy statement on the environment.
1970	Environment Policy Act adopted by the German Democratic Republic.
1971	Urban and rural renewal legislation introduced.
1972	Disposal of Wastes Act. Traffic in DDT Act.
1974	Federal Environmental Agency estab-lished.
1975	Principles relating to EIA adopted; Federal Forest Act; Federal Game Act; Plant Protection Act; Detergents Act.
1976	Federal Nature Conservation Act.
1977	Waste Water Act.
1980	Amendment of the Federal Nature Conservation Act.
1981	Federal Emissions Control Act, restrict-ing air pollution, noise, and vibration.
1983	Statutory restrictions on sulphur diox-ide emissions.
1986	Waste Avoidance and Waste Manage-ment Act. Gradual introduction of EIA throughout the Laender (state) in implementation of the European Com-munities Directive.
1988	Federal government endorses the Vienna Convention for the protection of the Ozone Layer; also the Montreal protocol.
1989	Amendment of Federal Nature Con-servation Act; large combustion plants ordinance.
1990	Environmental Impact Assessment Act; Federal Emissions Control Act; carbon dioxide reduction program; Radiological Protection Act.
1991	Environmental Impact Assessment Act applied to infrastructure projects; ordi-nances on the avoidance of packaging waste, on the prohibition of certain ozone-depleting substances, and the problem of discarded automobiles.
1992	Environmental Impact Assessment Act applied to industrial projects; adop-tion of a plan for eastern Germany.

be incorporated into the decision-making process. Environmental interests were to be treated on an equal footing along with other aims and responsi bilities of government. The overall objective, was a 'well-balanced harmonisation of interests'. The elements of this flow pattern are identified in checklist 6.5.

In 1990, the Environmental Impact Assessment Act was passed at federal level, brought into operation in two stages in 1991 and 1992; see checklist 6.5 on the evolution of environmental management. Other highly relevant and supportive legislation include the Federal Pollution Control Act, the Waste Avoidance and Waste Management Act, the Federal Water Act, and federal Acts governing forest management, railways, and highways.

For the Federal Pollution Control Act, a 'competent authority' is empowered to monitor compliance with limit values and other conditions of consent during project operation. If harmful effects to the environment are identified, further remedial measures can be required through the issue of subsequent directives. Failure to remedy these situations might lead to the revocation of the licence.

In most of the state of the Federal Republic of Germany, specific EIA administrative procedures exist on the compatibility of large projects such as highways, power plants, or harbours. In implementing the EC directive on EIA, these procedures are intended to form a two-stage EIA system, the second stage is in the subsequent licensing or permit procedures.

6.4   Italy

With a population exceeding 57 million and a population density of 190 persons per square kilometre, Italy industrially has developed rapidly since 1945, particularly in the north. Thus, while early pollution control legislation can be traced back to the 1930s, in recent years the main emphasis has been when more serious problems have tended to appear. See checklist 6.6.

The most important water pollution control legislation appeared in 1976. Its objective has been to control effluents of all types from all sources entering all waters; define criteria for water use; stimulate national restoration plans; and strengthen public agencies. Since then, EC directives, among other matters, have also been implemented about the quality of drinking water and recreational waters (Marchetti, 1989).

The principal air pollution control measure, introduced in 1966, required the adoption, in different parts of the country, of various measures

---

CHECKLIST 6.5

Germany: EIA procedures
Elements of the flow pattern

1   Preliminary approach

  (a)   task presentation

    •   technical objectives

    •   basic boundary conditions

    •   problems connected with the technical task

  (b)   presentation of technical measures

    •   possible solutions

    •   selection of measures

2   Examination of environmental relevance

  (c)   to establish whether or not harmful effects on the environment might occur, or are excluded

3   Assessment of environmental compatibility

  (d)   determination of environmental impact

    •   analysis of environmental conditions

    •   predictions about environmental conditions if measures are not taken

    •   predictions about environmental conditions if various measures are taken

    •   comparison of predictions

  (e)   evaluation of environmental impact

  (f)   PPA, and possible further measures

4   Weighing against other interests

(Derived from Federal Ministry for the Environment, Nature Conservation and Nuclear Safety)

---

according to the severity of pollution. Emission limits were set down for industrial plant and later for motor vehicles. Restrictions on the lead content in gasoline (petrol) were introduced in 1982.

However, public confidence was shaken when, on 10 July 1976, a major incident occurred at a multi-national chemical plant, Icmesa, at the village of Seveso, near Milan. A build-up of pressure in the process plant led to the release into the atmosphere of a vapour cloud containing a highly toxic dioxin. Within three weeks, 700 people had to be evacuated from the danger area (Gilpin, 1978)

Of those people evacuated, some 500 showed symptoms of poisoning. Pregnant women affected were advised to have abortions, for the chemical

---

CHECKLIST 6.6

Italy: evolution of environmental management

1865   Water Supply and River Management Act.

1902   Cultural Heritage Act.

1922   Parks and Nature Reserves Act: first national park.

1931   Fauna and Flora Act.

1934   Air Pollution Act.

1939   Coastal Protection Act; Cultural Heritage Act.

1941   Waste Pollution Act.

1942   Town and Country Planning Act.

1961   Water Pollution Act.

1966   Air Pollution Act.

1973   Environmental Impact Assessment Act.

1974   Toxic and Hazardous Substances Act.

1976   Water Pollution Act.

1977   Hunting and Wildlife Protection Act.

1979   Water Pollution Act.

1983   Air Pollution Act; Marine Pollution Act.

1984   Parks and Nature Reserves Act; Toxic and Hazardous Substances Act.

1985   Water Pollution Act.

1986   Ministry of the Environment created.

1988   Decree requiring an EIA for certain public and private projects.

1989   EIA legislation comes into force; EIA Commission created; introduction of public inquiries.

1992   EIA requirements extended; Minister of the Environment reviewing legislation to ensure full implementation of EC Directive 85/337.

---

was known to cause malformations in foetuses. More than 600 domestic animals were poisoned by the gas; all those that survived were destroyed. All contaminated crops were destroyed by fire over a zone extending 8 kilometres south of the factory. An expert called in by the Italian government advised that everyone in the area should undergo lifelong medical checks.

This event in 1976 led to a strengthening of air pollution control legislation. Increasing concerns about air pollution control led, in 1986, to the creation of the Ministry of the Environment.

Legislation on EIA had been introduced in 1973, but it was confined to the electricity industry. In 1985, the Italian parliament resolved to implement the EC directive of that year. Through Acts and decrees, EIA became effective for certain public and private projects in 1989. In 1991, EIA was extended to the full range of projects listed in the annexes of the EC directive. The principle of the public inquiry was introduced; the public were to become much better informed and encouraged to participate in the decision-making process. Some regions and provinces have enacted their own laws on EIS since 1989.

An improvement in the quality of environmental impact studies is evident. Between January 1989, when the EIA legislation came into force, and the autumn of 1991, 64 projects were subject to EIA procedure (Matarrese, 1991).

6.5   Austria

Austria has a population of about 8 million, more than half of whom live in cities; there are 93 people per square kilometre. Most of the country is alpine or subalpine, with heavily wooded mountains and hills. Manufacturing is the mainstay of the economy, and agricultural production meets most food needs.

In a number of areas, Austria's environmental policies have been quite successful, particularly about sulphur dioxide emissions, motor vehicle fuels, and lake protection; in other environmental areas, Austria has lagged, notably in waste prevention, chemicals policy, and EIA (Austrian Federal Government, 1992, p. 102).

Indeed, by 1992, Austria was only beginning to formulate a law on EIA for large-scale industrial and area-planning projects. However, some intensive studies have been undertaken by the Federal Environmental Agency for existing plants. For example, a study of the Treibacher chemical works, the Montanwerke Brixlegg copperworks, and the pulp and paper industry, and their effects on the environment have been done.

6.6   Belgium

Belgium has a population of 10 million, with a high density of 328 persons per square kilometre. Save for nuclear installations and the storage of radioactive materials, responsibility for EIA has been transferred from the national administration to the regions of Flanders, Wallonia, and Brussels. In Flanders, EIA became effective in 1989 through a series of administrative orders. In Wallonia, EIA was introduced by decree in 1985. By 1992, measures in Brussels had not been implemented.

In Flanders, in 1992, an intervarsity commission of experts in environmental law (known as the Bocken Commission) developed proposals for an updated and integrated revision of environmental legislation. It was recommended that EIA procedures should be applied to policies, plans, programs, and projects, with area-wide assessments of land-use plans. The proposals have been much discussed.

6.7   Commonwealth of Independent States affiliates

The former Soviet Union had embraced one-sixth of the world's land mass with a population of 289 million. It broke up in 1991; 11 republics later in the year formed the Commonwealth of Independent States; Estonia, Georgia, Latvia, and Lithuania chose not to join.

The broad notion of EIA had been mooted by the Soviet government in 1985. In 1988 a Central Administration of Environmental Impact Assessment was established with appropriate regional offices. Its principal task was to implement national EIA policies and programs. Since 1990, the finance for all projects and programs was initiated only after favourable EISs (Govorushko, 1990). It is clear, however, that while EIA had been initiated in the former Soviet Union, it had not been extensively applied.

However, in November 1991, an International Seminar and First Inter-Republican Conference on EIA was held in Moscow. The conference had been sponsored initially by the former Soviet Union and three UN agencies. It became clear at this conference that there had not been any adequate legal basis for EIA in the Soviet Union, let alone in the 11 sovereign republics that were then emerging.

The conference recommended that appropriate EIA legislation should be developed in each republic; that the principle should be applied to policies, programs, and projects; and that there should be uniform methodological approaches with development of databases. Public consultation as part of the EIA process, generally supported as desirable and even essential, had, like the EIA process itself, yet to be implemented.

Since that conference, EIA legislation has been enacted in Russia and several other republics. Legislation has also been introduced in the former Soviet republics of Estonia, Latvia, and Lithuania; and in a number of former members of the Soviet bloc, including Poland, Bulgaria, Hungary, Romania, and the Czech and Slovak Republics.

6.8   Czech and Slovak Republics

The population of former Czechoslovakia is more than 15.5 million, with 122 people per square kilometre. Before the Czechoslovakian revolution of 1989, the Czech and Slovak Federated Republic did not have a ministry for the environment, or other central authority responsible for environmental policies or programs. Following the revolution, however, three environmental bodies were created: the Federal Committee for the Environment (in effect a ministry); the Czech Ministry for the Environment; and the Slovak Commission for the Environment.

The federal committee became responsible for ecological policies, environmental relations, and for information about the environment; the Czech and Slovak ministries for carrying out environmental programs, and projects. An environmental board made up of representatives of the federal and republican ministries, an environmental committee of the federal parliament was formed, and advice was received from the private sector through an 'expert' board of 60 or 70 members drawn from citizens and academic groups.

In December 1991, the Czechoslovak federal assembly passed the Environmental Act. This Act defined basic concepts and determined fundamental principles to protect the environment, and support for the principle of sustainable development. The Act indicated the need for EIA and environmental planning. EISs would be required in future for major projects, before an approval for the project. The Act has a schedule of activities falling into this category.

In December 1991, the federal government approved the principles of state policy for the power industry, which set out the government's power industry policy objectives for the next 10 years. These major objectives were (1) a reduction of at least 35 per cent in the use of coal for power generation; (2) a reduction in power generation in north-west Bohemia (where environmental pollution is at its worst); (3) the introduction of desulphurisation and denitrification equipment into power plants; (4) a significant growth in the import of natural gas; (5) energy savings measures; and (6) increased reliance on nuclear energy.

This energy policy must be seen against a background in which Czechoslovakia's energy supply has been dependent on indigenous brown coal. This coal has a low-heat value and produces large amounts of sulphur dioxide. Also, 60 per cent of all electricity in the country has been produced by about six main power stations in the black belt of northern Bohemia, where pollution is worst. The power industry has contributed significantly to the damage to the forests, and to soil degradation, and river pollution (Federal Committee for the Environment, 1991).

In January 1993, Czechoslovakia peacefully split into two nations: the Czech and Slovak Republics. As such action did for Norway and Sweden, the tranquillity of the divorce augurs well for future environmental cooperation on the lines already established at the federal level.

6.9 Greece

Greece has a population of more than 10 million with a population density of 78 per square kilometre. The basis of EIA was created in 1986 when a measure to protect the environment was passed by the parliament. A system of environmental licences requiring EIA was established for new major projects or modifications, or activities that might significantly affect the environment. As much preparatory work was required, the law did not operate until 1990.

6.10 Ireland

Ireland has a population of only 3.5 million, and a population density of 50 per square kilometre. The EC EIA Directive 85/337 was brought into operation gradually in Ireland, over 1988 to 1990, through 12 statutory regulations. Of these, the most important were the European Communities (Environmental Impact Assessment) Regulations 1989 and the Local Government (Planning and Development) Regulations 1990. These regulations provide for the application of EIA procedures to all EC Annex 1 projects, and to most of the optional Annex 2 projects.

An Environmental Protection Agency has been created, essentially to control pollution through an integrated licensing system, and playing a significant role in the EIA process.

Ireland is particularly active in the area of EA; the number of EISs has been relatively high compared with, for example, Britain.

6.11 Luxembourg

With a population of only 387 000, Luxembourg has pressed on with the implementation of the EC directive. EIA is now essentially part of Luxembourg law for the control of dangerous, dirty, and noxious installations; the protection and conservation of nature, and natural resources; and the communication network. These laws came into

effect between 1967 and 1990. Further measures are planned to cover some EC directive provisions not yet incorporated in Luxembourg law.

6.12 Netherlands, The

The Netherlands has a population of 15 million with a high density of 447 people per square kilometre. In 1986, the Dutch parliament approved EIA legislation, as part of the Environmental Protection (General Provisions) Act. The Act stipulates the general requirements on the content of EIA documentation and procedural requirements. See checklist 6.7. A 'positive list' of works and activities requiring EIA has been a constant feature of this legislation. PPA is also required; these investigations must be carried out during or after the undertaking of the activity. PPA results are published periodically, thus ensuring public access to the information obtained.

Despite the comprehensiveness of the legislation, a review was done in 1991, with special regard to the precise requirements of the Directive 85/337; in 1992, the Dutch parliament endorsed the findings and recommendations. The results were some amendments to the Environmental Protection

---

CHECKLIST 6.7

The Netherlands: contents of an EIS

1. A statement of the purpose and rationale of the particular activity or project being proposed.

2. A description of the activity and reasonable alternatives to it, including the alternative that is the least harmful to the environment.

3. A description of the existing environment, including a projected description of the environment should the project not proceed.

4. A description of the environmental impacts of the proposed activity or project and its alternatives.

5. A comparison in terms of environmental impact between the proposed activity or project and its alternatives (including the do-nothing alternative).

6. Deficiencies in knowledge.

7. A non-technical summary.

(Derived from The Netherlands government, 1991)

(General Provisions) Act. The concept of compensation was introduced for remaining unavoidable impacts on the environment, after all reasonable preventive and mitigation measures had been adopted. EIA was to promote sustainable development, and by decree, EIA was extended to a greater range of industrial, transport, and land development projects.

6.13   Poland

Poland, with a population of 38.5 million, introduced EIA in 1989, incorporating these provisions in the Town and Country Planning Act, the Environmental Protection Act, and certain other Acts. EIA is compulsory for exceptionally polluting developments; these are identified through an executive order. The Minister of Environmental Protection, Natural Resources and Forestry is assisted by an EIA committee which reviews EISs. The process starts, however, with an application to a local authority, and advice is received from the EIA committee. The public are consulted at an early stage and a number of meetings are held. If an EIS is required, the contents are stipulated by the local authority. When completed, the EIS accompanies the siting application. The EIS might be reviewed by a local EIA committee; a siting licence might include conditions about, for example, the need for monitoring or for a PPA.

6.14   Portugal

Portugal has a population of close to 10 million, and 107 people per square kilometre. It entered the EC in 1986, one year after the EIA directive; EIA studies followed, taking the directive into account. In 1987, the Portuguese Environmental Act was passed, making specific provision for EIA. Decrees followed in 1990. These requirements make the proponent responsible for presenting the EIA study for the project to the competent authority (the licensing authority); the authority sends this to the Minister for the Environment. The minister delegates responsibility for further work, ensuring public consultation and participation; the emerging commentary determines the future of the project. The procedures in Portugal are mainly centralised.

6.15   Spain

Spain has a population of 39 million, and 78 people per square kilometre. It joined the EC in 1986. EIA measures were introduced in 1986 and 1988. All the project categories in Annex 1 of the EC directive are subject to EIA, but not yet all those in Annex 2. In addition to central legislation, many legal EIA provisions have been introduced at regional levels. The Autonomous Community of Madrid, and the Cantabria and Estremadura communities, have issued decrees.

6.16   Switzerland

With a population of just under 7 million and 168 persons per square kilometre, Switzerland has a range of laws about water pollution, nature and landscape protection, and land use. EIA requirements are found in the Federal Law on the Protection of the Environment, 1983, which came into operation in 1985. These are mainly framework laws. The cantons have a duty to promulgate their implementation. Initially in the process, only the proponent, decision-making authority, and Environmental Protection Agency, are involved. Once a decision is made, appeals might be possible, but the right of appeal is restricted to about 20 organisations explicitly listed in an ordinance. An EIA can be applied only to construction projects, not to planning or land-use schemes. Decisions are left to the canton. However, the central government issues a manual of guidance for the cantons. The EIA process in Switzerland is mainly about the protection of the natural environment and not at all with social and economic matters.

6A   Case study: Proposed 2 000 MW thermal power station, Ratcliffe-on-Soar, Britain

An application to the Minister of Power for consent to build a new coal-fired 2 000 MW power station in south Nottinghamshire was first made by the Central Electricity Generating Board (CEGB) in March 1960, when a station at Holmepierrepont was proposed. This application was subject to a public inquiry and was later rejected by the minister largely on environmental grounds of air pollution, aesthetics, and transportation of coal and ash.

In June 1962, the CEGB applied for consent for a similar station at Ratcliffe-on-Soar, just to the south of Nottingham. Because of the loss of the Holmepierrepont site, the atmosphere at CEGB headquarters was tense. A further public inquiry into these fresh proposals was held in Nottingham in January 1963. The inquiry, which lasted 14 days, was conducted by a deputy chief engineering inspector, Ministry of Power, and a principal planning inspector from the Ministry of Housing and Local Government. A senior medical officer, from the Ministry of Health, attended as a medical assessor.

In all, 84 written objections and a protest petition signed by 5 763 people, mostly residents of Long

Eaton nearby, or users of the recreational area of Trent Lock were submitted. Among the objectors were also Nottingham City Council, Beeston and Stapleford urban district council, Long Eaton urban district council, and Gotham parish council. Supporters of the CEGB application included Nottinghamshire County Council and the National Coal Board.

The case for the CEGB rested upon three main arguments: the rate at which the demand for electricity was increasing in Britain, the need to locate coal-fired power stations on the most economic sites, and the efficiency of pollution control. The dust arresters were to a minimum removal efficiency of 99.3 per cent; and the hot gases from a single stack 200 metres in height would effectively dilute pollutants and penetrate temperature inversions of all severities. The air pollution contributions to breathing levels were to be minimal during conditions of fog or inversion.

It was claimed by the objectors that the environmental assessment by the CEGB was unsatisfactory because: there was no 2000 MW power station in operation, consequently all estimates were extrapolations of figures obtained from small power stations; and there was insufficient knowledge of what might happen during certain meteorological conditions. The findings of the inspectors and the medical assessor covered all aspects of the chimney emissions: smoke, grit and dust, and sulphur dioxide. The medical assessor concluded that any health fears were groundless.

The inspectors agreed, however, that from an engineering standpoint it was impracticable for the CEGB to give an assurance that a collecting efficiency of 99.3 per cent could be achieved at all times, and continuous monitoring would be needed. However, the CEGB's calculations on the diffusion of sulphur dioxide were not effectively challenged by the objectors, and the theoretical calculations were reinforced by actual measurements taken around Castle Donington and High Marnham power stations for more than 20 years.

The inspectors concluded because of all the evidence that the objectors had not justified their submissions that the site of a power station of the size proposed should be well away from the urban areas at and near Nottingham on the grounds of possible atmospheric pollution. The counter-claim was that the location was much more favourable in all respects, including aesthetics, than the Holmepierrepont site.

After careful and full consideration, and after consultation with the relevant ministers, the Minister of Power consented to the construction of the power station, subject to the specifications and assurances given at the inquiry. The station was subject to the continuous surveillance of the chief alkali inspector, who would need to be satisfied before issuing a certificate authorising the operation of the power station. The four-unit power station, using low-sulphur coal from East Midlands collieries, was constructed and operates satisfactorily.

(Based on Gilpin, Alan, *Analysing the Ratcliffe Power Station inquiry*, News Letter No. 37, Central Electricity Generating Board, London, 1963, and original sources)

6B   Case study: Atmospheric emissions study for Kent County Council, Britain

During 1992, several proposals for nine new power generating installations and incinerators in the north Kent and east Thames Valley areas accentuated growing public concern about air quality. DNV-Technica Ltd were commissioned by Kent County Council to carry out an atmospheric emissions study to assess the long-term impacts of combined emissions from the proposed nine plants. Although the proponents were diverse, the proposals were treated as a single program with possible adverse cumulative effects.

The study area covered over 1 600 square kilometres of land, the ground elevations varying from the low-lying flat terrain adjacent to the River Thames and Medway Estuary to the raised area of the North Downs in Kent. The nine new proposed and imminent sources of air pollution were as follows:

- Barking power station (combined cycle gas turbines);
- AES Medway power station (combined cycle gas turbine);
- Kingsnorth power station (combined cycle gas turbine);
- Crossness sewage sludge incinerator;
- Beckton waste incinerator;
- Cory 'energy for waste' plant;
- Northfleet 'energy for waste' plant;
- Kemsley combined heat and power plant;
- SCA Aylesford cogeneration plant.

The above proposals were individually examined to establish typical pollutant emission rates representative of operations over one year, embracing normal operational practice and back-up/peak demand expectations.

Oxides of nitrogen and oxides of sulphur were the most significant pollutants for the study, while other pollutants might warrant later more localised studies. A standard Gaussian dispersion model (frequency distribution whose graph is a normal curve) was used to predict the annual average ground-level pollutant concentrations in the study area attributable to the principal emissions; results from individual sources were integrated to produce concentration isopleths or isograms (see glossary) across the study area. Annual average meteorological data was obtained for London and Manston, a coastal city in Kent, to provide representative long-term modelling conditions.

The results from the modelling study were compared with the available background monitoring data in each area; these findings were then considered in the context of air quality legislation and guidelines.

It was concluded that significant emissions of oxides of nitrogen would result in the south-east area of London, where the background levels of the pollutant were already high. Elsewhere in the study area, where background levels of oxide of nitrogen were not so high and the sources not concentrated together, the conclusion was that there would be no significant impacts associated with oxides of nitrogen emissions. It was also shown that the combined emissions of oxides of sulphur would not result in significant long-term impacts on ground-level concentrations; background levels of oxides of sulphur are relatively low.

The study provided a basis for decision-making in the region and for on-going air quality assessment; it highlighted the need to examine the impacts of combined emissions and cumulative effects from various plants as a supplement to isolated studies of individual plants. The study also illustrated the lack of adequate significant long-term background monitoring data in most industrial areas. The model developed is a useful tool to assist regional planners, assessing air quality.

(Derived from DNV-Technica Ltd, London, Britain)

6C   Case study: Hydroelectric and river diversion scheme, Greece

A scheme involving the construction of two large hydroelectric dams on the Achelous river has been proposed by the Greek government. As an adjunct to the dams, an 18-kilometre diversion tunnel would take one-third of the river's waters eastwards to irrigate the cotton fields of the Thessaly plains and help irrigate otherwise dry ground.

The Achelous is the longest river in Greece; it is 220 kilometres in length and rises in the Pindus mountains, falling into the Ionian sea. Its water is charged with fine mud, much of which is deposited along the banks in fertile marshy plains. At the mouth, the river is less than 1 metre deep, not navigable from the sea.

In winter, the river overflows the whole of the lower plain. The wetlands become the winter home

for several endangered bird species and the nesting ground for hundreds more. Rare Dalmatian pelicans are found there. Cutting the flow of the river could be critical to the grounds of migratory wildlife. Known as the Missolonghi wetlands, they are one of Europe's most treasured bird habitats and protected by the Ramsar Convention. This international convention, signed at Ramsar, came into force in 1975, to create reserves and to protect wetlands, including habitats for rare or migratory birds.

Greece has perennial problems with irrigation and drinking water which necessitates dam construction, and such activity facilitates the use of water power for electricity generation as a pollution-free natural resource.

However, this particular scheme has invoked considerable environmental opposition. Apart from the ecological implications for wildlife, the project will inundate hundreds of homes in the 14 villages scattered along the Achelous valley, a seventeenth-century monastery at Myrophilla in the Pindus mountains, several schools, and churches. The scheme has been condemned by environmentalists as one of the most 'hideously destructive projects' ever to have been planned in Europe.

The economics of the scheme have been challenged on the grounds that it will reduce production from three existing hydroelectric plants. The World Wide Fund for Nature has criticised the Greek government for not informing the nation about the project and its likely or certain impacts on the lives of Greek citizens. It appears that the rules of good EIA have not been complied with.

(Derived from the Greek government, *Report to the United Nations Conference on Environment and Development 1992*; *The European*, 24-27 June 1993, 'The dam that will drown a valley of nightingales'; and World Wide Fund for Nature)

6D   Case study: Baikal pulp and paper mill, Russia

Located in eastern Siberia, Lake Baikal contains about one-fifth of the world's surface fresh water; it is also the deepest continental body of water to be found. Flowing into Lake Baikal are 336 rivers and streams; the most important is the Selenga. Most of the outflow is through the Angara river. Fauna and flora life in the lake is rich and various; about three-quarters of the species are specific to Baikal.

Industries on the shores of the lake include mining (mica and marble), cellulose and paper manufacture, ship-building, fisheries, and sawmilling. There was a Soviet government decree of 1971 for the protection and rational use of resources, and the prevention of polluting emissions from cellulose and other industrial plants in Baikal. The Baikalsky nature reserve, on the southern shore of Lake Baikal, has been set aside for research in the natural sciences and into the ecosystem of southern Lake Baikal.

A government report of 1981 indicated that the condition of the lake was deteriorating, despite action to control pollution. Factories discharging effluents into rivers and watercourses serving the lake and paper mills, oil tankers, and the city of Slyudyanka, which discharged raw sewage were blamed.

The Baikal pulp and paper mill was constructed in 1966, at the southern end of the lake, to produce high-quality cellulose pulp. It was built with an elaborate three-stage waste treatment facility (mechanical, chemical, and microbiological). Yet the adverse effects of the mill on the environment and on the Lake Baikal ecosystem have been considerable.

The project was the subject of an environmental review process that took place during and after the construction of the waste treatment facility; the review was coordinated by an interagency commission, which organised regular scientific and public meetings. As a result of this review, several monitoring programs were introduced to obtain regular information of the state of the lake. Particular attention was paid to water quality, air quality, soils, and ground-water pollution. The program paid particular attention to the mill but did not focus solely on that project; all major sources of pollution were reviewed.

It was found that the environmental impacts of the mill were excessive. Further, public concern about these and other adverse effects had led to the popular slogan 'Hands Off Baikal'.

In 1987, the Soviet government decided to close the Baikal pulp and paper mill, substituting it with a non-polluting industry. This was to be done during the 5-year plan, 1991 to 1995.

(Derived from Gilpin, Alan, *Environmental planning: a condensed encyclopedia*, Noyes Publications, Park Ridge, New Jersey, USA, 1986; UN ECE, *Post-project analysis in environmental impact assessment* UN, New York, USA, 1990)

6E   Case study: Rudna copper mine in the Legnica–Glogow copper district, Poland

The province of Legnica, south-western Poland, has copper mines, food processing, and electrical machinery manufacturing. The provincial capital is Legnica and other principal cities include Glogow, Lubin and Jawor. Rudna, 32 kilometres north of Legnica city, is the site of Poland's largest copper mine, opened in 1974.

In 1977, a tailings pond was constructed to receive the flotation waste as a slurry from Rudna and two other smaller copper mines. Known as the Zelazny Most tailings pond, the slurry entering this pond contains mainly quartz and dolomite, with some copper and trace amounts of heavy metals; also flotation agents left after the separation of copper from the ore, in particular, carbon disulphide.

An environmental review was conducted earlier based on land-use planning, mining, and environment protection laws. As a result of the review, future monitoring of the identified environmental impacts was imposed. Monitoring networks were to measure the following: (1) mining damage and subsidence; (2) dust fall and fine particles; (3) sulphur dioxide, nitrogen oxides and carbon disulphide concentrations in the air; (4) surface and underground water quality; and (5) heavy metal concentrations in soil, and vegetation. A separate complementary network was established around the tailings pond for monitoring air, surface-water and ground-water pollution.

In addition, an area-wide EA of regional development in the Legnica–Glogow copper district was undertaken in 1979 in cooperation with the UN Development Program (UNDP) and WHO. The essence of this study was to compare the impacts of the Rudna mine with those predicted; it was in effect, a PPA.

This broader study was assisted because of baseline monitoring of the area that had begun before the mine started operation. The new study was able to use these results for comparative purposes. The results provided guidance for modification to the mine operations and to revise, at 5-year intervals, the environment protection program overall.

Beyond that, the studies were able to test, verify, and improve the methods used for predicting impacts so that future mines and similar projects could benefit and be subject to more significant environmental reviews.

For Rudna, the monitoring resulted in better techniques for back-filling, different construction techniques for the tailings pond, and a more environmentally sensitive ore treatment technology. The environmental review and monitoring program was also improved.

(Derived from UN ECE, *Post-project analysis in environmental impact assessment*, New York, USA, 1990)

CHAPTER 7

The Nordic countries

7.1 Denmark

The Kingdom of Denmark is made up of Denmark, the autonomous territories of the Faroe Islands, and Greenland. Denmark itself has an area of 43 000 square kilometres and a population of close to 5.2 million; the average population density is 120 people per square kilometre to no more than 592 persons per square kilometre in Greater Copenhagen itself. It has limited natural resources with an intensively cultivated agricultural sector; however, Denmark extracts oil and gas from the North Sea. The populations of the Faroe Islands and Greenland are very small.

The state of the environment in Denmark has been described (Ministry of the Environment, 1991a, 1991b). In 1971, Denmark created a Ministry of the Environment with a department and five agencies: the National Agency of Environmental Protection, the National Forest and Nature Agency, the National Agency for Physical Planning, the National Environmental Research Institute, and the Geological Survey of Denmark. The Ministry of Foreign Affairs gives high priority to international cooperation on the environment. The Danish Society for the Conservation of Nature is one of the largest voluntary interest groups in the kingdom.

In 1988, as a follow-up to the report of the UN World Commission on Environment and Development (1987), the Danish government prepared one of the first national action plans covering a number of areas vital to the environment: fishing, agriculture, industry, energy, transport, cities, and construction. In addition, the plan focuses on: administrative and economic instruments; decision-making processes; and education, training, information, and research. The action plan of more than 150 different initiatives, has become the framework of Danish environmental policy.

EIA

Environmental impact procedures came into force in Denmark in July 1989, in accordance with the 1985 EC directive. This procedure stipulates that large facilities and development projects that are likely to significantly affect the environment must be assessed for their total effect on the environment; they are subject to public hearings before they can be initiated.

EIA is required for new crude-oil refineries; nuclear power stations, and thermal power stations over 300 MW; iron and steel mills; large plants that recover and process asbestos; integrated chemical plants; large transport projects such as motorways, airports, and harbours; facilities that process hazardous and toxic waste or deposit radioactive or hazardous and toxic waste in the ground; enterprises that carry out especially hazardous activities; large drainage or irrigation projects and schemes for the cultivation of large natural areas; cement and lime works, certain types of extraction schemes; and large holiday or similar proposals in areas near the coast, or special natural areas. However some large development projects approved by special legislation passed by the Folketing (parliament) are not governed by this procedure (Ministry of the Environment, 1991c).

The procedure for EIA is outlined in checklist 7.1.

7.2 Finland

With a total population of 5 million, the Republic of Finland has an average population density of 17 people per square kilometre. Forests covering 65 per cent of the land area remain the mainstay of Finland's prosperity; wood, paper, and related

---

CHECKLIST 7.1

Denmark: environmental impact procedure

(Based on the National and Regional Planning Act, 1989 and the Environmental Impact Assessment Order, 1989)

1 A developer presents a project for approval.

2 The authorities decide whether this project requires an EIA.

3 If an EIA is required, the authorities determine the content and extent of the assessment.

4 The developer prepares a report (EIS).

5 The county or the Minister for the Environment assesses the environmental impact and prepares a regional plan supplement or national planning directive, which is then published.

6 A period of public consultation follows with public meetings and site inspections. Citizens can lodge objections to the project.

7 The authorities review and comment on the objections, and assess the need for changes to the project.

8 The material is sent to the national agency for physical planning which prepares a draft decision for the Minister for the Environment.

9 The municipality may adopt a local amended plan for the area.

10 The county and municipality may then grant the necessary approvals and permits, including an approval under chapter 5 of the Environmental Protection Act.

11 When the deadline for appeals against these approvals and permits expires and the appeals are determined in favour of the developer, construction can commence.

(Source: Ministry of the Environment, Denmark, *Environmental impact assessment in Denmark*, Ministry of the Environment/National Agency for Physical Planning, Copenhagen, 1991)

---

planning and building, housing matters, radiation studies, surveying, and environmental hygiene. On establishing the Ministry of the Environment in 1983, environmental affairs were brought under one administration. The ministry has four divisions: environmental protection, general management, physical planning and building, and housing.

EIA

EIA is acknowledged as an important tool in implementing and enhancing sustainable development in Finland. EIA principles have been applied to government policies, plans, and programs, or projects. However, there is no general EIA requirement, so not all activities which might have significant environmental consequences are systematically and thoroughly examined (Ministry for Foreign Affairs, 1991). The establishment of a statutory base for national environmental impact procedures is being pursued.

There are a number of Acts which contain provisions for the assessment of the effects of certain activities; Acts of major significance are the Planning and Building Act, the Water Act, the Public Health Act, Waste Management Act, and the Air Pollution Control Act. Environmental impacts are also studied during the planning of infrastructure and the drafting of land-use plans. There are some examples where the lack of EIA in the early planning stage has led to costly and time-consuming revisions of proposals. Also, the public have felt that, at times, there were inadequate opportunities to participate in, and influence, planning and decision-making.

Short of national EIA legislation, the Environmental Permit Procedure Act, 1992, does ensure a more comprehensive view of the impacts of a proposed project, in the course of permit procedures. The possibilities for public participation have been improved.

EIA principles have now been introduced into the drafting of policies, plans, and programs, or projects both at governmental and municipal level. During 1990, EIA was introduced at the policy level into work done by committees on draft legislation or government statements; and into the preparation of operational and economic plans, particularly about matters to be included in the annual national budget.

The National Board of Waters and the Environment is developing its expertise in the field of EIA. Finland is involved with the implementation of the UN ECE's convention on EIA in a transboundary context.

Extensive monitoring of the environment is carried out in Finland, and the overall strategy aims at

industries, account for a substantial part of export earnings. Finland has four nuclear power units meeting about one-third of the nation's electricity needs.

Environmental issues considered have been the use and management of water resources, hunting and recreational fishing, physical (environmental) a reduction of sulphur dioxide, nitrogen oxides, lead, and CFC compounds in the atmosphere; improved water pollution control, and waste management programs. The work of the Nordic Council is supported, particularly for cooperation in environmental protection and nature conservation. By 1992, Finland had contributed to the East European Action Plan, the implementation of which will reduce pollution in Finland. Finland has also endorsed many other international conventions about global environment.

7.3　Norway

Norway has a population of 4.3 million, with a low density of 13 persons per square kilometre; 37 per cent of this Scandinavian country remains forested and only a very small percentage is devoted to agriculture. Fish resources are crucial to coastal settlements, particularly in the far-flung northernmost part of the country. Norway possesses substantial energy reserves, in oil and gas. However, because of its mountainous topography Norway produces 99.9 per cent of all electricity from hydro power.

In Norway, the standard of living is high, as it is in the other Nordic countries and social welfare systems are well developed. The environment is annually subjected to an estimated 185 000 tonnes of sulphur and 88 000 tonnes of nitrogen through acid rain and dry deposition. Long-range air pollution from other countries is thought to contribute 90 per cent of the total acid precipitation. Damage caused by that air pollution is evident in forests and fisheries in southern Norway's fresh waters. However, the main contributions to water pollution are from industry, mining, agriculture, and municipal sewage.

Various regulatory measures have been progressively introduced to deal with the problems within Norway. One consequence is that the emission of sulphur dioxide from Norwegian sources has been halved since 1973. A specific carbon tax was introduced in 1991 and increased in 1992 to 12 US cents a litre for petrol; there is a similar charge on mineral oil.

EIA

Norway was one of the first countries to establish a Ministry of Environment. Since its creation in 1972, the ministry has played a major role in influencing national environmental protection and improvement. An extensive reorganisation of the ministry took place in 1989.

The Planning and Building Act of 1985 was extensively revised in 1989. It provides for public participation in decision-making processes and for EIA for major projects. These provisions ensure that the effects on the environment, natural resources, health, and society, are analysed and considered before approval of large public and private projects (Ministry of Environment, 1992). See checklists 7.2 and 7.3.

An early ad hoc EIA was carried out on a terminal facility for gas from the North Sea Statfjord field. The plant located in Karsto in western Norway receives, refines, and ships gas to European customers. The EIA was an input to the application for a licence to construct and operate a terminal. The licence was granted in 1981; construction was completed and the plant opened in 1985.

CHECKLIST 7.2

Norway: evolution of environmental management

1957　Open-air Recreation Act.

1964　Salmon and Freshwater Fishing Act.

1970　Nature Conservation Act.

1972　Establishment of Ministry of Environment.

1976　Product Control Act.

1977　Motorised Traffic in Marginal Land and Watercourses Act.

1978　Cultural Heritage Act.

1981　Pollution Control Act; Wildlife Act.

1983　Regulations concerning conservation of the natural environment in Svalbard.

1985　Planning and Building Act (EIA provisions).

1986　Regulations concerning conservation of the natural environment of Jan Mayen and its surrounding territorial waters.

1987　Gro Harlem Brundtland, Prime Minister of Norway, presents the report of the World Commission on Environment and Development, *Our Common Future*, to the General Assembly of the UN.

1989　Amendment of Pollution Control Act and the Planning and Building Act (EIA provisions); sale of detergents containing phosphates prohibited.

1990　ECE conference on Action for a Common Future held in Bergen.

1992　Amendment of Salmon and Freshwater Fishing Act and Cultural Heritage Act; plan for national parks presented to Parliament.

CHECKLIST 7.3

Norway: contents of EIA

1 Description of the project and plans for its implementation.

2 Description of practicable alternatives.

3 Land use and its relationship with municipal and county municipal planning.

4 The public and private measures necessary for the realisation of the project.

5 Permits required from public authorities.

6 Description of the environment, natural resources and social conditions in the areas affected by the project.

7 The significant effects of the project on the environment, natural resources, and the community, during the construction and operational phases, in the event of accidents, and in the event of closure.

8 Mitigation measures and their implementation.

9 An analysis and evaluation of any effects which may remain after the mitigation measures referred to in (8).

10 A proposed program for follow-up studies or assessments of the actual consequences of the project.

11 Relevant background material.

12 Short summary.

(Derived from Ministry of Environment, *Environmental impact assessment in Norway: provisions in the Planning and Building Act relating to environmental impact assessment*, ME, Oslo, Norway, 1990)

A condition imposed on the licence was that a major research program on the social and economic effects must be carried out; this program was financed equally by the proponent and the Norwegian government. This was undertaken, considering the possibilities of several gas terminals in the future. The issues addressed were labour market conditions and industrial life; social and cultural aspects; and municipal finances and expenditures. Compliance monitoring was also required.

7.4 Sweden

Sweden has a population of 8.7 million, with a density of 21 people per square kilometre. This is very low by European standards. However, about 84 per cent of the population live in urban areas, mostly in the southern one-third of the country, in the three main metropolitan areas of Stockholm, Göteberg, and Malmö. Sweden has one car for every three inhabitants.

Roughly 70 per cent of the total area of Sweden is covered with woodlands. The country's natural resources also include various types of ore, particularly iron ore, and hydro power.

Half the electricity is generated by hydro power, and about half from 12 nuclear power plants. Sweden is basically self-sufficient in major food products, though only about 4 per cent of the working population is engaged in agriculture. Sweden's base industries are forestry, mining, and steel; cars, machinery, electrical and communications equipment account for half of the nation's exports. Sweden has a small domestic market and depends on international trade.

Industrialisation in Sweden began in the 1870s with pulp and paper manufacturing, ironworks, mines, and the sugar-beet industry, all releasing substantial amounts of pollution into water and air. The rivers were increasingly harnessed for power production. Sewage discharges in urban areas also increased with improved domestic facilities. Pollution was further aggravated by the greater use of petroleum products in industrial processes, domestic heating, and in vehicles.

All these factors stimulated environmental awareness during the 1960s; and many earlier regulations about public health and water pollution were replaced by legislation to control emissions of all types from industrial plants and transport. In 1967, the National Environmental Protection Agency was set up to deal with environmental questions. A variety of other measures was adopted to reduce pollution and protect the natural environment (see checklist 7.4). International cooperation on the questions of transboundary pollution, particularly acid rain, the greenhouse, the ozone layer, and the protection of wildlife, have been central to Sweden's environmental and industrial activities.

Regulatory measures tended to dominate environment protection in Sweden; however, there is an increasing use of economic instruments; decentralisation of responsibility from central government to regional authorities, municipalities, and other agencies, to ensure that activities within their areas or sectors do not harm the environment; the polluter-pays principle and the precautionary principle are in place; and increasingly the policies embrace the principle of sustainable development.

The problems confronted by Sweden are examined in some detail in the nation's report to the UN Conference on Environment and Development, 1992 (Ministry of the Environment, Sweden, 1991).

CHECKLIST 7.4

Sweden: evolution of environmental management

1964	Nature Conservancy Act, superseding laws of 1909 and 1952.
1967	National Environmental Protection Agency created.
1968	Environmental Advisory Committee appointed; Sulphur Content in Fuel Oil Act.
1969	Environment Protection Act; the use of DDT in Sweden stopped, with some exemptions until 1975.
1971	Marine Dumping Prohibition Act; insecticides aldrin and dieldrin totally banned.
1973	Products Hazardous to Health and the Environment Act.
1975	Vehicle Scrapping Act.
1976	Sulphur Content in Fuel Oil Act amended.
1978	Environment Monitoring Program introduced.
1979	Forest Conservation Act; Cleansing Act.
1980	The Riksdag (parliament) voted to phase out nuclear power by 2010; Water Pollution from Vessels Act.
1985	Chemical Products Act.
1986	Building and Planning Act; Natural Resources Act; lead-free petrol introduced; Environmental Damage Act.
1987	Hunting Act.
1988	National phase-out plan adopted for CFCs.
1989	Catalytic conversion for car exhaust gases compulsory from 1989 models; Environment Protection Act amended.
1990	EIA requirements extended.
1991–92	EIA regulations introduced.

Procedures

The National Environment Protection Board (formerly Agency), the county administrative boards, and the municipal environment and health protection committees exercise supervision of environmentally hazardous activity. However, the Swedish government, under the Environmental Protection Act, may issue directives that factories or establishments of certain kinds (for example, nuclear) may not be constructed; that wastewater of a certain type, quantity, or composition, may not be discharged; that solid matter or waste may not be discharged or stored in a manner likely to contaminate land or water; and that changes to plants likely to affect the environment detrimentally cannot be undertaken without official approval.

The National Licensing Board for Environment Protection is responsible for granting permits for major, potentially polluting, activities. The board must undertake thorough examination of all applications before it. Under the Environment Protection Act, the board is required to advertise proposed activities to provide those people who might be affected, with an opportunity to express their views; consult the central and local authorities that have substantial interests in the matter; hold a meeting with the parties concerned and carry out on-site inspections; and keep the proponent, and all other interested persons, fully informed, with ample opportunity for further comment; and in detail. Permits may be granted for a limited period, but not for more than 10 years. Permits issued may later be partially or wholly revoked to protect the environment when unforeseen events occur. Annual reports might be required in particular circumstances. The legislation has been described in some detail (Ministry of the Environment, Sweden, 1990).

EIA

Municipal master plans, which are compulsory, play an important part in the realisation of the aims of the Environment Protection Act and the Natural Resources Act; that is, to conserve a good natural, physical, and cultural environment; to secure the long-term supply of the country's natural resources; to promote an equitable social structure; and to protect the right of public access to forests, lakes, and recreation areas. The planning process helps to raise public awareness and knowledge, and increase the ability of citizens to participate in discussions and debates on present and future municipal planning and environmental policies.

Within this context, the principle of EIA for potentially significant impacts on the environment has gained an increasingly important place in Sweden. For example, an application for permission to build a major industrial facility must always include an EIS to be assessed. EIAs are paid for by the proponent. Such matters as to whether a particular type of plant or class of activity should be considered at a local, county, or national level by the Licensing Board, are determined by rules made under various Acts such as the Environment Protection Act, Natural Resources Act, Water Act, Planning and Building Act, the Nature Conservancy Act, the Roads Act, the Electricity Act, the Aviation Act, the Minerals Act, and the Continental Shelf Act.

The coordinating responsibility for the implementation of EIA regulations lies with the National Board of Housing, Building and Planning; the Swedish Environmental Protection Agency; and the Central Board of National Antiquities.

The nuclear power referendum in Sweden

The nuclear power referendum in Sweden is a rare example of an EA carried out by the public, on the basis of general knowledge and belief, without any other formal procedure.

The Swedish nuclear program was launched in 1966 and was extended in 1975 by the Swedish government with the approval of parliament (Riksdag) and (presumably) a broad base of public opinion. The program was completed in 1985 when the latest of 12 nuclear power units was connected to the electricity grid. Today, nuclear power supplies about half the electricity used in Sweden.

Nuclear power first became a political issue in Sweden during the election of 1976, when the Social Democratic Party lost its majority in parliament and a minority faction of that party took up an anti-nuclear position. In 1979, following the Three Mile Island (USA) accident, the Swedish government decided to hold a referendum on the question of the use of nuclear energy in Sweden.

The choice offered to Swedish electors was limited to three nuclear options: (1) to decommission the 6 nuclear units already in operation over a period of 10 years; (2) and (3) to complete the nuclear program approved by parliament and decommission the 12 units at the end of their planned technical and economic lifetime (these options vary only in some details). Almost 76 per cent of the electorate participated in the referendum.

The first option received 38.7 per cent support, while options (2) and (3) together obtained 58 per cent of the votes. These results were interpreted by parliament as endorsing the completion of the 12 units, to be phased out by 2010. The nuclear program proceeded as originally planned.

However, the Chernobyl (Ukraine) accident and its impact on Swedish public opinion led the Swedish parliament in 1987 to decide to phase out 2 nuclear units by 1995. This was accompanied by a decision not to increase the consumption of oil and coal and to make available renewable sources of energy for electricity generation.

By the late 1980s, several official studies concluded that phasing out the 2 nuclear units could lead to a doubling of the price of electricity for heavy industry and to the loss of 100 000 jobs. Labour union leaders began to argue against phasing out the units. Conflicts in policies began to emerge, for there had been much opposition also to the development of hydro power on the major rivers.

In mid-1990, the Social Democratic government decided to look for a more coherent and integrated energy policy and to seek a broad consensus on the energy issue. A three-party agreement was announced in January 1991; this cancelled the decision to phase out 2 units by 1995, but maintained the date of 2010 for the final phasing out of nuclear power in Sweden.

More recent public opinion polls have shown that most of the Swedish population favours the use of the 12 units, even after 2010, as long as they remain competitive and safe. However, further deployment of nuclear energy in Sweden would require the endorsement of the public through a further referendum. By the time of the UN Conference on Environment and Development in 1992, the decision of the Swedish parliament remained that nuclear power in Sweden is to be phased out by not later than the year 2010 (Ministry of the Environment, Sweden, 1991).

7A   Case study: Underground natural gas-storage facility near Stenlille, Denmark

The sale of natural gas has increased sharply since it was first discovered in Danish territorial waters in the North Sea in 1984. Natural gas is extracted at a constant rate throughout the year, but consumption varies, and increases in the winter. One natural gas-storage facility had already been established in northern Jylland (Jutland), but Dansk Naturgas A/S decided that another storage facility was needed on Sjailland (Zealand).

After many site studies, an area near Stenlille was chosen to be suitable because of its particular geological formation.

Dansk Naturgas A/S prepared an EIS on the proposed site, and the National Agency for Physical Planning undertook an EIA of the proposal; all the relevant authorities were consulted. The EIA was exhibited for public comment from 22 August to 19 October 1990. The agency held a public meeting in Stenlille with the proponent and all the authorities involved. By the deadline of 19 October, the agency had received 19 objections.

The outcome of the EIA was that the building of the storage was justified and that the anticipated air pollution, noise, and waste, would not exceed the acceptable standards; further traffic to and from the facility would only be environmentally significant during the construction phase. However, because of the objections, one of the gas lines between the store and one of the well heads was to be moved, the restrictions in the safety zones were to be specified, and the facility was to be better adapted to the surrounding landscape.

After the Minister for the Environment issued a national planning directive and the National Agency for Environmental Protection approved the facility, construction began, the first phase coming into operation in 1994.

(Derived from Ministry of the Environment/National Agency for Physical Planning, *Environmental impact assessment in Denmark*, 1991, prepared by the Environmental Impact Assessment Research Centre, Royal Danish Academy of Fine Arts, in cooperation with the Environmental Impact Assessment Research Centre at Roskilde University Centre, with others)

7B   Case study: Highway Five, Finland

Highway Five is one of the main national roads in Finland, stretching from Helsinki to the north via the town of Kuopio and the municipality of Siilinjärvi, to the town of Kemijärvi. This case study deals with a 15-kilometre stretch passing through an esker area, a long narrow ridge of coarse gravel deposited by a stream.

In Finland, there has been no systematic EIA procedure for highways, though for large projects environmental matters must be considered in the planning process. The planning of the upgrading of Highway Five in this critical segment began in 1964, but a formal plan by the National Board of Roads and Waterways (NBRW) did not occur until 1982. This plan included three alternatives: to repair the existing highway, or to construct a new highway either to the west, or to the east of the existing highway. The plan described the environmental impacts of the three alternatives.

The western alternative would go through an esker area already in the National Esker Preservation Program and it would also cross an important recreational ground water area. Yet the NBRW had preferred this route for technical reasons and because of lower costs. Further studies were carried out, and subalternatives of the western route were considered by a supervising group, specially appointed. The group concluded that there was no acceptable solution for the highway in the area.

On the basis of comments from various agencies and organisations on the initial three environmental and further studies, a new alternative D was developed. Alternative D began at the same southern point as the other western subalternatives A, B, and C, but joined the existing highway before the

esker area, passing the centre of Siilinjärvi, only a short distance west of the existing highway. Alternative D was more expensive than the other western subalternatives, but comments on alternative D were invited, and all the previous agencies consulted.

Against all the background information and comment, the NBRW submitted a report to the Ministry of Communications which chose to consult the Ministry of the Environment. In the negotiations between the two ministries, alternative D was preferred as it would leave the esker untouched. The final opinion of the Ministry of Communications was that planning should proceed with alternative D, and the NBRW, advised late in 1984, decided to proceed with that alternative (see map 1).

The public participated through public meetings organised by the municipality of Siilinjärvi. Most people were mainly concerned about land and property values, and the possibility of increased traffic noise. The influence of the public on this issue does not appear to have been significant, yet the whole process went through an EIA process between 1982 and 1984.

(Derived from UN ECE, *Application of environmental impact assessment: highways and dams*, 1987, p. 84)

7C   Case study: Kobbelv hydro power project, Norway

This project, a hydroelectric plant of 300 MW, is situated near the Arctic Circle, in a mountainous area with peaks reaching to 1 500 metres. Two national parks are located in the area, Rago (Norway) and Padjelanta (Sweden). The area has several glaciers and many lakes; other nearby localities at lower altitudes have rich vegetation and are important habitats for both fish and wildlife.

The main area of conflict between this development and nature conservation has been, therefore, in the valleys. The phases and timing of the project, up to 1990, are set out in figure 13.

The proponent of this project was the Directorate of the State Power System, responsible for the preparation of the EIS. Most of the studies were carried out by consultants. The EIS offered three alternative locations, based on technical and economic evaluation.

The public was informed about the beginning of the planning process and the review by announcements in various local newspapers. One open public meeting was held as an information session. The Water Resources Department administered the review stage while many organisations, agencies, and institutions, commented on the plan.

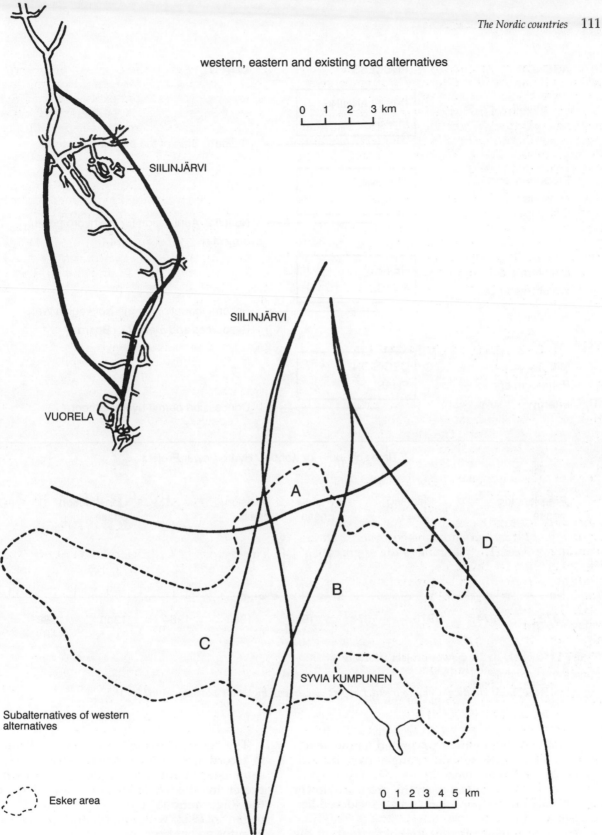

western, eastern and existing road alternatives

0   1   2   3 km

SIILINJÄRVI

SIILINJÄRVI

VUORELA

A

D

B

C

SYVIA KUMPUNEN

Subalternatives of western
alternatives

Esker area

0 1 2 3 4 5 km

Map 1 Highway Five, Finland: Alternative routes
(Source: UN ECE, *Application of environmental impact assessment: highways and dams*, 1987, p.84)

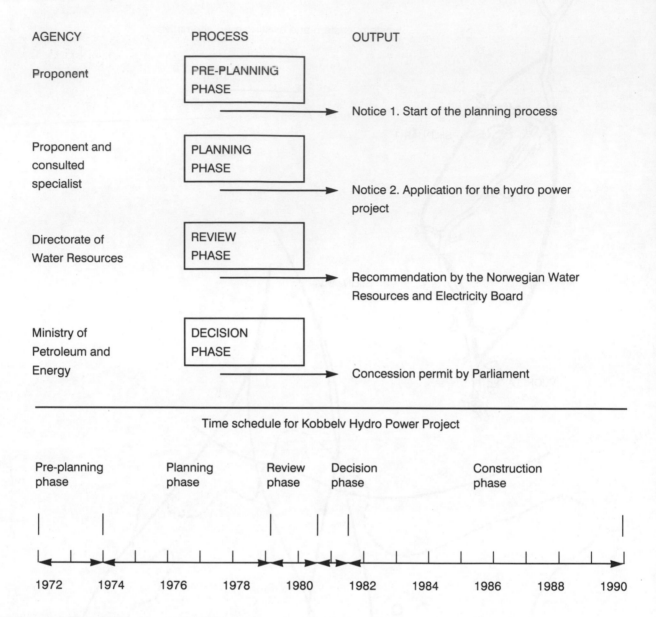

Figure 13 Kobbelv hydro power project, Norway
Phases and schedule
(Source: UN ECE, *Application of environmental impact assessment: highways and dams*, 1987, p. 182)

In 1981, the proponent presented a new development plan with several changes over the original. These changes were:
• exclusion of what had been the proposed 'lower fall' section of the project, now considered less economic;
• a related power plant at Reinoksvatnet, in the original concept, would not be built;
• the water level in the reservoir would be lowered 5 metres;
• the generating capacity in the Kobbelv plant would be increased from 270 MW to 300 MW.

The decision by the Norwegian parliament was in accordance with the revised scheme. However, some participants had argued unsuccessfully for preserving the whole area through enlargement of the Rago national park. The construction phase began in 1982, with completion in 1990. Careful monitoring has been necessary.

(Derived from UN ECE, *Application of environmental impact assessment: highways and dams*, 1987)

CHAPTER 8

North America

8.1 Canada

One of the largest countries, Canada, has a population of 27.7 million, and one of the lowest population densities, 3 people per square kilometre; however, the population is highly urbanised. Almost 90 per cent of the country is uninhabited.

Proximity to the immense US market and a wealth of natural resources have contributed greatly to Canada's well-being. The province of Ontario has the largest manufacturing base and agricultural sector, a population of 10 million and 40 per cent of the national gross domestic product (GDP).

Responsibility for environment protection and nature conservation in Canada is shared by the federal and provincial governments; the municipal governments have powers assigned to them at the discretion of the provincial legislatures. The federal government and most of the 10 provinces have created departments of the environment; all have created advisory bodies.

The Department of the Environment (Environment Canada) was created at the federal level in 1971; it has an overall responsibility for protecting the country's environment and natural resources. The department absorbed the functions of several other federal bodies for the environment. Environment Canada is organised into seven services: the environmental protection service develops and enforces environmental regulations, guidelines, codes, and protocols introduced under federal legislation for air and water pollution, solid waste management, and resource recovery, noise, contaminants, and EIA. The service liaises with provincial agencies, industry, other federal agencies, and the general public. Checklist 8.1 indicates the evolution of environmental management in Canada since 1868.

EIA

In December 1973, the federal cabinet decided to adopt an EIA and review process for projects initiated by federal departments and agencies, or those for which federal funds are allocated, or which involve federal property. Projects thought likely to have significant environmental effects were to be referred to an EA panel, established within the-then Department of the Environment. In special cases, the Minister of the Environment could establish an environmental review board outside the federal public service to carry out a formal review. The minister would then review the final assessment with the minister of the initiating agency; in the event of disagreement over the measures to be adopted the matter could be referred to cabinet for decision. The Federal Environmental Assessment Review Office (FEARO) was also established. Located in Ottawa, this agency undertakes the coordination of the process.

In 1984, the federal government issued EA and review process (EARP) guidelines which superseded the earlier cabinet decisions. Further change was contemplated. These guidelines indicated two phases: an initial assessment phase based on self-assessment; and the public review stage held by an independent EA panel. The initial assessment phase helps ensure that the environmental implications of an activity are considered early on in planning, and helps determine when a complete EIA and public review is necessary. FEARO has prepared a policy document, the initial assessment guide, to help federal agencies with their internal procedures.

All federal agencies must develop environmental screening procedures, which are incorporated in their normal decision-making process. Exclusion lists have been prepared which specifically exempt

---

CHECKLIST 8.1

Canada: evolution of environmental management

1868   Fisheries Act.

1909   Boundary Waters Treaty (USA–Canada).

1946   Atomic Energy Control Act.

1957   Fertilisers Act.

1970   Canada Water Act; Canada Shipping Act; Fisheries Act; Northern Inland Waters Act; National Parks Act.

1971   Clean Air Act; Department of Environment (Environment Canada) established.

1972   Great Lakes Water Quality Agreement (USA–Canada); Ministry of the Environment (Environment Ontario) established; Pest Control Products Act.

1973   Federal Environmental Assessment Review Office (FEARO) established.

1975   Environmental Contaminants Act; Ocean Dumping Control Act; Environmental Assessment Act (Ontario).

1980   Memorandum of Intent on Transboundary Air Pollution (USA–Canada).

1985   Amendments to the Canada Water Act, Clean Air Act, Canada Shipping Act, Fisheries Act, Northern Inland Waters Act, Pest Control Products Act, Environmental Contaminants Act.

1989   Environmental Protection Act.

1992   Canadian Environmental Assessment Act; creation of Canadian Environmental Assessment Agency.

---

particular activities of no environmental significance. If a project is not on an exclusion list, then it must be screened for its potential environmental impacts.

The relevant federal agency must come to one of the following decisions:
- the project has no environmental impacts, or has impacts which can be readily mitigated; the project may proceed;
- the likely impacts of the project, or ways to mitigate those impacts, are inadequately known and further study is needed; after this the project may be rescreened;
- the environmental impacts of the project are unacceptable; the project must be modified or abandoned;
- the project has potentially significant environmental impacts and might be an object of public concern; it must be referred by the initiating minister to the minister of the environment for a review by an independent EA panel.

The results of all screening decisions needed to be submitted in summary form to FEARO for publication in the *Bulletin of Initial Assessment Decisions*. The related documents also had to be available for scrutiny by the affected public. There have been panel reviews for: major harbour and airport developments; hydroelectric dams; offshore drilling; oil and gas pipelines; major highways and railways; nuclear power stations; uranium refinery projects; and mining and industrial developments; proposals that compete with existing land-use and water-use policy; proposals in ecologically sensitive areas; threats to agriculture, fishing, and other traditional methods of food production; and threats to the national heritage.

Until 1992, the federal EARP derived its authority from an Order-in-Council. This authority was superseded by the Canadian Environmental Assessment Act. The Act maintains most of the fundamental features of EARP, providing a sound legal basis for EIA. FEARO has been succeeded by the Canadian Environmental Assessment Agency (CEAA).

The Act requires that EAs will have to address need, alternatives, cumulative effects, and resource sustainability. The scope for public participation has widened and improved with greater emphasis on the effectiveness of public reviews. The environment minister's powers are enhanced for initiating public reviews, including joint public reviews with other jurisdictions. The new agency must report annually to the ministry on the process.

Apart from the Act, the Canadian cabinet has also ruled that all memoranda to cabinet (MCs) shall be accompanied by an EA. Thus all policy decisions by the Canadian federal government are subject to EIA.

To harmonise these new measures with those of other jurisdictions, negotiations began in 1993 with provincial and territorial administrations and with leaders of the emerging native self-government bodies.

The Canadian provinces derive their authority to carry out EIA from a variety of legal bases. Manitoba initially established an EARP by cabinet directive in 1975. New Brunswick adopted a similar policy in the same year, and Ontario passed specific EA legislation. Saskatchewan and Newfoundland followed suit in 1980. Earlier, in 1978, Quebec amended its Environmental Quality Act to allow for EIA. British Columbia supplemented the EIA procedures within existing statutes through the passage of the Environmental Management Act, 1981. Generally speaking, the provincial procedures and the federal procedures are similar, involving the stages described above.

8.2 United States of America (USA)

The population of the USA is about 255.5 million, with a density of 27 people per square kilometre of which 75 per cent is urban, and 25 per cent is rural.

In the USA, a federal republic, responsibility for environment protection and conservation is shared among the federal government and the 50 states. The federal government's role is not confined to matters of narrowly construed federal interest; it embraces a national leadership, standard-setting, target-formulating function. Coupled with the influence of federal funding in specific areas, direct responsibility for a large and important system of national parks and reserves, and regulatory control under, for example, the National Environmental Policy Act (NEPA), 1969, the federal role has more control than other federal systems, for instance, Germany and Canada where federal governments enjoy positive roles, and considerably more so than in Australia where the states remain supreme about many environment matters in their jurisdictions. Environmental concerns in the USA can be traced back through the decades to the clean-up campaigns in Pittsburg ('darkness at noon') and St Louis, and the protracted campaign against photochemical smog in Los Angeles (see glossary). Conflicts about national parks and natural resource conservation date back to the nineteenth century.

Since the 1970s, in the USA, pollution control, environment protection and conservation policies have become more vigorous than in previous years. See checklist 8.2. The US Environmental Protection Agency (EPA) was created as an independent agency in 1970, with a mandate to mount an integrated, coordinated attack on environmental pollution with state and local governments. The EPA became responsible for the federal programs for air and water pollution abatement, solid and toxic waste disposal, pesticide registration, setting radiation standards, and noise control; it is also responsible for the emerging policy of EIA. The agency also undertakes enforcement procedures.

NEPA created the EPA and the Council on Environmental Quality (CEQ). The CEQ was authorised to issue regulations to ensure the effectiveness of EISs and to reduce unnecessary paperwork. See figure 14.

EIA procedures

The CEQ held public hearings during 1977 on how the EIA procedures would work more efficiently. Regulations introduced set criteria for the preparation of EISs and the establishment of better procedures. The objective of CEQ is that EISs are concise, readable, and based upon competent professional analysis. The rules came into force in 1979. See checklist 8.3.

CHECKLIST 8.2

USA: evolution of environmental management

1872 Creation of Yellowstone national park.

1899 Refuse Act.

1908 State of the Union Message by President Theodore Roosevelt on the need for the conservation of natural resources.

1935 Historic Sites, Buildings and Antiquities Act.

1940 Bald and Golden Eagle Protection Act.

1946 Start of Pittsburgh clean-up.

1947 Los Angeles anti-smog program launched; Federal Insecticide, Fungicide and Rodenticide Act.

1948 Federal Water Pollution Control Act.

1956 Water Pollution Control Act re-enacted as a permanent measure; Fish and Wildlife Act.

1962 *Silent Spring* published by Rachel Carson; White House Conservation Conference.

1963 Federal Clean Air Act.

1964 Wilderness Act; National wilderness preservation system.

1965 Federal Water Quality Act; Solid Waste Disposal Act; further Clean Air Act; Anadromous Fish Conservation Act.

1966 EIA policy established; Clean Water Restoration Act; National Historic Preservation Act.

1967 Federal Air Quality Act.

1968 National Trails System Act; Wild and Scenic Rivers Act.

1969 National Environmental Policy Act; Council on Environmental Policy appointed.

1970 US Environmental Protection Agency (EPA) created; Environmental Quality Improvement Act; Water Quality Improvement Act; Clean Air Amendment Act; Mining and Minerals Policy Act.

1972 Noise Control Act; Coastal Zone Management Act; Clean Water Act; Marine Mammal Protection Act.

1973 Endangered Species Act.

1974 Safe Drinking Water Act; Solar Energy Research, Development and Demonstration Act.

1975 Energy Policy and Conservation Act.

1976 Toxic Substances Control Act; Resource Conservation and Recovery Act; Magnusan Fishery Conservation and Management Act; National Forest Management Act; Federal Land Policy and Management Act.

1977 Environmental impact procedures strengthened; Clean Water Act; Clean Air Amendment Act; Surface Mining Control and Reclamation Act; Soil and Water Resources Conservation Act; President's environmental message.

1978 EIA regulations promulgated; Renewable Resources Extension Act; Public Rangelands Improvement Act; Surface Mining Control and Reclamation Act; Cooperative Forestry Assistance Act; National Energy Conservation Policy Act; Solar Photovoltaic Research, Development and Demonstration Act; Uranium Mill Tailings Radiation Control Act; National Ocean Pollution Planning Act.

1979 Introduction by the US Environmental Protection Agency (EPA) of the 'bubble concept' for the management of pollution.

1980 Alaska National Interest Lands Conservation Act; Comprehensive Environmental Response, Compensation and Liability Act (Superfund); Wind Energy Systems Act; Low-level Radioactive Waste Policy Act; Act to Prevent Pollution from Ships.

1982 Coastal Barrier Resources Act; Reclamation Reform Act; Asbestos-in-schools rule; Nuclear Waste Policy Act.

1983 Times Beach found to be too contaminated with dioxins for human habitation.

1985 International Security and Development Act.

1986 Emergency Wetlands Resources Act; Right-to-Know Act.

1987 Water Quality Act; Driftnet Impact Monitoring, Assessment and Control Act.

1988 Ocean Dumping Ban Act.

1989 First nationwide survey of more than 320 toxic chemicals released to air by industry; tanker *Exxon Valdez* aground in Alaska; North American Wetlands Conservation Act; Marine Pollution and Research and Control Act.

1990 Clean Air Act to substantially reduce air emissions; California Air Resources Board introduces strictest vehicle-emission controls ever; Coastal Wetlands Planning, Protection and Restoration Act; Coastal Barrier Improvement Act; Oil Pollution Act; Food Security Act; Pollution Prevention Act; Antarctic Protection Act; Global Change Research Act.

1991 US signs UN ECE convention on EIA in a transboundary context.

1992 US Congress to mandate the analysis of the environmental effects of major US federal actions abroad.

(Derived from *United States of America national report to the United Nations conference on environment and development 1992*, Council on Environmental Quality [CEQ], Washington, DC, USA, and several other sources)

CHECKLIST 8.3

USA: contents of an EIS

1 Cover sheet

2 Executive summary, to describe in sufficient detail (10 to 15 pages) the critical facets of the EIS so that the reader can become familiar with the proposed project or action and its net effects, the alternatives and major conclusions.

3 Table of contents.

4 Purpose and need for the action.

5 Alternatives considered by the applicant (proponent), including the do-nothing alternative. The applicant's (proponent's) preferred alternative shall be identified. There must be a balanced description of each alternative.

6 The affected environment. The affected environment on which the evaluation of each alternative was based to include such matters as hydrology, geology, air quality, noise, biology, socio-economics, energy, land use, archaeology, and history. The total impacts of each alternative shall be presented for easy comparison.

7 Coordination. Full consideration must be given to the objections and suggestions made by local, state, and federal agencies, by individual citizens and environmental groups. The results of public participation through public meetings or scoping meetings shall also be included. A list of persons, agencies, and organisations, to whom copies of the EIS have been sent shall be included.

8 List of preparers of the EIS, and their qualifications. Persons responsible for a particular analysis shall be identified.

9 Index, commensurate with the complexity of the EIS.

10 Appendixes.

11 Material incorporated into an EIS by reference shall be included in a supplemental information document, available for review on request.

12 The format used for EISs shall encourage good analysis and clear presentation of alternatives, including the proposed action, and their environmental, economic, and social impacts.

13 The text of a final EIS shall normally be less than 150 pages, and for proposals of unusual scope or complexity shall normally be less than 300 pages.

14 EISs shall be written in plain language with readily understood graphics.

(Derived from NEPA and EPA (US) regulations and procedures, 1991)

One of the most significant innovations in the NEPA regulations is a process known as 'scoping'. When an agency decides that an EIS is necessary, it takes prompt action to identify those issues that require full analysis, and separate them from less significant matters that do not require so much detailed study. To ensure effective coordination, affected federal, state, and local agencies, and all interested members of the public are invited to participate in this scoping process. Pubic participation is a cornerstone of the NEPA process. See also Scoping, 2.3.

The NEPA process is made up of an evaluation of the environmental effects of a federal undertaking, and its alternatives. There are three levels of analysis: an undertaking might be excluded from detailed analysis as having no significant environmental impact; at the second level, a federal agency prepares a written EA to establish whether the undertaking might significantly affect the environment; and at the third level, if the EA reveals that the consequences might be significant, an EIS is prepared. If the EA reveals that, in fact, there is no significant impact, a finding of no significant impact (FONSI) will be issued.

During the latter half of the 1980s, about 450 draft and final EISs were prepared annually on proposed federal actions; during the same period, between 10 000 and 20 000 EAs were prepared annually (Economic Commission for Europe, 1991).

Following the passage of NEPA, which only applies to federal proposals, a number of states introduced laws to take into account the environmental effects of state actions.

The systems implemented by states, modelled on NEPA, became frequently known as 'little NEPAS' (NEPAs) though they varied a great deal in their legal basis, administration, and requirements. By 1992, 19 states, the District of Columbia and Puerto Rico, had enacted 'little NEPAS'. Some

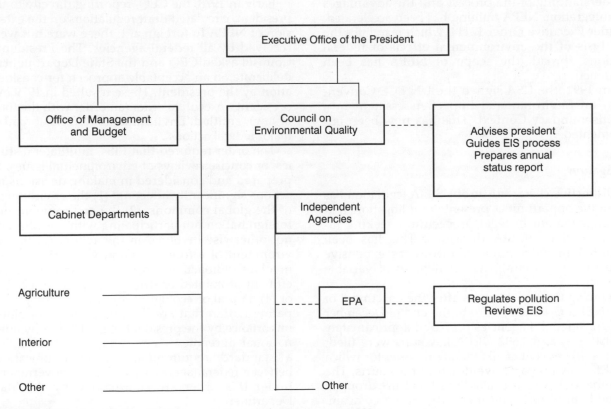

Figure 14 USA: organisation chart for environmental management, 1992

states, such as California, New York, and Washington, have established vigorous EIA systems, supported by comprehensive regulations and active judicial enforcement. Other states have systems that apply to a narrower range of activities, appearing to be less dynamic in their relationship with state decision-making (United States of America, 1992).

Recently, there has been a fresh surge of interest in the establishment of 'little NEPAS'. In 1986, the Montana Environmental Quality Council held a conference focusing on Montana's EIA process. In 1987, the CEQ co-sponsored with the Environmental Law Section of the New York State Bar Association, a conference focusing on the preparation and review of EISs at both the state and federal levels. The state of Washington undertook a major revision of its Environmental Protection Act in 1988, and, in 1989 the Council of the District of Columbia passed its first 'little NEPA' law. Also in 1989, the governor of New Jersey revised the state's executive order governing the New Jersey EIA process. Other states such as Michigan and Maine have their EIA procedures under review.

As NEPA enters into its third decade, there has been emphasis on improving compliance with the Act and addressing new environmental issues through this mechanism. The CEQ and the EPA have conducted workshops to promote a better understanding of the process and the advantages of integration. NEPA training has been accelerated. Under Executive Order 12114, which mandates the analysis of the environmental effects of federal actions abroad, the scope of NEPA has been widened.

In 1991, the USA signed the UN ECE Convention on Environmental Impact Assessment in a Transboundary Context. This has now been implemented.

Litigation

A distinctive characteristic of US EIA legislation has been the opportunities presented for litigation, that is, engagement in legal proceedings seeking judicial review of EIA decisions. This has been avoided in most other countries, as expensive and time-consuming, with outcomes of variable character.

During the first 13 years after the enactment of the NEPA (1 January 1970 to the end of December 1982), 70 federal agencies prepared approximately 16 000 EISs and 1 602 NEPA law suits were filed; that is, 10 per cent of all federal proposals for which an EIS was prepared went before the courts. The number of law suits peaked in 1974 at 189, dropped steadily until 1982, and then cases increased again. By 1987, the incidence of litigation had still not returned to the lower levels reached in the late 1970s (Kennedy, 1987).

These actions, often taken by US citizen action groups, were often based upon an assertion that an EIS had not been adequately prepared. Such actions were assisted by the US Freedom of Information Act, whereby American citizens have access to all planning documents. One of the outcomes is that recommendations and guidelines published by the US EPA, the CEQ, federal and state bodies, have tended to become embodied in law through court decisions.

EIA and foreign aid

The requirement of the US that all federal agencies prepare an EIS on 'major actions significantly affecting the quality of the human environment' immediately raised the question as to whether this applied to the action of providing foreign aid to countries outside US legal jurisdiction.

In 1975, the US Agency for International Development was sued by a public interest group to enforce the preparation of EISs on its loans and grants to other countries. As a consequence of this lawsuit the agency, in 1976, introduced a process of EIA on many of the projects with which it has been involved. Later, the US Export–Import Bank and the State Department were sued on similar issues.

Early in 1978, the CEQ, reporting directly to the president, circulated draft regulations on the extension of NEPA to foreign aid; these were not well-received by all federal agencies. The President's Counsel asked CEQ and the State Department to deliberate on an acceptable approach for consideration by the president. These resulted in 1979 in a president's executive order (an order with the force of law), entitled 'Environmental effects abroad of major federal actions'.

The order required that EISs, multilateral studies, or concise reviews of environmental issues, be prepared and considered in making decisions for actions significantly affecting: (1) the environment of the global commons; (2) the environment of a foreign nation not participating with the USA and not otherwise involved in the action; (3) the environment of a foreign nation when the activity involves radioactive substances or an emission of effluent prohibited or strictly regulated by US law; or (4) natural or ecological resources in the participating nation that are designated to be of global importance by the president of the USA or by international agreement. For category (1) an EIS is a standard requirement. All communications between federal agencies and foreign governments under this order are coordinated by the State Department.

Particular activities largely about national

security and arms transfers are exempted from this order. This is, however, consistent with the statement of objective of the order which is 'to further environmental objectives consistent with the foreign policy and national security policy of the United States'. Actions not having a significant effect on the environment, as determined by the involved agency, are also exempt.

8A   Case study: Banff national park, Canada: upgrading of Trans Canada Highway (TCH)

Banff national park is in south-western Alberta, Canada. Established in 1885 as the nation's first national park, it is located on the eastern slopes of the Rocky Mountains and embraces several large icefields and glacial lakes; by contrast, the area also contains numerous hot mineral springs. Originally only 26 square kilometres, Banff national park is now 6640 square kilometres. The park's vegetation includes flower-covered alpine meadows. The fauna include bears, elk, deer, moose, wild sheep, and goats. The great influx of visitors has created maintenance difficulties; rather than a strict conservation area it has become more of a recreation area.

The route of the Trans Canada highway (TCH) runs through this national park; indeed such routeing has been consistent with national parks policy. The highway was established in 1960. As early as 1972, discussions and preliminary studies began on the possibility of expanding the existing 2-lane TCH into a 4-lane limited access highway. The proposal was highly contentious and further work was delayed for a number of years. The upgrading was intended to apply to the 27-kilometre stretch through the national park area.

In 1978, however, a FEARO panel was appointed to review the environmental consequences of the Banff project; guidelines were issued for the preparation of an EIS. In the EIS the proponent, Public Works Canada, discussed several alternatives to twinning (that is, the construction of an additional two lanes) and provided a detailed environmental comparison for alternative feasible routeings. These are shown in figure 15; however, this EIS was confined to the first phase only, another EIS is required for the second phase.

The initial EIS was placed on public exhibition and advertised, with requests for comments; summaries of the EIS were sent directly to all those who had indicated interest. There were 15 written submissions received and these were circulated by the panel to the interested parties, before holding public meetings. During these public meetings, the panel and all participants had the opportunity for a period of questions and answers and to make short statements after each presentation. Representatives of the media were present at all public meetings. At the end of this process there had been 50 presentations and the proponent had submitted additional material, particularly for measures to address concerns about wildlife and erosion. Transcripts of the proceedings, over 1000 pages, were made available through FEARO.

As there were two EISs to cover the whole route, the consultation process was repeated.

The report of the EA panel concluded that: (1) the need for the additional highway capacity had been clearly demonstrated; (2) there were no viable alternatives to the project as proposed that would reduce negative environmental impacts; (3) the proposal was compatible with national, provincial, regional, and national park plans, and policies; (4) the proposed project could be constructed and operated with acceptable environmental disturbance, and; (5) the residual overall environmental impact of the proposed project would not be significantly detrimental.

The recommendation that the project could proceed was tempered by a number of conditions: the main condition of approval was a need for underpasses and overpasses and fencing to isolate the highway from ungulates (hoofed animals) and Chinaman's Creek had to be realigned. Also careful attention was needed in the design and construction of the extension to ensure that the project resulted in an aesthetically pleasing highway, consistent with park values.

The panel recommended that: a special committee be established to ensure the implementation of the mitigation and enhancement measures and those already identified in the EISs; an environmental coordinator be designated for the project to serve as a day-to-day contact for park wardens and other inspectors, and to ensure that operations were carried out using good environmental practices. Road construction proceeded and was completed in 1986.

The follow-up study indicated that coordination had been fairly successful in ensuring an environmentally sensitive design, with only minor disturbances during construction. The realignment of Chinaman's Creek had been successful, and measures to re-vegetate the disturbed areas had been undertaken. Mitigation had reduced vehicle and wildlife accidents.

(Derived from FEARO and UN ECE, *Application of Environmental Impact Assessment: Highways and Dams*, New York, 1987)

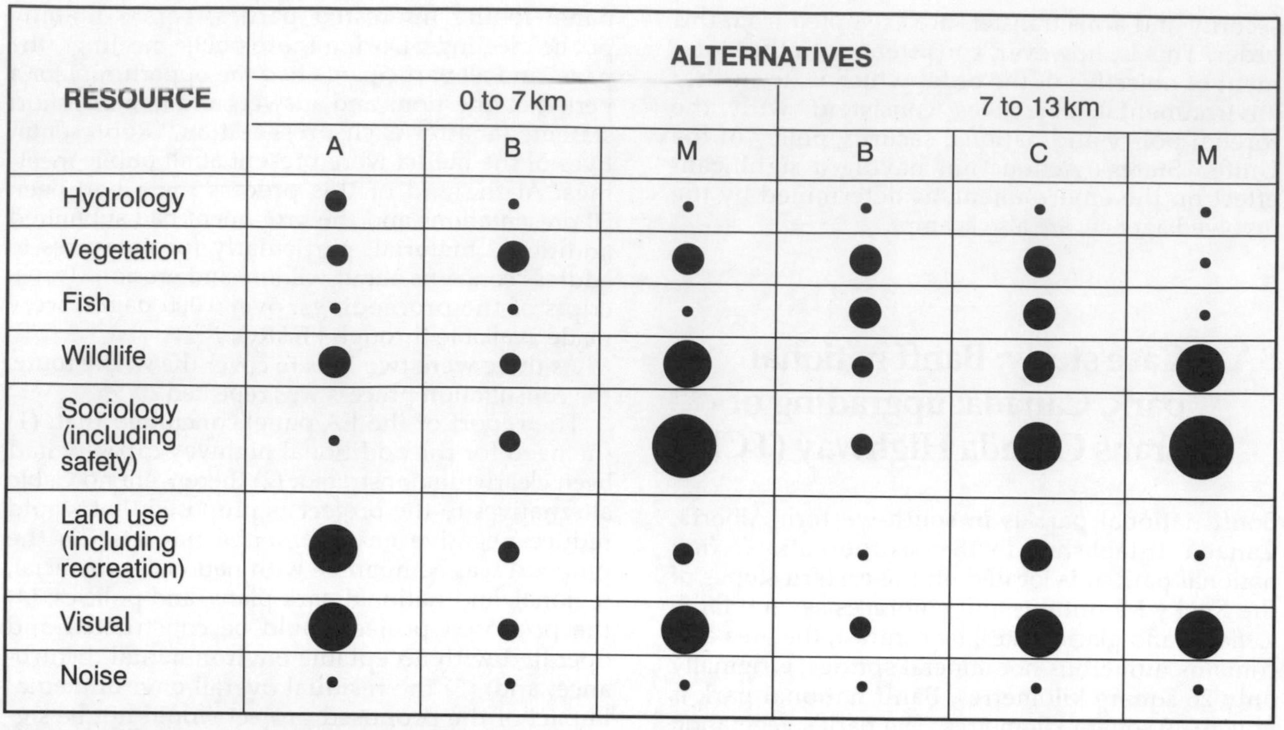

RESOURCE	ALTERNATIVES					
	0 to 7 km			7 to 13 km		
	A	B	M	B	C	M
Hydrology	●	·	·	·	·	·
Vegetation	●	●	●	●	●	·
Fish	·	·	·	●	●	·
Wildlife	●	·	●	·	●	●
Sociology (including safety)	·	·	●		●	●
Land use (including recreation)	●	·	·	·	●	·
Visual	●	·	●	·	●	●
Noise	·	·	·	·	·	·

Note: The larger the circle the more adverse the impact.
Alternative B is the preferred route.

ALTERNATIVE SCHEMES IN PRESENT CORRIDOR

Scheme	Description
0 km – 7 km	
A	Parallel to railway
B	Parallel to existing highway — wide median
C	Parallel to existing highway — barrier median
7 km – 13 km	
C	Moving the railway — new east-bound lanes on old railway line
B	Parallel to existing highway on north side — minimum median
M	Parallel to existing highway — barrier median

Figure 15 Banff national park: comparison of environmental impacts of alternative schemes

(Source: FEARO and UN ECE, *Application of environmental impact assessment: highways and dams*, New York, 1987, p. 67)

8B   Case study: Beaufort sea hydrocarbons project, Canada

From 1980 to 1984, the Canadian government carried out an environmental review of proposed oil and gas development in the Beaufort sea, in the western Canadian Arctic. In addition to substantial new investment, the development is likely to create 24 000 new jobs by the year 2000. The natural environment was largely unknown, hostile and fragile, and home to 30 000 people including many Inuit communities.

At the time of the review, the proposal was only at the conceptual stage, but it had the potential to introduce industrial and commercial activity on such a scale that could change forever the frontier nature of the land and its people.

Conducted under the provisions of the Canadian federal environmental assessment and review process (EARP) and the review, undertaken by an EA panel of 7 was to embrace the economic, developmental, technological, social, cultural, and environmental impacts.

The assessment team travelled throughout the

Arctic region and held consultations with 29 potentially affected communities (including indigenous peoples) over the 3 years of the review. The main recommendations of the panel were that there should be:

- a phased development of 'small' projects carefully controlled and monitored;
- no use of ice-breaking tankers at the current stage of knowledge;
- a progressively improved government administration system capable of ensuring safe transport by tankers and able to manage the social stresses and strains created.

The panel concluded that the local peoples should be able to manage the effects of the changes, while deriving long-term benefit from the development; and the degree of risk to renewable resources should prove acceptable to the northerners.

The panel also developed innovative procedures since accepted as procedures under EARP, which included:

- detailed rules of a non-adversarial character for the public hearings to follow;
- technical specialists to be available to all participants;
- publication of all material made available to the panel;
- public funding for groups with legitimate interests and a view to express.

The Beaufort sea panel review was deemed a success, the outcome became a blueprint for development, illustrating the value of early public participation; and it stressed that inadequacy of data can dictate a multi-stage EIA process.

(Derived from Department of the Arts, Sport, the Environment, Tourism and Territories, *Environmental impact assessment as a management tool: workshop proceedings*, November, DASETT, Canberra, Australia, 1987, pp. 39-40)

8C Case study: Wastewater treatment facilities, Everett, Washington, USA

The city of Everett is the seat of Snohomish County, north-western Washington on Puget Sound. Settled in 1862, it was initially promoted as a manufacturing centre, later exploiting local timber and agricultural resources. Its landlocked harbour has been developed as a cargo and commercial fishing port. The population of the metropolitan area is about 1.6 million.

In 1982, the city began to examine options for expanding its wastewater treatment facilities on Smith Island in the lower Snohomish river basin.

The preferred alternative was an expansion of the existing diked lagoon system into a wetland and the disposal of sludge on-site. It was anticipated that the city would apply to the federal government for a construction grant under the Clean Water Act, linked with an application under that Act for a dredge-and-fill permit.

In these circumstances, the US Environmental Protection Agency and the US Army Corps of Engineers requested the city to re-evaluate alternatives so that both agencies could ensure compliance with the requirements of the NEPA. The state's own Department of Ecology also needed further evaluation of alternatives to meet the requirements of the state's Environmental Policy Act.

Three environmental issues were of principal concern: (1) the effects of inundating and diking 30 hectares of wetland located in a 100-year flood plain near a major river that supports anadromous fisheries; (2) the potential impact of sludge disposal within such an area; and (3) the recurring violations of water discharge permit conditions at the existing plant. In addition, the project required coastal zone consistency approval.

Extensive consultations and negotiations took place among several agencies both at federal and state level; throughout the process, public meetings were held achieving significant input from the public. This wide consultation process resulted in substantial changes to the city's plan.

A new treatment and disposal alternative was selected that would affect only about 5 hectares, 3 hectares of which are wetland. This alternative would allow for an improved operating system with higher capacity. The facility was re-designed in compliance with federal flood insurance regulations. The city also selected a new method of sludge disposal by composting, with a later land application on off-site silvicultural or agricultural areas.

The revised plan reduced the negative effects on the environment; met water-discharge permit conditions; and was far more acceptable to the public. The adverse effects on the wetland area were mitigated by reclamation and enhancement of 5.3 hectares of disturbed wetland in the proximity, which satisfied resource agency concerns. The resolution of these issues enabled both the EPA and the Corps of Engineers to complete their EAs and to determine that the final project would not result in significant impact to the environment. The EPA (US) issued a FONSI (finding of no significant impact), and a construction grant was awarded to the city of Everett in 1988.

(Derived from CEQ and the USA national report to the UN Conference on Environment and Development, Rio de Janeiro, 1992).

8D   Case study: Wheeling Creek dam, West Virginia, USA

The Wheeling Creek watershed plan was authorised by the US Congress in 1966, in response to local political concern that the seasonal and flash flooding of the city of Wheeling from the overflow of Wheeling Creek should be reduced. Flood damage in Wheeling and adjacent suburban areas had been a frequent occurrence, damaging residences, businesses, roads, and bridges.

The plan originally included 6 floodwater retarding dams and a flood protection and recreation dam. The major beneficiary of the 7 dams was the city of Wheeling, located in the northern panhandle of West Virginia and several kilometres downstream.

By 1977, 5 of the 7 dams had been built, providing more than 60 per cent of flood protection. The proposal to build the remaining 2 dams, in Enlow Fork Valley and in Dunkard Fork Valley, both in Pennsylvania, provided controversy. There was concern at the possible effects of the former on natural resources, and of the possible impacts of the latter on cultural and social resources.

Opposition focused on the proposal to impound Enlow Fork and substantially increase the original planned pool to provide a water supply for a steel company wanting to begin coalmining in the valley. The EPA (US), the US Fish and Wildlife Service, the Pennsylvania Fish and Game Commissions, and local citizen groups, opposed any type of wet dam impoundment. Environmental impacts — and failure to establish the need for the project or to assess alternatives were views expressed.

The draft EIS prepared and released in 1979 was followed by further studies by the Soil Conservation Service with federal, state, and local agencies, voluntary organisations, and individuals. A second EIS was completed in 1982, after thorough review of the original proposal.

The outcome decided by the Wheeling Creek Watershed Commission was the construction of a single-purpose flood control dam on the Enlow Fork of Wheeling Creek; that is, a dry dam with no permanent pool of water impounded behind it. This would not have significant adverse impacts on water quality, air quality, archaeological or historic sites, the deer wintering area, wetlands, or any threatened or endangered species. The proposed multi-purpose dam on Dunkard Fork was eliminated from the program.

The Enlow Fork dam would be carefully monitored. There would be an evaluation of the effect of flood waters on aquatic and terrestrial resources. Close consultation with a landscape architect would help to blend the dam and spillway into its surroundings.

Scoping meetings and a public hearing on the draft EIS were held. The EIS was distributed to all interested parties of which government agencies, 13 public interest organisations, 4 private corporations, and 45 individuals were involved. That the EIS was available to the public was advertised through the media. All comments were considered in the final EIS, and summarised in an appendix.

(Derived from UN ECE, *Application of environmental impact assessment: highways and dams*, 1987)

8E   Case study: Franconia Notch Highway, New Hampshire, USA

Franconia Notch is a scenic pass between the peaks of the Franconia (east) and Kinsman (west) ranges in the White mountains, north-western New Hampshire. The area has a number of striking features and was dedicated a state park in 1925. The project proposed by the New Hampshire Department of Public Works and Highways and the United States Highway Administration (also the competent authorities to agree to the works) involved the construction of a highway to complete the interstate highway system in the White mountains region; of 18 kilometres through this important recreation and tourism area.

The proposed interstate highway was to replace an existing 2-lane highway, which was then considered insufficient to meet traffic needs. Almost half the projected traffic would be park visitors. A route through the park had been selected in 1958, but the concern about the possibility of landslides, damage to park scenery, and adverse impacts on recreation in the park with its many unique geological formations led to the proposal being deferred.

In 1973 the US Congress passed legislation allowing approval of a highway through Franconia Notch state park, with design standards to protect the environment. Work began in 1974 on the EIS, the content of which followed federal guidelines. In the draft EIS, several alternative routes were described as well as several alternative roadway configurations. The final EIS identified the preferred route and described the selected design concept.

A 4-lane expressway was proposed outside the park boundary; within the park, a 4-lane parkway with grass shoulders was proposed, tapering to a 2-lane undivided parkway in the most environmentally sensitive areas of the park. Access was provided to specific recreational areas. Mitigation measures were also described in detail: to follow ground contours as much as possible; to lower the speed limit; to minimise changes to streams and drainage patterns; to provide noise abatement measures where needed; and to control soil erosion during construction.

Throughout the development of the draft EIS and for many years before, there was great public interest in the proposal. During 1974, an intensive program of public involvement was undertaken. The EIS project team worked with interest groups and the local communities potentially affected. Public information meetings were held and the public were kept further informed through press statements and newsletters mailed directly. Comments were received from 200 agencies, local government bodies, interest groups, and individuals. Much interest was taken in the Franconia Notch and the geological feature, the Old Man of the Mountain. Most people favoured building in the Franconia Notch Corridor.

The final EIS was prepared by the state in cooperation with the Federal Highway Administration; and then submitted for review by the federal Office of the Secretary of Transportation. The EIS was approved in early 1979. Construction did not begin until 1984. The work was subject to monitoring.

(Derived from UN ECE, *Application of environmental impact assessment; highways and dams*, 1987)

8F   Case study: The Great Lakes ecosystem

Canada and the USA share an aquatic ecosystem which contains the largest area of fresh water, outside the polar icecaps; the Great Lakes comprise 20 per cent of the world's fresh water supply. About 30 million people live within the catchment area, which covers 767 500 square kilometres. The Great Lakes have had a major role in the development of both countries for shipping, as a major source of water for industrial processes and for drinking water, a source of commercial fishing, and an invaluable recreational resource. The Great Lakes offer a rich and diverse biological community.

However, by the twentieth century, immense tracts of forest had been cleared around the shores of the Great Lakes, overfishing had devastated the natural fisheries, and waterborne diseases such as typhoid and cholera had become a scourge in the lakeside human communities. The problem was aggravated through the further devastation of the fisheries by the coarse sea lamprey, nutrient overloading from agricultural and human wastes, and the introduction of toxic pollutants such as mercury and petroleum residues. By the mid-1960s, Lake Erie was considered dead, as a consequence of eutrophication; while the Cuyahoga river caught fire from heavy pollution by oil and flammable wastes. DDT and other pesticides were decimating wildlife populations.

In 1972, the Great Lakes Water Quality Agreement was signed by Canada and the USA to clean up the pollution of the Great Lakes, particularly lakes Erie and Ontario. The agreement was amended in 1978 and 1987. There was a massive public works program to construct municipal sewage treatment facilities, to be completed by 1983. There are specified targets to limit toxic substances such as arsenic, cadmium, chromium, copper, iron, lead, mercury, nickel, selenium, zinc, fluoride, and phosphorous discharge; and to limit 9 categories of organic pesticides. The industrial pollution control program was to be completed by 1985. The agreement introduced an annual public inventory of discharges and pollution control requirements, with an improved monitoring and surveillance system for water and airborne pollutants in the Great Lakes.

More than 1 000 sewage treatment plants along the shores and tributaries of the Great Lakes have been improved or replaced since 1983. In all, significant progress has been made in restoring the ecological integrity of the Great Lakes since the 1970s. Populations of predatory birds are once again present throughout the basin. Fires no longer occur on Great Lakes waterways!

However, significant problems remain: continued loss of habitat, the introduction of non-beneficial exotic fish species, the presence of persistent bio-accumulative toxic chemicals, and contaminated sediments. Airborne pollutants have been identified as one of the most significant sources of toxic pollutants. A sustained integrated approach is necessary at the federal, provincial, state and local government levels. Formally designated Areas of Concern will be subject to the development and implementation of Remedial Action Plans. Lakeside management plans are being developed for each of the Great Lakes. PPA is imperative, following a whole range of control projects.

(Derived from CEQ, and other sources)

CHAPTER 9

Asia and the Pacific

9.1 Australia

Australia has a population of 17.6 million, and one of the lowest densities, with 2 people per square kilometre. Most settlements are urban, making up about 87 per cent, and about 13 per cent in rural areas. As much of the continent is arid or semi-arid, most settlement is along the coastal fringes.

Australia is a federation of states with a written constitution of 1900. The constitution, among many other things, defines the various responsibilities of the commonwealth (federal) government; beyond these matters the states are supreme. The role of environmental protection is not mentioned in the constitution and hence becomes substantially a matter for each government. Consequently, the states of New South Wales, Victoria, Queensland, South Australia, Western Australia, and Tasmania, have enacted their own separate environmental protection legislation. The commonwealth exercises environmental responsibilities only in matters within its direct or indirect control. Sometimes the exercise of these responsibilities conflicts with the views of an individual state government, and the disagreement has to be resolved by the High Court of Australia.

The commonwealth government exercises an environmental protection role for the following: (1) territories partially under the control of the commonwealth, such as the Australian Capital Territory and the Northern Territory; (2) activities and projects carried out by the commonwealth including defence facilities, railways, national highways, factories, dockyards, airports, postal and telecommunication facilities, and other developments on commonwealth-owned land; (3) Australia's claimed share of Antarctica and marine waters outside of state limits, thus controlling the Great Barrier Reef marine park off the Queensland coast and the Nangaloo marine park off the Western Australian coast;

(4) matters in which commonwealth export licences are required as for woodchips, woodpulp, uranium, mineral sands, coal, iron ore, alumina, oil, and gas; (5) national programs in which commonwealth financial grants are made to the states for specific purposes; (6) matters requiring the approval of the Foreign Investment Review Board; and (7) matters for which the commonwealth has signed an international convention or agreement such as UNESCO World Heritage listings (see glossary).

Checklist 9.1 lists the principal EA legislation of the commonwealth and state governments of Australia; checklist 9.2 indicates the evolution of pollution control and environment protection legislation in Australia since 1958 from which EIA procedures have emerged (Gilpin, 1988; Gilpin and Lin, 1990).

The Commonwealth

The commonwealth government's Environment Protection (Impact of Proposals) Act was enacted in 1974 and amended in 1987. The Act seeks to ensure that environmental matters are examined and taken into account in the decision-making processes at the federal level. In summary, the Act and its associated administrative procedures set out:

- types and categories of activities to which the Act applies in both the public and private sectors;
- powers of the commonwealth environment minister to require the preparation of an EIS or shorter public environment report (PER);
- content of an EIS or PER;
- arrangements for public involvement in the assessment process;
- provisions for recommending environmental conditions to apply to approvals;
- arrangements for holding public inquiries.

CHECKLIST 9.1

Australia: EA legislation

Jurisdiction	*Legislation*
Commonwealth	Environment Protection (Impact of Proposals) Act, 1974–87.
New South Wales	Environmental Planning and Assessment Act, 1979–85.
Victoria	Environmental Effects Act, 1978.
	Planning and Environment Act, 1987.
Queensland	State Development and Public Works Organization Act, 1971–85.
South Australia	Planning Act, 1982–85.
Western Australia	Environmental Protection Act, 1986.
Tasmania	Environment Protection Act, 1973–85.
Northern Territory	Environmental Assessment Act, 1982–84.
Australian Capital Territory	Environmental Assessments and Inquiries Act, 1991.

CHECKLIST 9.2

Australia: evolution of environmental management

1958–64 Australian states introduce air pollution control legislation.

1964–79 Australian states introduce solid and liquid waste management and anti-litter legislation.

1970 New South Wales establishes the State Pollution Control Commission and the Metropolitan Waste Disposal Authority; Victoria establishes the Environment Protection Authority and the Land Conservation Council.

1970–71 Australian states introduce water pollution control legislation.

1971 Australian Environment Council established; Western Australia establishes Environment Protection Authority.

1972 South Australia establishes the Environment Protection Council.

1972–78 Australian states introduce noise control legislation.

1973 Tasmania establishes a Department of the Environment.

1974 Council of Conservation Ministers established; Commonwealth (federal) government introduces EIA legislation.

1975 Commonwealth government establishes the Great Barrier Reef Marine Park Authority and Australian Heritage Commission.

1978 Victoria introduces EIA legislation.

1979 New South Wales introduces EIA legislation and creates Department of Environment and Planning; South Australia creates Waste Management Commission; Northern Territory introduces environmental controls for uranium mining.

1980 Northern Territory establishes Conservation Commission.

1981 South Australia establishes Department of Environment and Planning.

1982 Northern Territory introduces EIA legislation.

1983 National Conservation Strategy adopted by commonwealth and most states; Victoria creates Ministry for Planning and Environment and Department of Conservation, Forests, and Lands.

1984 Australian Capital Territory (Canberra) creates ACT Pollution Control Authority.

1985 New South Wales introduces environmentally hazardous chemicals legislation; national unleaded petrol (gasoline) program inaugurated.

1987 Victorian State Conservation Strategy announced; Western Australia State Conservation Strategy announced; Murray–Darling Basin Commission established.

1989 Commonwealth government creates Resource Assessment Commission.

A program for the planting of one billion trees initiated by the commonwealth.

Ozone protection legislation introduced. National industrial chemicals notification and assessment scheme operational.

1992   Intergovernmental agreement on the environment between the commonwealth, states, territories, and local government.

The council of Australian governments agree on the objectives and guiding principles for ecologically sustainable development (ESD)

NSW creates the Environment Protection Authority, replacing the State Pollution Control Commission.

The commonwealth creates an Environment Protection Agency within the Department of the Arts, Sport, the Environment and Territories.

Commonwealth Endangered Species Protection Act; Natural Resources Management (Financial Assistance) Act.

The term 'environment' as used in the Act refers to 'all aspects of the surroundings of human beings'. It encompasses the natural environment (air, water, soils, flora, fauna), the built environment (buildings, roads, housing, and recreational facilities), and the social aspects of human surroundings.

The act is limited to matters that affect the environment to a 'significant' extent, and the Act only applies to proposals in which there is some involvement by the commonwealth government.

This EIA legislation is currently administered within the commonwealth Department of Environment, Sport and Territories (DEST). Within the department, the Environment Assessment Branch has 20 officers engaged in day-to-day administration. These officers have diverse professional backgrounds and include engineers, planners, and economists, as well as scientists in natural resource disciplines.

Following receipt of the statutory 'notice of intention' accompanied by a summary of the proposal, the Act provides for four levels of EIA:
• initial examination of the proposal by DEST without the preparation of an EIS or PER;
• assessment by DEST following the preparation and public review of a PER;
• assessment by DEST following the preparation and public review of an EIS;
• examination by a commission of inquiry.

The proponent is responsible for preparing an EIS or PER. Since 1974, more than 2 500 environmentally significant proposals have been submitted for assessment. By the end of 1988, more than 100 of these required the preparation of an EIS.

The PER was introduced in 1987. It is a report prepared by the proponent, briefly outlining the proposal, examining the environmental implications, and describing the safeguards necessary to protect the environment. This type of report is used where impacts are expected to be few or focused on a small number of specific issues, and the preparation of a full EIS is not warranted. A PER provides a more selective treatment of the environmental implications of a proposal than does an EIS; it allows a level of assessment below that of the EIS.

DEST consults with each proponent on the content and coverage of a draft EIS or PER in a scoping exercise, providing guidelines for their preparation, and seeking to ensure that such documents are suitable for public review. Subject to commercial confidentiality and national security, draft EISs and PERs are made available for public review and comment. The minimum period of review is 28 days. The minister can direct the department to hold 'round table' discussions with the proponent and members of the public following public review of a draft EIS or a PER.

After these procedures, DEST prepares an EIA report for the minister, taking account of all public comments. Copies of this are also made available to the public. A final EIS is then published.

To date, the commonwealth has conducted four public inquiries into environmental matters: including the Fraser Island Environmental Inquiry relating to sand-mining in 1975, and the Ranger Uranium Environmental Inquiry in 1977. Figure 16 outlines commonwealth EIA procedures.

New South Wales

Between 1971 and 1979, New South Wales had an EIA procedure based on a state cabinet directive. It was applied at the discretion of the Minister for Environment and implemented by the NSW State Pollution Control Commission (SPCC). The system lacked general acceptance, though much valuable work was done and 12 major public inquiries were conducted.

In 1979, the New South Wales government passed the Environmental Planning and Assessment Act, creating a Department of Environment and Planning, providing for state environmental planning policies, regional environmental plans, local environmental plans, and EIA procedures. EIA staff were transferred from the SPCC to the new department. The new system integrated EIA into land use, heritage, and environmental planning processes. Concurrent legislation created a NSW Land and Environment Court. In 1988, the department was split into a Department of Planning (with EIA responsibilities) and a Department of the Environment.

EIA is required for both public and private sector projects likely to have significant impacts on the

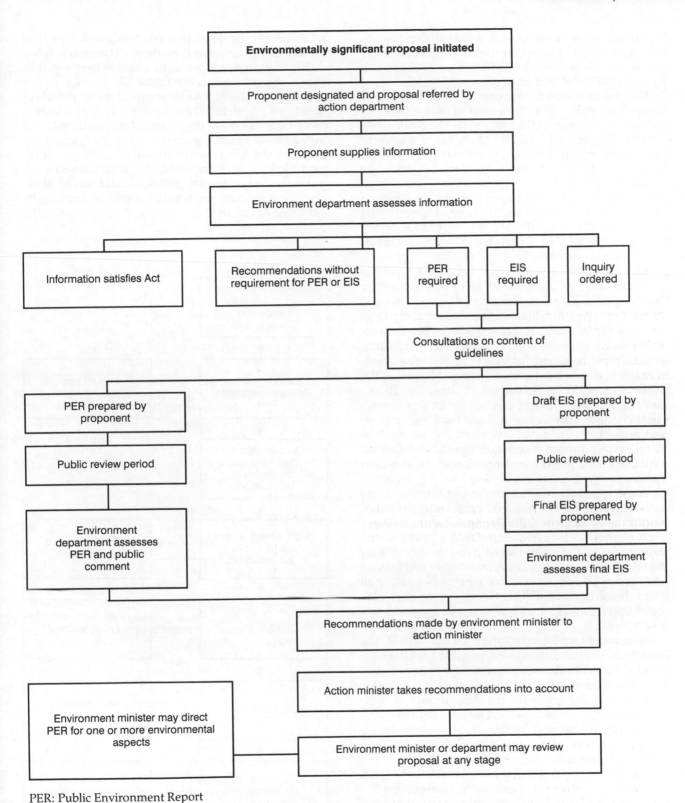

PER: Public Environment Report

Figure 16 Commonwealth (Australian federal) government: main steps under EIA procedures

(Derived from Department of the Arts, Sport, the Environment, Tourism and Territories, *Environmental Impacts Assessment As a Management Tool: Workshop Proceedings, November 1987*, Australian Government Publishing Service, Canberra, Australia, 1988)

environment — environment is here defined in the broadest terms. Opportunities are presented for public participation, public inquiries, and appeals to the NSW Land and Environment Court.

Unique in Australia, Section 123 of the Environment Planning and Assessment Act, 1979–85, allows any person to take action in the NSW Land and Environment Court and challenge if a government department or agency has adequately complied with the Act, without showing a financial or proprietary interest in the outcome. This is an important provision as it does not require a person to establish any 'standing' by way of a particular interest or other qualification before legal action can be initiated. More than half the actions taken have been successful.

EIA procedures have been applied to various projects such as aluminium smelters, coalmines (both open-cut and underground), sand and soil extraction, peatmining, shopping centres, local environmental plans, residential subdivisions, community centres, LPG installations, heavy industrial plants, grain-handling installations, high-rise developments, and petrochemical works. However, the New South Wales government has, on 10 occasions, legislated to get around the process that it itself created. This has been done for some important projects in Sydney, New South Wales, such as the Darling Harbour redevelopment, the central city monorail, and the Sydney Harbour (vehicular) tunnel.

As an example of the success of EIS procedures between 1980 and 1988, 900 EISs were prepared and publicly exhibited under the Act. About 80 per cent of the total were private sector projects, the remainder in the public sector. The quality of EISs has progressively improved, but it may still be said that some 50 per cent do not cover adequately all the relevant issues. This is usually remedied later by supplementary reports which add time and cost to the process.

In a recent and fairly rare instance (1988), the deficiencies of an EIS proved so great that the proponent submitted, on the opening day of a public inquiry, a supplementary document eight times longer than the original EIS. This attempt at compensating for deficiencies in the EIS had the effect of modifying the proposal, which had to be re-advertised. The adjournment cost the proponent a delay of 6 months.

Part IV of the Act relates to private sector proposals that require development consent from a local council (an elected body with planning powers under the Act), which is normally the appropriate body. However, the Minister for Planning may 'call in' projects or groups of projects of special regional or environmental importance. In such cases, the minister makes the decision on whether the project shall proceed, and if it proceeds, subject to what conditions. The public has a right, in many instances, to require that a public inquiry be conducted. See figure 17.

Part V of the Act deals with forms of development not requiring development consent from a local council — a state, statutory authority, or indeed local council proposal. Such projects, however, require approval from a determining authority following EIA procedures. Arrangements for public participation are provided, and the Minister for Planning may direct that a public inquiry be held. See figure 18.

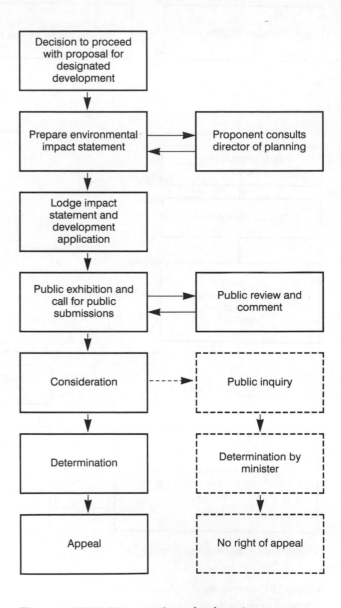

Figure 17 NSW: EIA procedures for the private sector (Source: NSW Department of Planning, 1992)

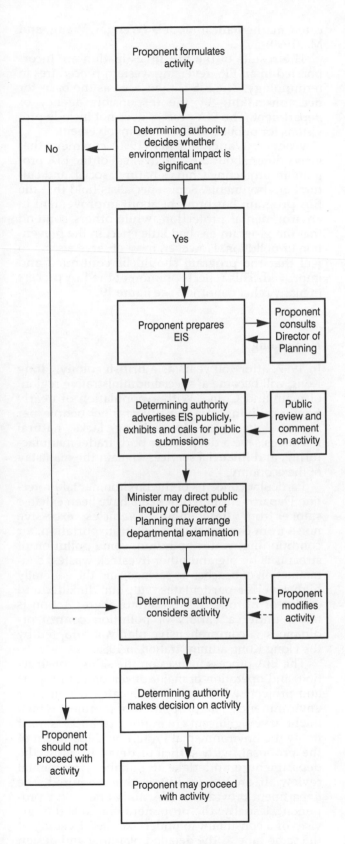

Figure 18 NSW: EIA procedures for the public sector
(Source: NSW Department of Planning, 1992)

A survey of the top 1 000 Australian companies and organisations by Cooper & Lybrand (1991) revealed that a considerable proportion of businesses are now recognising their environmental responsibilities; many are now undertaking audits with the objective of establishing environmental corporate policies. Formal environmental audits had been undertaken by the following industries: minerals/chemicals manufacturing sector (75 per cent); mining sector (59 per cent); metal goods, engineering, and vehicle industry (53 per cent).

Major aspects in audits included: compliance with legislation; monitoring systems and procedures; possible site contamination; and product use and disposal.

An example of a corporate policy is that adopted by ICI Australia about EIA:

GS 13 Each location shall prepare and maintain an up-to-date assessment of the environmental impact of its activities. This assessment shall take into account, but not be limited to, solid, liquid and gaseous wastes produced and the measures for their disposal; as well as any land contamination issues and/or any unplanned releases of materials or energy.

9.2 China

China is home to more than one-fifth of the human race, more than 1.3 billion people with a density of 122 people per square kilometre. It remains one of the poorest nations and it will be a long and arduous haul to achieve individuality and prosperity. Enough food or better food, acceptable living space or a little more living space, more clothes, and more mobility, are still the main targets for most Chinese people (Zhou, 1991).

Before 1980, few people in China thought about environment protection issues as a matter of public policy, although the management and disposal of hazardous wastes or emissions had a long history, mainly through industry. Gradually, environment protection was seen as something closely related to economic and social development as a whole.

Initially, an Environment Protection Office (EPO) was set up by the State Council as the first national environment protection organisation. Later this was replaced by the National Environment Protection Bureau (NEPB). Then, NEPB became part of the former Ministry of Urban and Rural Construction and Environment Protection. This arrangement was superseded by the creation of a National Environment Protection Agency (NEPA) (China), an independent agency, responsible for making environment protection policy and maintaining its management in China. NEPA has a semi-ministry position in the hierarchy of central government, reporting directly to the State Council.

In each province there are environment bureaus, responsible for provincial environment issues; these report to provincial governments and directly to NEPA (China). In cities and counties, there are also bureaus or offices of environment protection which report to the local governments and environment protection bureaus at the regional and national level.

In all ministries responsible for industry, a division or special office is responsible for environment protection; this extends to the enterprises owned by the central government. The enterprises themselves have offices of environment protection, or a specially appointed person in the case of small enterprises. Environment protection bureaus are authorised to supervise, monitor, and enforce the various regulations promulgated.

A revised environment protection law was adopted and promulgated in 1990 by the standing committee of the National People's Congress. This law authorised NEPA (China) to supervise and implement environment protection management throughout the country. National standards must take account of the national economic and technical context. This law is to be tried and tested over the next 10 years.

There can be no doubt that China has established a well-organised system of environmental management, and perhaps a rapid deterioration of environmental quality has been slowed, but no more. Air pollution is still the dominant problem in urban areas, particularly in the northern part of China in the winter; in some cities vehicle emissions are also a problem. Acid rain affects extensive areas. Most wastewater from industry and households drains into rivers untreated. Noise remains an urban problem. Deforestation, and soil and land erosion continue.

EIA

EIA procedures have developed in the People's Republic of China since the mid-1980s. The impetus was provided by the environmental protection law adopted by the Fifth National People's Congress in 1979. Since then EIA has been applied to major construction projects (Wang and Bi, 1993).

Four stages are typically involved in an EIA investigation: (1) the design of the investigation; (2) evaluation of background environmental quality; (3) prediction of the environmental impacts; and (4) an assessment and analysis of the environmental impacts. Various approaches are used for predicting and analysing environmental impacts, ranging from ad hoc methods to fairly sophisti-

cated mathematical models (Wenger, Wang, and Ma, 1990).

The results of the EIA investigation are incorporated in an EIS, reversing western procedures in terminology. The EIS is then used as the basis for decision-making by the responsible agency or department. The EIA process does not include provisions for public notification or involvement.

Wenger, Wang, and Ma (1990) comment that views differ about the effectiveness of the EIA program in protecting China's natural, social, and cultural environments. Some specialists hold that the EIA program has brought about improvement in environmental protection, while others contend that the program has had little effect in the prevention of pollution. However, most observers seem to feel that the program should be continued and improved. This reflects opinion of the EIA process in many other countries. See figure 19.

Hong Kong

In 1997, after 150 years as a British colony, Hong Kong will become a 'special administrative region' of mainland China. With a population of nearly 6 million living at a density of 5399 people per square kilometre, Hong Kong lacks natural resources save a deep-water port; trade, manufacturing, and financial services, remain the mainstay of the economy.

Particular concerns of the Environmental Protection Department in recent years have been exhaust smoke from diesel-engined vehicles; excessive noise from construction work, transportation, air conditioning; water pollution; some pollution of streams is by pig and other livestock wastes; contamination of beaches by sewage; and the generally high level of particulates, sulphur dioxide, and oxides of nitrogen, in the atmosphere. Action is taken under a variety of pollution control ordinances. A comprehensive plan was adopted by the Hong Kong administration in 1989.

The EIA process focuses on the siting, construction, and operation of major development projects and projects which might be located in sensitive environments. The proponent of a project which might have significant environmental impacts must notify the Environmental Protection Department of the proposal, with sufficient detail to allow the department to undertake an initial environmental review. If an EIS or EIA is then required, the department provides an EIA study brief to the proponent. Usually, the proponent employs the services of a consultant to undertake the EIA study at the same time as the detailed planning and design work for the project.

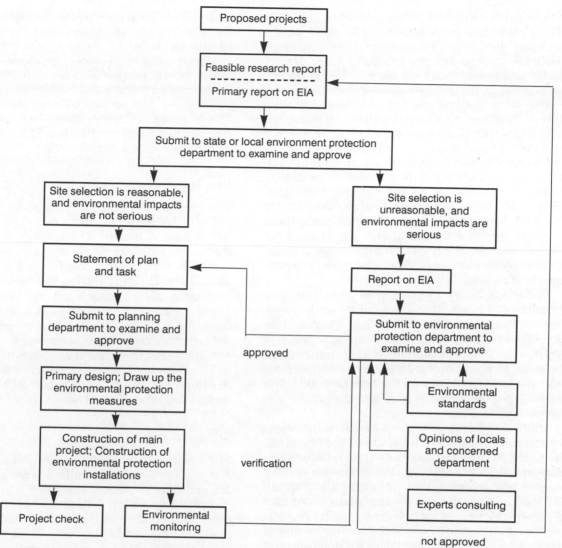

Figure 19 China: EIA procedures
(Source: Wang, H. and Ma, X., 'Progress of environmental impact assessment in China', in *Proceedings of the international symposium on environmental impact assessment*, Beijing Normal University, Beijing, China, 1987, p. 22)

In 1991, the Hong Kong administration decided to make the results of EIA studies available to the public; this was the first step in an evolving approach to public consultation on EA matters. Under those improved procedures, EIA studies have been conducted for a major proposed power station at Black Point, an expansion of the power station on Lamma Island, a chemical waste treatment facility, marine borrow areas, strategic landfills, refuse transfer stations, and port and airport development projects including a new international airport at Chek Lap Kok (Environmental Protection Department, 1992).

9.3   Indian subcontinent

India

With a population of some 890 million and a density of 281 people per square kilometre, India is a federal republic with 25 states, each with its own elected legislature. To the south of the Himalayas a wide and densely populated alluvial plain contains the Ganges, Indus, and Brahmaputra rivers. Peninsular India consists of the Deccan plateau, fringed by a coastal plain.

As at independence, in 1947, nearly all of India's

people work small plots of land and live in simple village communities; poverty and insecurity are the dominant facts of life. Poor environmental management has caused serious problems with deforestation and loss of vital top soils. Economic progress has been slow, though firmly based.

The Department of the Environment is responsible for promoting EIA principles and has been involved with the assessment of major industrial projects, thermal power, hydro power, river basin development, and mining. Environmental implications are considered in the formulation of all new development projects, often with statutory authorities and major departments which are directly involved. The views of the general public and those of environmental organisations are heeded. In some cases, special expert committees might be set up to explore, in greater detail, the environmental aspects of a project.

The Silent Valley hydroelectric project became the subject of much controversy in the early 1980s. The southern state of Kerala had proposed to develop a part of the Silent Valley, a densely forested area, to increase electricity production in the state. This was met with great opposition from both environmentalists and the general public. The central government intervened and the project was stopped on environmental grounds.

Another major involvement has been the water resources development program of the Narmada basin; the River Narmada rises at Amarakantak in Madyapradesh flowing 1 300 kilometres west to the Arabian Sea, its catchment embracing three states. The water development program plans eventually to construct 29 major (and several smaller) projects to utilise vast amounts of energy for irrigation and power, as well as to deliver water for domestic and industrial purposes. EIAs are in progress for the catchment area, the dam environs, submergence areas, and downstream river areas, the implications for resettlement and rehabilitation, and how to achieve these.

Various recommendations have emerged about soil and moisture conservation measures such as terracing, check dams, and grassland improvement; conservation, improvement of existing natural forests and plantations, and soil conservation; and the encouragement of public participation in the planning phase.

The World Bank was, for a time, heavily involved in this project. In 1993, the Indian government cancelled the proposed World Bank loan unhappy, at least in part, with the bank's exacting environmental and resettlement standards. The project itself, however, is still to proceed.

Pakistan

A federal republic since 1947, Pakistan has a population of 130 million and 148 people per square kilo-

metre. The Himalayas, in the far north, feed rivers that run through a scrubby plateau to the flat alluvial plain of the Indus.

Wheat is the main food crop; cotton is grown for the domestic market and for export. Industry is dominated by textiles and food processing.

There are four provincial assemblies in Pakistan. The Pakistan Environmental Protection and Improvement Agency handles EIA procedures for all major development projects.

Bangladesh

The People's Republic of Bangladesh has a population of 110.5 million and a density of 768 people per square kilometre. The country is mostly flat, low-lying, with extremely fertile flood plains and deltas, notably of the Ganges and Brahmaputra. Storms and flooding during the monsoon seasons have often taken a terrible toll on life and property. There are many deaths and countless people are rendered homeless, dependent on welfare relief. Subsistence crops are destroyed. Bangladesh remains one of the poorest countries in the world.

The Planning Commission carries out the EIA of development projects on behalf of the Environmental Pollution Control Board.

Sri Lanka

The Democratic Socialist Republic of Sri Lanka has a population of 17.5 million and a density of 266 people per square kilometre. It is an island state of south-east India. Sri Lanka has diversified its economy which had been traditionally based on rice-growing and tea exports, with the development of light industry, and tourism.

A National Environmental Authority requires EIA procedures for all major manufacturing projects. The Mahaweli Ganga development program, an accelerated development program for most of the country, has completed the most comprehensive EIA in the region. This has provided guidelines and impetus for the development of EIA in Sri Lanka.

The Mahaweli Ganga accelerated development program includes a whole range of such facilities as hydroelectric dams, irrigation systems, and canals. The studies have been integrated, using external consultants, and have been coordinated by the Ministry of Mahaweli Development.

Some of the matters investigated have been hydrology, land use, soils, watershed management, forestry, wildlife, water quality, fisheries, wetlands, aquatic vegetation, pest management, public health, social problems, and economic questions. Potential beneficial and adverse impacts on both the human and natural environments have been identified and evaluated: land-use changes, losses to forestry and wildlife, erosion, changes in water quality, hydrological effects on wetlands, effects on fishing and shrimp resources, spread of aquatic weeds, potential rise in the incidence of malaria and waterborne communicable diseases, alteration of population centres, and the integration of various ethnic, religious, and language groups.

Local residents have been interviewed to determine how the development program would affect their reliance on fisheries resources, use of wetland grazing areas, drinking water supplies, health care services, sources of firewood and timber, and crop damage as a result of wildlife encroachment. A whole range of environmental planning and mitigative measures has evolved as a result of people's input (Tippetts et al, 1980).

9.4   Indonesia

The Republic of Indonesia is made up of 13 670 islands, 930 of them inhabited. Most are rugged, sometimes volcanic, and covered with rainforest. The population is 184.8 million with an average density of about 96 people per square kilometre. Most people live in the river valleys, alluvial coastal plains, or on terraced mountain sides. Indonesia has still a low per capita income, but has been able to reduce the population living in poverty from 58 per cent in 1970 to 17 per cent in 1987. However, the total number living below the poverty line in 1987 was estimated to be about 30 million (Salim, 1990a).

Indonesia's development policy aims to promote growth with an eye to equity. Yet the country's extensive resources and distribution over many islands at varying levels of socio-economic development, pose a range of environmental impacts (Tarrant, 1987). First, much of the oil, gas, coal, and other minerals, are located in sparsely settled areas where any industry would heavily affect forest, coastal, and marine environments, through the intrusion of access roads, railways, surface mining, processing, storage, and power facilities. Second, the rapid development of forestry product industries in Kalimantan and Sumatra disrupts fragile forest environments, causing soil erosion, and problems with waste handling and disposal. Third, dams and irrigation systems constructed on the rain-fed uplands, are often a significant contributory cause of landslides, and soil erosion. In Java, the steady increase in the number of very large dams for power, flood control, fisheries, and water supply, has encroached significantly on agricultural land and displaced people. Fourth, there have been adverse effects of land displacement and erosion, leaks, and explosions, and aesthetic losses from the construction of pipelines,

roads, and telecommunication facilities, in Java and elsewhere.

Finally, the major cities in developing areas have been facing serious health and environmental problems owing to lack of waste disposal and sanitation systems, or their inadequate maintenance. The main causes of morbidity in Indonesia are diarrhoeal and infectious diseases, respiratory infections, skin and eye infections, intestinal parasites, and vector-borne diseases, especially malaria. In summary, it would appear that many problems are a result of development; yet another range of problems arises from lack of development.

The Indonesian government has many policies: for forests, for example, a policy of sustainable yield is being pursued to conserve forest in the interests of soil conservation, biological diversity, watershed protection, and the maintenance of hydrological cycles, and still drawing on the forests for timber and other forest products, and clearing some forest for the purposes of agriculture, industry, and settlements. To achieve these conflicting purposes, forests have been divided into protected forests and national parks for conservation; and into production and conversion forest for exploitation. Major reforestation programs are in hand (Salim, 1990).

EIA

Some guidelines for state environmental policy were adopted by Decree 4 of the general session of the Consultative People's Assembly in 1978. These guidelines related to the need for the adequate evaluation of natural resources; the maintenance of the quality of natural resources and the environment; the proper evaluation of the effects of development on the human environment and devising the best possible safeguards against adverse effects; the rehabilitation of impaired natural resources; the need for integrated approaches to river basin management and land-use generally; the careful use of water resources and coastal regions; and the need, with new settlements, to improve the living environment of low-income people. The adoption of this statement corresponded with the setting up of the Ministry for Population and Environment.

In 1982, the Indonesian government enacted a basic law dealing with the principal provisions of environmental management. Among other things, this law created an EIA process. Regulations were enacted in 1986 to reinforce this measure. EIA procedures were to be established by all ministries by 1987.

The coordination of the EIA process was initially the responsibility of the ministry for Population and Environment. In 1990, this responsibility was transferred to the Environmental Impact Management Agency. However, the actual authority for the implementation lies with both the central and provincial levels of government: at the central level with 14 sectoral government departments and non-departmental government institutions, and at the regional level with the 27 provincial governments of Indonesia.

The goal of EIA in Indonesia is to facilitate and expedite economically sound, environmentally and socially acceptable, development ventures. Initial documents in the process might supply preliminary environmental information, an environmental evaluation study, or a full EIS essentially according to the prospective status of the project, or activity. A complete guide has been published by the Environmental Impact Management Agency (1991). Figure 20 also illustrates the procedure.

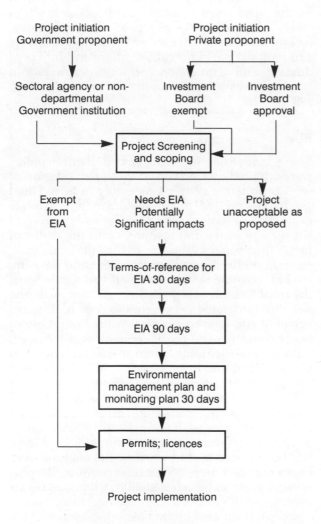

Figure 20 Indonesia: EIA procedures
(Source: BAPEDAL — Environmental Impact Management Agency)

The types of projects and activities which are likely to need a full EIS and EIA include: the building of roads, dams, railways; mining and forest exploitation; the clearing of forest; major land-use changes; major energy projects; activities which might cause changes or deviations in the value system, outlook and/or lifestyle of the local people; activities, processes and products which might cause pollution, damage to a natural reserve area and/or pollution to a cultural reserve area; the introduction of new plants or microorganisms which might cause new diseases to vegetation; the introduction of new species of animals which might affect the ecosystem of existing animals; the application of living (bionic) and non-living (abiotic) substances which might include the concept of mutation; and the application of technology which might cause a negative environmental impact on health.

Environmental impact analysis is regarded as a tool for decision-makers to consider the consequences that might arise from a project or activity on the environment in order to prepare measures to mitigate the negative impacts and enhance the positive impacts (Ministry for Population and Environment, 1991, 1B Elucidation of Government Regulation no. 29, 1986, p. 21). A later ministerial decree provides guidelines for the determination of significant impacts, discussed elsewhere in this work. In 1987 guidelines were published for the analysis of environmental impacts of proposed projects and the preparation of EISs; also procedures for the mitigation of pollution and damage to the environment.

Permit and licence conditions provide for environmental mitigation and monitoring requirements developed in the EIA process to be legally enforceable in the event of non-compliance by the project proponent. The use of water effluent and air emission standards are critical to the effectiveness of the EIA process; national noise standards have been prepared. EIA guidelines have been issued by many of the sectoral ministries.

Regulations in Indonesia required initially that companies publish an audit of current environmental performance by December 1992. Legislation in 1993 requires all companies to produce environmental audit reports on a 5-year cycle. Indonesia has the only system worldwide of compulsory environmental audit.

9.5   Japan

Japan's population increased from 73 million in 1940 to 124.3 million in 1992, with an average density of 328 per square kilometre. Much of the land is mountainous and in effect the density is closer to 1600 per square kilometre.

In Japan, health facilities improved rapidly after the Second World War. A public sanitation bureau was created within the Ministry of Welfare. Striking improvements in living standards took place, with consumer expenditure shifting in emphasis from food towards clothing and durable goods. Yet a penalty of progress has been the general neglect of environmental considerations, but for natural parks where progress has been continuous since the 1930s. It was 1967 before Japan introduced the Basic Law for Environmental Pollution Control. By 1971, however, the creation of the Japan Environment Agency brought environment administration under centralised coordination. See checklist 9.3.

In 1972, Japan contributed significantly to the UN Conference on the Human Environment with thorough documentation and many frank admissions of failure; the facts on air and water pollution were outlined with detailed description of two pollution-related afflictions: itai-itai disease and minamata disease as a result of cadmium and organic mercury respectively. The mayor of Kobe in his address at Stockholm described graphically the environmental pollution problems that had developed in and around Japan's major cities.

A serious problem lies in the inadequacy of the sewerage system. Improvements have been promoted through a series of 5-year plans raising the percentage of those served by sewers and sewage treatment plants from 23 per cent in 1975 to about 44 per cent in 1990. The objective in 1991 was to increase the percentage of the population served by sewers to 55 per cent by the end of 1995. In those areas not provided with sewerage, there exist dip-up lavatories and the use of septic tanks for the treatment of night soil alone. Where these systems are used, untreated sullage water from kitchens and bathrooms is discharged into rivers and lakes (Japan, 1991).

Environmental disputes and public participation

Japanese citizens, in the past, have had little opportunity to influence or directly participate in policy-making processes. However, during the 1960s citizens began to organise in an attempt to influence decisions, through confrontation, litigation, and political controversy, particularly those decisions about pollution control and environment protection. The most widely publicised demonstrations in recent years have been those against the Narita airport in Tokyo.

Environmental issues have been raised effectively through litigation. Three significant court decisions were achieved between 1971 and 1973 dealing with cadmium poisoning in Toyama (itai-itai disease), mercury poisoning in Niigata and Kumamoto (minamata disease), and pollution-

related asthma in Yokkaichi. The decisions, in which polluters were to compensate environmental victims, in effect placed upon enterprises a duty to monitor all the risks of pollution and to adopt the best control technology available. These are known as the 'big three' pollution cases. By 1980, lawsuits had become much more commonplace (Edmunds, 1982).

CHECKLIST 9.3

Japan: evolution of environmental management

1918 Wildlife Protection and Hunting Law.

1957 Natural Parks Law.

1962 Smoke Control Law.

1965 Japan Environment Corporation established to finance pollution control projects.

1967 Basic Law for Environmental Pollution Control.

1970 Water Pollution Control Law; Soil Pollution Control Law; Waste Disposal and Public Cleansing Law.

1971 Japan Environment Agency established; Offensive Odour Control Law; amendment of Agricultural Chemical Regulation Law.

1972 Air Pollution Control Law; Nature Conservation Law; Adoption by cabinet of EIA procedures for major public projects.

1973 Pollution-related Health-damage Compensation Law; Chemical Substances Control Law; amendment of Nature Conservation Law and Natural Parks Law.

1984 Adoption by cabinet of EIA, for general application.

1986 National survey of the natural environment (the Green Census); revision of Chemical Substances Control Law.

1987 Comprehensive Resort Area Development Law; amendment of Pollution-related Health-damage Compensation Law.

1988 Protection of the Ozone Layer Law.

1989 Amendment of Water Pollution Control Law.

1990 Revision of Nature Conservation Law and Natural Parks Law.

1991 Revision of Wildlife Preservation Law; objective of seventh 5-year program (1991–95) to increase the percentage of the population served by sewers to 55 per cent; Recycling Resources Law.

In the 1990s a new agency was created called the Environmental Disputes Coordination Commission. Its function is to attempt to resolve disputes through a process of conciliation, mediation, and arbitration. However, only the more serious disputes come before this commission; less serious matters are dealt with at the prefectural level through the mechanism of an Environmental Disputes Council.

EIA

In 1972, a cabinet resolution introduced environmental impact procedures for large-scale public works. In consequence, a large number of projects have been reviewed; public hearings often are part of the procedures. Since 1977, through local ordinances, municipalities began to require public hearings as part of the assessment procedure for local projects. In 1980, citizen groups held demonstrations against the public hearings being conducted as part of the EA process for new nuclear power stations.

In the mid-1970s, the government began drafting legislation for a comprehensive EIA system; in 1981, the bill was submitted to the Diet but it was rejected. In 1984, attempts to have the bill adopted were abandoned and the bill was withdrawn. However, in the same year a cabinet resolution entitled 'Implementation of environmental impact assessment' was carried, immensely broadening the scope of EIA procedures. At the same time, practical guidelines were laid down and issued. By 1991, the broadened procedures had been applied to 123 projects. See checklist 9.4, table 2, and figure 21.

These cabinet-adopted procedures are reinforced by existing laws. For example, an assessment of a harbour and landfill project was facilitated by the Port and Harbour Act and the Public Water Area Reclamation Act. The whole EIA procedure is being strengthened by the progressive development of regional environmental control plans embracing whole communities and urban areas. Nevertheless, the absence of national EIA laws remains a handicap.

9.6   Korea, South

The population of South Korea is 43.7 million, with a population density of 440 people per square kilometre, one of the world's highest. Despite this, about two-thirds of the land area is often mountainous and forest; only 21 per cent of the land is cultivable. Rice is the single major crop.

South Korea's environmental problems have been largely because of rapid industrialisation and urbanisation since the 1960s. The government's

---

CHECKLIST 9.4

Japan: projects subject to EIA

1   Construction or reconstruction of national expressways, national roads, and other major roads.

2   Construction of dams and waterworks on rivers, prescribed by the River Law.

3   Construction or improvement of railways.

4   Construction and major modification of airports.

5   Waste dumping and reclamation works.

6   Land readjustment projects, prescribed by the Land Readjustment Law.

7   Residential area developments, prescribed by the New Residential Built-up Area Development Law.

8   Industrial estate projects, prescribed by legislation in the national capital and Kinki regions.

9   Urban infrastructure development projects, prescribed by New Cities legislation.

10 Distribution business centres, prescribed by the Construction of Distribution Business Centres Law.

11 Projects implemented by corporations established by special legislation to promote residential, industrial, business, and agricultural development.

12 Other projects designated by a competent minister in consultation with the Minister of the Environment Agency.

(Derived from Japan national report to the UN Conference on Environment and Development 1992, p. 227)

Table 2 Japan

Number of projects subject to EIA procedures by cabinet decision

Year	Road	Dam	Airport	Reclamation	Others	Total
1986	1	–	–	2	–	3
1987	4	1	1	3	–	9
1988	23	–	–	3	3	29
1989	12	3	2	1	3	21
1990	39	1	–	2	3	45
1991	47	1	1	2	3	54
Total	126	6	4	13	12	161

(Source: Environment Agency, Japan, 1992)

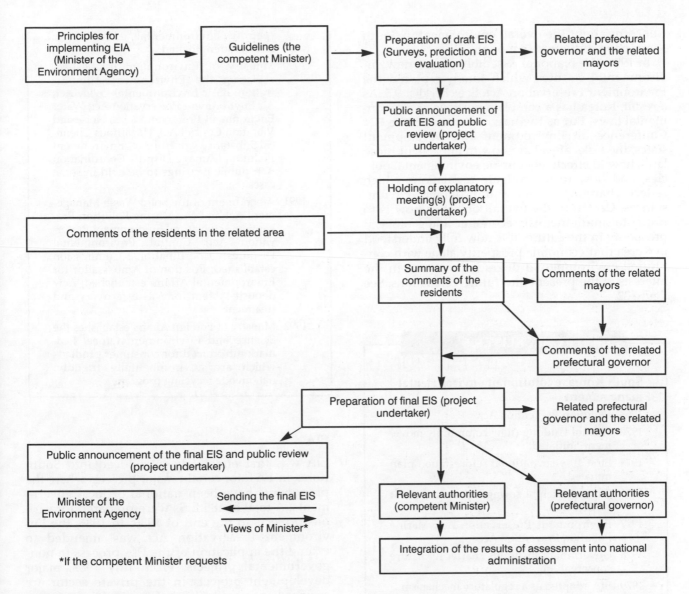

Figure 21 Japan: EIA procedures
(Source: Japan national report to the UN Conference on Environment and Development, Rio de Janeiro, 1992, p. 226)

position of favouring industrialisation above all else relaxed in the late 1970s. In late 1977, the first major environmental statute, the Environment Preservation Act was enacted, while in 1980 the Environment Administration was established. In fact in the 1982 to 1986 5-year plan a new explicit conservation objective became part of the official objective for national economic development. The Ministry of Environment replaced the Environment Administration in 1990.

In metropolitan Seoul, which accommodates 10.6 million people, measures against air pollution began in 1981 and the city changed to using low-sulphur fuel oil instead of coal for heating, which

was prohibited in commercial buildings and office buildings, and cluster housing. In 1988, the use of liquefied natural gas (LNG) became compulsory for new commercial and office buildings. Sulphur dioxide pollution has been halved. Much remains to be done to combat water pollution. The quality of drinking water has been impaired by the pollution of water supply reservoirs and the erosion of water supply pipes; treatment standards have not kept up with this. The rate of installation of sewerage systems has increased, but by the end of 1990 no more than 31 per cent of the population were connected to sewers (Ministry of Environment, 1991). Rivers and coastal waters continue to be polluted.

Concerns about the overall environment in South Korea have continued to mount.

In 1990, the National Assembly passed new environmental statutes which totally replaced the Environment Preservation Act. See checklist 9.5. As a result, Korea has a complete portfolio of environmental laws. But as the national report to the UN Conference on Environment and Development states, the tasks ahead are how to implement those laws, how to effectively pursue environmental policies, and how to promulgate regulations which reflect changing social and economic circumstances. Certainly the overall objective now is to promote simultaneously economic and ecological prosperity in the future. It is now fully understood in Korea that economic prosperity alone with continuing environmental degradation is not in the interests of the present and future generations. See figure 22.

CHECKLIST 9.5

South Korea: evolution of environmental management

1963 Pollution Prevention Act.

1970 Saemol Undong (new community movement) initiated.

1973 First 10-year national reforestation plan initiated.

1976 First municipal sewage treatment plant constructed.

1977 Environment Preservation Act; Marine Pollution Prevention Act.

1978 Government institutes charter for nature conservation.

1979 EIA adopted as a regulatory mechanism.

1980 Environment Administration established; New Constitution adopted guaranteeing the right to live in a clean and healthy environment; Korea Resource Recovery and Reutilisation Corporation established.

1981 Environment Preservation Act amended to introduce an emission charge system to enforce the measurement of emission standards; low-sulphur fuel oil policy for large cities; EIA process introduced.

1986 Solid Waste Management Act; six regional offices of the Environment Administration established; Environment Preservation Act amended to extend the application of the EIA process to non-governmental projects.

1987 Environmental Management Corporation established new emission standards for cars; introduction of unleaded gasoline

(petrol); environmental education in schools strengthened.

1990 Ministry of Environment established, replacing the Environment Administration; Basic Environmental Policy Act; Air Environment Preservation Act; Water Environment Preservation Act; Noise and Vibration Control Act; Hazardous Chemical Substance Control Act; Environment Pollution Damage Dispute Coordination Act; public hearings to be held in some cases.

1991 Amendment of the Solid Waste Management Act and the Marine Pollution Prevention Act; Natural Environment Preservation Act; Central Environmental Disputes Coordination Commission established; Position of Ambassador for Environmental Affairs established; new deposit system for waste recovery and treatment.

1992 Ministry of Foreign Affairs establishes the Science and Environment Office; Eco-mark introduced for consumer products which are environmentally friendly; nationwide recycling program.

EIA

EIA was first effectively introduced into South Korea in 1981, for certain major projects where the proponents have been national or local governments. A total of 185 EISs were prepared for various projects to the end of 1986. In 1986, the Environment Preservation Act was amended to extend the application of the EIA process to non-governmental projects. From July 1987, major development projects in the private sector are required to submit EISs before final approval of these projects by the relevant government agencies. In 1989, 120 EISs in the public and private sectors were prepared, followed by 212 in 1990. The main problem with the established EIA system, however, was that public participation was not provided for.

The Basic Environmental Policy Act of 1990 remedied this deficiency as it requires that EISs are brought to the notice of the public and that public hearings are held in certain cases. Further, the Ministry of Environment is in a position, unlike its predecessor, to request other agencies to take remedial measures, or even stop the construction of projects not undertaken in accordance with the approved EISs or conditions imposed. It is anticipated that EIA will become a more effective tool for the realisation of ecologically sustainable development.

These developments must be seen in perspective. In the 1960s Korea was one of the poorest agricultural countries and had a small, stagnant

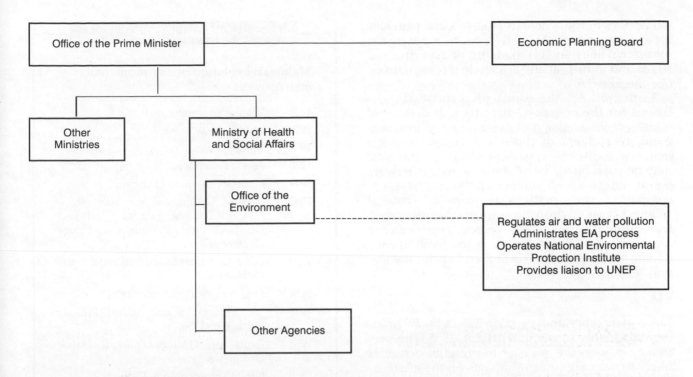

Figure 22 South Korea: organisation chart for environmental management
(Source: Minister of Environment, South Korea, 1992)

economy. It is now one of the most dynamic economies. A marked improvement in the people's welfare has evolved with economic growth. This is evident in medical insurance, a national pension system, and a minimum wage requirement. Among the negative effects of growth has been environmental deterioration caused by rapid industrialisation, urbanisation, and an increasingly affluent urban lifestyle.

One of the major EIAs conducted in South Korea has been the Han River Basin Development of the 1980s. The study area covered one-quarter of the land area of the Republic of Korea including the Han river drainage basin; it embraced Seoul and Incheon, the two largest cities, and 46 smaller cities and towns with a population of about 14 million.

The major fields of study included topography, geology and soils, climate, meteorology, hydrology, water quality (surface and ground), air quality, natural areas, biological resources, social resources, land use and human resources, demographics, public health, social and family patterns, economic development and finance, and laws and institutions. Water quality, air quality, and solid waste management models, were developed.

The Master Plan took development through the 1980s. The river bed was dredged, and many rec-reational facilities including sports grounds and Olympic stadiums were provided. Large grassed areas with nature study gardens, fishing grounds and ponds were established. Riverside roads were constructed and navigation extended. In order to collect domestic sewage and industrial wastewater, interceptors were installed, cutting off the inflow of wastes into the river; new treatment facilities are to be installed before the end of the century (Office of Environment, 1983).

9.7 Malaysia

With a population of 18.6 million, Malaysia is modestly populated with 57 people per square kilometre. Malaysia is endowed with abundant natural resources. It is the largest producer of rubber and palm oil, and the second largest producer of tin; it has begun to exploit its plentiful oil and timber reserves. Almost three-quarters of the land area is tropical rain forest or swamp forest. Manufacturing has become a key economic sector, with a drive to create heavy industries.

The Environmental Quality Act 1974 is a comprehensive piece of legislation, which enables the minister to make regulations for the implementation of the general policies defined in the Act. The

Act applies to the whole of Malaysia and provides for an Environmental Quality Council to advise the minister. The council is made up of departmental heads and industrial and academic representatives. See checklist 9.6.

Under this Act, the minister has specified regulations for the emission, discharge, or deposit of wastes, or the emission of noise into any area, segment, or element of the environment; in some instances a discharge, or deposits, or an emission may be prohibited. The Act also provides powers for dealing with oil spills. Regulations have encompassed such matters as palm oil, natural rubber, licensing, clean air, sewage effluents, industrial effluents, and motor vehicle exhausts. The Department of Environment is the main agency administering pollution control and environmental policies.

EIA

EIA is mandatory under section 34A of the Environmental Quality (Amendment) Act, 1985. This section empowers the minister to prescribe activities likely to have significant impacts on the environment and therefore requiring an EIA; prescribed activities were listed in regulations in force from 1988.

EIA reports are reviewed by an EIA technical committee, which seeks opinions from other government agencies and the private sector as necessary; independent review panels appointed for specific projects are also used. During 1989, 106 EIA cases were monitored by the department (Department of Environment, 1989); efforts are made to monitor projects before they reach the formal EIA stage. The department actively promotes incorporating environmental dimensions in project planning. This includes various infrastructural schemes such as sewerage and forestry. See figure 23.

The application of EIA in planning; specific guidelines for various activities to minimise adverse environmental impacts; and incorporating environmental considerations into development planning, are the main strategies adopted by the Department of Environment towards achieving the objectives of sound and sustainable development. These complement the on-going programs of pollution control through the enforcement of the Environmental Quality Act and its regulations.

9.8   New Zealand

With a population of 3.5 million, mainly European and Maori, New Zealand's pristine mountains, relatively clean air, unpolluted rivers and unspoiled beaches are greatly valued; but constant vigilance

---

CHECKLIST 9.6

Malaysia: evolution of environmental management

1920	Waters Enactment.
1929	Mining Enactment.
1934	Mining Rules.
1935	Forest Enactment.
1949	Natural Resources Ordinance 1949.
1952	Poisons Ordinance; Merchant Shipping Ordinance; Sale of Food and Drugs Ordinance; Dangerous Drugs Ordinance.
1953	Federation Port Rules; Irrigation Areas Ordinance.
1954	Drainage Works Ordinance.
1956	Medicine (Sales and Advertisement) Ordinance 1956.
1958	Explosives Ordinance; Road Traffic Ordinance.
1960	Land Conservation Act.
1965	National Land Code; Housing Development Act.
1966	Continental Shelf Act.
1968	Radioactive Substances Act.
1969	Civil Aviation Act.
1971	Malaria Eradication Act.
1972	Petroleum Mining Act.
1974	Environmental Quality Act; Geological Survey Act; Street, Buildings and Drainage Act; Aboriginal People's Act; Factories and Machinery Act; Pesticides Act.
1975	Destruction of Disease-Bearing Insects Act; Municipal and Town Boards Act.
1976	Protection of Wildlife Act 1976; Antiquities Act; Local Government Act; Town and Country Planning Act.
1980	Malaysian Highway Authority Act; Pig Rearing Act.
1984	Atomic Energy Licensing Act; Exclusive Economic Zone Act; National Forestry Act.
1985	Fisheries Act.
1988	EIA becomes mandatory; 19 categories of industry required to submit EIA reports.
1991	331 major projects have now been subject to EIA.
1991–95	Sixth Malaysia Plan.

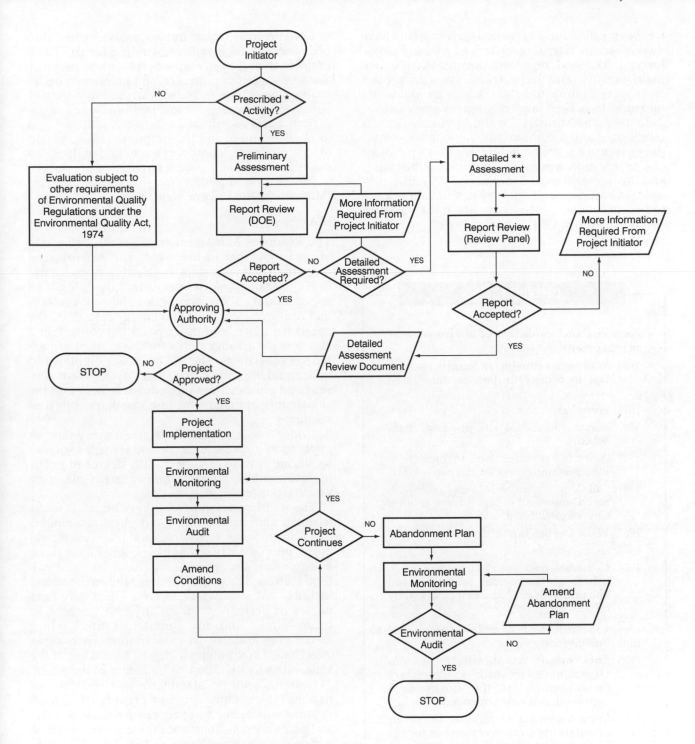

* Environmental Quality (Prescribed Activities)
  (Environmental Impact Assessment) Order 1987
** Consultation with Department of Environment on Terms of Reference

Figure 23 Malaysia: outline of EIA procedure
(Source: Department of Environment, Kuala Lumpur, Malaysia, 1992)

has been called for. Successive governments have developed an extensive system of national parks, forest parks, and reserves, throughout the two main islands; and have taken steps to protect endangered fauna and flora. Clean air and water measures have been implemented for many years.

In 1986, the Ministry for the Environment was established and a parliamentary commissioner for the environment appointed. In 1987, a Department of Conservation was set up to protect public lands and to manage coastal areas. In 1974 EIA procedures had been endorsed by cabinet; these were to become statutory requirements in the Resource Management Act, 1991. See checklist 9.7.

CHECKLIST 9.7

New Zealand: evolution of environmental management

1854 Wellington provincial council passes a law to control thistles, an introduced weed.

1874 Forest Act.

1894 Tongariro national park (the first) established.

1907 Animals Protection Act, to protect indigenous animal species and native birds.

1941 Soil Conservation and Rivers Control Act; Soil Conservation and Rivers Control Council established.

1967 Water and Soil Conservation Act, 1967.

1972 Clean Air Act.

1974 Commission for the Environment established; environmental protection and enhancement procedures introduced by cabinet (EIA procedures).

1977 Town and Country Planning Act.

1981 Public Works Act.

1986 Environment Act; Ministry for the Environment established; Parliamentary Commissioner for the Environment appointed; Forest Act amended.

1987 Conservation Act; Department of Conservation set up; creation of clean air zone in Christchurch; unleaded petrol available.

1989 Tasman Conservation Accord, to safeguard 52 areas of native forest throughout New Zealand.

1990 Ozone Layer Protection Act.

1991 Resource Management Act (EIA); New Zealand signs Antarctica protocol and ratifies the convention for the prohibition of fishing with long driftnets in the South Pacific; additional tax on lead in petrol.

Concurrently, social impact analysis came into prominence as a means of planning for the social impacts arising from major development projects. The steps taken to protect communities from undesirable effects have included: early identification of issues and planning; compilation of a sound information base; coordination between national and local government and the proponent involvement of local people in identifying issues and in decision-making, and the subsequent monitoring of impacts.

EIA is now applied throughout New Zealand (Ministry for the Environment, 1991).

EIA

The Resource Management Act, 1991, came into effect in October of that year. The Act replaced more than 20 major statutes affecting resource use in New Zealand, such as statutes governing land use and land subdivision; water and soil; geothermal resources; minerals and energy resources; the coast; air, noise, and other pollution control; and also sets up arrangements for the control of hazardous substances. The Act created both plan and policy-making procedures, and development consent and enforcement procedures to promote the sustainable management of natural and physical resources.

Under the Act, an EIA is required every time an application for a resource consent is made. Another significant feature of the Act is the degree of public involvement in resource management planning and decision-making.

The word 'environment' is very broad; it refers to much more than natural and physical elements as it also embraces ecosystems and their constituent parts, people and communities; amenity values; and relevant social, economic, aesthetic, and cultural matters. The word 'effect' for the environment includes any positive or adverse effect, any temporary or permanent effect; any past, present, or future effect; and any cumulative effect which arises over time or in combination with other effects; and any potential effects, regardless of the scale, intensity, duration, or frequency of the effect.

National policy statements on matters of national importance are also provided for; local government agencies must ensure their policies and plans are consistent with these statements. The national government retains the right to call in applications of national significance and make a decision, subject to appeals to the planning tribunal. Hearings and mediation of disputes are a feature of procedures; public submissions are sought as part of any inquiry, though the minister must make the decision on the application. A hierarchy of management plans and policy statements will exist from central government to district council level; this includes regional and district management plans.

The Act foresees that greater efficiency will come from incorporating EIA into the development consent process. A primary aim is to resolve problems in the first instance, avoiding trouble later on.

9.9 Philippines, The

The Republic of the Philippines is an island group made up of about 7000 islands and islets. The population is about 63.6 million, with an average density of population of 212 people per square kilometre. The country ranks high in the list of disaster-prone areas: an annual inventory of natural disasters invariably includes typhoons, excessive monsoon rains, earthquakes, and volcanic eruptions.

Metropolitan Manila is characterised by great disparities in income and living standards. About one-third of the city's population live in slums and squatter areas which lack sanitation facilities; there are high levels of malnutrition, infant mortality, and parasitic and intestinal diseases.

Water pollution in metropolitan Manila and other major urban and regional centres is caused by the general public and, to a lesser extent, by the industrial sector. All metropolitan areas in the Philippines lack efficient sewage collection and treatment, except in some affluent subdivisions with residents who can afford an expensive sewage treatment facility. Only about 12 per cent of metropolitan Manila's population is served by a sewerage system; the balance of unserved areas contribute about 70 per cent of all the biodegradable organic pollutants that flow into the different river systems in Manila. Untreated or partially treated industrial wastewater is also discharged into rivers and lakes, accounting for the other 30 per cent of the organics that have all but killed metropolitan Manila's water systems (Department of the Environment and Natural Resources, 1990).

Most of the toxic and hazardous wastes from industry are apparently discharged untreated into natural water bodies and coastal waters. Municipal solid wastes usually find their way into the river system, through open canals and culverts. Efforts are being made to improve the situation, including the demolition of slums.

The National Environmental Protection Council was created by presidential decree in 1977, as the central authority to promote and implement the Philippines government environment program in much the same way as the National Economic and Development Authority promotes the country's economic development. In the same year, the Philippine Environment Code was proclaimed. Within this framework, the National Pollution Control Commission became responsible for establishing standards for air and water pollution, and noise. The siting of industry was to be influenced by social, economic, geographic, and environmental considerations. See figure 24.

The code embraced natural resources management and conservation to achieve optimal benefits, having regard to present and future generations; the protection of mangrove areas, marshes and sensitive inland areas, coral sea areas and islands; the

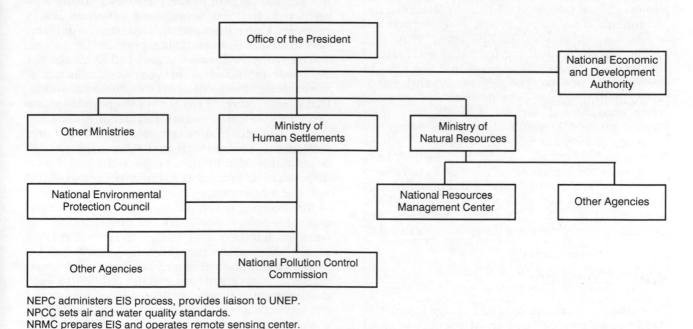

NEPC administers EIS process, provides liaison to UNEP.
NPCC sets air and water quality standards.
NRMC prepares EIS and operates remote sensing center.

Figure 24 Philippines: organisation chart for environmental management, 1992

protection of habitats and the control of methods of catching and hunting; forestry and soil conservation; the use of fertilisers and pesticides; flood control; the promotion of solar, wind and tidal energy; the conservation and utilisation of surface water and ground water; the protection of threatened species; and the rational and efficient use of mineral resources.

EIA

Presidential decree no. 1586 (1977), established an EIS system; an overriding responsibility of the National Environmental Protection Council was to ensure that an EIS was undertaken in the case of all projects likely to have an effect on the ecological and environmental balance. The council issued guidelines for the implementation of the system. The presidential proclamation no. 2146 prescribed certain areas and types of projects as 'environmentally critical' and within the scope of the system.

The procedure has required a draft EIS to be prepared and circulated to government agencies and interested parties; the council collates all comments on the draft, and decides whether to hold a public hearing into the matter. With or without a public hearing, the proponent then proceeds to prepare a final EIS. This document is then presented to the council for approval. Once approved, with or without amendment, the council issues the proponent with a 'certificate of compliance with the EIS system'. This enables the project to proceed. To ensure compliance with the conditions imposed by the process, the council monitors the progress of the project at least once every 3 months (National Environmental Protection Council, 1977; Department of Environment and Natural Resources, 1990).

The Department of Environment and Natural Resources (1990, p. 6) concedes that the EIS/EIA system has not worked efficiently and needs strengthening. Major development undertakings have encountered serious difficulties as their impacts on the surrounding environment have not been adequately considered. Some projects have been found to be unsustainable because they have led to resource depletion. Other projects have been abandoned because of public opposition, financial encumbrance by unforeseen costs, very high liabilities arising for damages to natural resources, and the disastrous accidents the projects have caused.

9.10   Singapore

This island republic of only 622 square kilometres has a population of 2.8 million, at a density of about 4489 people per square kilometre.

Since Singapore split from the Malaysian federation in 1965 it has enjoyed substantial economic growth, to become one of the richest of the Asian 'Little Dragons'. Yet in the beginning, newly independent Singapore's population of 1 million lived in largely unsewered, overcrowded slums, without piped water or proper refuse collection systems. Serious infectious diseases such as malaria, cholera, and typhoid fever were commonplace. The annual rate of population growth at that time was over 4 per cent.

The industrialisation of Singapore began with the development of an industrial estate in Jurong. The chemical and electronic industries grew rapidly during the 1970s. Later developments took place in software design, precision machinery, aerospace research, and other high value-added activities.

Singapore is now malaria-free; childhood diseases such as poliomyelitis and diphtheria no longer exist. Plague and smallpox were eradicated long ago. Infant mortality is among the lowest in the world. Every household enjoys piped, fully potable tap water. All wastes and refuse are collected and treated. The city is virtually squatter-and slum-free. There has been a conscious effort throughout Singapore to combine development with environment protection in a balanced manner.

An anti-pollution unit was formed in 1970 and a Ministry of the Environment in 1972. In 1986, the anti-pollution unit was absorbed by the ministry. The Clean Air Act 1971 was introduced with regulations to control emissions at source. Open burning of industrial and trade waste was banned, and the sulphur content of fuels used by industry was restricted. In 1990, overall air pollution levels remained low, within international standards (Ministry of the Environment, Singapore, 1992).

The Water Pollution Control and Drainage Act 1975 was intended to prevent the pollution of watercourses by the discharge of human or industrial waste. Today, 97 per cent of the population are served by sewers, and all industrial estates are sewered. Industrial wastewater must be pretreated; raw sewage is treated at six major sewage treatment works. Refuse is collected, treated, and disposed of daily from all premises; over half of this refuse is incinerated.

The 'Keep Singapore Clean' campaign has been maintained since 1968. Since 1970, tree planting has been undertaken and nature reserve lands of nearly 3000 hectares have been designated.

The environmental impact of all proposed developments is assessed and considered before each development is allowed to proceed. The Ministry of the Environment is consulted by the planning and development control authorities. The ministry checks these proposals, assesses the possible impacts on the environment, ensuring that new industrial and residential developments are properly sited and are compatible with surrounding land use.

Regular monitoring of the ambient air, inland coastal waters, is carried out to assess the adequacy and effectiveness of control programs. The quality of water in inland waters is good and supports aquatic life. The coastal waters meet the standards for recreational use. Air pollutants remain at a satisfactory level and there is no photochemical smog.

These achievements in Singapore have been reviewed independently (Australian Trade Commission, 1991) and described in Singapore's national report to the UN Conference on Environment and Development, 1992 (Singapore Inter-Ministry Committee, 1991).

9.11 Taiwan

The Republic of China, off the south-east coast of mainland China, of 36 000 square kilometres, has a population of 20.7 million; the average population density being 576 people per square kilometre, one of the highest in the world. However, as about two-thirds of Taiwan is mountainous or hilly, much of it forested, densities above 1 000 people per square kilometre in the coastal plains and basins are common. Industrial progress since 1960, despite modest mineral resources, has ensured Taiwan a place as one of the richest Asian 'Little Dragons' (South Korea, Singapore, and Hong Kong are others).

However, as a result of this rapid economic growth, the expansion and urbanisation of the population, there have been increases in the use of chemical fertilisers and pesticides, the growth in the number of motor vehicles, the rapid acceleration in energy consumption, and environmental pollution. Since the introduction of chemical fertilisers, night soil has been disposed of mostly into rivers and streams instead of being applied to the land. The sewerage system is quite inadequate; untreated municipal wastes have become a serious problem (Hung and Chou, 1989).

Measures taken in Taiwan to reduce the effects of pollution have included: discouragement of migration from country and outer urban areas into central city areas to ease the problems of over-crowding, congestion of streets, drainage and sewerage, and garbage collection and disposal. The action has enveloped environmental and city planning, emphasising zoning for polluting industries, providing buffer zones, landscaping, and planting of trees and shrubs; set limits for polluting gases in the general atmosphere and for pollutants in water; prevention of massive pollution from livestock farms; the adoption of wastewater treatment and

recycling; progressive planning and construction of municipal sewage treatment plants and sewerage systems; comprehensive water quality management for designated rivers and regions; and monitoring air and water quality and noise levels. Some of the legislative measures are indicated in checklist 9.8 (Gilpin and Lin, 1990).

CHECKLIST 9.8

Taiwan: evolution of environmental management

1967 Taiwan provincial government assigns air and water pollution control to the Taiwan Institute of Environmental Sanitation and the Taiwan Water Pollution Control Agency, respectively.

1974 Water Pollution Control Act.

1975 Water Pollution Control Regulations announced for Hsintien river.

1976 Water pollution control measures announced for Taiwan Province and Taipei Municipality; Water Pollution Control Regions announced for Keelung and Tamshui rivers.

1979 Executive Yuan issues an order that government departments are to undertake EIAs for proposed major projects, to reconcile growth and development with social and environmental considerations.

1980 Executive Yuan instructs the Taiwan Power Company (Taipower) to undertake EIAs for all future nuclear power plants.

1981 Atomic Energy Council establishes a Radioactive Waste Unit.

1982 Department of Health establishes a Division of Toxic Substances Control.

1983 Executive Yuan issues an order (Executive Order 1854) that EIAs are to be conducted not only for major government projects but also for major private sector projects including scenic and recreational site developments, which are otherwise likely to cause environmental pollution and deterioration.

National Park Law stipulated the undertaking of EIAs and a requirement for licences for specified developments and activities within national park areas.

Taiwan Environmental Protection Bureau established, consolidating the functions of the Taiwan Institute of Environmental Sanitation and the Taiwan Water Pollution Control Agency; City Environmental Protection Bureau established for Taipei and Kaohsiung.

1985 Atomic Energy Council imposes a requirement that EIA for nuclear power stations shall include a safety analysis report.

Taiwan Environmental Protection Bureau formulates a tentative national EIA Program for 1985–90.

1986 Hill Land Preservation Regulation stipulated that proposed developments involving 100 acres (40 hectares) or more of hill land shall be subject to EIA before approval.

Public demonstration against a proposed titanium dioxide plant at Lukang.

1987 Environmental Protection Administration established (superseding the Bureau) to control air, water, and noise pollution, and hazardous wastes, under the jurisdiction of the Executive Yuan.

1991 Amendments to the Air Pollution Control Act and the Noise Control Act. Settlement Law for Public Nuisance Disputes introduced to help resolve controversies involving pollution. Paper recycling plan a success.

1992 Afforestation campaign launched. Hsuehpa national park to be established. Villagers claim compensation for damage to health from thermal power stations. Sixth naphtha cracking plant endorsed after EIA. Residents protest against location of fourth nuclear power station.

The increasing deterioration of the environment and resulting pollution problems are of great concern to the general public about the 'quality of life' in Taiwan. A 1986 survey revealed that more than 60 per cent of the people favoured protection and conservation of the natural environment rather than the unrestricted pursuit of economic growth (Min-der Foundation, 1986). Since then, there have been public expressions of disquiet about specific proposed industrial developments, and the possibility of additional nuclear generating capacity.

EIA

The concept of EIA was first mooted in Taiwan during a 1974 symposium on modern engineering technology (Environmental Protection Administration, 1989). Subsequently, a national construction committee concluded that the use of EIAs was necessary; at this stage the Bureau of Environmental Protection (under the Department of Health) actively promoted it. An EIA bill was drafted and reviewed in 1982 by the Executive Yuan. However,

the Executive Yuan recognised the lack of experience and skilled human resources available in Taiwan then for that purpose, and recommended a progressive program to be developed over 5 years. The Executive Yuan is responsible for policy and administration; and the Legislative Yuan is the main law-making body.

The Executive Yuan had already applied the principle to various segments of the economy since 1979, with particular reference to nuclear power plants. In 1985, the Bureau of Environmental Protection finalised a tentative national EIA program for 1985 to 1990; this was approved by the Executive Yuan on 17 October 1985.

In sum, EIA legislation in Taiwan has yet to be fully established (Gilpin and Lin, 1990). The whole procedure is under the regulation of several Executive Orders, and parts of Acts and Regulations such as the National Park Law and the Hill Land Preservation Regulation. Between 1985 and 1990, more than 50 EISs were assessed about the petroleum, petrochemical, cement, steel, and pesticide industries; major infrastructure projects such as power plants, dams, highways, ports and harbours, ocean outfall sewerage systems, solid waste treatment and disposal facilities, mass transit systems, and new community development projects; large-scale resource extraction projects such as major mining activities, logging, and ground water irrigation projects; and projects adjacent to, or within, environmentally sensitive areas including national parks, wetlands, deep-slope areas, tidal lands, natural preservation areas, and areas of unique, historical, archaeological, scientific or educational value.

The emerging flow chart for the EIA process is presented in figure 25. Problems and difficulties in its implementation still exist. See also figures 26 and 27.

9.12　Thailand

Thailand has a population of 56.8 million, with an average of 111 people per square kilometre; metropolitan Bangkok has a population of about 6.5 million. Rice remains the mainstay of the domestic economy and chief export, with newer crops growing such as maize, sugar, and tapioca. Rubber, tin, and teak are other valuable exports. Heavy industries such as cement and petrochemicals are now developing. Thailand's forests have suffered extensively from over-use and mismanagement. Forests covered over 50 per cent of the total land area in the early 1960s and forests are now only 28 per cent of the total land area. Uncontrolled logging and land clearance for farming have been the two factors responsible (Thailand, 1992).

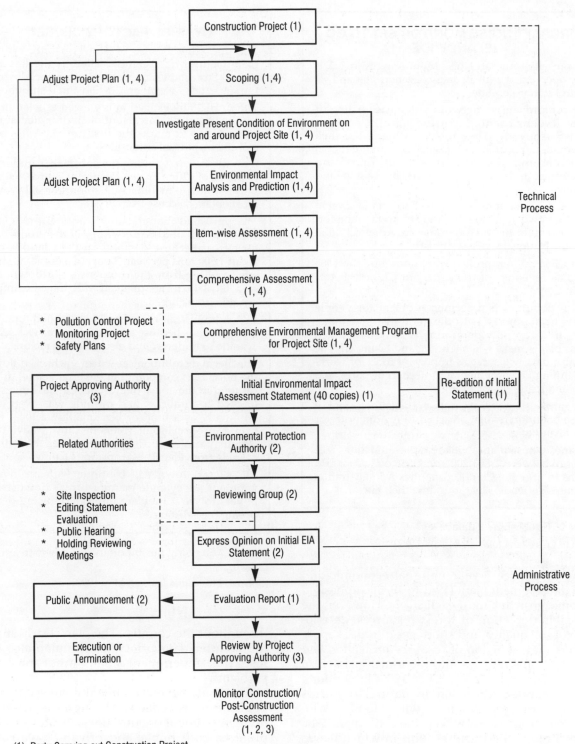

Notes:
(1) Party Carrying out Construction Project
(2) Environmental Protection Authority
(3) Project-Approving Authority
(4) Party Performing EIA

Figure 25 Taiwan: flow chart for the environmental impact process

(Source: Environmental Protection Administration, *An introduction to environmental protection in the Taiwan area, Republic of China*, EPA, Taipei, 1989, p. 15)

AIRCRAFT NOISE MONITOR SET TO GO ISLANDWIDE

Taiwan's first Aircraft Noise Monitoring Network is now operational with 59 data-collection sites and six control stations on-line.

The comprehensive network will measure aircraft noise level by scientific instruments at several airports islandwide. They include Chiang Kai-shek International near Taipei, Hsiao-kang International in Kaohsiung, domestic airports in Taipei and Taichung, and military airports in Tainan and Hualien.

It took the Environmental Protection Administration just over two years to plan and set up the monitoring system for the Civil Aeronautics Administration and the National Defense Ministry.

The US$5 million project was funded by the 1988 surplus revenues of the state-run Chinese Petroleum Corp.

Noise pollution is a serious problem for people living near airports. With the multi-instrument system, EPA can now determine exactly how much noise planes make when landing and taking off. The reliable data will serve as important tools for working through environmental protection disputes, and for conducting city planning.

The new system will strengthen the enforcement of noise pollution regulations, said EPA Administrator Jaw Shau-kong.

Airlines whose planes violate noise guidelines face fines of between US$1,200 and US$6,000 Also, EPA plans to urge the Civil Aeronautics Administration to punish offenders by grounding their aircraft.

Figure 26 Establishing a database
(Source: *Free China Journal*, 24 July 1992)

CYANIDE FACTORY CLOSED

The operating license of Taiwan's only cyanide manufacturer has been cancelled by the Environmental Protection Administration in a crackdown on the substance's illegal production and distribution.

The April 28 investigation is viewed as a landmark for the island's enforcement of environmental protection laws. It marks the first time EPA has been assisted by judicial authorities.

Cyanide is listed among the substances under the Republic of China Toxic Chemicals Control Act. Any firm wishing to manufacture, import or sell cyanide must obtain a license from EPA.

The punished manufacturer's annual production was in excess of 8,000 tons. Most of the product was for export because demand on the island is only about 1,500 tons per year. To avoid a domestic shortage resulting from the company's shutdown, EPA said local factories in need will have to import cyanide from abroad.

EPA Administrator Jaw Shau-kong called for a halt on operations because the manufacturer was selling cyanide to underground electroplating factories.

The illegal distribution caused an unchecked flow of the poisonous compound in the local market. It also resulted in the abuse of cyanide. Careless ingesting has led to fatalities, and cyanide was even used criminally as a tool for blackmailing a local food firm. Moreover, some rivers in Taiwan have been seriously polluted by waste water containing cyanide from illegal electroplating factories.

EPA's crackdown will continue with an investigation of the cyanide manufacturer's downstream buyers to see if they are improperly using or disposing the substance.

Figure 27 Stressing the importance of downstream policing
(Source: *Free China Journal*, May 1992)

The first three 5-year national economic and social development plant (1961 to 1976) emphasised economic growth almost exclusively. However, the noticeable depletion of forest resources, deterioration of soil quality, and shortages of water supply led to the introduction of resource protection and rehabilitation strategies into the fourth plan (1976 to 1981). The fifth plan (1981 to 1986) hoped for a more integrated approach to natural resources development coordinated with local socio-economic progress. However, the sixth plan (1986 to 1991) marked a turning point in which it was recognised that the depletion of the resource base might act as a constraint to development.

At the same time, escalating urban environmental problems such as air pollution, water pollution, and the growing volume of hazardous wastes, raised problems as pressing as natural resource depletion. The seventh plan (1991 to 1996) has set definite targets to improve environmental quality throughout the country. The plan clearly supports the polluter-pays principle. The plan also recognises that government alone cannot solve all the problems.

The growing environmental consciousness of Thai society is reflected through the activities of non-government organisations. A number of large projects, both public and private, have run into strong opposition from a collective concern by these voluntary organisations and the media.

Progressive measures are being taken against air pollutants. Catalytic converters are required on all new cars using only unleaded fuel. There is also an annual inspection program for vehicle emissions. National ambient air quality standards have been established.

Domestic sewage and sullage effluents are a major source of water pollution problems; less than 2 per cent of the population of Bangkok is connected to a sewage treatment system. Industrial wastewater may contain toxic concentrations of organic and inorganic chemicals, although pollution from sugar factories has been much reduced. The seventh plan sets out defined targets to improve water quality, with particular emphasis on the estuaries of the major rivers and the tourist areas. Measures are also being taken against hazardous and toxic wastes.

At present, the number of natural conservation and recreation areas in Thailand totals 226, covering 12.7 per cent of the country. Thailand has one of the highest ratios of protected area to total land area in the world. The seventh plan seeks to raise this ratio to 25 per cent.

In 1992, the Thai government strengthened its environmental legislation with the National Environmental Act and the Wildlife Conservation Act.

EIA

The Office of the National Environment Board (ONEB) is responsible for the administration of the EIA process in Thailand, which has slowly evolved over the years. The National Environmental Quality Act was revised in 1992, to improve the operation of the system. The proponent for a project may be a government agency, state enterprise, or private company or corporation; the proponent is responsible for the preparation of an EIA report.

Whoever is the final decision-maker, all EIAs must be routed through the ONEB.

Since 1984, it has been a requirement that EIA reports have to be prepared by consultancies registered with ONEB; these firms alone have the right to conduct EIA. Once submitted to ONEB, a review team is set up to ensure impartial and well-qualified review. Clearly, in Thailand, an EIA is what is described elsewhere as an EIS. Terms of reference (amounting to scoping) are defined through discussion with ONEB before the preparation of an EIA. For public projects, the final decision-maker is the cabinet. See figure 28.

The kinds of projects to which EIA applies include the following: dam or reservoir, irrigation scheme, airport, hotel or resort facility, mass transit system, expressway, mine, industrial estate, port or harbour, power plant, oil refinery, natural gas plant, iron or steel works, cement works, and pulp mill (Office of the National Environment Board, 1988).

One of the EIA studies in the 1980s was the Nampong basin project in the Udon-Thani, Loei, and Khon Kaen provinces in Thailand, carried out by the Mekong Committee in three phases. The project consisted of a high rockfill dam, a hydro power station, and a network of irrigation canals. This multi-purpose project for power, irrigation, and flood control, was completed in 1966. The PPA which included the operational experience of this project, was conducted over a 5-year period in three different phases.

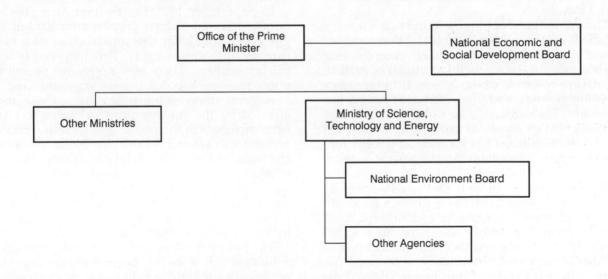

NEB sets pollution control standards, administers the EIA process, and provides liaison to UNEP

Figure 28 Thailand: organisation chart for environmental management, 1992

Specific EIA studies have been on plant diseases, livestock diseases, land use, soil physics and chemistry, insects and pests, human health and nutrition, socio-economic characteristics, weeds, hydrological studies, water quality, fish and plankton. Phase 3 included the planning and implementation of an 'integrated management-oriented simulation model of the Nampong basin'.

9A   Case study: Proposed Bayer Australia facilities for the formulation and storage of agricultural and veterinary products at Kurnell, Sydney, Australia

This controversial DA was 'called in' by the Minister for Planning and Environment and was subject to a public inquiry. Reporting in early 1987, the Commission of Inquiry recommended that the DA be refused. The minister, as consent authority, endorsed this recommendation. The residents of Kurnell village regarded the outcome as a major victory.

The DA and its accompanying EIS were placed on public exhibition by the Sutherland Shire Council for 6 weeks in 1986. It was then referred by direction to the minister. The public inquiry was held in 1986; more than 300 parties registered for the inquiry, which with adjournments, stretched over 3 months.

The Commission of Inquiry found that it was not satisfied, on the evidence, that the Bayer project would operate without harmful effect on the local environment of the Kurnell Peninsula; in particular, nature reserves, oyster leases, fishing, prawn breeding grounds, and the wetlands of Botany Bay generally. The evidence had not established with certainty that emissions of toxic chemicals, even at low levels, would not have a detrimental environmental impact, particularly for the aquatic environment.

Further, spillages of toxic chemicals were likely to occur on Captain Cook Drive through accidents, the spillages being incapable of containment. Road improvements would not eliminate this risk, but Bayer objected to undertaking such works, and to a number of suggested environmental controls. The State Pollution Control Commission stressed the difficulties of adequate independent and constant supervision of the proposed high-temperature incinerator.

The commission found that alternative sites for the project had not been adequately explored. It was noted with regret by the commission that Bayer Australia had spent funds on the acquisition and upgrading of both buildings and site, before the determination of their DA.

A consequence of the refusal of the development application was the rezoning by the minister of the controversial site and surrounding area, restricting it to general industry only. It had been argued by the commission that the conservation of the wetlands at Kurnell should have priority so those wetlands are protected from environmental damage likely to be caused by the location of new hazardous industries at Kurnell.

(Derived from Report of the Commission of Inquiry into the proposed Bayer Australia facilities for the formulation and storage of agricultural and veterinary products at Kurnell, Office of Commissioners of Inquiry, Sydney, January 1987)

9B   Case study: Proposed third runway, Sydney (Kingsford Smith) Airport, Australia

The further development of Sydney airport versus the development of a new international airport elsewhere in the Sydney region, to meet the growing demand for air travel, had been a controversial issue for years, with governments, both federal and state, and local councils taking up various positions.

In September 1990, the Federal Airports Corporation issued a draft prepared by Kinhill Engineers Pty. Ltd. for the construction of a third runway at Sydney airport. This followed federal EIA procedures. There was a 3-month period for public review. No public inquiry was conducted.

A great many submissions from those most affected by the runway proposal were received from members of the public, conservation bodies, and councils around Botany Bay. Noise was a central issue. In 1991, the federal government decided to proceed with the third runway, while making a start with a new international airport at Badgerys Creek. New South Wales EIA legislation was not relevant to this project, though close consultation took place between the two governments.

The principal issues raised by people opposed to a third runway were the effects of aircraft noise, the preference for early development of an airport at Badgerys Creek, the increased risk of air crashes, and air pollution effects. The issues most frequently put by those supporting the third runway included the convenient access to Sydney airport, the distance of Badgerys Creek from the city centre, and the need to increase airport capacity to enhance the tourism industry, in particular, and the economy, in general.

On the central issue of noise, it became clear that many residents would benefit as the existing east-west runway would eventually be used much less. Then residents to the north might well experience greater noise. Special measures were contemplated to deal with this. After years of debate, a third runway at Sydney airport was inevitable, not because it was ideal, but because within the time constraints then presented, it became the only available practicable solution.

The EIS was one of the longest and probably most complex in Australia's assessment history, of 680 pages. The public's contribution, however, greatly exceeded this. In principle, it was an issue of alternative sites; in practice, it was a matter of the greatest complexity.

(Derived from Federal Airports Corporation *Proposed Third Runway Sydney (Kingsford Smith) Airport: Draft Environmental Impact Statement*, Kinhill Engineers Pty. Ltd., September 1990, and subsequent documents and announcements)

9C Case study: Mount Piper to Marulan transmission line, NSW, Australia

In the late 1980s it became necessary to identify a route for a major electricity transmission line from the new 1 320 MW Mount Piper power station to Marulan, a distance of 160 kilometres. The Electricity Commission of New South Wales (Elcom) chose a route for this transmission line. However, at a public meeting to describe this route there was vehement opposition from the local residents. In the face of this opposition, the proposed route was withdrawn.

In 1990 Elcom prepared alternatives with a different strategy for presentation, avoiding the idea of arbitrary selection or preference. Professional judgement about routes was set aside, and a comprehensive graphic overlay procedure was developed. This involved:

- defining the outer limits of the geographic area for a possible route;
- listing all of the factors that might influence the final choice of route, including engineering, economic, social, and environmental factors;
- establishing a suitable indicator for each factor and applying the indicator over the entire geographic area for potential routes;
- ascribing relative weights to each indicator for route selection;

- combining the weighted indicators by computer to produce composite maps;
- selecting routes on the composite maps.

Local community groups and conservation interests were invited to participate in this new route selection process. They were asked to review and modify, if appropriate, the factors selected and to choose the relative weightings of the factors. They could produce their own composite maps, the selection of factors and weights influencing the outcome.

What was particularly interesting in this exercise, was that the local community group opposed to the initial previously rejected Elcom proposal chose, using their own factors and weights, a route that was almost identical. However, the general preference was for an alternative route involving variations from the original proposal. The methodology proved both open and transparent.

Another interesting feature of this exercise was that electromagnetic radiation (emr) was not well known and was not included in the NSW Department of Planning's stipulations for the contents of the EIS. Despite this lack of interest, an analysis of emr was included in the EIS and the route selection criteria. Just before the construction of the line, when emr had become a recognised issue, local community interests then challenged the adequacy of the EIS before the NSW Land and Environment Court. The court found the EIS to be adequate, clearing the project for construction. The absence of discussion of emr could have proved a fatal flaw.

(Derived from Pacific Power, author: Jenkins, B. 'Integrating environmental considerations into the development of major projects', presented at a conference on *Facilitating major projects* April, Sydney, Australia, 1992)

9D Case study: The Three Gorges water conservation and hydroelectric project, China

The Changjiang (the Yangtze) river, more than 6 300 kilometres, is the longest river in both China and Asia. It rises in the Tibetan highlands, traverses 12 Chinese provinces or regions, reaching the sea near Shanghai. Intensive cargo and passenger traffic travels 2 700 kilometres of the river's course. Large ships reach Wuhan, 1 000 kilometres up-river from the coast. The Changjian basin is the granary of China, on which almost half the crops of the country grow. The potential resources for the generation of electrical energy from the river are very great.

The mountainous Three Gorges of Tsyuytan, U, and Silin, are located in the middle course of the Changjiang river, an area of great natural beauty. A proposal for a major hydroelectric scheme could yield up to 40 000 MW, and could help control destructive floods and lead to the development of new agricultural land. The development of the project is now in its earliest stages, and it remains highly controversial. It commanded 10 papers at the 1993 Annual Meeting of the International Association for Impact Assessment held in Shanghai.

The project has been listed in the 10-year Program for Economic and Social Development of China, 1991 to 2000. It involves the construction of a dam, a reservoir, a hydroelectric station, a navigation lock, and other necessary auxiliary facilities. Apart from its advantages for flood control, power generation, and navigation, the project is intended to bring benefits in irrigation, aquatic cultivation, tourism, and economic development, in general, in the regions along the whole middle reaches of the Changjiang. The project was reaffirmed, despite reservations, at the Fifth Plenary Session of the Seventh National People's Congress of China in Beijing in April 1992.

The total length of the reservoir created by the dammed section of the river will be 600 kilometres. Consequently about 725 000 people need to be resettled; more than 54 per cent of whom are residents of towns and cities; the rest are rural residents. About 33 800 hectares of farmland will be flooded in the territory in 19 counties and cities in the provinces of Sichuan and Hubei. The major construction program is expected to take 15 years. The hydroelectric station with its 26 hydraulic generators would be completed in that time. Over half the cost of the total project will be absorbed in the resettlement program. It is now 70 years since the Three Gorges was first proposed.

The technical and economic feasibility study for the project was financed initially by the Canadian International Development Agency and completed by a Canadian consortium called the Canadian Yangtze Joint Venture (CYJV). Barber (1993) argues that the project was inadequately assessed by the CYJV and that the consequences to the lives, health, and properties of those directly affected by the dam was underestimated. Bi (1993), while recognising the immense economic and social benefits, stresses also the obvious, irreversible, ecological impacts.

Chen (1993) has concluded that the natural beauty of the Three Gorges will be seriously damaged with other adverse ecological effects. In common with Bi, Chen argues that some, though not all these, adverse effects could be mitigated.

Yang (1993) emphasises that the Three Gorges is among the 10 most famous scenic regions in China, and that the development proposal will have a great adverse affect on this area. Hence, this aspect should be clearly taken into account by the Chinese government.

Questions have been raised about soil quality in that area, and the adverse social, economic, and cultural effects. There has also been criticism of the Canadian feasibility studies. It has been argued constructively that a number of smaller schemes would be preferable with more reliable control of flooding and much reduced social and environmental impact with less severe implications for existing industries. Objectors to the larger project have not always been kindly treated.

The Three Gorges development project clearly offers comprehensive benefits for flood prevention, power generation, and transportation; and while measures may be adopted to minimise the adverse effects of large-scale migration, ecological damage, and soil erosion, there will be many environmental management problems and social penalties in the short term. This issue illustrates the difficulties of balancing short- and long-term losses against prospective benefits maybe 15 years into the future. Clearly, the proposal should be kept under continuous review and its alternatives closely examined.

(Derived from the *Proceedings of the 13th Annual Meeting of the International Association for Impact Assessment*, Shanghai, China, 12-15 June 1993, and other sources)

9E   Case study: Fushun West open-pit mine, China

The Fushun West open-pit mine is located in the western part of the Fushun coalfield, 900 kilometres north-east from Beijing. The mine lease covers about 17 square kilometres. The Hwunhe river, the major river of the region, flows along the north side of the mine; close to the eastern boundary runs the Guching creek which joins the Hwunhe river. The production of the mine in the 1980s was about 3 million tonnes each year.

Each year 35 million to 40 million cubic metres of overburden are stripped away. About 8 million tonnes of this consists of rich oil shale which is processed in an oil distillation plant near the mine. The pit is now about 300 metres deep, with 28 benches. Water must be continuously pumped from the pit; discharged at the surface it flows into Guching creek before entering the Hwunhe river. A coal preparation plant was built adjacent to the pit some years ago, made up of baum jigs and heavy-medium washers.

Three spoil areas have been established outside the mine area; some beans, corn, and wheat, have been grown on parts to improve the environment. In 1970, re-vegetation was attempted on parts of the eastern spoil area. Rehabilitation of the open pit is impossible before the mine is exhausted.

Water pollution arises from three sources: seeping water from spoil areas, de-sliming water from the coal preparation plant, and drainage water from the open pit. It adversely affects farmlands and water wells, growth of plants, and the health of residents. Commune members have protested strongly against these hazards.

The People's Government of Liaoning province decided that compensation should be paid for each tonne of de-sliming water drained into the creek. In consequence, a monthly payment is received from the mine. Later, part of the de-sliming water was diverted to the Wangliang spoil area to irrigate a paddy field there. The aim now is to recover 60 000 tonnes of coal slime each year and alleviate the blocking of the river and canal.

Other problems have been associated with chimney effluents, few boilers having dust-removal equipment. Other sources of dust at the mine have included unsealed roads, stockpiles of coal slime, and blasting. Silicosis is still a problem among the miners.

Monitoring arrangements have been introduced for vibration, and shock waves, and noise. Fines are imposed by the province where noise limits are exceeded.

By 1981, it had become apparent that a major reconstruction plan was needed with adequate environment protection measures.

The lesson here is that a mine was established with no environment protection measures, environmental management plan, without controls and monitoring in place. The need to pay compensation to the province on the one hand, and the need for expensive major reconstruction on the other, illustrates the need for the early EIA of major projects, and subsequent PPA.

(Source: Gilpin, Alan (1985) *The human environment: the world after Stockholm*, unpublished manuscript)

9F   Case study: New international airport, Hong Kong

The international airport at Kai Tak, located on the eastern fringe of Kowloon, is to be replaced by a new international airport with two independent runways at Chek Lap Kok to the west of Hong Kong island. Land for the airport will be formed by levelling the islands of Chek Lap Kok and Lam Chau just off Lantau Island and by using excavated material from marine borrow areas.

The airport master plan study began in 1990, establishing a basic airport configuration. The configuration selected involved the dredging and disposal of more than 70 million cubic metres of marine mud and a requirement for over 150 million cubic metres of fill. An early decision was taken to retain a sea channel between the airport island and the coast of North Lantau; this enabled the natural coastline west of Tung Chung to be largely preserved allowing also for tidal flushing of a potential bay area to the east of Chek Lap Kok.

An early EIA study of construction impacts identified a number of significant impacts. About 70 dwellings would be adversely affected by noise. The construction program started in 1992 on a 24 hour basis. The Hong Kong Executive Council granted exemption from the Noise Control Ordinance for the construction program to proceed round the clock. However, this exemption was subject to conditions, including provision for the installation of air conditioners in affected dwellings allowing windows and doors to be closed to shut out noise. In addition, a temporary 10-metre earth bund was installed along the southern edge of the airport island as a barrier to construction noise.

Dust has been the main pollutant arising from construction activity, with rock-blasting producing the greatest impacts. Little could be done to reduce dust emissions from blasting operations.

The destruction of the two islands and their terrestrial and marine life, necessitated a number of compensatory conservation measures, among them the rescue, study, and possible reestablishment of the rare Romer's tree frog.

The EIA study otherwise confirmed that the airport island will have an insignificant effect on water quality, bulk flow and tidal regimes, subject to the preservation of a sea channel to assist tidal flushing some 200 metres wide. Aircraft noise impacts were predicted for various assumed aircraft fleet mixes using Noise Exposure Forecast contours. It was predicted that by the year 2000 an acceptable level would only be exceeded for a small number of dwellings at Sha Lo Wan on North Lantau, west of Tung Chung. These villagers were to be relocated and all new noise-sensitive land uses to be excluded from the airport vicinity.

(Derived from Environment Protection Department, Environment Hong Kong 1992, Government Printer, Hong Kong, 1992)

9G   Case study: Population and family health project, Bangladesh

The People's Republic of Bangladesh has a population of 110.5 million, with a density of 768 people per square kilometre; it is one of the poorest and most densely populated countries in the world. It has an agricultural economy based on rice-growing in the Ganges delta. The country is heavily dependent on foreign aid.

Political conflicts have often been overshadowed by the natural elements. Storms and flooding during the monsoon season take a huge toll on life and property annually. Malnutrition is widespread with high infant and child mortality. Life expectancy at birth is about 56 years. More than 80 per cent of the population has less than the required energy input in their diet.

Without moderation in population growth, the number of people in Bangladesh will increase by about 18 million people between 1993 and 2000. The social and economic cost of absorbing this population increase will be enormous. The government of Bangladesh has given high priority to the population control program. The aim is to achieve a net reproduction rate of one child per couple by the year 2000. At present it is 4.9 per child-bearing woman.

There has been a decline in mortality and fertility rates in Bangladesh through the implementation of the government's 5-year plans. A primary target is to improve women's education and devolve responsibility for family planning from the government to the community. Should these plans succeed, there will be a substantial positive impact on the human and natural environment in Bangladesh.

The third 5-year plan aimed to consolidate gains made in the family planning, service delivery, and maternal child health services. It pursued programs for immunisation, diarrhoea management, the supply of medicines for maternity and child health, and birth control education. It gave assistance to non-government organisations which promote and provide family planning services. Additional field workers were provided to increase effective cover in the rural areas. Training and retraining was also promoted.

Precise measurement of the environmental benefits of these programs is unavailable because of a deficiency in the statistics on health and birth rates.

However, Bangladesh now enters its fourth 5-year program in this crucial area. It illustrates that environmental considerations do not just relate to projects, but also to policies and programs which can deliver positive environmental benefits when seen in that context.

(Derived from Australian International Development Assistance Bureau, 1991)

9H   Case study: The Semerak rural development project, Malaysia

This case study relates to the EIA of a watershed development. The Semerak rural development (SRD) project has been promulgated by the Malaysian government on behalf of the Kelantan state government; its purpose is to develop the north Kelantan alluvial flood plain into one of the country's major agricultural productive areas, particularly as a 'rice bowl'.

The SRD project has enveloped major flood mitigation, irrigation, and drainage schemes to substantially reduce annual flood damage and through irrigation, to enable double cropping. It encompasses the entire Semerak river basin and the whole of the district of Pasir Puteh. See map 2.

The EIA report identified a number of environmental impacts likely to arise from the flood mitigation and irrigation works:
- The two quarry sites for the supply of stone are located in a designated forest reserve; denudation of forest cover, erosion of the denuded hill, and loss of terrestrial habitats would occur. There will also be adverse changes to the hydraulic characteristics of the Yong river.
- The construction of a new flood channel by excavation will require the disposal of 1.5 million cubic metres of spoil; this will be dumped within nearby wetlands. These areas will be lost as wetlands, the height being raised by about 2 metres.
- When the new flood channel is constructed, the progressive littoral drifts along the coastline are expected to gradually silt up the mouth of the river and pollute the waterway, with reduced flushing action.

The EIA report proposed a variety of mitigation measures:
- For the quarry operations the proper planning and designing of blasting operations would minimise the amount of explosive; the quarries should be sited at least 500 metres away from residences; airborne dust removal equipment should be adopted at the site; wet methods should be used to control fugitive dust; truck speeds should be limited; and the quarry sites eventually rehabilitated.

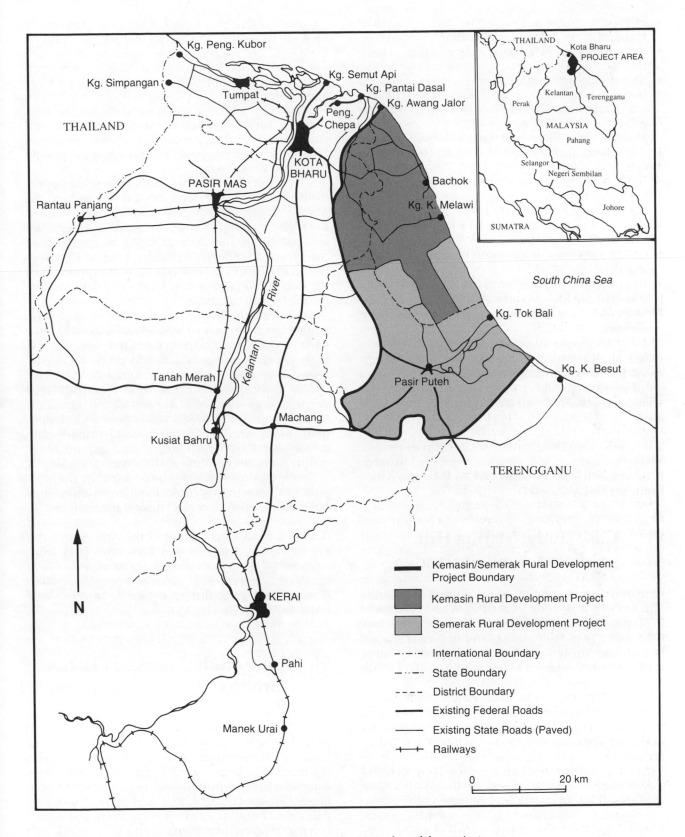

Map 2 The Semarak rural development project, Malaysia: location plan of the project area

- Spoil should be redirected to sites other than wetland areas so far as practicable.
- A decision should be made as to whether to keep the river mouth open; or whether to close it.
- Monitoring and surveillance measures should be instituted to measure the consequences of specific environmental modifications induced by the project.

However, the EIA report, later reviewed by Zain and Ibrahim, apparently failed to address several issues:

- neither the problem of over-drainage of the Gelam forest area was not examined, nor the issue of high salinity;
- the impacts of closing the river mouth were not examined;
- the implications of alternative areas for dumping;
- the potential impacts from the proposed activities, that are likely to affect fisheries and the viability of fishing villages, have yet to be taken into account.

Despite shortcomings, the EIA report still provided an opportunity to rectify various environmental problems arising from the project, proving a good planning tool for the promotion of sustainable development in an agriculturally productive area.

(Derived from Department of the Environment, Malaysia, *Berita, EIA newsletter no. 1*, January–June, an article by O. Zain and A. Ibrahim, Kuala Lumpur, Malaysia, 1991)

9I   Case study: Martha Hill goldmine, New Zealand

One of a new generation of goldmines, the Martha Hill project was to be located at Waihi, a town of 3500 population 150 kilometres south of Auckland, principal city of the North Island of New Zealand. Waihi had grown up around a previous large underground goldmine during the years 1882 to 1952.

An audit team was established under New Zealand's environmental protection and enhancement procedures, to serve both environmental and planning approval purposes. The team was led by an officer from the Commission for the Environment, a commission created by the New Zealand government in 1973. Membership of the team included the proponent, and representatives from government departments, the scientific community, and local residents.

The proponent established a liaison forum with the local community, keeping the public well-

informed about planning for the project. Chaired by a townsperson, the forum met on 22 occasions from 1982 to 1987 during the planning, approvals, and construction phases. These forums were open to all; reports from government departments were another feature.

However, bilateral meetings between the proponent, various government departments, and community groups, provided the main source of the environmental conditions attached eventually to the project approvals.

The proponent concluded that the wide opportunities for public discussion did not reduce the number of objections (about 150), but they resulted in excellent relationships between all of the parties and contributed in the end to the acceptability of the project. Similarly, community representatives found the forum established a good rapport from the outset. All parties saw great value later during the bilateral netotiations.

However, the lengthy period (27 months from application to approval) was acknowledged to have been too long and the direct and indirect costs too high. On the other hand, the EIA process was perceived as credible, unbiased, and fair.

The Department of Scientific and Industrial Research was involved at various stages of the EIA, in the scoping of technical issues from an independent standpoint. The department identified some critical issues, in particular river and ground water quality, which were subjected to baseline studies.

Some environmental groups felt that the proponent's consultants could have given more serious consideration to project design alternatives.

(Derived from Department of the Arts, Sport, the Environment, Tourism and Territories [1987] *Environmental impact assessment as a management tool: workshop proceedings*, November, Australian Government Publishing Service, Canberra, Australia, 1987, pp. 40–41)

9J   Case study: Formosa Plastics Group (FPG) naphtha plant, Taiwan

In January 1992, the government of the Republic of China finally granted approval for the sixth naphtha plant to be constructed in Taiwan, subject to an extensive list of anti-pollution conditions. The Formosa Plastics Group (FPG) had faced 5 years of delay because of the sustained protests and opposition of local environmentalists.

The decision followed a report by the 29-member screening committee of the Environmental

Protection Administration, which finally recommended conditional approval after a thorough EIA.

The FPG naphtha cracker will break down crude oil to produce ethylene and other byproducts important to the petrochemical industry. However, the EPAs screening committee requires this plant to be built in stages to allow for close monitoring by environmental officials.

In the west coast county of Yunlin is the third alternative site for its cracker nominated by FPG. The facility will comprise 23 production plants. The land requirement for the initial phase will be augmented by landfill by 1997.

The project is scheduled for completion in 4 or 5 years. By then, the complex will be manufacturing oil byproducts for medium-sized petrochemical manufacturers and downstream industries that produce a wide range of goods.

FPG first proposed to build its naphtha cracker in 1986 in the Kuanyin industrial zone, Taoyuan county. The proposal had the initial blessings of government authorities, but environmental opposition spread into the streets as residents near the proposed site rallied against the construction of the cracker.

The company then embarked on a public education program to convince people that the naphtha plant could be designed and operated in such a way as to maintain clean air, clean water, and green pastureland. The attempt failed. FPG next tried to convince the Litze residents in Ilan county, but these negotiations also failed. FPG continued to try to improve its public image through the media.

However, most people of underdeveloped Yunlin county have welcomed the project. During the construction phase, about 10 000 workers are required, 10 times the number required for the construction of Taiwan's fifth naphtha cracker, operated by the state-run Chinese Petroleum Corporation. In the long-term, about 100 000 jobs will be available.

(Derived from *Free China Journal*, 31 January 1992, and other sources)

9K   Case study: Tin smelter, Thailand

The Kingdom of Thailand has a population of just under 56.8 million, with a density of 111 people per square kilometres. The wealth of the country traditionally rested on growing rice and exporting the surplus. In 1985, textiles overtook rice as the leading export. Other valuable export commodities are rubber, tin, and teak. Heavy industries are now developing. However, inadequate infrastructure imposes a constraint on growth, particularly in metropolitan Bangkok, with its population of 6.5 million.

Of the heavy industries, the only tin-smelting and refining plant in Thailand is located at Ao Kham Bay on the south-east shore of Phuket Island, off the south-west coast. It produces about 20 per cent of current world output of refined tin. The industry produced three types of waste: liquid, solid, and gaseous. Air pollution is the greatest hazard of the three.

The tin smelter was established in 1964; in 1984 the industry decided to conduct an EIA. The small EIA team used a methodology developed by the Battelle Institute and the US Army Corps of Engineers in which environmental resources are classified and evaluated under four general headings namely: (a) natural physical resources; (b) natural ecological resources; (c) economic development resources; and (d) quality-of-life values.

The team noted that most complaints on record were about blasting noise from slag granulation, and smoke from blasting, and stacks. Noise had adversely affected most of the residents of the villages and dust emissions were much complained of. The smelter air emissions had caused significant reduction in the yields of coconut plantations.

On the other hand, the team identified a number of beneficial effects from the operation of the smelter. There was an improved water supply to the villages, improved job opportunities and incomes, and there was economic growth.

The only adverse effects were about air and noise pollution from the plant. Air pollution caused damage to vegetation, and left deposits of dust in living quarters. Many thought these elements could be detrimental to human health, though the evidence was not clear on this point.

For air emissions, the cyclones, baghouses and electrostatic precipitators were generally performing well, though some maintenance measures could be improved. Some of the baghouses, however, lacked stacks, the emissions going straight to atmosphere after filtering. Also some of the equipment needed additional controls to reduce arsenic trioxide emissions. Gas cooling was suggested here. An improvement in shopfloor working conditions could also be achieved by better procedures and improved maintenance. The frequency of slag explosions needed to be substantially reduced. Improvements in all areas were introduced during 1986 to 1987, coupled with an environmental monitoring program.

(Derived from UN ESCAP, 1991)

CHAPTER 10

Towards the twenty-first century

Clearly, EIA, particularly at the project level, will not change the world; nor is it designed to. For this reason, it is held in disdain by certain fundamentalist groups in the environmental movement. Such groups sometimes refuse to participate in scopings and assessments, or in commissions of inquiry. The failure of EIA is regarded as turning on two basic points; first, EISs, in either the private or public sectors, are prepared by the proponent and hence are distrusted; and, second, reviews of EISs and public inquiries are often conducted by government servants and hence are equally to be distrusted. Even outside reviewers are looked on as hand-chosen by government and that part of the culture which needs drastically revamping.

EIA procedures are seen simply as a servant, smoothing the more jarring aspects of development, and few projects are rejected. Assessments, it is felt, are undertaken within a short-term framework, excluding those long-term aspects upon which sustainable development depends.

International conferences such as the UN conferences of 1972 and 1992 are seen as talkfests, at which plenary speakers before, or after splendid meals, repeatedly declare 'I speak with sincerity'. Many delegates are selected by governments for their ability to speak, rather than to act; and at home, for skill not so much in conservation, as in handling and keeping ahead of conservationists. Besides, EIA commanded no separate chapter in Agenda 21, and appeared in the final declaration of principles only through the alertness of a Harvard-trained member of the secretariat. These views might be termed those of 'the left', though not in any distinct political sense. There is also 'the right'; the fundamentalist business element with its political allies that resents the entire EIA process on the grounds that it adds another bureaucratic layer to the whole process of conducting business, involving as it does planning permission, consents, permits, and licences. It is not the direct cost of EA that

is the greatest concern, but the indirect costs of unexpected delays, preventing more efficient plant or procedures coming on stream. It was about 1960 when the construction of a thermal power station in Britain, previously taking 5 years became 7 years or more, as a result of increasingly sophisticated environmental opposition.

EIAs can be frustrating. A company might select a correctly zoned site, indicate its willingness to meet all pollution control and environment protection standards for that site, consult at all stages with the planning, environmental, and other agencies concerned, talk to the public, and yet be met with a wall of public opposition to the proposal. The company might then face a full-scale public inquiry with development approval finally refused.

Or if approved, it will be accompanied inevitably by a raft of conditions and restraints, with requirements for regular reporting, post-project monitoring and auditing, perhaps of an independent kind.

The lack of certainty about standards to be achieved, conflict or confusion between governments at various levels (local, state, or provincial, and national), might lead to the loss elsewhere of important enterprises. The relationship between 'the left' and 'the right' is essentially polarised.

There is also much effective criticism from 'the centre'; for example, about the quality of EISs, the viability of scientific predictions in such documents, the inadequacies of the databases, lack of time for preparation of responses, the cost of obtaining copies of an EIS, the conduct of public inquiries, the absence of adequate scoping meetings, a sense of 'whitewash' about some issues at some times, and occasionally with a lack of confidence in the decision-making bodies.

However, it remains an important conclusion that at no stage have 'the left', 'the right', or 'the centre', suggested the abolition of EIA; all would simply seek its reorientation, shortening, or improvement. Its extensive and increasing application in Europe, North America, the Pacific region, and Asia, gives it a momentum based on practical success.

The UN Conference on Environment and Development in 1992, recommended the global application of the EIA technique. Principle 17 of the final agreement stated:

> Environmental impact assessment, as a national instrument, shall be undertaken for proposed activities that are likely to have a significant adverse impact on the environment and are subject to a decision of a competent national authority.

The drafting might have been improved, for EIA may need to be introduced not only federally but at state and provincial levels (as in Australia, Canada, the USA, and other federal systems); and this means that the competent authority may not be national, but competent, nonetheless. EIA also needs to be applied to policies, plans, programs, and projects, and not simply to 'activities'.

The general application of EIA principles across nations has much to commend it, though the challenge is immense. EIA is unlikely to have a comfortable passage in countries dominated by dictatorships or in countries positively opposed to democracy. It is hardly likely to flourish in countries where all criticism is suspect and opposition seen as akin to treason. A 'fair-go' is unlikely in countries riven by ancient hatreds and deep ethnic divisions. It will lack balance in all societies where women are not encouraged to have a full share of society's responsibilities. EIA seems inappropriate in countries racked by civil war, dogged by starvation, crop failures, droughts, and floods. It appears irrelevant in all those societies or segments of society where the primary concern is the next meal; some of these conditions have been described in summary in this book by the Economic and Social Commission for Asia and the Pacific (ESCAP).

Yet many Asian countries from unpromising beginnings in the early 1960s, have shown what can be achieved, and from the fruits of that achievement find the resources neceessary to combat pollution and introduce EIA procedures. In Africa, the roots of EIA are planted in Nigeria, Ghana, and Egypt. Like democracy, it might now progressively spread; more walls may fall, not simply in physical terms. North Korea and South Korea might yet be unified, so that all Korean people might join in a celebration of democracy and environmental progress. The unification of Hong Kong with China might have far-reaching and unexpected results in that vast nation. Taiwan struggles openly with the question in a small island

of a fourth nuclear power station and a fourth great national park; EIA is quite definitely 'in', with people's marches and demonstrations.

The essential ingredients of successful EIA have been reviewed in this book. It requires:

- a legislative basis;
- a schedule of those works and activities requiring an EIS;
- adequate environmental databases;
- a high level of competence in the physical and social sciences, engineering, planning, and environmental management;
- integrity in its participants;
- active public participation;
- avenues of appeal against decisions;
- avenues for remedying breaches of the legislation by any person;
- the ability for any person to require, in certain circumstances, a public inquiry;
- competent multi-disciplinary teams for the preparation of EISs and the review of such statements;
- the ready availability to the public of all relevant documents;
- the conduct of scoping meetings;
- the clear allocation of responsibilities for the enforcement of any conditions attached to a statutory development consent;
- project and post-project monitoring and auditing;
- annual reports on the conduct of the venture;
- the application of the principle to all policies, plans, programs, and projects, likely to have adverse effects on the environment;
- the clear support of regional environmental plans, and state and national policies.

Above all, EIA requires integrity in government; far too often governments introduce measures considered to be necessary for political survival, but in which the parliamentary party of the governing party as a whole does not genuinely believe. Governments than appoint suitable people to implement those policies while standing on their necks behind closed ministerial doors. Examples spring to mind!

None of the EIA systems reviewed in this book approach all the ideal requirements outlined above; nevertheless in 35 countries systems are established, some are performing well, others are gaining experience. It has hopes in the Commonwealth of Independent States affiliates and the People's Republic of China.

The first national legislation was the National Environmental Policy Act 1969 of the USA, applying to federal activities only; Japan and Singapore quickly followed in 1972, though Japan did with cabinet directives only. During the 1970s, Canada, Australia, France, Germany, the Philippines, and

Table 3 Life expectancy at birth (years), 1972, 1992, males and females

Country	1972		1992	
	M	F	M	F
Australia	67.9	74.2	73.3	79.6
Austria	66.5	73.3	72.5	79.0
Bangladesh	45*		56.4	55.4
Belgium	67.7	73.5	72.4	79.1
Britain	68.7	74.9	72.4	78.0
Canada	60.8	75.2	73.3	80.0
China	59*		68.4	71.4
Czechoslovakia	67.3	73.6	–	–
Czech and Slovak Republics	–	–	68.9	75.1
Denmark	70.7	75.4	72.0	77.7
Finland	65.4	72.6	70.8	78.9
France	68.0	75.5	72.7	80.9
Germany	–	–	72.1	78.7
Greece	67.5	70.7	72.6	77.6
Hong Kong	66.7	73.3	75.0	81.0
Iceland	70.8	76.2	75.7	80.3
India	41.9	40.6	58.1	59.1
Indonesia	47*		55.6	58.9
Ireland	68.1	71.9	71.0	76.7
Italy	67.2	72.3	73.2	79.7
Japan	69.1	74.3	75.9	81.8
Korea, South	51.1	53.7	67.4	75.4
Luxembourg	70*		70.6	77.9
Malaysia	62*		68.8	73.3
Netherlands, The	71.0	76.4	73.7	80.2
New Zealand	68.4	73.8	72.0	77.9
Norway	71.0	76.0	73.4	79.8
Pakistan	53.7	48.8	59.3	60.7
Philippines, The	57*		62.7	66.5
Poland	66.9	72.8	66.8	75.5
Portugal	60.7	66.4	70.6	77.6
Russia	–	–	63.9	74.3
Singapore	68*		70.3	75.8
Spain	67.3	71.9	73.3	79.7
Sri Lanka	64*		69.1	73.4
Sweden	71.9	76.5	74.4	80.3
Switzerland	68.7	74.1	74.0	80.8
Taiwan	65.8	70.4	71.3	76.8
Thailand	53.6	58.7	65.1	69.2
USA	66.6	74.0	72.0	78.8
USSR	65.0	74.0	–	–
West Germany	67.6	73.6	–	–
*mean				

(Sources: *Britannica* Year Books, *World Bank Atlas*, and UN *Demographic Statistics*)

Taiwan, adopted appropriate measures. During the early 1980s, Korea, Indonesia, Thailand, and Malaysia, joined the EIA club; later in the 1980s, the rest of Europe and the Nordic countries embraced EIA legislation.

Nevertheless, there has been some debate about where the roots of EIA are really to be found, for several countries had well-developed planning systems which took account of environmental considerations before 1969. Public inquiries into proposed slum-clearance schemes were being conducted in Britain during the early 1900s. The first public inquiry under the Clean Air Act was conducted in West Bromwich in 1956, to deal with challenges to the first segment of a smoke control program. During the very early 1960s, major public inquiries were conducted into proposed power stations at Holmepierrepont, Ratcliffe-on-Soar, and Fiddler's Ferry. All of these inquiries had the characteristics of EIA reviews. A fair judgement is that the USA developed EIA as a separate statutory procedure and Britain pioneered public participation and the public inquiry into controversial environmental issues.

So how will EIA go in the twenty-first century? Certainly, the signs are favourable. All the countries which have adopted EIA systems have invariably made significant advances in economic growth since the 1970s, reflected in improved material well-being and health of entire societies. Over time,

roughly between the UN Conference on the Human Environment held in Stockholm in 1972 and the UN Conference on Environment and Development held in Rio de Janeiro in 1992, the expectation of life in the more advanced countries improved by 4.5 years, and in the less advanced countries (such as China, India, Bangladesh, and Indonesia) by between 7 and 15 years. See table 3 based on figures from the UN demographic division. A life span of between three-score years and four-score years is now common in many countries.

This increase in life expectancy, coupled with continuing population growth in many countries, emphasises the need for closer attention to the optimal use of resources, to the careful identification of all costs, and all benefits. The days have gone when satisfactory development decisions could be made behind closed ministerial and cabinet doors; when it was thought that the only rights people had, in many countries, was to come out every few years to pass judgement on the quality of government, and lacking adequate means to do so. For success, the achievement of sustainable development for the twenty-first century demands everyone's contribution.

EIA has proved in practice to be the best of approaches to making decisions about policies, plans, programs, and projects; and it is a most important ingredient of democracy in practice, majority rule with respect for minority rights.

Chapter 1: EIA approaches

Australian and New Zealand Environment and Conservation Council (1991) *A national approach to environmental impact assessment in Australia*, ANZECC Secretariat, Canberra, Australia.

Canadian Council of Ministers of the Environment (1991) *Cooperative principles for environmental assessment*, 6-7 May, Ottawa, Canada.

Council on Environmental Quality (1986) *Regulations for implementing the procedural provisions of the National Environmental Policy Act*, 40 CFR Parts 1500–1508 with particular reference to 1508.27 Significantly. CEQ, Washington, DC, USA.

Environment Canada (1983) *Environmental planning for large-scale development projects: recommendations and actions for implementation*, proceedings of an international workshop, 2-5 October, EC, Vancouver, British Columbia, Canada.

Gilpin, A. (1973) *Report on the environmental effects of the proposed Newport D power station*, Government Printer, Melbourne, Australia.

— (1980) *The Australian environment: twelve controversial issues*, Sun Books, Melbourne, Australia, chapter 4.

— (1986) *Environmental planning: a condensed encyclopaedia*, Noyes Publications, Park Ridge, New Jersey, USA.

Kennedy, W. V. (1987) 'EIA in global perspective: does it work?', in *Environmental impact assessment as a management tool*, workshop proceedings, November, Department of the Arts, Sport, the Environment, Tourism and Territories, Canberra, Australia.

Ryding, S-O. (1991) 'Environmental priority strategies in product design', in *Integrated Environmental Management*, issue 4, November, University of Sheffield, Sheffield, Britain.

United Nations Conference on Environment and Development (1992) *Agenda 21*, UN, New York, USA.

United Nations Economic Commission for Europe (UN ECE) (1987) *Application of environmental impact assessment: highways and dams*, UN ECE, New York, USA.

World Commission on Environment and Development (1987) *Our common future*, Oxford University Press, Oxford, Britain, p. 63.

Chapter 2: EIA procedures

Australian International Development Assistance Bureau (1991) *Annual audit of the environment in the Australian international development cooperation program*, Australian Government Publishing Service, Canberra, Australia.

Bass, R. (1990) 'California's experience with environmental impact reports', *Project Appraisal*, 5(4), 220-224.

Bureau of Industry Economics (1990) *Environmental assessment: impact on major projects*, research report no. 35. Australian Government Publishing Service, Canberra, Australia.

Commission of Inquiry (1988) *Extraction of sand and soil. Menangle: a report to the Minister for Planning* (Commissioner Dr A. Gilpin), Office of Commissioners of Inquiry, Sydney, Australia.

Commission of the European Communities (1992) *Report from the Commission of the European Communities to the United Nations Conference on Environment and Development 1992*, Brussels, Belgium.

Couch, W. (1991) 'Recent EIA developments in Canada', *EIA Newsletter 6*, EIA Centre, Department of Planning and Landscape, University of Manchester, Manchester, Britain, pp. 17-18.

Department of Planning (1985) *Manual for environmental impact assessment*, Department of Environment and Planning, Sydney, Australia.

Environmental Protection Administration (1985) *Technical guidelines for conducting EIAs*, Taipei, Taiwan, Republic of China.

Gilpin, A. (1990) *An Australian dictionary of environment and planning*, Oxford University Press, Oxford, Britain.

Kennedy, W. V. (1987) 'EIA in global perspective: does it work?' in *Environmental impact assessment as a management tool*, workshop proceedings, November, Canberra, Australia.

Kinhill Engineers (1990) *Proposed third runway Sydney (Kingsford Smith) Airport: Draft environmental impact statement*, Kinhill Engineers and Federal Airports Corporation, Sydney, Australia.

Lee, N. and Colley, R. (1990) *Reviewing the quality of environmental statements*, Department of Planning and Landscape, University of Manchester, Manchester, Britain.

Lee, N. and Walsh, F. (1992) 'Strategic environmental assessment: an overview', *Project Appraisal* 7(3).

Mathews, W. H. and Carpenter, R. A. (1981) 'The growing international implications of the US requirements for environmental impact assessments', *Environmental Law and Policy in the Pacific Basin Area*, University of Tokyo Press, Tokyo, Japan, pp. 159-169.

NSW Science and Technology Council (1983) *The science and technology of environmental impact assessment, with particular reference to methods used in New South Wales*, a report by FEARO, Canada, NSWSTC, Sydney, Australia.

Overseas Development Administration (ODA) (1992) *Manual of environmental appraisal*, ODA, London, Britain.

Smyth, R. B. (1987) *The Environmental Planning and Assessment Act as a management tool*, seminar on environmental legislation and its impact on management. The Institution of Engineers Australia Department of Environment and Planning, Sydney, Australia.

United Nations Economic Commission for Europe (1990) *Post-project analyses in environmental impact assessment*, environmental series 3, UN, New York, USA.

— (1992) *Application of environmental impact assessment principles to policies, plans and programs*, environmental series 5, UN, New York, USA.

Chapter 3: EIA methodologies

Ahmad, Y. J. and Sammy, G. K. (1985) *Guidelines to environmental impact assessment in developing countries*, United Nations Environment Program, Nairobi, Kenya.

Andrews, R. N. L. and Waits, M. (1978) *Environmental values in public decisions*, School of Natural Resources, University of Michigan, Ann Arbor, USA.

Barnett, H. J. and Morse, C. (1963) *Scarcity and growth: the economics of natural resources availability*, Johns Hopkins Press, Baltimore, USA.

Battelle Pacific Northwest Laboratories (1974) *Environmental assessment manual, Columbia River and tributaries*, prepared for US Army Corps of Engineers, North Pacific Division, Seattle, USA.

Baumol, W. J. (1968) 'On the social rate of discount', *American Economic Review*, vol. 58.

Baumol, W. J. and Oates, W. E. (1979) *Economics, environmental policy, and the quality of life*, Prentice-Hall, New Jersey, USA.

Beder, S. (1989) *Cost-benefit analysis: an explanation using the Sydney Harbour Tunnel as a case study*, Environmental Education Project, University of Sydney, Sydney, Australia.

Bisset, R. (1980) 'Methods for environmental impact analysis: recent trends and future prospects', *Journal of Environmental management*, 11 (1), pp. 27-43.

Blamey, R. K. (1991) *Contingent valuation and Fraser Island*, 20th Annual Conference of Economists, University of Tasmania, Hobart, Australia.

Brady, G. L. and Bower, B. T. (1981) *Air quality management: quantifying benefits*, Research Paper 7, Environment and Policy Institute, US East-West Center, Honolulu, Hawaii, USA.

Burchell, R. W. and Listokin, B. (1975) *The environmental impact handbook*, Center for Urban Policy Research, Rutgers University, New Brunswick, USA.

Canter, L. W. (1977) *Environmental impact assessment*, McGraw-Hill, New York, USA.

Ciriacy-Wantrup, S. V. (1968) *Resource conservation: economics and policies* (3rd edn), University of California Press, Berkeley, USA.

Department of Finance (1991) *Handbook of cost-benefit analysis*, Australian Government Publishing Service, Canberra, Australia.

Department of Home Affairs and Environment/Environment Protection Authority, Victoria (1980) *Costs and benefits of environment protection*, National Conference on the Costs and Benefits of Environment Protection, Australian Government Publishing Service, Canberra, Australia.

Department of Science and the Environment (1979) *Environmental economics*, National Environmental Economics Conference, Australian Government Publishing Service, Canberra, Australia.

Dixon, J. A. and Hufschmidt, M. M. (eds) (1986) *Economic valuation techniques for the environment: a case study workbook*, Johns Hopkins Press, Baltimore, USA.

Dorfman, R. (ed.) (1965) *Measuring benefits of government investments*, Brookings Institution, Washington, DC, USA.

Eckstein, O. (1958) *Water resource development: the economics of project evaluation*, Harvard University Press, Cambridge, USA.

Economic and Social Commission for Asia and the Pacific (1985) *Environmental impact assessment: guidelines for planners and decision-makers*, UN publication ST/ESCAP/351, UN, New York, USA.

— (1990) *Environmental impact assessment: guidelines for industrial development*, UN publication ST/ESCAP/784, UN, New York, USA.

Environment and Policy Institute (1980) *Report of the proceedings of a workshop on case studies and a training manual for extended benefit-cost analysis*, US East-West Center, Honolulu, Hawaii, USA.

Fabos, J. G. Y., Greene, C. M., and Joyner, S. A. (1978) 'The METLAND landscape planning process: composite landscape assessment, alternative plan formulation and plan evaluation', *Research Bulletin 653*, University of Massachusetts Agricultural Experiment Station, Amherst, USA.

Fisher, A. C. (1981) *Economic efficiency and air pollution control*, Research Paper 8, Environment and Policy Institute, US East-West Center, Honolulu, Hawaii, USA.

Fisher, A. C. and Peterson, F. M. (1976) 'The environment in economics: a survey', *Journal of Economic Literature*, 14 (1) March, 1-33.

Freeman, A. M. (1979) *The benefits of environmental improvement: theory and practice*, Johns Hopkins Press, Baltimore, USA.

Gilpin, A. and Hartmann, H. (1981) *Air pollution and energy in Australia: economic and policy implications*, Research Paper 6, Environment and Policy Institute, US East-West Center, Honolulu, Hawaii, USA.

Hammond, R. J. (1958) *Benefit-cost analysis and water pollution control*, Stanford University Press, Stanford, USA.

Herfindahl, O. C. and Kneese, A. V. (1965) *Quality of the environment: an economic approach to some problems in using land, water, and air*, Resources for the Future, Washington, DC, USA.

— (1974) *Economic theory of natural resources*, Charles E. Merrill Publishing, Columbus, USA.

Holling, C. S. (ed.) (1978) *Adaptive environmental assessment and management*, Wiley-Interscience, New York, USA.

Hufschmidt, M. M. (1980) *New approaches to the economic analysis of natural resources and environmental quality*, a report of the proceedings of a conference on extended benefit-cost analysis, US East-West Center, Honolulu, Hawaii, USA.

— (1981) *The role of benefit-cost analysis in environmental quality and natural resource management*, Environment and Policy Institute, US East-West Center, Honolulu, Hawaii, USA.

Hufschmidt, M. M. and Hyman, E. L. (eds) (1982) *Economic approaches to natural resource and environmental quality analysis*, Bray Co. Tycooly International, Wicklow, Leinster, Ireland.

Hufschmidt, M. M., James, D. E., Meister, A. D., Bower, B. T., and Dixon, J. A. (1983) *Environment, natural systems, and development: an economic valuation guide*, Johns Hopkins Press, Baltimore, USA.

Hyman, E. L. (1981) 'The valuation of extramarket benefits and costs in environmental impact assessment', *Environmental Impact Assessment Review*, vol. 2.

Hyman, E. L. and Stiftel, B. (1981) 'Retrospective of a research program on the theory and practice of environmental impact assessment methodologies', *Environmental Impact Assessment Review*, vol. 2.

Imber, D. (1991) *Observations on contingent valuation*, 20th Annual Conference of Economists, University of Tasmania, Hobart, Tasmania, Australia.

Industry Commission (1991) *Costs and benefits of reducing greenhouse gas emissions*, vol. 1 Report; vol. 2 Appendices, Industry Commission, Canberra, Australia.

Interim Mekong Committee (1979) *Environmental management and water resource development in the Nam Pong basin of northeastern Thailand.*

— (1982) *Environmental impact assessment: guidelines for application for tropical river basin development*, Mekong Secretariat, Economic and Social Commission for Asia and the Pacific, Bangkok, Thailand.

James, D. and Boer, B. (1987) *Application of economic techniques in environmental impact assessment: a report to the Australian Environment Council*, AEC, Canberra, Australia.

Jones-Lee, M. W. (1976) *The value of life: an economic analysis*, Martin Robinson, London, Britain.

Kneese, A. V. and Bower, B. T. (1968) *Managing water quality: economics, technology, institutions*, Johns Hopkins Press, Baltimore, USA.

Kneese, A. V., Ayres, R. V., and D'Arge, R. C. (1970) *Economics and the environment: a materials balance approach*, Resources for the Future, Washington, DC, USA.

Kneese, A. V., Rolfe, S. E., and Harned, J. W. (eds) (1971) *Managing the environment: international economic cooperation for pollution control*, Praeger Publishers, New York, USA.

Krutilla, J. V. and Eckstein, O. (1958) *Multiple purpose river development: studies in applied economic analysis*, Johns Hopkins Press, Baltimore, USA.

Krutilla, J. V. and Fisher, A. C. (1975) *The economics of natural environments: studies in the valuation of commodity and amenity resources*, Johns Hopkins Press, Baltimore, USA.

Lapping, M. (1975) 'Environmental impact assessment methodologies: a critique', *Environmental Affairs*, vol. 4, pp. 123-134.

Lave, L. B. and Seskin, E. P. (1977) *Air pollution and human health*, Johns Hopkins Press, Baltimore, USA.

Leopold, M., Clarke, F. E., Hornshaw, B. R., and Balsley, J. R. (1971) 'A procedure for evaluating environmental impact', *Circular 645*, US Geological Survey, Washington, DC, USA.

Little, I. M. D. (1957) *A critique of welfare economics*, (2nd edn), Oxford University Press, Oxford, Britain.

Little, I. M. D. and Mirlees, J. A. (1974) *Project appraisal and planning for developing countries*, Basic Books, New York, USA.

Lohani, B. N. and Kan S. A. (1983) 'Environmental evaluation for water resources in Thailand', in *Water Resources Development*, 1(3), 185-195.

Maass, A. A., Hufschmidt, M. M., Dorfman, R., Thomas, H. A., Marglin, S. A., and Fair, G. M. (1962) *Design of water-resource systems*, Harvard University Press, Cambridge, USA.

McHarg, I. L. (1969) *Design with nature*, Natural History Press, New York, USA.

McKean, R. (1958) *Efficiency in government through systems analysis*, John Wiley & Sons, New York, USA.

Mishan, E. J. (1976) *Cost-benefit analysis* (2nd edn), Praeger Publishers, New York, USA.

Mooney, G. H. (1977) *The valuation of human life*, Macmillan, London, Britain.

National Environment Board (1979) *Manual of NEB guidelines for the preparation of environmental impact evaluations*, Bangkok, Thailand.

National Environment Board/Seatec International Consulting Engineers (1986) *Eastern seaboard regional environmental management planning project: final report* (12 vols), Bangkok, Thailand.

Nichols, R. and Hyman, E. L. (1980) *A review and analysis of fifteen environmental assessment methodologies*, Center for Urban and Regional Studies, University of North Carolina, Chapel Hill, North Carolina, USA.

    (1982) 'Evaluation of environmental assessment measures', *Journal of the Water Resources Planning and Management Division*, Proceedings of the American Society of Civil Engineers, New York, USA, 108 (WR1), March.

Organisation for Economic Cooperation and Development (1974) *Environmental damage costs*, OECD, Paris, France.

— (1976) *Economic measurement of environmental damage*, OECD, Paris, France.

— (1977) *Pollution control costs in the primary aluminium industry*, OECD, Paris, France.

— (1981) *The costs and benefits of sulphur oxide control*, OECD, Paris, France.

Pearce, D. W. (ed.) (1978) *The valuation of social cost*, George Allen & Unwin, London, Britain.

Pigou, A. C. (1946) *Economics of welfare* (4th edn), Macmillan, New York, USA.

Prest, A. R. and Turvey, R. (1965) 'Cost-benefit analysis: a survey', *Economic Journal*, 75, December, 683-735.

Rowe, W. D. (1977) *An anatomy of risk*, John Wiley & Sons, New York, USA.

Scott, A. (1955) *Natural resources: the economics of conservation*, University of Toronto Press, Ontario, Canada.

Sinden, J. A. (1991) *An assessment of our environmental valuations*, 20th Annual Conference of Economists, University of Tasmania, Hobart, Australia.

Sinden, J. A. and Worrell, A. C. (1979) *Unpriced values: decisions without market prices*, John Wiley & Sons, New York, USA.

Solomon, R. C., Colbert, B. K., Hansen, W. J., Richardson, S. E., Canter, L. W., and Vlachos, E. C. (1977) 'Water resources assessment methodology (WRAM): impact assessment and alternative evaluation', *Technical Report Y-77-1*, US Army Engineer Waterways Experiment Station, Vicksburg, USA.

Squire, L. and van der Tak, H. (1975) *Economic analysis of projects*, Johns Hopkins Press, Baltimore, USA.

Stiftel, B. and Hyman, E. L. (1980) 'Assessment of environmental quality in a democratic state', *Environmental Professional*, 2, 306-314.

United Nations Environment Program (1980) *Guidelines for assessing industrial environment impact and environmental criteria for the siting of industry*, UNEP, Nairobi, Kenya.

United States Geological Survey (USGS) (1971) *A procedure for evaluating environmental impact*, circular 645, Washington, DC, USA.

Water Resources Council (1973) 'Water and related land resources: establishment of principles and standards for planning', US *Federal Register*, vol. 38, 10 September, pp. 24778-24869.

— (1978) 'Final rule: principles and standards for water and related land resources planning', US *Federal Register*, vol. 43, 29 November, pp. 55977-56007.

White, G. (1972) *Organising scientific investigations to deal with environmental impacts*, paper presented to the Careless Technology Conference, Washington, DC, 1968, The Natural History Press, New York, USA.

Chapter 4: Public participation, inquiries, and mediation

Boer, B., Craig, D., Handmer, J., and Ross, H. (1991) *The potential role of mediation in the Resource Assessment Commission Inquiry Process*, discussion paper no. 1,

January, Resource Assessment Commission, Canberra, Australia.

Coulson, R. (1989) *Business mediation: what you need to know*, American Arbitration Association, New York, USA.

Gilpin, A. (1963) *Control of air pollution*, Butterworths, London, Britain.

— (1963b) 'Analysing the Ratcliffe Power Station Inquiry', *Central Electricity Generating Board Newsletter 37*, October 1963.

— (1990) 'The role of the public inquiry in the resolution of environmental conflict', proceedings of the *Eighteenth Australasian Chemical Engineering Conference*, 27-30 August, Auckland, New Zealand, pp. 152-161.

Office of the Commissioners of Inquiry (1988) *Commissions of inquiry for environment and planning: how they work*, OCI, Sydney, Australia.

Priscoli, J. D. (1987) 'Conflict resolution for water resource projects: using facilitation and mediation to write section 404 general permits', *Environmental Impact Assessment Review*, p. 313.

Street, L. (1990) 'The Court system and alternative dispute resolution procedures', *Australian Dispute Resolution Journal*, 1(1), 5.

Chapter 5: International organisations

5.1 European Community

Commission of the European Communities (1986) *EEC fourth environmental action program 1987-1992*, CEC, Brussels, Belgium.

— (1992a) *Report from the Commission of the European Communities to the United Nations Conference on Environment and Development 1992*, Brussels, Belgium.

— (1992b) *Towards sustainability: a European Community program of policy and action in relation to the environment and sustainable development*, COM (92) 23 final: vol. 2, CEC, Brussels, Belgium.

Council of Europe (1980) *Model outline environmental impact statement from the standpoint of integrated management or planning of the natural environment*, Nature and Environment Series 17, Council of Europe, Strasbourg, France.

Gilpin, A. (1986) *Environmental planning: a condensed encyclopedia*, Noyes Publications, Park Ridge, New Jersey, USA, p. 103.

5.2 Nordic Council

Lind, T. (1992) *Nordic cooperation on environmental impact assessment*, Department of Regional Planning and Resources Management, Ministry of Environment, Oslo, Norway.

5.4 Organisation for Economic Cooperation and Development (OECD)

Organisation for Economic Cooperation and Development (1979) *The assessment of projects with significant impact on the environment*, recommendation adopted on 8 May C(79)116, OECD, Paris, France.

— (1985) *Environmental assessment of development assistance projects and programs*, recommendation adopted on 20 June C(85)104, OECD, Paris, France.

— (1986) *Measures required to facilitate the environmental assessment of development assistance projects and programs*, recommendation adopted on 21 November C(86)26, OECD, Paris, France.

5.6 UN Economic and Social Commission for Asia and the Pacific (ESCAP)

Economic and Social Commission for Asia and the Pacific (1990) *Ministerial declaration on environmentally sound and sustainable development in Asia and the Pacific*, ESCAP, New York, USA.

— (1991) *Regional strategy on environmentally sound and sustainable development in Asia and the Pacific*, ESCAP, New York, USA.

— (1990) *State of the environment in Asia and the Pacific 1990*, ESCAP, New York, USA.

— (1985-90) Environment and development series *Environmental impact assessment*
  (1) *Guidelines for planners and decision-makers*.
  (2) *Guidelines for agricultural development*.
  (3) *Guidelines for industrial development*.
  (4) *Guidelines for transport development*.
  (5) *Guidelines for water resources development*.
  UN, New York, USA.

— (1992) *The Asian and Pacific Input to the United Nations conference on environment and development*, Brazil, 1992, ESCAP, New York, USA.

5.7 UN Environment Program (UNEP)

Htun, N. (1988) *EIA and sustainable development*, presentation to the seventh annual meeting of the International Association of Impact Assessment, 5-9 July Griffith University, Queensland, Australia.

United Nations Environment Program (1982) *Guidelines on risk management and accident prevention in the chemical industry*, UNEP, Paris, France.

— (1987a) *Goals and principles of environmental impact assessment*, UNEP, Nairobi, Kenya.

— (1987b) *Environmental guidelines for settlements planning and management*, UN Centre for Human Settlements (Habitat), Nairobi, Kenya, vols 1, 2, and 3.

— (1990) *An approach to environmental impact assessment for projects affecting the coastal and marine environment*, UNEP regional sea reports no. 122, Nairobi, Kenya.

5.8 Asian Development Bank (ADB)

Asian Development Bank (1986) *Manual of environmental guidelines for development projects*, series of 12 manuals, ADB, Manila, Philippines.

— (1987) *Environmental guidelines for selected agricultural and natural resources development projects*, ADB, Manila, Philippines.

— (1988a) *Guidelines for integrated regional economic-cum-environmental development planning: a review of regional environmental development planning studies in Asia*, ADB, Manila, Philippines, vol. 1, 125 pp.; vol. 2, 240 pp.

— (1988b) *Training workshop on environmental impact assessment and evaluation: proceedings and training manual*, ADB, Manila, Philippines, vol. 1, 402 pp.; vol. 2, 389 pp.

— (1990a) *Environmental guidelines for selected infrastructure projects*, ADB, Manila, Philippines.

— (1990b) *Environmental guidelines for selected industrial and power development projects*, ADB, Manila, Philippines.

— (1991a) *Guidelines for social analysis of development projects*, ADB, Manila, Philippines.

— (1991b) *Environmental risk assessment: dealing with uncertainty in environmental impact assessment*, ADB, Manila, Philippines.

Dixon, J. A., Carpenter, R. A., Fallon, L. A., Sherman, P. B., and Manipomoke, S. (1988) *Economic analysis of the environmental impacts of development projects*, Earthscan Publications, London, Britain.

5.10 World Health Organisation (WHO)

Environmental Resources Ltd (1985a) *Environmental health impact assessment of urban development projects: guidelines and recommendations*, WHO, Regional Office for Europe, Copenhagen, Denmark.

— (1985b) *Assessment of irrigated agricultural development projects: guidelines and recommendations*, WHO, Regional Office for Europe, Copenhagen, Denmark.

World Health Organisation (1987) *Health and safety components of environmental impact assessment*, WHO, Regional Office for Europe, Copenhagen, Denmark.
— (1989) *Environmental impact assessment: an assessment of methodological and substantive issues affecting human health considerations*, WHO report 41, University of London, London, Britain.

Chapter 6: Europe

6.1 Britain
Department of the Environment/Welsh Office (1989) *Environmental assessment: a guide to the procedures*, HMSO, London, Britain.
Department of the Environment (1990a) *This common inheritance: Britain's environmental strategy*, HMSO, London, Britain.
— (1990b) *Monitoring environmental assessment and planning*, HMSO, London, Britain
— (1991) *Policy appraisal and the environment*, HMSO, London, Britain.
Evelyn, J. (1661) *Fumifugium: or the smoake of London dissipated*, National Society for Clean Air, London, Britain.
Gilpin, A. (1963) *Control of air pollution*, Butterworths, London, Britain.

6.2 France
Turlin, M. and Lilin, C. (1991) 'Les études d'impact sur l'environnement: l'expertise francaise', *Aménagement et Nature*, 102, pp. 4-7.

6.3 Germany
Federal Republic of Germany (1975) *Resolution on adopting environmental assessment principles*, 22 August, Bonn, Germany.
Ministry of the Interior (1972) *Report of the Federal Republic of Germany on the Human Environment*, Bonn, Germany.

6.4 Italy
Benedetto, C. and de Blasis, M. R. (1991) 'Environmental problems related to the transport system in Italy', *VIA*, 18, pp. 16-35.
Berrini, M., Fraternali, D., and Zambrini, M. (1991) 'From projects to plans', *VIA*, 17, pp. 48-61.
Gilpin, A. (1978) *Air Pollution* (2nd edn), University of Queensland Press, St Lucia, Brisbane, Australia, p. 36.
Marchetti, R. (1989) 'Italy', in E. J. Kormondy (ed.), *International handbook of pollution control*, Greenwood Press, New York, pp. 199-208.
Matarrese, G. (1991) 'Environmental impact assessment in Italy', *EIA Newsletter 6*, EIA Centre, Department of Planning and Landscape, University of Manchester, Manchester, Britain.

6.8 Czech and Slovak Republics
Federal Committee for the Environment (1991) *Strategy for caring for the environment in Czechoslovakia*, FCE, Prague, Czechoslovakia.
Chapter 6 Case study. 6D: Baikal pulp and paper mill, Russia
Govorushko, S. M. (1989) *Environmental impact assessment in the USSR: the current situation*, Pacific Institute of Geography, Far East Branch, The USSR Academy of Sciences, Vladivostok, USSR.

Chapter 7: The Nordic countries

7.4 Sweden
Ministry of the Environment (1990) *Swedish environmental legislation*, ME, Stockholm, Sweden.
— (1991) *Sweden: national report to the United Nations conference on environment and development 1992*, ME, Stockholm, Sweden.
Chapter 7 Case study. 7A: Underground natural gas-storage facility near Stenlille, Denmark
Ministry of the Environment (1991a) *National report to the United Nations conference on environment and development 1992*, Danish State Information Office, Copenhagen, Denmark.
— (1991b) *The state of the environment in Denmark*, Danish State Information Office, Copenhagen, Denmark.
— (1991c) *Environmental impact assessment in Denmark*, ME, Copenhagen, Denmark.
Chapter 7 Case study. 7B: Highway Five, Finland
Ministry for Foreign Affairs (1991) *Finland national report to the United Nations conference on environment and development 1992*, MFA, Helsinki, Finland.
Chapter 7 Case study. 7C: Kobbelv hydro power project, Norway
Ministry for the Environment (1992) *Norway's National Report to the United Nations Conference on Environment and Development*, 1992, Oslo, Norway.

Chapter 8: North America

Economic Commission for Europe (1991) *Policies and systems of environmental impact assessment*, UN Economic Commission for Europe, Geneva, Switzerland/UN, New York, USA.
Kennedy, W. V. (1987) 'EIA in global perspective: does it work?', in *Environmental impact assessment as a management tool*, workshop proceedings, November, Department of the Arts, Sport, the Environment, Tourism and Territories, Canberra, Australia.
United States of America (1992) *National report to the United Nations conference on environment and development*, CEQ, Washington, DC, USA.

Chapter 9:   Asia and the Pacific

9.1 Australia
Australian and New Zealand Environment and Conservation Council (1991) *A national approach to environmental impact assessment in Australia*, ANZECC Secretariat, Canberra, Australia.
Coopers & Lybrand (1991) *Environmental management practices: a survey of major Australian organisations*, C & L, Sydney, Australia.
Department of the Arts, Sport, the Environment, Tourism and Territories (1987) *Environmental impact assessment as a management tool*, workshop proceedings, November, Canberra, Australia.
Gilpin, A. (1989) 'Australia', in E. J. Kormondy (ed.), *International handbook of pollution control*, Greenwood Press, New York, USA.
Gilpin, A. and Lin S. J. (1990) *Environmental impact assessment in Taiwan and Australia: a comparative study*, Environment and Policy Institute, US East-West Center, Hawaii, USA.
Holliday, S. (1988) *A review of environmental impact procedures in New South Wales*, Environmental Law Association (NSW) conference, 12-13 August, Sydney, Australia.
Smyth, R. B. (1987) *The Environmental Planning and Assessment Act as a management tool*, seminar on environmental legislation and its impact on management, The Institution of Engineers Australia/NSW Department of Planning, 22-23 October, Australia.

9.2 China

Ashcroft, B. C. (1987) 'Environmental impact assessment in Hong Kong: an outline of procedures and a selected case study', in *Proceedings of the international symposium on environmental impact assessment*, Institute of Environmental Sciences, Beijing Normal University, Beijing, China, pp. 24-40.

Environmental Protection Department (1992) *Environment Hong Kong 1992*, EPD, Hong Kong.

Wang, H. and Bi, J. (1993) 'Development of environmental impact assessment in China' in *Development and the Environment*, the proceedings of the 13th Annual Meeting of the International Association for Impact Assessment, Shanghai, China, 12-15 June, IAIA, p. 123.

Wang, H. and Ma, X. (1987) 'Progress of environmental impact assessment in China', in *Proceedings of the international symposium on environmental impact assessment*, Institute of Environmental Sciences, Beijing Normal University, Beijing, China, pp. 14-23.

Wenger, R. B., Wang, H., and Ma, X. (1990) 'Environmental impact assessment in the People's Republic of China', *Environmental Management*, 14 (4), 429-439.

Zhaoqiu, Cao (1981) *Mining and the environment at the Fushun West open pit mine*, workshop on the increased use of coal in Asia and the Pacific: achieving energy and environmental goals, Environment and Policy Institute, US East-West Center, Hawaii, USA (workshop held in Canberra, Australia).

Zhou, D. (1991) 'The power industry in China: institutional changes and environmental protection', *Electricity and the environment: background papers for a senior expert symposium*, Helsinki, 13-17 May. International Atomic Energy Agency IAEA-TECDOC-624, Vienna, Austria, pp. 553-562.

9.3 Indian subcontinent

Banerjee, A. N. (1988) *Environmental impact of a coal mining project: Singrauli Mines, Uttar Pradesh and Madhya Pradesh*, India, Asian Development Bank, Manila, Philippines.

Bowonder, B. and Arvind, S. S. (1989) 'Environmental regulations and litigation in India', *Project Appraisal*, 4 (4): 182-196.

Khanna, P. (1988) *Environmental impact assessment in land use planning and urban settlement projects in India*, Asian Development Bank, Manila, Philippines.

Maudgal, S. (1988a) *Environmental impact assessment in India: an overview*, Asian Development Bank, Manila, Philippines.

— (1988b) *Environmental impact of a thermal power station in Bombay, India*, Asian Development Bank, Manila, Philippines.

Tippetts et al (1980) *Environmental assessment: accelerated Mahaweli development program*, Ministry of Mahaweli Development, Colombo, Sri Lanka.

9.4 Indonesia

Environmental Impact Management Agency (Bapedal) (1991) *EIA: a guide to environmental assessment in Indonesia*, Jakarta, Republic of Indonesia.

Ministry for Population and Environment (1991) *Documents relating to the environmental impact analysis process in Indonesia* (2nd edn), Jakarta, Republic of Indonesia.

Republic of Indonesia (1978) *Guidelines for State environmental policy: decree 4 of the general session of the Consultative People's Assembly*, Jakarta, Republic of Indonesia.

Salim, E. (1988) *Social impact assessment: the Indonesian experience*, presentation to the seventh meeting of the International Association of Impact Assessment, 5-9 July, Griffith University, Queensland, Australia.

— (1990a) *Alleviating poverty through sustainable development*, paper presented in Perth, Australia, Jakarta, Republic of Indonesia.

— (1990b) *The environment and the third world*, paper presented in Canberra, Australia, Jakarta, Republic of Indonesia.

Tarrant, J., Barbier, E., Greenburg, R. J., Higgins, M. L., Lintner, S. F., Mackie, C., Murphy, L., and van Veldhuizen, H., (1987) *Natural resources and environmental management in Indonesia: an overview, United States Agency for International Development*, Jakarta, Indonesia.

9.5 Japan

Barrett, B. F. D. and Therivel, R. (1991) *Environmental policy and impact assessment in Japan*, Routledge, London, Britain.

Edmunds, C. M. Webb (1984) 'The politics of public participation and the siting of power plants in Japan', *The environmental professional*, 6(3/4), 292-302.

Environment Agency (1991) *Quality of the Environment in Japan*, EA, Tokyo, Japan.

Japan (1991) *Environment and development: Japan's experience and achievement*, Ministry of Foreign Affairs, Tokyo, Japan (being the Japan national report to the UN Conference on Environment and Development, 1992).

9.6 Korea, South

Ministry of the Environment (1991) *National report of the Republic of Korea to the United Nations Conference on Environment and Development 1992*, Seoul, Korea.

Office of Environment, Bureau of Planning and Coordination, Republic of Korea (1983) *Han River Basin Environment Master Plan: Final Report*, Seoul, Korea.

9.7 Malaysia

Department of Environment (1989) *Environmental Quality Report*, Kuala Lumpur, Malaysia.

— (1990a) *Environmental impact assessment (EIA): procedure and requirements in Malaysia*, Ministry of Science, Technology and the Environment, Kuala Lumpur, Malaysia.

— (1990b) *A handbook of environmental impact assessment guidelines*, Ministry of Science, Technology and the Environment, Kuala Lumpur, Malaysia.

— (1991a) *Berita EIA: the environmental impact assessment (EIA) newsletter no. 1*, January–June, Department of Environment, Kuala Lumpur, Malaysia.

9.8 New Zealand

Ministry for the Environment/Ministry of External Relations and Trade (1991) *New Zealand's National Report to the United Nations Conference on Environment and Development 1992*, Wellington, New Zealand.

9.9 Philippines

Department of Environment and Natural Resources (1990) *Philippine strategy for sustainable development: a conceptual framework*, DENR, Quezon City, Philippines.

— (1992) *DENR administrative order amending the environmental impact statement system*, DENR, Quezon City, Philippines.

National Environmental Protection Council (1977) *The environmental impact statement system*, NEPC, Quezon City, Philippines.

Official Gazette (5 June 1978) *Rules and regulations of the national pollution control commission*, Manila, Philippines.

9.10 Singapore

Australian Trade Commission (1991) *Protection and conservation of the environment in Singapore*, Austrade, Singapore.

Chow, Kuan-Hon (1989) 'Singapore', in E. J. Kormondy (ed.), *International handbook of pollution control*, Greenwood Press, New York, USA, pp. 377-392.

Ministry of the Environment (1992) *Environmental management in Singapore*, ME, Singapore.

Singapore Inter-Ministry Committee (1991) *Singapore's*

national report to the United Nations conference on environment and development 1992, SIMC, Singapore.

9.11 Taiwan

Chien, E. (1990) *Working towards environmental quality in the 21st century*, Environmental Protection Administration, Taipei, Republic of China.

Environmental Protection Administration (1985) *A national EIA program*, EPA, Taipei, Republic of China.

Environmental Protection Administration (1988) *Environmental protection in the Republic of China*, EPA, Taipei, Republic of China.

Gilpin, A. and Lin, S. J. (1990) *Environmental impact assessment in Taiwan and Australia: a comparative study*, Environment and Policy Institute, US East-West Center, Hawaii, USA.

Hung, Tsu-Chang and Chou, Chang-Hung (1989) 'Taiwan', in E. J. Kormondy (ed.), *International handbook of pollution control*, Greenwood Press, New York, USA.

Min-der Foundation (1986) *Survey of the general public on Taiwan's current and living quality trends*, MF, Taipei, Taiwan.

9.12 Thailand

Office of the National Environment Board (1988) *Environmental impact assessment in Thailand*, Bangkok, Thailand.

Thailand (1992) *National report to the United Nations conference on environment and development 1992*, Bangkok, Thailand.

Chapter 9. Case study 9D: The Three Gorges water conservation and hydroelectric project, China

Barber, M. S. (1993) 'Inadequate IA threatens life, health and property: the Three-Gorges water control project feasibility study', in *Development and the Environment*, the proceedings of the 13th Annual Meeting of the International Association for Impact Assessment (IAIA), Shanghai, China, 12-15 June, IAIA, p. 5.

Bi, J. (1993) 'Study on ecological impacts of the Three-Gorges project', in *Development and the Environment*, the proceedings of the 13th Annual Meeting of the International Association for Impact Assessment, Shanghai, China, 12-15 June, IAIA, p. 12.

Chen, G. (1993) 'Impacts of the Three-Gorges project on the eco-environment and countermeasures', in *Development and the Environment*, the proceedings of the 13th Annual Meeting of the International Association for Impact Assessment, Shanghai, China, 12-15 June, IAIA, pp. 18-19.

Yang, H. (1993) 'Analysis and assessment of impact of the Three-Gorges project on natural scenery of the Three-Gorges', in *Development and the Environment*, the proceedings of the 13th Annual Meeting of the International Association for Impact Assessment, Shanghai, China, 12-15 June, IAIA, p. 138.

Agenda 21 A document adopted by the UN Conference on Environment and Development meeting in Rio de Janeiro in June 1992, representing a program for the twenty-first century. The conference was held on the twentieth anniversary of the UN Conference on Human Environment which met in Stockholm in June 1972. Agenda 21 reviewed and developed the achievements of that first conference.

alternatives In EIA, an examination of alternative locations, methods, and techniques for a particular project, including the alternative of not proceeding. It may be demonstrated that a project is not actually needed if demand–management approaches (for example, curbing the demand for water or electricity) are adopted or strengthened. At regional and national levels, a choice of policies, plans, and programs, may be presented, with a range of environmental impacts and mitigation measures.

applicant The proponent or developer seeking approval or consent for a proposed project, or seeking the issue of a permit or licence.

Australian Design Rule (ADR) Rules adopted by the Australian Transport Advisory Council with which new vehicles, sold in Australia, must comply; for example, in respect of emissions and noise.

beneficial use In the context of environmental planning, a use of the environment or any element or segment of the environment that is conducive to public benefit, welfare, safety, or health, and which requires protection from the effects of waste discharges, emissions, deposits, and despoliation.

best practicable means (BPM) A commonly used approach to pollution control requirements from industrial and other premises; the word 'practicable' is taken to mean 'reasonably practicable' having regard to the state of technology, to local conditions and circumstances, and to the financial implications. The concept is much easier to administer than the ambient quality approach. Other approaches include 'best available control technology', 'good control practice', and 'maximum available control technology'.

billion In this work, one thousand million.

biological diversity Or biodiversity, an umbrella term to describe collectively the variety and variability of nature; it encompasses three basic levels of organisation in living systems: the genetic, species, and ecosystem levels. Plant and animal species are the most commonly recognised units of biological diversity, thus public concern has been mainly devoted to conserving species diversity. This has led to efforts to conserve endangered species and to establish specifically protected areas. However sustainable human economic activity depends upon understanding, protecting, and maintaining the world's many interactive, diverse ecosystems with their complex networks of species and their vast storehouses of genetic information.

borrow pit or area An excavation from which material such as sand or gravel is removed to assist an industrial development.

bund An earthwork or wall surrounding a tank or tanks to retain the contents in the event of the fracture of the tank; or an earthwork or screen separating a source of noise from residences to mitigate impact.

conservation Defined by the World Conservation Strategy of 1980 as 'the management of human use of the biosphere so that it may yield the greatest sustainable benefit to present generations while maintaining its potential to meet the needs and aspirations of future generations'. Conservation is, therefore, something positive embracing preservation, maintenance, sustainable utilisation, restoration, and enhancement of the natural environment. This theme was further endorsed by the World Commission on Environment and Development (Brundtland Commission) in its 1987 report to the UN.

cost-benefit analysis (CBA) Or benefit-cost analysis, the identification and evaluation of all costs and all benefits attributable to a policy, plan, program, or project, over time being reduced by discounting to a present worth. Generally, the greater the benefit/cost ratio, the more attractive the proposal. Originally confined to those proposals in which the costs and benefits could be readily measured in monetary terms, the principle has been gradually extended to proposals in which there are significant intangibles not readily measured in such terms.

cumulative effects Progressive environmental degradation over time arising from a range of activities throughout an area or region, each activity considered in isolation being possibly not a significant contributor. Such effects might arise from a growing volume of vehicles, multiple sources of power generation or incineration, or increasing application of chemicals to the land. The solution is better regional planning and control.

dB(A) Or decibel (A-scale), an international weighted scale of sound levels or noise providing a good correlation with subjective impressions by individuals, in most cases, of loudness and sense of annoyance. Nearly all audible sound lies between 0 and about 140 dB(A). The B, C, and D scales are used for more specialised noise measurements; for instance, the D-scale is used for measurement of jet engine noise at airports.

decision-maker   The body or person responsible for deciding whether a project shall proceed or not, or proceed subject to conditions and constraints. The decision-maker is usually an elected body or responsible agency or minister, the decision-making being essentially a function of government.

developer   The initiator of a project; also called the proponent, or applicant, for development consent.

development   The application of human, financial, and physical resources to satisfy human needs; inevitably, development involves modification of the biosphere and some aspects of development detract from the quality of life locally, regionally, nationally, or globally. The breadth of development is not always appreciated as the word applies not only to the growth of industry, commerce and infrastructure, but to sanitation, education, medicine, health, housing, national parks, tourist, and recreational facilities.

EC EIA directive   The directive of the EC of 27 June 1985 (85/337) requiring the 12 members of the EC to introduce and bring into operation EA procedures. All have now done so.

ecosystem   The plants and animals of an ecological community, and their environment, forming an interacting system of activities and functions regarded as a unit. There are innumerable ecosystems: for example, marine, freshwater, terrestrial, forest, and grassland. All ecosystems together comprise the biosphere, that part of the Earth's crust and atmosphere inhabited by living things. Ecology is the study of the relationship between an animal or plant and its surroundings.

endangered species   Fauna and flora likely to become extinct as a result of direct exploitation by humans, intrusion into highly specialised habitats, threats from other species, interruption of the food chain, pollution, or a combination of such factors.

environment   A concept which includes all aspects of the surroundings of humanity, affecting individuals and social groupings. The EC has defined the environment as 'the combination of elements whose complex interrelationships make up the settings, the surroundings and the conditions of life of the individual and of society, as they are or as they are felt'. The environment may be regarded as a parcel of things which render a stream of beneficial services and some disservices to people, though largely unpriced, and which take their place alongside the stream of goods and services rendered by real income, houses, infrastructure, transport, and other people.

environmental auditing   A management tool consisting of an evaluation, periodic and objective, of an organisation and its installations to assess compliance with regulatory requirements; an important aspect of post-project analysis.

environmental health impact assessment (EHIA)   A subset of EIA, an assessment of the impacts on the environment and people of aspects of a project recognised as having potentially adverse health effects. In 1982, WHO recommended that EHIA studies should be conducted for all major development projects. Many consider that the adverse effects of the Aswan High Dam in Egypt, such as the spread of bilharzia, were neglected in the EIA.

environmental impact assessment (EIA)   The critical appraisal of the likely effects of a policy, plan, program, project, or activity, on the environment. To assist the decision-making authority, assessments are carried out independently of the proponent, who may have prepared an EIS. The decision-making authority might be a level of government (local, state, or federal) or a government agency (at local, state, or federal level). Assessments take account of any adverse environmental effects on the community; any environmental impact on the ecosystems of the locality; any diminution of the aesthetic, recreational, aesthetic, scientific, or other environmental values of a locality; the endangering of any species of fauna or flora; any adverse effects on any place or building having aesthetic, anthropological, archaeological, cultural, historical, scientific, or social significance; any long-term or cumulative effects on the environment; any curtailing of the range of beneficial uses; any environmental problems associated with the disposal of wastes; any implications for natural resources; and the implications for the concept of sustainable development. EIA extends to the entire process from the inception of a proposal to environmental auditing and PPA.

environmental impact statement (EIS)   A document, prepared by a proponent, describing a proposed activity or development and identifying the possible, probable, or certain effects of the proposal on the environment; examining the alternatives to the proposal; setting out the mitigation measures to be adopted; proposing a program of environmental management; provisions for monitoring, PPA or auditing; and plans for decommissioning and rehabilitation. An EIS should be prepared following scoping exercises to identify the key issues. It should be objective, thorough and comprehensive, but without superfluous material. EISs are usually prepared by consultants working for the proponent presenting what has been described as an ethical dilemma; however, the ultimate test is not pleasing the proponent in the short-term, but achieving development consent after rigorous examination by a government agency and the public. This has ensured an increasing degree of integrity in the preparation of EISs. An EIS is often a key document in the EIA process.

environmental management   A concept of care applied to individual premises, corporate enterprises, localities, regions, catchments, natural resources, areas of high conservation value, lifetime cycles, waste handling and disposal, cleaner processing and recycling systems, with the purpose of protecting the environment in the broadest sense. It involves the identification of objectives, the adoption of appropriate mitigation measures, the protection of ecosystems, the enhancement of the quality of life for those affected, and the minimisation of environmental costs.

environmental planning system   An organisational and legislative structure within which the environmental decision-making process takes place. In a generalised way, the system's objective is to provide the best framework for making planning decisions based on economic, social, and environmental aims, providing for public involvement, promoting the guiding rather than the restrictive aspects of planning. Decisions need to be made at a policy, plan, program, and project level, providing for the involvement of all tiers of government.

greenhouse effect   In the general atmosphere surrounding the Earth, a warming effect as a result of the presence of certain gases such as carbon dioxide, methane, nitrous oxide, ozone, and water vapour; these greenhouse gases prove transparent to incoming short-wave solar radiation but relatively opaque to long-wave radiation reflected from the ground, the result is a long-term warming or greenhouse effect. Policies to combat the greenhouse effect will need to be considered in EIA procedures.

habitat Or living space; all the things which collectively make up the place in which organisms, creatures or humans live. Habitat includes non-living influences such as soil, light, temperature, humidity, and other abiotic factors; and biotic factors dependent on the activities of individuals and communities. In 1976, a UN conference on human settlements took the title 'Habitat'.

hazard and risk assessment An essential component of many EISs. Such an assessment embraces the potentially adverse effects of a project involving fire, heat, blast, explosion or flood, arising from a manufacturing plant or transportation system. An assessment reveals hazards to life and limb and property, and is expressed in the form of risk probability. Safety depends on the location of a plant, the safety precautions, back-up arrangements adopted, and the degree of training and alertness in the plant. Buffer zones and correct routeing of vehicles are also essential.

health Defined by WHO as 'a state of complete physical, mental and social well-being and not merely the absence of disease or infirmity'. However, most assessments of health still rely upon morbidity and mortality statistics, such as infant and child mortality rates, and average expectations of life in different countries.

isopleth An imaginary line connecting points of equal value for various climatic variables.

jurisdiction The geographical area in which a government (local, provincial, state, or national) exercises authority; or a sphere in which a government agency operates. Conflicts relating to jurisdiction might arise between levels of government and between government agencies. Nations might accept the jurisdiction of a multinational body such as the EC which issues directives binding on its members; the international courts and the UN.

mine bonding The depositing of a sum of money (the posting of a bond) with a consent authority (government agency) by a mining company before beginning operations. The deposit is intended to guarantee the reclamation and rehabilitation of the area to be mined. If a miner goes bankrupt or fails to comply with the conditions imposed, the mining company forfeits the bond to the consent authority which then becomes responsible for the rehabilitation of the mine site.

mitigation measures Action taken to prevent, avoid, or minimise the actual or potential adverse effects of a policy, plan, program, or project. Measures might include abandoning or modifying a proposal, or relocating it; substitution of techniques; cleaner methods; recycling; pollution control methods; closure of older plant; landscaping and rehabilitation; acquisition of properties; and better programming.

monitoring A combination of observation and measurement for the performance of a project and its compliance with development consent conditions. Instrumentation might be required in relation to air, water, and land pollutants; noise and blasting; radiation; transport movements; and land subsidence. Records might be required for materials movements, raw materials, products, wastes, complaints and investigations, instrument and analysis results.

NIMBY and BANANA Acronyms for some attitudes to development: 'Not in my backyard' and 'Build absolutely nothing anywhere near anybody'. Both fall short of opposing any development anywhere and do not reflect a belief in zero economic growth shared by others.

nuisances Accumulations, deposits, effluvia, infestations, sources of odour and noise, which might be detrimental to the health of the public.

optimum The best or most favourable condition, degree, quality, or quantity, achievable in a particular situation.

post-project analysis (PPA) An environmental study undertaken during the operational stage of a project or program to assess compliance with the terms imposed by the EIA process and to consider the quality and possible improvement of environmental management. It has broader aims than environmental auditing.

precautionary principle A guiding rule in EIA to protect people and the environment against future risks, hazards, and adverse impacts, tending to emphasise safety considerations in the occasional absence of clear evidence.

program An array of projects, which might proceed concurrently or sequentially, such as an energy program or transport program.

project A proposed installation, factory, works, mine, highway, airport, or scheme, and all activities with possible impacts on the environment.

proponent The proposer (or applicant) of an activity, policy, plan, program, or project in the private or public sectors; a proposal usually requires official approval or consent and during the process of obtaining this, the public have increasing opportunities to voice opinions of support and objection.

public inquiry or hearing An opportunity for members of the public, voluntary bodies, and government agencies, to express opinions before an independent and impartial commissioner of inquiry, to enable issues about a controversial proposed development to be fully discussed. The usual outcome is the submission of a report by the commissioner with recommendations to a decision-making body or minister, the report becoming immediately a public document. The success of the public inquiry hinges upon the choice, integrity, and independence of the commissioner; and upon a political and social context which encourages full participation by all citizens, without fear of reprisal or discrimination. The public inquiry often stands at the apex of EIA processes.

quality of life In current usage, a concept embracing a miscellany of desirable things not always recognised, or adequately recognised, in the marketplace. It embraces such highly relevant matters as real income, housing, and working conditions, health, and educational services, and recreational opportunities which might be regarded as the general standard of living. Other highly relevant matters include community relationships, race relationships, civil liberties, compassion, justice, freedom, and fair play, safety and security, law and order, and environmental conditions.

sanitation An important health-related branch of development embracing drainage and sewerage, sewage and sullage treatment and effluent disposal, safe and adequate domestic water supplies, avoidance of public nuisances and uncontrolled tipping, and drainage facilities for floodwater and surface run-off. Few countries renowned for high-tech achievements have been able to resolve the basic requirements of sanitation, relying on primitive methods (or none).

scoping A procedure, carried out as early as possible, to help ensure that an EA focuses on key environmental issues associated with a proposed activity or development; scoping involves meetings between the proponent and planning or environmental agencies, members of the public, and other interests likely to be affected. The result should determine the scope and depth of the significant issues to be examined in the forthcoming EIS.

smog   A word first used early in the twentieth century to describe a mixture of smoke and fog; subsequently the word has been applied to air pollution generally, including photochemical smog which contains neither smoke nor fog.

social impact assessment (SIA)   A subset of EIA, an assessment of the impact on people and society of major policies, plans, programs, activities, and developments. Social impacts or effects are those changes in social relations between members of a community, society or institution, resulting from external change. The changes might be physical or psychological involving social cohesion; general lifestyle; cultural life; attitudes and values; social tranquillity; relocation of residents; and severance or separation. For example, in the construction of large hydro-electric dams, large populations are relocated into unfamiliar environments. The consequences have been social discontent, unhappiness, increased illness, and a loss of productivity and income.

strategic EIA (also SEA)   The application of EIA not only to individual projects, but to policies, plans, programs, activities, and regional land-use objectives. There is a growing conviction that matters cannot be completely resolved at project level when many matters have been decided already at a higher level. Matters difficult or impossible to settle at the project level relate to the cumulative effects of other projects within the same or related programs; to transportation decisions governing the modal split between road and rail movement; to energy policies relating to power generation; to greenhouse strategies; and to natural resource conservation and management.

sustainable development   Development which provides economic, social, and environmental benefits in the long-term, having regard to future generations. To achieve this, sustainable development considers both the living and non-living resource base for conservation and the advantages and disadvantages of alternative courses of action for future generations. It allows the use of depletable resources in an efficient manner with an eye to the substitution of other resources in due course.

world heritage listings   Those assets considered by the UN Educational, Scientific and Cultural Organisation (UNESCO) to be of 'outstanding universal value, the destruction or disappearance of which would constitute a 'harmful impoverishment of the heritage of all nations of the world'. Thus many items of the world's cultural and natural heritage have been preserved. Such listings must be carefully respected in EIAs.

Aguilo, M., Alonso, S., Blair, W., et al (1986) *Foundations for visual project analysis*, John Wiley & Sons, London, Britain.

Ahmad, Y. J. and Sammy, G. K. (1984) *Guidelines to environmental impact in developing countries*, Hodder and Stoughton, London, Britain.

Armour, A. (1988a) *Integrating impact assessment in the planning process: from rhetoric to reality*, presentation to the seventh annual meeting of the International Association of Impact Assessment, 5-9 July, Griffith University, Brisbane, Australia.

— (1988b) 'Methodological problems in social impact monitoring', *Environment Impact Assessment Review* 8 (3); 249-265.

Asian Development Bank (1990) *Environmental guidelines for selected industrial and power development projects*, Environment unit, Asian Development Bank, Manila, Philippines.

— (1991) *Guidelines for social analysis of development projects*, Infrastructure Department, Asian Development Bank, Manila, Philippines.

Atelier Central de l'Environnement (1990) *Environmental impact assessment: the French experience*, ACE, Neuilly, Paris, France.

Atkinson, S. F. (1985) 'Habitat-based methods for biological impact assessment', *The environmental professional* 7 (3), 265.

Australian Bureau of Agricultural and Resource Economics (1990) *Mining and the environment: resource use in the Kakada conservation zone*, a submission to the Resource Assessment Commission, Australian Government Publishing Service, Canberra, Australia.

Australian Conservation Foundation (1975) *The EIS Technique*, ACF, Melbourne, Australia.

Austrian Federal Government (1992) *Austria: National report to the United Nations Conference on environment and development 1992*, Austrian Federal Ministry of Environment, Youth and Family, Vienna, Austria.

Bailey, J. and English, V. (1991) 'Western Australian environmental impact assessment: an evolving approach to environmentally sound development', *Environmental and Planning Law Journal*, 8, (3), 190-199.

Baille, P. and Chemin, J. L. (1991) Études d'impact sur l'environnement: réflexions sur la pratique française' *Aménagement et Nature*, 102, p. 12.

Ball, S. (1991) 'Implementation of the environmental assessment directive in Britain', *Integrated Environmental Management*, 5, pp. 9-11.

Bamber, R. N. (1990) 'Environmental impact assessment: the example of marine biology and the UK power industry', *Marine Pollution Bulletin*, 21 (6), 270-274.

Barke, S. (1990) 'Swedish EIA policy', *VIA* (Italy), 16, pp. 26-29.

Bass, R. (1990) 'California's experience with environmental impact reports', *Project appraisal*, 5 (4), 220-224.

Bass, R. E. and Herson, A. I. (1992) *Successful California Environmental Quality Act compliance: a step-by-step approach*, Solano Press, Point Area, California, USA.

Beanlands, G. E. and Duinker, P. N. (1983) *An ecological framework for environmental impact assessment in Canada*, Federal Environmental Assessment Review Office, Quebec, Canada.

Becker, H. A. and Porter, A. L. (eds) (1986) *Methods and experiences in impact assessment*, D. Reidel Publishing Company, The Netherlands.

Bennett, J. and Carter, M. (1991) *Recent developments in contingent valuation in Australia*, June, a paper presented to the European Association of Environmental and Resource Economists, Stockholm, Sweden.

Bingham, G. (1986) *Resolving environmental disputes: a decade of experience*, The Conservation Foundation, Washington, DC, USA.

Biswas, A. K. and Agarwala, S. B. C. (eds) (1992) *Environmental impact assessment for developing countries*, Butterworth–Heinemann, Oxford, Britain.

Black, P. (1981) *Environmental impact analysis*, Praeger Publishers, New York, USA.

Bloom, S. G., Cornaby, B. W., and Martin, W. E. (1978) *A guide to mathematical models used in steam electric power plant environmental impact assessment*, Battelle Columbus Laboratories, Columbus, Ohio, USA.

Boes, M. (1990) 'Environmental impact statements in Belgium', *Northwestern journal of international law and business*, 10 (3), 522-540.

Bolton, K. F. and Curtis, F. A. (1990) 'An environmental procedure for siting solid waste disposal sites', *Environmental impact assessment review*, 10, pp. 285-296.

Boon, P. J. (ed.) (1990) *Environmental impact assessment and the water industry: implications for nature conservation*, Nature Conservancy Council, Peterborough, Britain.

Bradley, K., Skehan, C. and Walsh, G. (eds) (1991) *Environmental impact assessment: a technical approach*, DTPS Ltd, Dublin, Ireland.

Breton, F., de Miro, M., and Sauri, D. (1991) 'Les études d'impact en Espagne et en Catalogne', *Aménagement et Nature*, 102, p. 27.

British Columbia (1976) *Guidelines for coal development*, Environmental Land-Use Committee, Government Printer, Victoria, BC, Canada.

British Standards Institute (1992) *BS7750 British standard for environmental management*, BSI, London, Britain.

Bronfman, L. M. (1991) 'Setting the social impact agenda: an organisational perspective', *Environmental impact assessment review*, 11 (1), 69-80.

Brown, L. R., Durning, A., Flavin, C., French, H., Jacobsen, J., Lenssen, N., Lowe, M., Postel, S., Renner, M., Ryan, J., Starke, L., and Young, J. (1992) *State of the world 1991: a Worldwatch Institute Report on progress toward a sustainable society*, W. W. Norton & Co. Inc., New York, USA.

Buchan, D. and Rivers, M. J. (1990) 'Social impact assessment: development and application in New Zealand', *Impact Assessment Bulletin*, 8 (4), 97-105.

Buckley, R. (1988) 'Critical problems in environmental planning and management', *Environmental Planning and Law Journal* (Australia), September, pp. 206-225.

— (1989) *Precision in environmental impact predictions: first national environmental audit, Australia*, Centre for Resource and Environmental Studies, Australian National University, Canberra, Australia.

Burchell, R. W. and Listokin, D. (1975) *The environmental impact handbook*, Rutgers, State University of New Jersey, New Jersey, USA.

Bureau of Industry Economics (1990) *Environmental assessment — Impact on major projects*, research report no. 35, Australian Government Publishing Service, Canberra, Australia.

Bureau of Land Management (1988) *National environmental policy act handbook* (author: Williams, D. C.), Bureau of Land Management, US Department of the Interior, Washington, DC, USA.

Burke, A. (1990) 'Learning to live without nuclear power: Sweden's decision to phase out its twelve reactors is put to the test', *Current Sweden no. 372*, The Swedish Institute, Stockholm, Sweden.

Canada (1991) *Canada's national report to the United Nations conference on environment and development 1992*, Ministry of Supply and Services, Ottawa, Canada.

Canadian Environmental Assessment Research Council (1988) *The assessment of cumulative effects: a research prospective*, CEARC, Quebec, Canada.

Canelas, L. D. (1991) 'Implementation of the EEC directive in Portugal: a case study', *Impact Assessment Bulletin*, 9 (3), 75-83.

Canter, L. W. (1977) *Environmental impact assessment*, McGraw-Hill, New York, USA.

— (1979) *Water resources assessment: methodology and technology sourcebook*, Ann Arbor Science, Michigan, USA.

— (1985) *Environmental impact of water resource projects*, Lewis Publishers, New York, USA.

— (1990) *Environmental monitoring in environmental impact studies*, Environmental and Groundwater Institute, University of Oklahoma, Oklahoma, USA.

Canter, L. W., Robertson, J. M., and Westcott, R. M. (1991) 'Identification and evaluation of biological impact mitigation measures', *Journal of environmental management*, 33 (10), 35-50.

Cheremisinoff, P. N. and Morresi, A. C. (1977) *Environmental assessment and impact statement handbook*, Ann Arbor Science, Ann Arbor, Michigan, USA.

Clark, B. D., Bisset, R., and Wathen, P. (1980) *Environmental impact assessment: a bibliography with abstracts*, Bowker, New York, USA.

Clark, B., Gilad, A., Bisset, R., and Tomlinson, P. (eds) (1984) *Perspectives on environmental impact assessment*, D. Reidel Publishing Company, The Netherlands.

Clark, M. and Herington, J. (eds) (1988) *The role of environmental impact assessment in the planning process*, Mansell Publishing, London, Britain.

Cocklin, C. (1989) *Methodological approaches to the assessment of cumulative environmental change*, Environmental Science Occasional Publication, no. CEC-02, University of Auckland, Auckland, New Zealand.

Cocklin, C. and Parker, S. (1990) *Cumulative environmental change: concepts revisited and a case study*, Environmental Science Publication no. CED-03, University of Auckland, Auckland, New Zealand.

Cohrssen, J. J. and Covello, V. (1989) *Risk analysis: a guide to principles and methods for analysing health and environmental risks*, The National Technical Information Service, US Department of Commerce, Springfield, Virginia, USA.

Colombo, A. G. (ed.) *Environmental impact assessment*, Kluwer Academic Publishers, Dordrecht, The Netherlands.

Commission for Environmental Impact Assessment (1990) *Advice for guidelines on the content of the environmental impact statement about the construction of a pipeline through the Wadden area*, CEIA, Utrecht, The Netherlands.

Commission of Inquiry into the Conservation, Management and Use of Fraser Island and the Great Sandy Region/ Cabinet Office of New South Wales (1990) *Public issue dispute resolution: a joint discussion paper*, Government Printer, Brisbane, Australia.

Cooper, C. (1981) *Economic evaluation of the environment*, Hodder & Stoughton, London, Britain.

Council on Environmental Quality (1978a) *Regulations for implementing the procedural provisions of the National Environmental Policy Act*, Washington, DC, USA.

— (1978b) *Preparation of environmental impact statements guidelines*, Washington, DC, USA.

— (1986) *Regulations for implementing the procedural provisions of the National Environmental Policy Act*, Washington, DC, USA.

— (1987) *Memorandum to Agencies: Forty most asked questions concerning CEQ's National Environmental Policy Act Regulations*, Washington, DC, USA.

— (1989) *Inventory of federal agency activities on cumulative impact assessment and summary of 1988 interagency meeting on cumulative impact assessment* (author: Rodes, B. K.), Washington, DC, USA.

— (1991) *Environmental quality: twenty first annual report*, Executive Office of the President, CEQ, Washington, DC, USA.

Culhane, P. J., Friesma, H. P., and Beecher, J. (1987) *Forecasts and environmental decision-making: the predictive accuracy of environmental impact statements*, Westview Press, Denver, Colorado, USA.

Czechoslovak Economic Digest 3/91 (1991) *The ecological dimension of economic reform in Czechoslovakia*, Prague, Czechoslovakia.

Délégation à la Qualité de la vie (1983) *Etudes d'impact sur l'environnement: guide des procédures administratives et recueil des textes d'application*, Cahiers Techniques de la Délégation à la Qualité de la Vie, Ministère de l'Environnement, Paris, France.

Denver Research Institute (1982) *Socioeconomic impacts of power plants*, DRI, Denver, Colorado, USA.

Department of Agriculture (1982a) *A national program for soil and water conservation: final program and environmental impact statement*, US Government Printing Office, Washington, DC, USA.

— (1982b) *Guidelines for economic and social analysis of programs, resource plans and projects: final policy*, Federal Register, 47 (80), 17940-17954, US Government Printing Office, Washington, DC, USA.

— (1983) *Final environmental impact statement: Black Hills national forest*, US Forest Service, South Dakota, USA.

Department of Defense (1979) *Environmental effects in the*

United States of Department of Defense Actions, Department of Defense Directive 6050.1 DOD, Washington, DC, USA.

Department of Environment (1990) *Progress in Malaysia towards environmentally sound and sustainable development (ESSD) 1976-1990*, Kuala Lumpur, Malaysia.

— (1991) *Malaysia: environmental quality report 1990*, Ministry of Science, Technology and the Environment, Kuala Lumpur, Malaysia.

Department of Home Affairs and Environment (1983) *Economics and environment policy: the role of cost-benefit analysis*, Australian Government Publishing Service, Canberra, Australia.

Department of Housing and Urban Development (1981) *Areawide environmental impact assessment: a guidebook*, DHUD, Washington, DC, USA.

— (1985) *Handbook 1390.2 Environmental assessment guide* (author: Prybyla, W.), DHUD, Washington, DC, USA.

— (1986) *Environmental review guide for community development* (author: Prybyla, W.), DHUD, Washington, DC, USA.

Department of the Army (1975) *Handbook for environmental impact analysis*, DA, Washington, DC, USA.

Department of the Environment (1992) *Ireland: National report to the United Nations Conference on environment and development*, Dublin, Ireland.

Department of the Interior (1973) *A methodology for assessing the environmental impact of water resources development*, US Department of the Interior, Washington, DC, USA.

Department of the Navy (1983) *Environmental assessments and impact statements*, DN, Washington, DC, USA.

Deutsche Gesellschaft für Technische Zusammenarbeit (1987) *Sector catalogues for the identification of environmental effects*, GTZ, Germany.

Devuyst, D. and Hens, L. (1991) 'Environmental impact assessment in Belgium: an overview', *The environmental professional*, 13 (2), 166-173.

Dirección General del Medio Ambiente (1984) *Curso sobre evaluaciones de impacto ambiental*, Ministerio de Obras Publicas y Urbanismo, Madrid, Spain.

— (1989) *Guias metodológicas para le elaboración de estudios de impacto ambiental: 1 carreteras y ferrocarriles; 2 grandes presas*, MOPU (DGMA), Madrid, Spain.

Dixon, J. A. and Hufschmidt, M. M. (1986) *Economic valuation techniques for the environment: a case study workbook*, Johns Hopkins Press, Baltimore, Maryland, USA.

Draper, D. W. (1984) 'Siting of coal-fired power plants near environmentally sensitive areas in Canada', *The environmental professional* (USA), 6 (3/4), 303-315.

Eastern European Newsletter (1989) *Note on Czechoslovakia* (Britain), 3, (23).

Economic and Social Commission for Asia and the Pacific, environment and development series (1985-90) *Environmental impact assessment*

(1) *Guidelines for planners and decision-makers.*
(2) *Guidelines for agricultural development.*
(3) *Guidelines for industrial development.*
(4) *Guidelines for transport development.*
(5) *Guidelines for water resources development.*
UN, New York, USA.

Environment and Policy Institute, US East-West Center (1982) *Proceedings of conferences on air quality and the siting of coal-fired power stations*, held in Seoul and Daejon, Korea, 17-28 May, EWC, Hawaii, USA.

Environment Canada and Transport Canada (1988) *Environmental monitoring and audit: guidelines for post-project analysis of development impacts and assessment methodology*, Environment Canada, Ottawa, Canada.

Environmental Protection Administration (1985) *Technical guidelines for conducting EIA-requiring projects*, Taipei, Taiwan, Republic of China.

Environmental Protection Agency (1979) *Implementation of procedures under the National Environmental Policy Act, Federal Register*, 44 (216), 64174-64193, US Government Printing Office, Washington, DC, USA.

— (1984) *Policy and procedures for the review of federal actions impacting the environment*, EPA, Washington, DC, USA.

— (1990a) *Bibliography and abstracts of environmental impact assessment methodologies*, EPA Office of Federal Activities, Washington , DC, USA.

— (1990b) *Environmental investments: the cost of a clean environment*, EPA, Washington, DC, USA.

— (1991a) *Cross-cutting environmental laws: a guide for federal/state project officers*, EPA, Washington, DC, USA.

— (1991b) *Procedures for implementing the requirements of the Council on Environmental Quality on the National Environmental Policy Act*, EPA, Washington, DC, USA.

Environmental Research Unit (1992) *Inventory of environmental impact statements submitted between July 1988 and December 1990: also submitted during 1991*, ERU, Dublin, Ireland.

Environmental Resources Ltd (1981a) *Methodologies: studies on methodologies, scoping and guidelines*, Ministry of Public Health and Environment, The Hague, The Netherlands.

— (1981b) *Environmental impact assessment: studies on methodologies, scoping and guidelines*, ERL, London, Britain.

— (1981c) *Environmental impact assessment: final report on methodologies, scoping and guidelines*, Ministry of Health and Environmental Protection/Ministry of Culture, Recreation and Social Welfare, Leidschendam, The Netherlands.

— (1984) *Prediction in environmental impact assessment: a summary report of a research project to identify methods of prediction for use in environmental impact assessment*, ERL, London, Britain.

— (1985) *Handling uncertainty in environmental impact assessment*, Ministry of Public Housing, Physical Planning and Environmental Protection, The Hague, The Netherlands.

Erbguth, W. and Schink, A. (1992) *Gesetz uber die Umweltvertraglichkeitsprufung: Kommentar*, C. H. Beck'sche Verlagsbuchhandlung, Munich, Germany.

Erickson, P.A. (1979) *Environmental impact assessment: principles and applications*, Academic Press, New York, USA.

Essex County Council (1992) *The Essex guide to environmental assessment*, ECC, Chelmsford, Essex, Britain.

Falque, M. (1990) *L'étude d'impact sur l'environnement*, Somi Consultants, Paris, France.

Farmer, A. (1980) *Habitat evaluation procedures*, US Fish and Wildlife Services, Washington, DC, USA.

Federal Aviation Administration (1985) *Airport environmental handbook*, Federal Aviation Administration Order 5050.4A FAA, Washington , DC, USA.

— (1986) *Policies and procedures for considering environmental impacts: federal aviation administration order 1050.11*, Washington, DC, USA.

Federal Energy Regulatory Commission (1990) *Environmental report checklist (revision 6) and recommended mitigation procedures* (author: Hoffmand, R. R.), Washington, DC, USA.

Federal Environmental Assessment and Review Office (1984) *Improvements in the federal environmental assessment and review process*, FEARO, Ottawa, Canada.

— (1985) *Environmental assessment in Canada: summary of current practice*, FEARO, Ottawa, Canada.

— (1986) *Initial Assessment Guide*, FEARO, Ottawa, Canada.

— (1987) *Reforming federal environmental assessment: a discussion paper*, FEARO, Quebec, Canada.

— (1988) *Manual on public involvement in environmental assessment: planning and implementing public involvement programs*, FEARO, Calgary, Canada.

— (1991) *Developing environmentally responsible policies: a guide to environmental assessment of policy*, FEARO, Ottawa, Canada.

Federal Republic of Germany (1990) *Environmental policy: environmental report 1990 by the federal minister for the environment, nature conservation and nuclear safety*, FRG, Bonn, Germany.

— (1991) *National report to the United Nations conference on environment and development 1992*, FRG, Bonn, Germany.

— (1992) *Global change: our world in transition*, Federal Ministry for research and Technology, Bonn, Germany.

Finsterbusch, K., Llewellyn, L. G., and Wolf, C. P. (eds) (1983) *Social impact assessment methods*, Sage Publications, London, Britain.

Fisher, R. and Ury, W. (1981) *Getting to yes*, Hutchinson, London, Britain.

Forsgren, B. (1992) *EIA in the Swedish planning and decision-making system*, Swedish Environmental Protection Agency, Department of Natural Resources, Stockholm, Sweden.

Fortlage, C. A. (1990) *Environmental assessment: a practical guide*, Gower Publishing, Aldershot, Britain.

Fowler, R. J. (1982) *Environmental impact assessment, planning and pollution measures in Australia*, Australian Government Publishing Service, Canberra, Australia.

Fuggle, R. F. (1988) *Integrated environmental management: an appropriate approach to environmental concerns in developing countries*, presentation to the seventh annual meeting of the International Association of Impact Assessment, Griffith University, Queensland, Australia, 5-9 July.

Furtrell, J. W. et al (1981) *NEPA in action: environmental offices in nineteen federal agencies; a report to the Council on Environmental Quality*. US Government Printing Office, Washington, DC, USA.

German Foundation for International Development (1985) *Environmental impact assessment for development*, Deutsche Stifting für Internationale Entwicklung, Feldafing, Germany.

Gilpin, A. (1990) *An Australian dictionary of environment and planning*, Oxford University Press, Oxford, Britain and Melbourne, Australia.

Gittinger, J. P. (1982) *Economic analysis of agricultural projects*, Johns Hopkins Press, Baltimore, Maryland, USA.

Go, F. C. (1987) *Environmental impact assessment: an analysis of the methodological and substantive issues affecting human health considerations*, Monitoring and Assessment Research Centre Report no. 41, London, Britain.

Gonzales, A. S., Aguilo, M., and Ramos, A. (1987) *Direcrices y tecnicas para la estimacion de impactos*, Trabajos de la Catredra de Planificacion, Escuela Tecnica Superior de Ingenieros de Montes, Universidad Politecnica, Madrid, Spain.

Goudie, A. (1986) *The human impact on the natural environment*, MIT Press, Massachusetts, USA.

Government Printing Office, Netherlands, The (1992) *Prediction in EIA*, 10 volumes on the prediction of effects in: air; surface water; soil and ground water; flora, fauna and ecosystems; landscape; the acoustic environment; radiation; risks; and health; plus an introductory volume, Government Printing Office, Amsterdam, The Netherlands.

Government Printing Office, The Netherlands (1992

Govorushko, S. M. (1989) *Environmental impact assessment in the USSR: the current situation*, Pacific Institute of Geography, Far East Branch, The USSR Academy of Sciences, Vladivostok, USSR.

Heer, J. E. and Haggerty, D. J. (1977) *Environmental assessments and statements*, Van Nostrand Reinhold, New York, USA.

Henderson, J. E. (1982) *Handbook of environmental quality measurement and assessment: methods and techniques*, Instruction Report E-82-2, US Army Engineer Waterways Experiment Station, CE, Vicksburg, Mississippi, USA.

Herson, A. and Bogdan, K. M. (1991) 'Cumulative impact analysis under NEPA: recent legal developments', *The environmental professional*, 13(2), 100-106.

Hills, O. and Ramani, K. V. (eds) (1990) *Energy systems and the environment: approaches to impact assessment in Asian Developing countries*, Asian and Pacific Development Centre, Kuala Lumpur, Malaysia.

Holling, C. S. (ed.) (1980) *Adaptive environmental assessment and management*, John Wiley, Chichester, Britain.

Howe, C. P., Claridge, G. F., Hughes, R., and Zuwendra (1991a) *Manual of guidelines for scoping EIA in tropical wetlands*.

— (1991b) *Manual of guidelines for scoping EIA in Indonesian wetlands*.

PHPA/AWB Sumatra wetland project reports nos 5 and 6b. Asian Wetland Bureau — Indonesia and Directorate-General of Forest Protection and Nature Conservation, Department of Forestry, Bogor, Indonesia.

Hufschmidt, M. M., James, D. E., Meister, A. D., Bower, B. T., and Dixon, J. A. (1983) *Environment, natural systems and development: an economic valuation guide*, Johns Hopkins Press, Baltimore, Maryland, USA.

Hufschmidt, M. M. (1985) 'The environmental dimensions of water resources management: application in developing countries', *The environmental professional*, 7 (4), 318-324.

Hundloe, T. (1986) *Environmental impact assessment: the basic concepts*, Institute of Applied Economic Research, Griffith University, Brisbane, Australia.

Hundloe, T. (1990) 'Measuring the value of the Great Barrier Reef', *Australian Parks and Recreation*, 26 (3), 11-15.

Hundloe, T., McDonald, G. T., Ware, J., and Wilks, L. (1990) 'Cost-benefit analysis and environmental impact assessment', *Environmental Impact Assessment Review*, 10 (1/2), 55-68.

Hyde, L. W. (1974) *Environmental impact assessment by use of matrix diagrams*, Alabama Development Office, State Planning Division, State Office Building, Montgomery, Alabama, USA.

Hyman, E. L. (1981) The valuation of extramarket benefits and costs in environmental impact assessment, *Environmental Impact Assessment Review*, 2, pp. 226-258.

Hyman, E. L. and Stiftel, B. (1988) *Combining facts and values in environmental impact assessment*, Westview Press, Boulder, Colorado, USA and London, Britain.

Imber, D., Stevenson, G., and Wilks L. (1991) *A contingent valuation survey of the Kakadu conservation zone*, Research paper 3, Resource Assessment Commission, Canberra, Australia.

Interim Committee for Coordination of Investigations of the Lower Mekong Basin (1982) *Nampong Environmental Management Research Project: Final Report for Phase 3*, Bangkok, Thailand.

International Atomic Energy Agency (1991) *Electricity and the environment*, IAEA-Tecdoc-624, Background papers for a senior expert symposium held in Helsinki, 13-17 May, IAEA, Vienna, Austria.

International Council of Scientific Unions (1987) *Environmental impact assessment*, ICSU, Washington, DC, USA.

International Institute for Environment and Development/World Resources Institute (1992) *World Resources 1992*, Basic Books Inc., New York, USA.

International Seminar and First Inter-Republican Conference

(1991) *Environmental impact assessment: methodology and applications*, 25-29 November, UNESCO/UNEP/UNDP/USSR, Moscow, USSR.

Jacobs, P. and Sadler, B. (eds) (1990) *Sustainable development and environmental assessment: perspectives on planning for a common future*, Canadian Environmental Assessment Research Council, Quebec, Canada.

Jain, R. K., Urban, L. V. and Stacey, G. S. (1977) *Environmental impact analysis: a new dimension in decision-making*, Van Nostrand Reinhold, New York, USA.

Jänicke, M., Mönch, H., Ranneberg, T., and Simonus, U.E. (1987) *Improving environmental quality through structural change: a survey of thirty-one countries*, Research Unit Environmental Policy, International Institute for Environment and Society, Berlin, Germany.

Jones, C. E., Lee, N., and Wood, C. (1991) *UK environmental impact statements 1988-1990; an analysis*, Department of Planning and Landscape, University of Manchester, Manchester, Britain.

Kennedy, W. V. (1986) *Environmental impact assessment and highway planning: a comparative case study analysis of the United States and the Federal Republic of Germany*, Rainer Bohn Verlag, Science Centre, Berlin, Germany.

Kent County Council (1991) *Kent Environmental Assessment Handbook*, KCC, Maidstone, Kent, Britain.

Krutilla, J. V. and Fisher, A. C. (1975) *The economics of natural environments*, Johns Hopkins Press, Baltimore Maryland, USA.

Lee, N. (1989) *Environmental impact assessment: a training guide*, (2nd edn) Department of Planning and Landscape, University of Manchester, Manchester, Britain.

Lee, N. and Colley, R. (1990) *Reviewing the quality of environmental statements*, Department of Planning and Landscape, University of Manchester, Manchester, Britain.

Lee, N. and Walsh, F. (1992) 'Strategic environmental assessment: an overview', *Project Appraisal*, 7 (3).

Leon, B. F. (1989) *A survey of analyses in environmental impact statements*, Quadrant Consultants, New York, USA.

Leopold, L. B., Clarke, F. E. Hornshaw, B. R., and Balsley, J. R. (1971) *A procedure for evaluating environmental impact*, US Geological Survey circular 645, Washington, DC, USA.

Little, I. M. D. and Mirrlees, J. A. (1976) *Project appraisal and planning for developing countries*, Heinemann, London, Britain.

Lohani, B. N. (1988) *Environmental assessment and management in the Bank's developing member countries*, Asian Development Bank, Manila, Philippines.

Lönnroth, Måns (1992) 'Sweden and the European environment', *Current Sweden no. 390 June 1992*, Stockholm, Sweden.

Maclaren, V. W. and Whitney, J. B. (eds) (1985) *New directions in environmental impact assessment in Canada*, Methuen, London, Britain.

McCold, L. N. (1991) 'Reducing global, regional, and cumulative impacts with the National Environmental Policy Act', *The environmental professional* 13 (2), 107-113.

McHarg, I. L. (1969) *Design with nature*, Natural History Press, New York, USA.

Maki, A. W. (1991) 'The Exxon Valdez oil spill: initial environmental impact assessment', *Environmental science and technology*, 25 (1), 24-29.

Meadows, D. H., Meadows, D. L., Randers, J., and Behrens, W. W. (1972) *The limits to growth: a report for the Club of Rome's project on the predicament of mankind*, Pan Books, London, Britain.

Mesarovic, M. and Pestel, E. (1975) *The second report to the Club of Rome*, Hutchinson, London, Britain.

Michel, P. (1988) *L'étude d'impact des ports de plaisance*, Délégation à la Qualité de la Vie, Paris, France.

Ministry for Planning and Environment (1985) *Review of seven environmental assessments carried out between 1975 and 1982*, MPE, Victoria, Australia.

— (1990) *Planning and Environment Act 1987: social, economic and environmental effects*, MPE, Victoria, Australia.

Ministry for the Environment (1988a) *Draft guide for scoping and public review methods in environmental impact assessment*, ME, Wellington, New Zealand.

— (1988b) *Impact assessment in resource management*, Resource management law reform working paper 20, Wellington, New Zealand.

Ministry for the Environment (1990a) *Environmental impact assessment in Norway: provisions in the Planning and Building Act relating to EIA*, The State Pollution Control Authority, ME, Oslo, Norway.

— (1990b) *Environmental impact assessment in Norway*, ME, Oslo, Norway.

— (1990c) *Report on the regional conference at ministerial level being the follow-up to the report of the World Commission on Environment and Development (the Brundtland report) in the ECE region*, ME, Bergen, Norway.

Ministry for the Environment (1991) *Guide for scoping and public review methods in environmental impact assessment*, ME, Wellington, New Zealand.

Ministry of Development Cooperation (1990-92) *Environmental impact assessment of development aid projects: initial environmental assessments: 1 to 6*, NADC (NORAD), Oslo, Norway.

Ministry of Foreign Affairs (1992) *Malaysia's report to the United Nations Conference on Environment and Development 1992*, Kuala Lumpur, Malaysia.

Ministry of Housing, Physical Planning and Environment (1989) *National environment policy plan: to choose or to lose*, MHPPE, The Hague, The Netherlands.

Ministry of the Environment, Physical Planning and Public Works (1991) *National report of Greece to the United Nations Conference on environment and development*, Athens, Greece.

Mitre Corporation (1975) *Guidelines for the environmental impact assessment of small structures and related activities in coastal bodies of water*, Mitre technical report MTR-6916 for the US Army, New York, USA.

Morris, M. L. (1991) 'Environmental impact assessment: current problems in Australia and prospects for improvement', Master's degree thesis, University of Adelaide, South Australia.

Munn, R. E. (ed.) (1979) *Environmental impact assessment* (2nd edn), John Wiley, New York, USA.

National Academy of Sciences (1985) *Safety of dams: flood and earthquake criteria*, NAS, Washington, DC, USA.

National Oceanic and Atmospheric Administration (1984) *NOAA directives manual* (author: Cottingham, D.), NOAA, Washington, DC, USA.

National Park Service (1982) *NEPA compliance guideline NPS-12* (author: Virstrait, J.), Washington, DC, USA.

Neuhold, J. M. (1989) 'United States', in E. J. Kormondy (ed.) *International handbook of pollution control*, Greenwood Press, New York, USA, pp. 95-112.

Neve, T. L. (1991) 'Including NEPA in Department of Defence decision-making', *The environmental professional*, 13 (2), 145-153.

Nichols, R. and Hyman, E. L. (1980) *A review and analysis of fifteen methodologies for environmental assessment*, Center for Urban and Regional Studies, University of North Carolina, Chapel Hill, North Carolina, USA.

Norton, G.A. (1984) *Resource economics*, Edward Arnold, London, Britain.

Norton, G. A., Clark, B. D., and Gilad, A. (1984) *Perspectives on environmental impact assessment systems analysis and environmental impact assessment*, Reidel, New York, USA.

NSW Science and Technology Council (1983) *The science and technology of environmental impact assessment, with particular reference to methods used in New South Wales*, a report by FEARO, Canada, NSWSTC, Sydney, Australia.

Office of Commissioners of Inquiry (1980 to present) *Reports of Commissions of Inquiry*, Sydney, Australia.

Organisation for Economic Cooperation and Development (1979) *Environmental impact assessment* (also in French), OECD, Paris, France.

— (1992) *Environment and development: The OECD approach*, a report prepared by OECD for the UN Conference on Environment and Development, Rio de Janeiro, Brazil, 3-14 June, OECD, Paris, France.

O'Riordan, T. and Sewell, W. R. D. (eds) (1981) *Project appraisal and policy review*, John Wiley & Sons, Chichester, Britain.

Ortolano, L. (1984) *Environmental planning and decision-making*, John Wiley & Sons, London, Britain.

O'Sullivan, M. (1990) *Environmental impact assessment: a handbook*, Resource and Environmental Management Unit, University College, Cork, Ireland.

Overseas Development Administration (1992) *Manual of environmental appraisal* (rev. edn), ODA, London, Britain.

Panyarachun, A. H. E. (1992) 'Business and environment: time for action', keynote address at an international conference on Merging business and the environment, 23 January, Bangkok, Thailand.

Paschen, H. (ed.) (1989) *The role of environmental impact assessment in the decision-making process*, Erich Schmidt Verlag GmbH, Berlin, Germany.

Pearce, D. W. (1978) *The valuation of social cost*, Macmillan, London, Britain.

— (1983) *Cost-benefit analysis*, Macmillan, London, Britain.

Pearce, D. W. and Nash, C. A. (1981) *The social appraisal of projects: a text in cost-benefit analysis*, Macmillan, London, Britain.

Pinho, P. and Pires, A. R. (1991) 'Social impact analysis in environmental impact assessment: a Portuguese agricultural case study', *Project appraisal*, 6 (1), 2-6.

Planning and Environment Commission, New South Wales (1980) *Environmental impact assessment: ICI Australia Pty Ltd proposed LPG storage facilities at Botany Bay*, Report no. 80/13, NSW Planning and Environment Commission, Sydney, Australia.

Porter, C. F. (1985) *Environmental impact assessment: a practical guide*, University of Queensland Press, St Lucia, Brisbane, Australia.

Portugal, Government of (1989) *Proposals for an EIA system in Portugal*, Government of Portugal, Lisbon, Portugal.

Prybyla, W. (1985) *Environmental assessment guide for housing projects: handbook 1390*, US Department of Housing and Urban Development, Washington, DC, USA.

Ramamoorthy, S. and Baddaloo, E. (1991) *Evaluation of environmental data for regulatory and impact assessment*, Elsevier, Oxford, Britain.

Ramsay, C. G., Clark, B. D., and Gilad, A. (1984) *Perspectives on environmental impact assessment: assessment of hazard and risk*, Reidel, New York, USA.

Rau, J. G. and Wooten, D. C. (1980) *Environmental impact analysis*, McGraw-Hill, New York, USA.

Riverin, G. (1988) *Environmental impact assessment: a planning tool for port development projects*, Occasional paper no. 15, FEARO, Quebec, Canada.

Roberts, R. D. and Roberts, T. M. (eds) (1984) *Planning and ecology*, Chapman and Hall, London, Britain.

Robinson, R. M. (1985) *The federal role in environmental assessment*, Occasional paper no. 11, FEARO, Quebec, Canada.

Rodes, B. K. (1989) *Inventory of federal agency activities on cumulative impact assessment*, CEQ, Washington, DC, USA.

Rosen, S. J. (1976) *Manual for environmental impact evaluation*, Prentice-Hall Inc., New York, USA.

Ryding, S-O. (1991) 'Environmental priority strategies in product design', *Integrated Environmental Management*, Blackwell, Oxford, Britain, issue 4, November, pp. 18-19.

Rzeszot, U. and Wood, C. (1992) 'Environmental impact assessment in Poland: an emergent process', *Project Appraisal* 7 (2), 83-92.

Sammarco, P. and Scarlett, C. (1991a) *Environmental impact assessment in Australia: a compendium of procedures at three levels of government*, Resource Assessment Commission, Canberra, Australia.

— (1991b) *Environmental impact assessment in Australia: some major issues*, Resource Assessment Commission, Canberra, Australia.

Saw, J. and Saddler, H. (1980) *Environmental evaluation to assist in the formulation of energy policies and programs*, Centre for Resource and Environmental Studies, Australian National University, Canberra, Australia.

Schaeffer, D. L. (1980) *A model evaluation methodology applicable to environmental assessment models: ecological modelling*, Elsevier Scientific Publishing, New York, USA.

Schibuola, S. and Byer, P. H. (1991) 'Use of knowledge-based systems for the review of environmental impact statements', *Environmental impact assessment review*, 11 (1), 11-28.

Scholten, J. L. (1988) *Current developments in environmental impact assessment in The Netherlands and its application to bilateral assistance projects and programs*, The International Association for Impact Assessment, Vancouver, BC, Canada.

Shears, J. (1992) 'Environmental management in the Antarctic', *NERC News*, October, Natural Environment Research Council, Swindon, Britain.

Sinden, J. A. (1991) *An assessment of our environmental valuations*, Twentieth Annual Conference of Economists, Hobart, Australia.

Sinden, J. A. and Worrell, A. (1979) *Unpriced values: decisions without market prices*, Wiley-Interscience, New York, USA.

Smith, L. G. (1991) 'Canada's changing impact assessment provisions', *Environmental impact assessment review*, 11 (1), 5-10.

Soil Conservation Service (1977) *Guide for environmental assessment*, SCS, Washington, DC, USA.

— (1990) *SCS technical guide policy* (author: Bouchard, C. E.), SCS, Washington, DC, USA.

Squire, L. and van der Tak, H. G. (1976) *Economic analysis of projects*, World Bank, Johns Hopkins Press, Baltimore, Maryland, USA.

Standing Advisory Committee on Trunk Road Assessment (1992) *Assessing the environmental impact of road schemes*, Department of Transport, HMSO, London, Britain. Also *The British Government's response to the SACTRA report*, HMSO, London, Britain.

Star Newspaper (1991) 'Ministry to compile list of EIA experts', Kuala Lumpur, Malaysia, 11 December, p. 3.

Stern, A. J. (1991) 'Using environmental impact assessments for dispute management', *Environmental impact assessment review*, 11 (1), 81-88.

Stiles, R., Wood, C., and Groome, D. (1991) *Environmental assessment: the treatment of landscape and countryside recreation issues*, Countryside Commission, Manchester, Britain.

Storm, P. C. and Bunge, T. (eds) (1988) *Handbuch der umweltverträglichkeitsprüfung*, Erich Schmidt Verlag, Berlin, Germany.

Sugden, R. and Williams, A. (1978) *The principles of practical cost-benefit analysis*, Oxford University Press, Oxford, Britain.

Sunkel, O., Gligo, N., Koolen, R., Ballesteros, R. B., Leal, J., and Vidal, O. R. S. (1990) *The environmental dimension in development planning*, HMSO, London, Britain.

Thomas, I. (1987) *Environmental Impact assessment: Australian perspectives and practice*, Graduate School of Environmental Science, Monash University, Melbourne, Australia.

Thompson, M. A. (1990) 'Determining impact significance in EIA: a review of twenty-four methodologies', *Journal of Environment Management*, 30 (3), 235-250.

Tomlinson, P. (1987) *Environmental and planning regulatory background to onshore exploration and production*, Environmental report no. 2A/87, Environmental Affairs Department, Shell UK (Exploration and Production), London, Britain.

Treasury Board (1978) *Benefit-cost analysis guide*, Ministry of Supply and Services, Hull, Quebec, Canada.

Turnbull, R. G. H. (ed.) (1992) *Environmental and health impact assessment of development projects: a handbook for practitioners*, Elsevier Applied Science, London, Britain.

United Nations Conference on Environment and Development (1992) *Agenda 21*, as adopted by the plenary session in Rio de Janeiro on 14 June 1992, UN, New York, USA.

United Nations Economic Commission for Europe (1987-1991) Environment series:

1. *Application of environmental impact assessment: highways and dams* (1987).
2. *National strategies for protection of flora, fauna and their habitats* (1988).
3. *Post-project analysis in environmental impact assessment* (1990).
4. *Policies and systems of environmental impact assessment* (1991).
5. *Application of environmental impact assessment principles to policies, plans and programs* (1992).

Economic Commission for Europe, Geneva, Switzerland, UN, New York, USA.

United Nations Environment Program (1988) *Environmental impact assessment: basic procedures for developing countries*, UNEP, Bangkok, Thailand.

United States Geological Survey (USGS) (1971) *A procedure for evaluating environmental impact*, circular 645, Washington, DC, USA.

UVP Reports (1991-92) *Information on environmental impact assessment*, UVP, Dortmund, Germany.

van der Staal, P. M., and van Vught, F. A. (eds) (1989) *Impact forecasting and assessment: methods, results, experiences*, Delft University Press, Delft, The Netherlands.

Vig, N. J. and Kraft, M. E. (eds) (1990) *Environmental policy in the 1990s*, CQ Press, Washington, DC, USA.

Vos, J. B., Feenstra, J. F., de Boer, J., Braat, L. C., van Baalen, J., (1985) *Indicators for the state of the environment*, Institute for Environmental Studies, Free University, Amsterdam, The Netherlands.

VROM (1981a) *Methodologies, scoping and guidelines: conclusions and recommendations*, Ministry of Public Housing, Physical Planning and Environmental Affairs, Leidschendam, The Netherlands.

— (1981b) *Scoping and guidelines*, Ministry of Public Housing, Physical Planning and Environmental Affairs, Leidschendam, The Netherlands.

— (1981c) *Methodologies*, Ministry of Public Housing, Physical Planning and Environmental Affairs, Leidschendam, The Netherlands.

— (1984) *Prediction in environmental impact assessment*, Ministry of Public Housing, Physical Planning and Environmental Affairs, Leidschendam, The Netherlands.

Walton, T. (1989) *The World Bank operational manual*, World Bank, Washington, DC, USA.

Wang, L. S. (1985) *A plan for the implementation of EIA in Taiwan*, Environment and Policy Institute, US East-West Center, Hawaii, USA.

Ward, B., Dubos, R., Heyerdahl, T., Myrdal, G., Miro, C., Zuckerman, Lord, and Peccei, A. (1973) *Who speaks for earth?*, W. W. Norton & Co. Inc., New York, USA.

Ward, B. and Dubos, R. (1972) *Only one Earth: the care and maintenance of a small planet*, W. W. Norton & Co. Inc., New York, USA.

Ward, D. V. (1978) *Biological environmental impact studies: theory and methods*, Academic Press, New York, USA.

Warner, M. L. and Bromley, D. W. (1974) *Environmental impact analysis: a review of three methodologies*, Wisconsin University, Wisconsin, USA.

Wathern, P. (ed.) (1988) *Environmental impact assessment: theory and practice*, Unwin Hyman, London, Britain.

Westman, W. E. (1985) *Ecology impact assessment and environmental planning*, John Wiley & Sons, London, Britain.

White, G. (1972) *Organising scientific investigations to deal with environmental impacts*, paper presented to the Careless Technology Conference, Washington, DC, 1968, The Natural History Press, New York, USA.

Whitney, J. B. R. and Maclaren, V. M. (eds) *Environmental impact assessment: the Canadian experience*, Institute for Environmental Studies, Toronto, Canada.

Williams, D. C. (1990) *Integrating environmental assessment into resource management planning*, US Bureau of Land Management, Department of the Interior, Washington, DC, USA.

Wood, C. and Djeddour, M. (1992) 'Strategic environmental assessment: EA of policies, plans and programs', *Impact assessment bulletin*, 10 (1), 3-22.

Wood, C. and Jones, C. E. (1991) *Monitoring environmental assessment and planning*, HMSO, London, Britain.

Wood, C. and Lee, N. (eds) (1991) *Environmental impact assessment training and research in the European Communities Department of planning and landscape*, University of Manchester, Manchester, Britain.

World Bank (1985) *Manual of industrial hazard assessment techniques*, World Bank Office of Environmental and Scientific Affairs, Washington, DC, USA.

— (1989) *The World Bank operational manual: operational directive 4.00* (author: Walton, T.), Washington, DC, USA.

— (1991) *The World Bank and the environment: a progress report fiscal 1991*, World Bank, Washington, DC, USA.

— (1992a) *World development report*, World Bank, Washington, DC, USA.

— (1992b) *Environmental assessment sourcebook, World Bank technical papers nos 139 and 140*, World Bank, Washington, DC, USA, vol. 1, 227 pp., vol. 2, 282 pp.

World Commission on Environment and Development (Brundtland Commission) (1987) *Our common future*, Oxford University Press, Oxford, Britain.

Wright, D. S. and Grace, G. D. (1987) *An environmental impact assessment methodology for major resource developments*, Academic Press, London, Britain.

Yang, E. J., Dower, R. C., and Menefee, M. (1984) *The use of economic analysis in valuing natural resource damage*, Environmental Law Institute, Washington, DC, USA.